Women and the Olympic Dream

Women and the Olympic Dream

*The Continuing Struggle
for Equality, 1896–2021*

Maria Kaj

McFarland & Company, Inc., Publishers
Jefferson, North Carolina

ISBN (print) 978-1-4766-8647-9
ISBN (ebook) 978-1-4766-4874-3

LIBRARY OF CONGRESS AND BRITISH LIBRARY
CATALOGUING DATA ARE AVAILABLE

Library of Congress Control Number 2022024173

© 2022 Maria Kaj. All rights reserved

No part of this book may be reproduced or transmitted in any form or by any means, electronic or mechanical, including photocopying or recording, or by any information storage and retrieval system, without permission in writing from the publisher.

Front cover image: Mary Lou Retton, circa 1984 (Photofest)

Printed in the United States of America

*McFarland & Company, Inc., Publishers
Box 611, Jefferson, North Carolina 28640
www.mcfarlandpub.com*

To the women who made nuisances of themselves,
then showed us how fast, how high,
and how strong we all can be.

Table of Contents

Acknowledgments	ix
Introduction	1
PART I—GAINING ENTRY	
One. Refused Admission at the Dawn of the Modern Games (1896)	10
Two. Getting in the Game: The Pioneers (1900–1912)	26
Three. The Road from Alice to Amsterdam (1912–1928)	39
PART II—TAKING AIM	
Four. Let 'Er Fly: Babe Didrikson and Exceptionalism (1930–1932)	58
Five. Pariahs (1932–1936)	73
Six. The Cold War and the Feminine Mystique (1948–1968)	89
Seven. The Other Cold War: Winter Games (1924–1956)	108
Eight. Olympic Gigantism and the Zero-Sum Game (1924–1976)	120
PART III—FIGHTING FOR ACCESS	
Nine. Nationalism and the Rise of the Teams (1964–1976)	134
Ten. Not So Fast: The Tortuous Journey of Title IX (1972–2000)	145
Eleven. See How She Runs: Gender Politics and Racing (1948–1984)	157
Twelve. Them's Fighting Words (1988–2012)	175
PART IV—BEING SEEN	
Thirteen. The Camera Changes the Narrative: Gymnasts, Skaters, Racers, Villains (1972–2000)	194
Fourteen. Showing the World (1988–2016)	211
Fifteen. Erasing the Specter of Lesbianism (1896–2016)	227
Sixteen. Femininity Control (1936–…)	239

Afterthoughts: On Visibility 259
Further Reading 262
Appendix: Charts 263
Chapter Notes 269
Bibliography 287
Index 289

Acknowledgments

Writing is a fairly lonely business: one woman, one screen, one blinking cursor. Yet, it would have been impossible to write a book like this without standing on the shoulders of hundreds of helpers. A few I even know personally.

I am eternally grateful for the patience and encouragement from my wife, who always listened—sometimes even with interest—to my "Did you know…" daily Olympic tidbits. Her advice on photos, marketing, and the business end of writing was likewise invaluable.

I also greatly appreciated the input from my beta readers. Even those who didn't get through it all provided encouragement that was sorely needed. Thanks to the pickleball posse—Tea, Dar, Peggy, Rich—who were always willing to let me tell yet another story. In particular, I would definitely not have written the book without the warmth and enthusiasm from Shawn-Marie Bryan. Especially useful editorial feedback came from my youngest, Lee, who highlighted several bumpy parts. The ride will be smoother for all because of these key insights.

Thanks to McFarland Publishing and especially to Susan Kilby, who probably has no idea how much inspiration can come from a terse email that basically said, we don't like this, but what else ya got? I had no idea that this book, this can of worms, was sitting around waiting to be opened until that point.

I could not have completed the project without the efforts of so many who provided Olympic material online. The academics, like Cecile Houry, Heather Dahl, and Gerd von der Lippe, provided studies which applied brilliant feminist theory to place the facts in social context. Wikipedia gets a bad rap, but the folks who update the Olympic data treat it with the proper respect and always cite their sources. Stuck in a COVID lockdown and unable to go to actual libraries, using these connections was critical for my work. The statisticians of Olympedia and olympanalyt.com further let me slice and dice to my analytics heart's content. United in data are we!

The LA84 Digital Foundation, which houses all the official reports, some of the original documents, and dozens of fascinating rabbit holes of research on individual sports and athletes, is the Twelfth Wonder of the World. I never knew how intriguing meeting minutes from 1957 might be. Still, I had a professor who taught Organizational Policy once, who showed us how to use changes in organization charts to find out what's really going on in a company. So, too, do those meeting minutes tell us what really went on to get women in or keep women out of the Games. Wouldn't it be the bomb-diggety to have the transcript of the conversation of when Michel Breal proposed the marathon? Perhaps LA84 Digital archaeologists may someday come upon it lying in a vault somewhere in 1894.

Lastly, I continue to be astounded by the performances and perseverance of the athletes. As I apply the finishing touches here, it is exactly ten days after the end of Tokyo 2020, which provided a plethora of staggeringly beautiful moments. The Games almost didn't happen and those who competed had to endure more than just a year of waiting. For me, watching this time and knowing how much had to be done to get them into the stadium—not just hand-washing and face masks, but all the years of lobbying and persuasion—made me more appreciative of what they accomplished. Their deeds always leave me breathless and inspired.

Introduction

"That the Olympics are a great international gathering of the best athletic stars of the entire world no one can deny.... But that they have succeeded in becoming a beneficial force in the spreading of peace and good will throughout the world, or that they bring together the various competitors in friendly social intercourse, is not so certain ... the history of the Olympic Games since their arrival in 1896 has been marked by sporadic dissension, bickering, heartburn, and one or two old-fashioned rows....

Surely the acme of absurdity was reached with the inclusion of women's teams from several nations in the swimming events. For not only were the Games in Sparta limited to men competitors; but for many years attendance even was restricted to the male sex."
—John R. Tunis, "The Olympic Games," 1928[1]

The Acme of Absurdity

In a review of the 1928 Amsterdam Olympics for *Harper's Magazine*, sportswriter John Roberts Tunis launched a diatribe on everything that had gone wrong with the modern Olympic Games in its first thirty years. He criticized the disgusting rise of professionalism, the use of team tactics to win medals, and the addition of events outside the ancient track and field disciplines to broaden participation. However, the worst sin of all committed by the modern Games, said Tunis, was in allowing athletes that the Greeks had excluded: women.

While there's some debate about whether the Greeks completely excluded women,[2] Tunis had plenty of company in his beliefs. In opposing the staging of those very same Games, a speaker in the Dutch Parliament warned that "women seized by the mania of sport will lose their feeling of modesty and virtue."[3]

Another journalist pointed out an obvious problem with females spending time on the field: "these girls ... have the heavy part of the household work in their own homes to perform ... washing clothes or scrubbing floors ... a fine exercise [and] somewhat 'self-sufficing' for an athletic point of view." Thus, women who turn their focus to Olympic athletic pursuits might either turn into fallen women or, worse, lack the energy to scrub floors.

The battle for women to get past such prejudice and on to the track or into the

Introduction

pool at the 1928 Games—at any Games—has been long and arduous. It's easy nowadays to look back and see participation as a steadily rising graph, as shown below.[4]

It's satisfying to cheer at the 2020 declaration from Thomas Bach, president of the International Olympic Committee (IOC): "At the Olympic Games [for] Tokyo 2020 … we will have reached gender balance, with 48.8 percent women competing."[5]

However, that view blurs the challenges that women have had to overcome to get there. Rather than through some planned steady, straightforward rise, the increase of women's Olympic sports has been achieved through battle after battle.

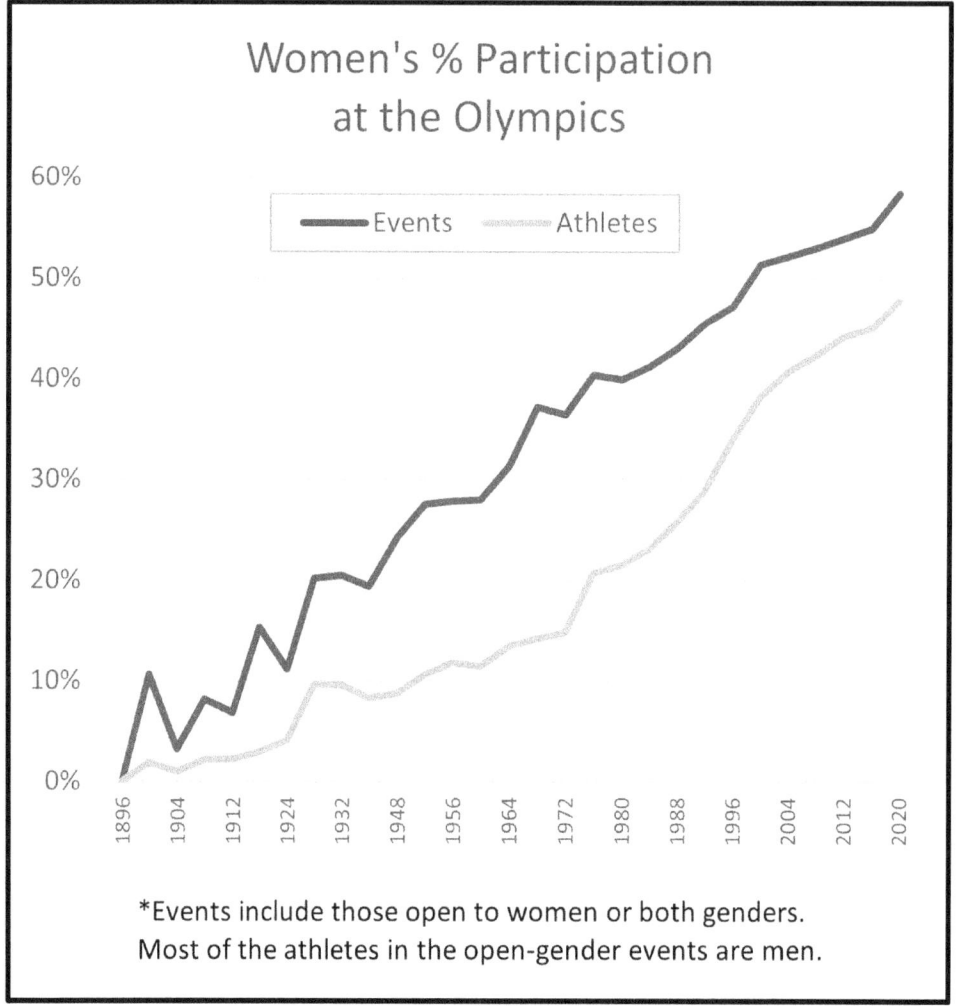

Chart One. The rising number of women in the Olympics masks the myriad of efforts required to gain entry to events (author's chart design based on data compiled from Olympanalyt.com, Olympedia, Wikipedia, and the Official Olympic Reports).

Consider the successive barriers women have encountered when trying to enter the Games:

- Not allowed to compete at all (1896)
- Not allowed to swim (1896–1908)
- Not allowed in track and field (1896–1924)
- Not allowed to compete in more than three events (1896–1948)
- Not allowed to run the 800 m (1932–1960)
- Not allowed to compete against men (1908–1952)
- Not allowed to compete as a team (1896–1964)
- Not allowed to run the marathon (1896–1984)
- …to cross-country ski (1928–1952)
- …to speed skate (1928–1960)
- …to play water polo (1896–2000)
- …to lift weights (1896–2000)
- …to wrestle (1896–2004)
- …to box (1904–2012)
- …to ski jump (1932–2014)
- …to compete if they looked too much like a man (1936–1968)
- …to compete if they had too much testosterone (1968–??)

Only twenty years ago, women pole vaulters were still being told they didn't have the upper-body strength and were just "not made to do it."[6] As late as 2005, the International Ski Federation (FIS) still banned women's ski jumping entirely because it "seems not appropriate for ladies from a medical point of view."[7] When boxing was finally added for women in London 2012, the worldwide boxing federations insisted that women wear skirts in order to tell them apart from the men. Meanwhile, even in 2021, the Norwegian women's beach handball team at the Youth Olympics was penalized for wearing swim shorts instead of bikinis.

Every time women have challenged a particular ban and finally won the right to act as athletes, another barrier pops up or another restriction is added back. Despite the glowing rhetoric about the rise of women athletes, resistance has been met all along that long way, baby. Thus, instead of the having the arcing trajectory of a baseball in flight, women's entry to the Olympics has been more like a never-ending race of hurdles, with no apparent finish line. As soon as one is passed, here comes another.

Be the Change, Ride the Change

Two elements have been key in helping women pass these barriers. The first reflects actions by individual heroines and heroes, advocates behind the scenes and athletes on the field. When organizing committees created rules limiting women, specific people challenged those legal and bureaucratic barriers. The efforts of women like Alice Milliat and Dutee Chand opened the doors for countless others. Chapter Three in this book will highlight Milliat's Women's World Games, which persuaded the IOC to allow women's participation in track events. Chapter Sixteen will explain how Chand's appeal to the Court of Arbitration for Sport (CAS) overturned long-held notions that chromosomes equal performance.

At the same time, inspiring efforts by women in the arena, by athletes like Madge Syers and Joan Benoit, have demonstrated that dazzling performances can erase the preconceived notions of female "natural fragility." The success of individual athletes, detailed throughout the book, helped convince the rule-setters that limitations were unnecessary.

Yet, the rise of the female celebrity athlete both accelerated and slowed progress for women. Consider a Babe Didrikson, labeled the greatest female athlete of the 20th century. Didrikson's ability to win multiple medals and cross with ease from track to golf wowed the crowds at the Olympics and on the LPGA circuit. But athletes of the century only come along once in a century. By focusing on star qualities of only a few women athletes, as Chapter Four suggests, the model of exceptionalism made it more difficult to see all women as potential athletes. If the greatest female medalist is an exception to the rule, then the rules stay in place.

While exceptionalism was working against athletes, historical forces helped move them forward as well as backward and sideways. The civil rights and women's protest movements significantly broadened women's athletic participation. After all, Title IX, which benefited team sports as explained in Chapter Ten, was an amendment to a civil rights act. But the execution of Title IX wasn't like the flipping of a light switch that opened all sports to women.

Meanwhile, other countries had their own reasons to include and exclude women from their favorite sports. The paths of volleyball in Japan or handball in Norway show that promoting civil rights wasn't always the reason. Another force at play was Olympic nationalism, which treated sports as a proxy for national supremacy or even war. When the "feminine mystique" urged women to leave the athletic field for the kitchen after World War II, the success of Olympic Soviet athletes convinced Western nations that women should put down the pots and pans and get back on the track. Under such changing attitudes, a team like the Tigerbelles could shine above systemic racism, while athletes like Larisa Latynina and Tamara Press could show how the Soviets raised the bar for everybody. Chapter Six illustrates such examples in detail.

Thus, the book as a whole traces the transition of women into the Games over time, illustrating how both individual actions and broader social forces combined to provide the opportunity for stellar female performances. Changing media, especially from the growth in televising the Games themselves, created both more opportunities and more barriers. Slowly but surely, female athletes had to take matters into their own hands, crafting their own definitions of muscular femininity for the camera and learning to control their public image.

Sometimes it's about winning a cultural war, sometimes about pressuring through the courts, and sometimes just creating the right nickname.

Whatever, say Rusty Kanokogi, Earlene Brown, Fanny Blankers-Koen, Kasai Masae, and Stamata Revithi. If someone wants to superimpose the image of suffragettes over the U.S. women's soccer team getting the gold in order to sell women's deodorant, so be it. If a country suddenly decides to praise Olympic medal-winning mothers because their robust health may produce better soldiers, let the Games begin. The compromises required for social change aren't always pretty. The social change part remains non-negotiable.

Neither are the Olympic Games always a shining example of athletic prowess and perfect sportsmanship. There's plenty to complain about in a sporting environment that has been plagued with scandal, over-emphasized winning, and fostered inane and jingoistic media coverage. Such critiques are well covered in other excellent Olympic history books.[8] This book is neither an indictment nor an endorsement of all aspects of the Games themselves.

In addition, the premise here is that women want to compete. Whether that's always a good idea can also be debated. Competition can be harmful, and many elite Olympic athletes lead lives of stress and injury, both women and men. The experience of gymnast Simone Biles in Tokyo illustrates the positive and negative sides of being the world's best athlete. This is not an assessment of the pros and cons of competing.

Finally, this is neither a manifesto nor a clarion call to action. The focus is on the history of athletes, a history that has taken its own strange twists and turns. Some of those who felt compelled to prevent women from competing had good reason; many did not. Some who helped put women on the track were neither altruists nor feminists. Exploring all of the reasons can further understanding of the impact of social change on sports.

This is the point: the fastest kid in a neighborhood, in a high school district, in a state, or in a country ought to be able to go to the Olympics and prove that they are the fastest in the world, if they so desire. And not be banned from doing so because they are female.

Nothing Like a Little Umbrage

I bumped into this topic quite by accident. That may seem ridiculous if I mention that I am an Olympics dork (working on my third book on the subject), an ardent feminist, and a blogger who frequently writes about sports history. The trifecta! Still, this book was nowhere on my horizon until July of 2020. I was minding my own business, looking for a quote for an Olympic-themed blogging exercise, primarily as a distraction during the spring COVID lockdown. I came across Mr. Tunis's article in *Harper's* and was amused at how his rant illustrated that attitudes for and against the Games haven't really changed in a hundred years.

But just for fun, I decided to print out the whole article and see what was making him so cranky. I read to the end, came across the passage that lauded the Greeks for excluding women, and nearly spit out my diet Mountain Dew.

Those words about the "acme of absurdity" stuck in my craw. I was incensed, as any 21st-century fan of sports would be. I started digging into how women had made their way into the Olympics of 1928—Mr. Tunis's Games—to see what all the fuss was about. I came across the Women's World Games and Alice Milliat, and I was spellbound at what she had accomplished.

I also laughed at the free spirits of Eleanor Holm and Babe Didrikson, women I had researched before. I had already been a huge fan of Earlene Brown, the beautician-turned-Tigerbelle. Especially fascinating to me was the story that shot put medalist Brown had once brought her Soviet Olympic rivals to Compton for a friendly game at the Bowlarama.

The picture started coming together. Here was a Greek woman who had run the first marathon, against the rules. There was Joan Benoit, finally winning the first official Olympic women's marathon, though misinformation about a dehydrated runner threatened to postpone the event again. I listened to the autobiography of Ginny Gilder, who wrote of rowing at Yale right after the passage of Title IX. There was Great Britain's Madge Syers, the first woman to medal in figure skating, who beat men before the skating federation decided to ban women from entering.

Lastly, I was struck by the contrast between Kerri Strug and Simone Biles. Strug's "vault for gold" is one of the most iconic stories in U.S. Olympic history. Many complain that Strug's vault on an injured ankle should never have been "allowed," but she has always brushed aside such criticisms. Strug argues that anyone on the men's team would have been expected to make the vault and thrilled to do it, if it earned the team gold medal.

In comparison, Biles took criticism for choosing *not* to compete after feeling disoriented in the compulsories. Still, she stood her ground until she felt she could flip across the balance beam safely. She was ultimately praised for acknowledging her vulnerability. The transition of the gymnasts from ballerinas to pixies to respected athletes has paralleled women's demand for acceptance at the Games as a whole.

All these women across the variety of sports had that one thing in common. They just wanted to compete on their terms. Perhaps it's just as well that an obnoxious quote from the 1920s bothered me so much. There's nothing like righteous anger to help a person attach seat to chair and begin writing. Ultimately, whatever made its way onto the page, I was amazed at what so many Olympic women athletes had accomplished and wanted to make sure I did them justice.

A Few Words on Approach

This book is organized roughly in chronological order, but "rough" is the key adjective here. The intent was to look at trends rather than to adhere to a strict time sequence or to cover all the Olympiads. Some of the time periods overlap, and history is revealed in clumps to make a point. Just as women's advances in the Games were not always linear, the story is not told in a straight line.

Part I addresses what women had to do just to get inside the Olympic stadium in the first place, which was no easy task. As the earliest women showed their prowess on the field, there was resistance to more, and Part II describes the successive waves of athletes who displayed feats of amazement, endured public censure, and persuaded with charm. When that didn't work, they went to court or appealed to national pride, as Part III explains. Lastly, Part IV illustrates how just getting on the field did not end the fight for equal treatment, as the rise of media and social attitudes about gender required women to battle repeatedly over how they would be seen.

In addition, I should emphasize that my educational background is in accounting and literature. I approached history as a fan would, rather than as a trained historian. A number of people—mostly women—have made available their outstanding academic research on women in sports, and making use of their work has been an ongoing reminder that this is more a labor of love than of scholarship. There will be no "epistemological ascendancy" found here. However, the work by these excellent researchers has inspired me to pursue a master's degree in history, so perhaps I may eventually wax lyrical about "sportification."

Also, I tried my best to stomp on my American bias whenever it reared its head. For American readers, there may be more emphasis here on other countries than is typical. For those outside the U.S., you might occasionally frown at my use of yet another American example. It does vary by sport; I am a big fan of the "little sports." Never fear, you will learn plenty about Norwegian handball and Japanese wrestlers. Also, apologies that I just cannot get my head around calling the world's most popular game "football," instead of "soccer." Forgive me when my flag is showing.

Lastly, this is by no means an exhaustive review of what women have accomplished at the Olympics. I don't cover all the sports and taking on challenges faced by Paralympians would call for another book. I don't even review examples of the best performances. For example, Jenny Thompson is the most decorated Olympic female swimmer (12 medals, 8 gold), but her performances didn't necessarily illustrate my explanations, so she is not mentioned. Once, on a family vacation trip with my seven-year-old, we drove out of the South Dakota hills to see a majestic herd of bison appear. At the time, the children were playing travel bingo in the back seat, and my youngest responded to our excited pointing and shouts with "They're not on my bingo card." I'm sorry, Jenny Thompson, Birget Fischer (12 canoeing medals/Germany), and Polina Astakhova (10 gymnastics medals/USSR), but you're not on my bingo card.

For those who would like to orient themselves to the overall Olympic timeline, with women's participation highlighted, there is a handy chart in the Appendix listing the Games by date, city, and sports, with differences highlighted between men's and women's events.

Ultimately, the troubled months of late 2020 and early 2021 may have been the right time to take this deep dive into how women overcame such opposition. Women athletes have advocated for social change with remarkable courage and persistence. After these recent years, which themselves have seemed so full of hurdles—the pandemic, political divisions, climate change, and xenophobia—it may be the perfect time to learn more about the women who hurdled themselves into Olympic competition. They provide a model of endurance that demonstrates what is possible.

Part I

Gaining Entry

ONE

Refused Admission at the Dawn of the Modern Games (1896)

On April 11, 1896,[1] as the early morning shadows began to retreat from across the beaten rocks of Marathon bridge, a slight figure strode confidently toward the appointed spot, about to break precedent and make history, the first in a long line of women who would do so. A wind from the hills was kicking up little swirls of dust. It blew a stray length of her blond hair out of its loose braid, and she tucked it back as she walked, determined to look fresh and confident to the trio of well-dressed men standing near a grove of olive trees.[2]

One of them, the mayor, doffed his hat in warm recognition. She had spent the previous two nights with his family, incessantly chattering about this crazy plan, a plan he found bizarre but fascinating. He was both surprised and relieved that she still intended to go through with it.

The day before had been chilly for April. Today should be warmer as the morning fog was drifting back out to the Petalioi Gulf. Whether the day would be hot or cold, the woman was dressed in the same threadbare long-sleeved blouse that she'd worn since showing up in town earlier that week, the only one she apparently owned. Her underskirt was tucked up to her waist, somewhat immodestly showing her ankles, like a farmer's wife preparing to work in the fields. In her hand were those ravaged shoes, one with a distinct hole visible in the sole and the other riddled with cracks.

Two or three reporters were there as well, returning after the uproar yesterday. It was a little too early now for a smoke or a drink, and none had eaten more than a bite of roll. They hoped she'd start soon, so they could go back to a proper breakfast.

The woman was cheerful and chatted briefly with them, explaining her plan. She expected to run the route in about three hours, she said. She'd done it many times. Well, not this route exactly, she admitted, but she had walked the 43 km from Piraeus to here already and that was longer. The reporter from *Estia*, the national Greek newspaper, didn't know what to make of her. It was a strange idea, but it would sell papers, whether she finished or not. If she was doing it to gain attention, it was working.

The morning quiet was broken only by a handful of hoopoes announcing spring across the trees, a stark contrast to the noise of the last few days. Two days ago, this undernourished woman had come in a cart with the others, in the rain. She had carried a toddler on her hip and had settled with him at a spot right over there, until the mayor had gone over to speak with her.

After that, she and the mayor had been seen walking up the street to his house, a modest mansion by Athenian standards but still one of the biggest in town. He had apparently taken an immediate liking to her brashness. Besides, his wife would have given him an earful had he not brought the woman and baby in out of the drizzle for a hot meal. After all, he was wining and dining several other runners as well, so there was plenty to go around.

By yesterday afternoon the mud had dried, and the town square and road to the bridge had been crammed with bicycles, horses, and local rubberneckers, all surrounding a handful of men dressed as lightly as this woman, in rolled-up pants and thin shirts. There had been seventeen of them, setting off in the afternoon on that long run, more than 40 kilometers off to the capital.

The woman had tried to argue her way into the group, but the Marathon Organizing Committee disapproved of her boldness. They had no intention of letting her run. It was against the rules. She had gone to the priest, Yanni Velioti, in his dark robes and long white beard, to ask for a special prayer. The priest had refused to give her one because she was not one of the official athletes. She claimed she had registered, but she had no card to prove it.

The organizers insisted that they had no record of such a thing. Besides, she hadn't been blessed. Her shoes were falling apart, and she was dressed immodestly. The other men wouldn't allow it, they said. No matter how she pleaded, they repeatedly shook their heads.

Nevertheless, the wiry woman remained determined. She pointed out that there were no specific rules against women running. She had spoken to the other runners when they rode together into town, and, though they had teased her, they didn't mind her running. She could run behind them. She had walked here for six hours with her baby, hearing of the race. This was a chance for her, perhaps for someone to hear about the deed and give her a job.

But the officials simply folded their arms and frowned. One of them finally grabbed her arm and pushed her roughly back. They would not admit her without an entry form. Then, as the others set off down the road, followed by their trailing entourage, the officials said her time for entry had expired, and they would hear no more.

With all the hullabaloo over, the locals had gone back to their work. Many had, quite frankly, forgotten about it. While they were lingering over a late-afternoon glass of beer, one of the horses had come galloping back into town with the rider shouting about a Greek, a water carrier. Then, it had been pandemonium, at least for an hour. A good excuse to buy another round of beer.

Today, the woman was back. A new day; a different plan. She could still run the route, with someone watching to verify her time. She asked the men in the dark suits—the mayor, the school master, the magistrate—to put their names on her card, underneath the date and time that she had written, in a careful if childish script. She showed the card to the journalists from *Estia* and *Asty*. Whether her plan was crazy or not, they were now witnesses to the insanity and could help prove her case.

Time to go. With one last wave and a shy smile to the reporters, she walked to where the rocky track meandered off under a row of trees toward the gentle slopes.

Days later, some of the papers would refer to her as a woman called Melpomene, the Greek's Muse of Tragedy. Melpomene was a good fit for one who was penniless and unemployed, though the vibrancy in her eyes and determination in her shoulders were tenacious rather than tragic. It's not clear whether Melpomene was a name she gave at the time. Years later, scholars would argue about whether there were two women who had tried to run. There might have been.

What is known is that there was a woman named Stamata Revithi, who started at 8 a.m. from Marathon to Athens, the day after the first marathon took place at the dawning of the modern Olympics.

In the dust, haze, and chirping on that Saturday morning, Revithi began to run.

Where Are All the Marble Statues?

The road for Revithi's marathon started near the Marathon town bridge[3] and would wend its way through the hills and towns southwest to Athens, to the Panathenaic Stadium. The journey that brought the modern Olympic Games to Athens in the first place was just as circuitous. For nearly a century, interest had been growing in holding an international sporting contest, a new Olympiad. But bickering among the organizers, lack of funding, and indifference from the general public delayed the resurrection. It was as much a miracle for the Games to take place in April 1896 as it was for Revithi to attempt a marathon in the first place. The controversy over whether to allow women was just one of many.

Much of the credit for rekindling the Games—and much of the blame for everything that was wrong about them in the early days—has been given to Baron Pierre Fredy de Coubertin. Coubertin, a French aristocrat, provided the mix of philosophical vision and patrician arm-twisting that was needed to build the right coalition of supporters. He was ultimately responsible for proposing the date and the place to hold this new set of sporting contests. Still, the Games did not spring whole cloth from Coubertin's head. The Olympics of 1896 came to life in Athens after decades of random events coalesced into a lucky set of circumstances.

Naturally, the ancient Olympics themselves formed the historical model, even though the site of Olympia was originally religious, a sacred grove (Altis) dedicated to a cult of Zeus. At some point around 776 BCE, between the priestesses pouring wine and the acolytes chanting, a race was added to honor the gods. A ceremonial path was carved out for a 200 m contest and, eventually, a stadium built around it.

Over the centuries more running and throwing events were added, in what would be recognized today as track and field. Historians know this, or think they know this, because it's painted on the urns. Combat and equestrian events followed suit, more buildings were erected, and the whole complex sprawled across nearly 250 acres by 393 CE, when Christian emperors began banning pagan celebrations. After more than a thousand years, the party was over.

Much of this became guesswork after Olympia fell into ruins. Milton and

Shakespeare both mention "Olympic games" in their texts, so stories must have been passed down after the buildings were long gone. An English antiquarian rediscovered the Greek site in the late 1700s, and a French team of archaeologists began planning an excavation of the area in 1829.

Even before the archaeologists had uncovered the temples, the very idea of the Games caught international fancy. Greece was finally able to throw out their Ottoman overlords. Waxing patriotic and nostalgic in 1833, a Greek poet named Panagiotis Soutsos sent out an appeal to his countrymen: "Where are all your theaters and marble statues?"[4]

Apparently, some were in Sweden. Professor Gustav Schartau of Lund had reacted to the news of Olympia's excavation by forming a Swedish "Olympic Union" and staging Scandinavian "Olympiads" in 1834 and 1836. Soutsos's poem also caught the eye of a wealthy Greek businessman, Evangelis Zappas, who offered to put up a million drachmas if competitions were restored in Athens. The Grecian government took him up on the offer and started making plans.

At roughly the same time, in 1849, a physician in the hills of Shropshire near the English-Welsh border dreamed up his version of an Olympic festival. Dr. William Penny Brookes was one of many who advocated physical fitness for the benefit of the general population, way before Coubertin had even been born. The Much Wenlock Games, named after Brookes's hometown, was his inspired creation.

The core of the events was "athletics"—the English, and later Olympic, term for track and field. However, the Much Wenlock Games also included cricket, tennis, tilting, and even artistic competitions. Like a country fair on steroids, the Much Wenlock Games admitted old and young, gentlemen and the working class, and men and women. It did not discriminate.

As it happened, Dr. Brookes came across a news clipping from Greece describing the efforts of Zappas and the governments to stage contests in Athens in 1859. Two months before the planned reboot of these Games, Brookes added the name "Olympian"[5] to his creation in solidarity. Those Much Wenlock Olympian Games have continued into the present day.[6]

The 1859 Athenian contests did take place, although for Greeks only. They were often referred to as the "Zappas Olympic Games," and the million drachmas was put to use constructing a stadium. Public interest in the contests, however, started to wane about the time the building was ready, primarily because the lack of international competition made the events less than riveting. Dr. Brookes wrote letters to the Greek government, suggesting the combining of forces for an international set of competitions, but his letters went unanswered, and the Greek cycle was discontinued in 1888. They all seemed to be talking at cross-purposes.

Thus, although historians grumble that Baron de Coubertin gets too much of the credit for reviving the Games, he did seem to provide the glue that slapped all this raw material together. In retrospect, the Frenchman was probably the perfect candidate to gather all these ideas under one roof.

Born in 1863, Coubertin grew up during a revival of interest both in the classics and in adding physical education to the schools. Part of the objective was to prepare young men to be better soldiers, a motivation that would continue well into the late

Fig.1. The egalitarian Much Wenlock Olympian Games have always included men and women across their 134 annual athletic contests. Pictured is champion tilter Charles Ainsworth (center) from 1887, surrounded by unnamed officials and being crowned with olive leaves (courtesy of the Wenlock Olympian Society).

20th century. The baron himself was not interested in pursuing a military career, despite his infatuation with the idea of a soldier-athlete.

Instead, he was educated by the Jesuits, at St. Ignace, and his parents hoped that he might be called toward the priesthood. But Coubertin's studies pushed him toward a career as "an intellectual," a notion which seems quaint today but neatly fit a philosophically minded 20-year-old aristocrat with a passion for the classics and a lot of time on his hands.

The baron was captivated reading as a teenager about the excavation of the ruins at Olympia and spoke of how "nothing in ancient history had given me more food for thought than Olympia."[7] He read eagerly in 1875 that a German team had begun uncovering the site in earnest,[8] as their discoveries were widely reported in the press.

However, Coubertin was just as fascinated with the rigors of physical education and the role sports could play in schooling. After traveling across England to view the public schools, especially the famous Rugby School, he became fixated on the value of athletics and how "organised sport can create moral and social strength."[9] Eventually, Coubertin struck up a friendship with Dr. Brookes, who even held a special Much Wenlock Games in the baron's honor in 1890.

Coubertin was himself also an avid sportsman, at least for those sports near and dear to the heart of any aristocratic athlete. He rowed, he cycled, he played tennis, and he shot pistols. While the ancient Greeks might not have put those at the top of the sporting lists, Coubertin would have considered them essential to developing the gentleman amateur.

Having money was a key component, too. While Coubertin wasn't interested in personally building stadiums or financing competitions, he had the money to travel extensively and underwrite fledgling organizations. After developing many friendships with men interested in bolstering international sporting associations, the next logical step was to create one. Thus, in 1887, Coubertin helped found the *Union des Societes Francaises de Sports Athletiques* (USFSA), whose role was initially directed toward the "propagation of physical education."[10]

By the time the USFSA's fifth anniversary rolled around, though, Coubertin thought the audience might be ripe for his "new" big idea. He began his campaign for a new international competition with a major keynote speech in 1892: "Let us export rowers, fencers, and runners: there is the free trade of the future, and … the cause of peace will have received a new and mighty stay. This is enough to encourage your servant to dream now … [of] the restoration of the Olympic Games."[11]

Uninteresting, Unaesthetic, and Improper

The first reaction to Coubertin's call to restore the Olympics was polite applause and confusion, with a bit of joking about whether contestants would be naked. Besides, weren't the Greeks already doing something? There was no immediate groundswell of acclaim for such a revival under the auspices of the USFSA. But once the topic was on the table, the baron kept circulating the idea for the next two years, until he had gathered similar thinkers to his cause.

The plan for the 1894 USFSA conference was to address amateurism. The gentlemen-sportsmen wanted to expand sports but still keep them for the gentlemen. Similar amateur-devoted organizations were popping up all over the place, like the Amateur Athletics Union (AAU) in the United States. All wanted to ensure contests remained aimed at the right kind of athletes. But Coubertin had another item to discuss along with the growing "problem" of professionals in sports.

As the agenda filled with speeches and events devoted to amateurism, organizers changed the title of the conference to the "Congress for the Re-establishment of the Olympic Games." Over lavish dinners with handpicked supporters sprinkled among the attendees, he pushed again for a new Olympics. This time, there was general agreement, and the focus turned to a discussion from "whether" to "where" and "when."

The baron proposed Athens, although London and Paris were also suggested and rejected as alternatives. It might seem a curious notion that a primarily French organization would take over a part of Greece. Moreover, the suggestions came from men who had never staged a competition, while those who had (e.g., Brookes) were absent. But the other French intellectuals at the meeting loved it, and the snowball began rolling downhill.

At the grand banquet, Michel Bréal, another classics scholar, offered his own proposal. Bréal pledged a prize cup for the winner of a special race, an ancient run inspired by the classic story of the Battle of Marathon in 490 BCE. Somewhere in those discussions over cigars and cognac, the idea of this race—this marathon—became intertwined with the restoration of the Olympic Games.

Thus, it's important to note, in exploring the history of women in the Olympics, or in exploring any kind of history related to the Games, that the modern Olympic tradition began as a collection of fanciful notions dreamed up in a haze of alcohol and cigar smoke. So many rules and traditions related to the Games—the length of the marathon, the restriction of athletes to amateurs, and the exclusion of women—were based on individual ideas and opinions. Other ideas are possible. Opinions can be changed.

Coubertin himself provided neither funding nor arrangements for the competitions to be staged in Athens. He had, however, persuaded a Greek writer living in Paris, Dimitrios Vikelas, to attend the USFSA meeting. Vikelas expressed enthusiasm about the revival of the Olympics. He soon found himself chair of the brand-new International Olympic Committee (IOC) and was "vol-untold" to work out all the pesky details.

When Vikelas took the proposal home to Athens, his government and the Zappas Foundation wanted no part of this new plan. They had neither the money nor the interest in creating more competitions at the whim of some other committee. However, after more Coubertin arm-twisting and a personal appeal to the Greek government, Crown Prince Constantine stepped in to make the arrangements and save the day. The Games did take place, with 241 athletes from 14 nations competing in 43 events.

The one thing that Coubertin did provide, aside from the design of the newly minted IOC of which he became general secretary, was an underlying philosophy that established four important ideas. The first two sounded so noble that they practically fly as a banner today above the five-ringed Olympic flag. The second two, however, caused heartache and discord for decades.

The first idea of Coubertin's was a continuation from his famous "export rowers" speech. Peace, he said, could be obtained through this international sporting contest. The Greeks had supposedly laid down arms and called a truce during times of war to hold their Olympiads. So should the modern world, said Coubertin. Over time, though, the Games have not "enforced peace" and have been canceled and disrupted by two world wars, terrorists, local armed conflicts, boycotts, and a pandemic. Whether peace and harmony can be obtained through sports is still a work-in-progress.

Coubertin's second piece of intellectual capital has probably become his most well-known:

> The important thing in the Olympic Games is not to win, but to take part; the important thing in life is not the triumph, but the struggle; the essential thing is not to have conquered but to have fought well.[12]

The baron had been influenced by Monsignor Ethelbert Talbot, whose sermon before the London Games emphasized that the "Games themselves are better than the race or the prize."[13] Coubertin quoted Talbot and then further framed the philosophy upon which the IOC was built.

Whether pipe dream or not, this description of sportsmanship forms what is now called "Olympism," and it has even led to an Olympic prize awarded when athletes demonstrate outstanding "fair play." In contrast, Coubertin's other two ideas, both born out of the elite world in which he was raised, created problems that lasted for most of the 20th century.

One of these problematic notions was the insistence that athletes must be amateurs. While Brookes of Much Wenlock had opened his games to all, and while the Greeks in the Zappas Games made no distinction between amateurs and professionals, Coubertin and his associates took a hard-nosed stand. They even went so far as to argue that amateurism was necessary for sportsmanship because "amateurism was defended with the argument that fair play and good sportsmanship are possible only when sports are an athlete's *avocation*, never his or her *vocation*."[14]

Of course, such an ideal could only come from someone with the independent means to indulge in the love of sports while being able to quote Pindar that "the gods are the friends of the games."[15] The strict insistence on amateurism would wreak havoc in competitions down the years, and great performers like Jim Thorpe and Paavo Nurmi would be punished for accepting money.

The other notion that Coubertin stubbornly asserted concerned half the population. He was unwilling to let women compete.

Coubertin's ideas about women, like his other ideas about the Games, were philosophical and adamantine. There was no *under certain circumstances* or *it's okay for women to be limited to feminine sports*. He was against women participating in his hallowed games from the very beginning, and, if anything, hardened his position as time went by. Even twenty years later, he would declaim after the 1912 Stockholm Olympics: "An Olympiad with females would be impractical, uninteresting, unaesthetic, and improper."[16]

As with amateurs, not everyone was against having women participate. Brookes had let the women of Much Wenlock compete. The baron himself had even suggested that physical activity *in school* for boys and girls was important in developing robust health for adults. Hence, women could play at a sport, "provided that they do not make a public spectacle of themselves." Never in public and certainly not at the Games! "In the Olympic Games, as in the contests of former times, their primary role should be to crown the victors."[17]

Coubertin, like the journalist Tunis, had plenty of chauvinists for company. Such sentiments were the norm at the time rather than the exception. Latter 19th-century researchers of anthropology and social psychology were still claiming that science proved women were less intelligent. A typical scientist, for instance, suggested that women's brains developed along the line of gorillas rather than "male crania."[18]

The typical sportswriter of the Victorian era would wonder in print how women could even accomplish a walking race: "How do these ladies propose to walk? If in petticoats, they will soon tire, if in bloomer costume they will not make very extraordinary time, but if they strip to tights and trunks, and go for putting on a record, they will expose themselves to criticism."[19]

It was in that environment where Coubertin was able to express a clear denial to women participants: "The Olympic Games must be reserved for men.... We must continue to try to achieve the following definition: the solemn and periodic

Fig.2. Charles Pierre de Frédy, Baron de Coubertin (1863–1937) put an indelible imprint on the Modern Olympics from 1894 to 1925. He welcomed women who wanted to box, row, or even play rugby, as long as they did not compete in public (courtesy of the International Olympic Committee).

exaltation of male athleticism, with internationalism as a base, loyalty as a means, art for its setting, and female applause as its reward."[20]

While Coubertin's influence would dissolve enough to let women trickle in eventually, especially for non-athletic events in the early years, the IOC and the organizing committee for Athens 1896 adopted a completely rigid stance. At the dawn of their newly initiated contests, there would be no women competing, period.

Reverse Image

> "[F]or the male athlete, sport is like cruising in a motorboat down an often-traveled river with his friends; the banks of the river where the cheering audience stands clearly mark his passage to a familiar and comfortable place. The female athlete has cast herself, for the first time, upon a stormy sea in a sailboat without a compass, map, or companion. A few onlookers watch, some proudly, some anxiously, some condescendingly as she journeys, little by little toward a distant, unfamiliar, and perhaps hostile destination."—Susan J. Bandy[21]

In a way, Stamata Revithi was the exact opposite of the Olympic athlete which Coubertin and his newly formed IOC had envisioned. Not only was this international brotherhood supposed to be brothers only—*no girls allowed in the tree house*—but the emphasis on gentleman amateurs would have pushed out anyone seeking employment as a reward for competing.

Recreating the track and field events in 1896 was a clear nod to the classical runners and throwers seen on those Grecian urns. But track and field for a gentleman athlete had to be approached a certain way. Those who have watched *Chariots of Fire* may remember the character of Lord Lindsay,[22] whose butler sets up champagne glasses on hurdles laid out in the garden. That was the ideal: the athlete-aristocrat. Running ought to take place across the grounds of an extensive estate or else around the courtyard of Oxford when the noon bell strikes.

The list of other events on tap for Athens were also those of the gentleman athlete: fencing, shooting, gymnastics, and tennis. Such sports required special equipment and training that only gentlemen athletes could afford. There was an awful lot of overlap between the list of events and the specific favorites of Coubertin and the other IOC members.

On the other hand, Revithi was—according to newspaper accounts compiled by historian Athanasios Tarasouleas—as much the opposite of Lord Lindsay as could be. There were no champagne glasses to be set on hurdles. Not only was she female, but she was poor. She was the mother of two, one child dead before age eight and the other accompanying her on the long walk from her home in Piraeus.

She was also looking for work. She said as much to a traveler on the road to Athens, and he mentioned the upcoming big race. The fellow suggested such a run might lead to fame and fortune. Here was at least one Greek who did not expect women to be banned from competing.

When Coubertin had spoken glowingly about the "free trade of the future," those rowers, fencers, and runners, he and his cronies meant "young men from the cultured class,"[23] not the working-class men who had populated the first two Zappas Games. When Coubertin wrote a poem on how sports was the "pleasure of the Gods, essence of life.... At your behest flesh dances and eyes smile; Blood runs abundantly through the arteries,"[24] he was not envisioning a thirty-something impoverished widow seeking a job.

Yet though Revithi wasn't the picture of the classical gentleman athlete, she had the boldness and arrogance of the athlete-aristocrat. For instance, when describing her plan to join the race, one of the other runners had teased: "Aren't you afraid you may enter the Stadium when all the spectators have gone?"

She'd replied in all seriousness, "Don't demean us women when you men have been demeaned by the Americans!"

This was a pointed reference to the Americans besting the field by winning 11 of the 43 events to date—more than the Greeks—despite being in the minority. Muhammad Ali would have smiled at her response, a "mic drop" of 1896.

Revithi *had* come all the way from Piraeus to Marathon. It was not unusual in those days to for a person to walk several miles daily looking for work. A 40 km run would not have been impossible for a hardy Mediterranean woman, especially one perked up by a hot meal at the mayor's house.

She had also described her crazy visions to the journalists, like a dream where she carried "an apron full of gold and guilded [*sic*] sugar almonds. Who knows?"[25]

Who knows, indeed, what dreams one might have after walking hungry from Piraeus to Marathon?

Who knows if the reverie continued while she ran through the hills in the April mid-morning sun? Passed occasionally by horses or travelers going out to the coast, she probably found the air fresh and the road pleasant. Trees still lined the rough road as it continued to twist through the low rocky hills near Pikermi, at the halfway point. At least it was still spring. Summer through these low rises would turn the flowers to gray stalks, bleak and depressing, and the noon sun would beat down with a different feel.[26]

Passing through Palini at 25 km, Revithi stopped to buy an orange with a coin pressed into her hand by one of the men earlier that morning. The triumphal arch was still standing from the day before, when a much bigger crowd had watched the batch of intrepid men run through.

The fruit seller told her that it was nearly eleven already, and she knew she would not finish in the three hours that she had boasted. Plus, the hills were getting steeper. Might as well sit for a drink, then, and create an excuse for taking her time. Today's contest was not about beating someone's time, not even her own prediction. This race was brand-new. No one had ever even run it before last month.

Surely just finishing would make history.

A Greek Wins the Marathon

So many marathons have gone into the history books since 1896 that it's hard to imagine the seat-of-the-pants nature of that very first one. But to put Revithi's historic run in perspective, it's helpful to take a look at that actual first marathon and understand how improvisational it was at the time.

Every Google search of the marathon, whether it's the Boston, New York, or Olympic version, mentions its connection to the Greek victory of the Battle of Marathon. Yet historians generally agree that the run to the death after that battle, described by Greek satirist Lucian six centuries after the event, didn't actually happen. Lucian, the Mark Twain of first-century Rome, was probably exaggerating.

Many running enthusiasts also don't know that the race was dreamed up by a French professor of classics over a dinner in 1894. Even the length of the marathon today—26.2 miles—wasn't standardized for a dozen years. The 26-mile, 385-yard length happened to be the distance from Windsor Castle to the 1908 Olympic Stadium in London, with the finish line directly in front of the royal box. Forever afterward, that oddball distance was used as the standard, even though they could at any time have rounded it to 26 miles.

While the organizers at the starting point in Marathon had spoken authoritatively about rules to Stamata Revithi, the truth was that the ink was barely dry on those rules. The organizers had only even decided on the course the week before.[27]

But Michel Bréal's flight of fancy had become everyone else's. When the list of Olympic events was announced for Athens, including fencing, tennis, discus, and sprints, the one event that everyone seemed excited about was this 40 km race. Of all the events, the marathon attracted the most spectators, as 80,000 fans packed the stands of the new Panathenaic Stadium in Athens. Spectators were willing to wait for more than three hours to see who might still be running after that distance.

Seventeen runners started. Thirteen were from Greece; none were from Great Britain or Germany. The non–Greeks included Arthur Blake (USA), Edwin Flack (AUS), Albin Lermusiaux (FRA), and Gyula Kellner (HUN). Blake, Flack, and Lermusiaux had taken prizes in the 1,500 m days before, though none had ever run a long distance. The concept of pacing and wristwatches was still decades away, and the racers would pay for that lack of experience.

Among the group of Greeks was another decidedly non-gentleman amateur. Spiridon Louis was a water carrier from a small village, Amarousian. Given that he had no history of racing, it's unknown why he decided to do it, other than for fame and fortune, like his female Grecian counterpart.

While Revithi was still stubbornly trying to argue her way onto the route, the motley group of runners took off from Marathon. The experienced Lermusiaux took an early lead, blazing down the road and quickly leaving the pack in the dust. The Frenchman passed under the triumphal arch constructed by the villagers in Palini at the 25 km mark, several minutes ahead of the others. The villagers slowed him down long enough to give him a victory wreath and a drink, and then he was off again. However, he began slowing down in the next big climb, was passed at 30 km, and collapsed before making it to Papagou at 35 km. Lermusiaux thus was the first of many runners who "race in haste, repent at leisure," a favorite motto of marathon coaches.

Blake, the only American, was also done after 90 minutes, along with four of the Greeks. The Australian Flack, who had passed Lermusiaux, was slowing, too. Louis and the rest of the field caught Flack shortly before Papagou. By 37 km, Flack was delirious and stumbling. He ended up punching a spectator who came to help. Eventually, the Australian also had to be carted off in a carriage and revived with some brandy.

At Panathenaic Stadium, the partisan audience had lapsed into silence at the advance news that an Australian was in the lead. But soon, Major Papadiamantopoulos, who had started the day back in Marathon with the starter's pistol, came galloping into the arena. The crowd perked up. It was hard to hear what he said as he approached the royal boxes, but suddenly a shout went up: *"Hellene! Hellene!* (A Greek! A Greek!)."

By the time Louis came trotting in, the crowd had reached fever pitch, and many locals came running behind, almost overtaking the marathoner. The officials pushed them back, although spectators in the stands also jumped down to add to the crowd. Even the prince and crown prince came down to run alongside Louis to the finish.

As Louis was hoisted on shoulders, exhausted but waving his hands with a mixture of pride and adrenaline, the last finishers entered onto the track. Second and third place went to two Greeks, Charilaos Vasilakos and Spiridon Belokas. The final non–Greek, the Hungarian Kellner, finished fourth, and only three more managed to come in behind. News soon followed, however, that Belokas had been given a ride part of the way. When the officials questioned him a few days later, he quickly admitted the truth, and Kellner took third place, the only non–Greek among the finishers.

Louis, of course, was the new favorite son, hometown winner of what was now an authentic, ancient hometown race. At the formal dinner, he received his laurel wreath, the silver cup promised by M. Bréal, a painted replica of a Greek vase, and a gold watch.[28]

Had the Greeks really thought this through, however, they might have realized that having two Greek winners, a man and a woman, would have raised Louis and Revithi practically to the status of modern gods.

Still, the race organizers had remained steadfast against allowing any women. So only Spiridon Louis is mentioned in the official record.

For the Record

Yet "official records" are less carved in stone than might be believed. Aside from the tissue-paper excuse for planning that formed the rationale for the 1896 Olympics in the first place, the idea that rules and records were treated as official at the time seems fairly laughable.

Consider the designation of the Olympiads themselves. Three sets of Zappas Games had already taken place prior to the 1896 competitions, not to mention the Swedish "Olympic Union" Games or the Much Wenlock versions. None of them were counted as Olympics because the Olympic Committee hadn't been formed. In other words, they aren't considered "Olympics" today because Coubertin and the USFSA hadn't yet proposed a revival of Games, when those Olympic-like contests took place.

The next two Olympiads after 1896 were designated for Paris and St. Louis. As the next chapter explains, both cities ended up combining the Games with World's Fairs, with competitions that were barely recognizable as a formal tournament. Local athletes won the vast majority of the medals. Olympic historians often even ignore those contests entirely when writing recaps of the Games.

Meanwhile, the Greeks enjoyed their 1896 success so much that they voted unilaterally among themselves to host the Olympics forever more. The IOC unilaterally disagreed. Nevertheless, Athens held another Olympic Games in 1906. This event was even better attended by fans and athletes than the first three. For instance, 20 nations sent 887 athletes to Athens in 1906—twice the number of countries that had gone to St. Louis, just two years before.

In many respects these 1906 Games were "paradoxically … the Olympics that came closest to Coubertin's vision."[29] They fit the model that the French intellectuals, the British athletes in Much Wenlock, and the Greek tycoons all had in mind. However, the IOC didn't organize them, so they were never called Olympiads and have always been referred to as the Intercalated Games. Their records don't count.

Being a stickler about who ran in the official race also doesn't limit stories of participation by athletes. Another of the strange but true stories in Olympic history was of two German oarsmen who rowed in the 1896 Pairs-Sculling race. Berthold

One. Refused Admission at the Dawn of the Modern Games (1896)

Kuttner and Alfred Jaeger took off from the Neo-Phaleron dock and rowed for victory. They even had a photo taken.

Kuttner further detailed in his journal his extensive training, the journey from Germany to Athens, the weather on race day, and the results. He recounted that he and Jaeger "won the race" and presented themselves to the prince, even noting that the prince's entourage had made fun of their rude clothing: "After the official salutation and presentation in the Court Loge, where many of the attendees could not hide a laugh about my clothing, Prince George, President of the Committee, praised me for our appearance at the racing track and presented me with the winners medal in bronze."[30]

Kuttner's journals surfaced during publicity before the 1936 Berlin Games, and his articles were extensively reprinted in *The Journals of Olympic History* in 2012.

There was only one problem: high winds and inclement weather had canceled all the rowing events. There *were* no official 1896 rowing events. The breezes had been so strong that dust clouds blew through the city, and some of the launch piers ended up thrown up onto the shore. But what's a little cancellation to a pair of athletes, ready to go? The German rowers' approach has itself made its way into the public record, if not the official one.

Additionally, the official report from Athens[31] still mentions the Greek Belokas "winning" third place in the marathon. There's no asterisk noting that he was stripped of his award when it was found he had ridden part of the way. In that sense, even official records can be in error.

Only amateur gentlemen athletes were supposed to be allowed, and at least one Greek runner had been turned away because he was a professional runner. Furthermore, a priest, Prosper Matzakos, was banned from taking part because his religious calling took him out of the ruling class. Yet Spiridon Louis, who was a working farmer by trade and not a gentleman athlete, was also allowed to run and hailed as the peasant victor. Rules were then—as they are now—subject to interpretation.

Some historians claim that no evidence supports a woman running in the Olympic marathon,[32] but multiple others have provided details about Revithi and the mysterious Melpomene, even in the IOC's official publication.[33] While Revithi is not listed in the marathon record books, her effort in the days before and after the marathon were chronicled in the local news.

Over the decades, fans have found Revithi's story so intriguing that many include her tale in their essays or anthologies, sometimes picking and choosing from the multiple reports of 1896.

One noteworthy example was on cable, a show called *Warehouse 13*, which centered around detectives searching for historical artifacts, some of which gave power to the finder. Among those artifacts was Stamata Revithi's registration card, filled out in Greek. It's still in the wiki for *Warehouse 13*, alphabetically nestled between St. George's ring and Stan Lee's pen in glorious Technicolor.[34]

The Olympics are, after all, based on ideas extracted from paintings on the sides of storage jugs and plant holders. A fictitious entry card might be the same as the artistic license taken and shown on those urns.

In the first modern Games, women—at least one in particular—were refused at

Fig.3. An (unknown) artist's rendering of Stamata Revithi, who ran the Athenian marathon the day after the 1896 Olympic contest, as reported by several Greek newspapers (courtesy of Running Heroes blog).

the starting line, but Revithi was not the only person not allowed to run. She was the only one who came back the next day to try again.

History records more than just the list of winners.

Melpomene's Legacy

At half past one on that Saturday in 1896, early diners enjoying a plate of bread and olives in an Athenian cafe near the Panathenaic Stadium would have seen a figure trotting toward them from the east, perhaps stopping for directions before heading their way. It turned out to be a woman, covered in dust and perspiration after five and a half hours on the road.

Revithi's pace after 40 km was steady but slow, though as she got closer to the stadium walls, she straightened and moved to a brisk trot. The handful of finishers the day before had done that, too.

One. Refused Admission at the Dawn of the Modern Games (1896)

Just as at the starting line the day before, she was stopped before entry. A pair of Greek military officers refused to allow her entry into the stadium, even though it was empty. It was a great disappointment, as she would have liked to finish on the track, but she recovered quickly and asked them to sign her record, confirming the time she arrived.

One of the officers, as if talking to a child, asked why she had run all that way:

—So that the king might award a position to my child. I am now going straight to Timoleon Philimon (the secretary general of the Greek Olympic Committee) to let him know how long it took me to run from Marathon, and tell him that whoever wishes may come to compete with me.
—Were you running quickly?
—You should have seen me! I stopped at various shops on the way. If I had run straight, I would have finished in three hours at the most.[35]

Despite the challenges, Revithi had completed the run. Half the runners who started the "official" marathon of the day before did not finish.

Columnist Jere Longman in the *Times* wondered why Revithi did it. "Why would anyone run 24 miles for a civil service job?"[36] Clearly Longman, like the Athenian Organizing Committee, the USFSA, and Coubertin, missed the point. One might as well ask why anyone would run, not for money, but for the glory and accomplishment? Surely, a woman might want that as much as any man.

Revithi showed up to run, and rules were invented to prevent her. She ran anyway.

Given how much she interacted with the reporters, she likely knew it might be scoffed at as a publicity stunt, but she didn't appear to mind. She probably knew, as she meandered through the dust and rocky hills, that there'd be no civil service job forthcoming, but she kept going. Her child had been left in Marathon, so if she made it to Athens, she would have had to travel the distance in reverse. She ran anyway.

In the years to follow, many women would boast, cajole, argue, plead, and run to prove their point, following in the footsteps of Stamata Revithi. As a man famously once said, it's not about the triumph but the struggle.

Revithi proved several things to the world at large. She proved that women could run. Women could finish. And she proved unequivocally that women were not going to go away.

Two

Getting in the Game
The Pioneers (1900–1912)

Despite being banned from the 1896 Olympics, women crept into the Games of 1900 and 1904, although hardly anyone noticed. They competed in lawn games developed by and for the wealthy, like croquet and tennis. Often they competed with family, like cousins, brothers, and husbands. Eventually, they were even permitted activities that emphasized their forms, as "bathing beauties" or shapely gymnasts.

At the same time, men's track and field events more than doubled in size and scope in the first two Olympiads, sill considered sacred competitions reserved for gentleman athletes. The organizing committees remained steadfast in their opposition to any participation of women in track and field.

Like the marchers for suffrage that accompanied the era, women athletes would have to protest in large numbers and in unique ways. As with the demands for suffrage, the push to let women into the Games would require decades of pressure. But what were a few more years after centuries of history? Women had been running—and winning—races already, for a long, long time.

Girls Allowed

Historians often imply that women barely participated in sports until they suddenly emerged, all at once, running and swimming into the arenas of the 20th century. The Victorians were notorious for suggesting that the skirts of *pedestriennes* prevented them from movement or that girls should refrain from sports because they needed to scrub the floors. Yet history has been full of examples of women competing.

Start with the Greek myths. Even if the Greeks curtailed women athletes, they wrote stories which recognized their capabilities. The goddess Artemis was an archer and huntress. The Amazons were fearsome on horseback.

The swift warrior Atalanta bargained with her father to remain unmarried as long as she could defeat all suitors in a footrace. Dozens lost the race and their lives, since losing meant death. Hippomenes decided to use his brain rather than physical skill and threw golden apples ahead of her to slow her down. She married him then but gained a substantial dowry. Atalanta was bested by cunning, not speed. Even among the ancients, women could compete and win.

Women weren't athletes just in the stories, either. In the friezes painted on the Minoan palace walls at Crete (~1600 BCE), both adolescent boys and girls practice in bull-leaping, grabbing a bull's horns from the front, then flying over its back. Centuries later, the Greeks banned women from the Olympiads—but only in the Games of Zeus. They held separate Games for Hera, which featured running contests specifically for young and adolescent girls.

Spartans also held contests for women, reasoning that healthy mothers gave birth to healthy warriors. Rome had female gladiatrices. Overall, even though women were kept out of the Olympics, ancient narratives were full of examples of female athletes.

European nobility took up plenty of sporting pastimes. Although men did the jousting, medieval women were expected to be excellent falconers and huntresses. Queen Elizabeth I was renowned on horseback,[1] while her cousin Mary Queen of Scots was painted playing golf, the national sport. Queen Victoria had a "bathing machine," a little house rolled into the water where she could change into a bathing costume and emerge straight into the water to stroke around the seaside.

The non-aristocratic classes also engaged in physical activity. From the Middle Ages forward, local boys and girls played "folk football" (the precursor to soccer) and "stoolball" (the precursor to cricket and baseball). In the 19th century, calisthenics and gymnastics came into vogue. Chapter Six will show how many countries picked up this gymnastics torch.

Meanwhile, the Industrial Age books were full of diagrams demonstrating how to exercise with a variety of physical contraptions, with pictures showing both genders. James Chiosso's *Polymachinon*,[2] for example, was the predecessor to the Bowflex, an 1850s all-in-one weight machine. Meanwhile, though 19th-century gentlewomen didn't play folk football or hang out at the gymnasium, they did add tennis, archery, and croquet to their repertoire of birding and horseback riding.

Improvements in nutrition and health meant women and men were eating more, living longer, and working less. Exercise as a pastime became increasingly popular. The strong push against women's participation in sports toward the latter part of the Victorian era was partly a counteraction against the strong and visible increase in their activity. By the start of the 20th century, plenty of women were running, jumping, bicycling, shooting, and swimming, not to mention playing golf, basketball, and tennis.

The response, by organizing committees and athletic unions, was to ban women from competitions. But it was trying to put the genie back in the bottle. As of 1897, the passion for sports was spreading widely, wider perhaps than even the enthusiasm for reviving the Games, which still waxed and waned.

Those first Olympic Games of 1896 were deemed both success and failure. The enthusiasm for international participation in Athens had been strong among those classical scholars sitting around the banquet table, but someone had forgotten to tell the participants. Only the United States and Hungary had sent all-around teams to Greece, and most contests were dominated by locals. The organizers were thrilled they pulled it off, and a grand party was had by all, but even the shopkeepers were disappointed when only about a thousand out-of-towners came to watch.

The plan for the next two Olympiads looked good on paper. Attach them to a World's Fair—upcoming ones were proposed for Paris and Chicago—and the international throngs would already be there, ready to buy souvenir programs. Coubertin was French, so naturally he pushed for a strong Olympic program to be included in Paris. He would later regret the move, when the sports were overshadowed by the fair as a whole.

To start with, the 1900 Paris World's Fair—*now with Olympics!*—took place over several months, from mid–May to October. There were no opening or closing ceremonies. The sports were sprinkled among the exhibitions, sometimes in bizarre categories. Skating and fencing were categorized as subsections of cutlery. The rowing events took place among the lifesaving displays. Track and field were a part of "providential" (voluntary) societies.

Although the IOC, formed in 1894, believed it was still in charge, the overall design of the athletic program was left to the head of the French Shooting Association, Daniel Merrillion. The result was rightly termed a "disaster."[3] Running events took place on a muddy field. The hammer and discus had to be thrown through a clump of trees. Broken telephone poles were used as hurdles.

No one still knows definitively which events were part of the Olympic program. For example, the Official Paris 1900 Olympic report includes a 90-page section on the balloon races, which sound kind of fun, though the IOC now excludes them from the official website. As historian David Goldblatt puts it : "To this day, it remains a matter of some dispute as to precisely which events were Olympic and which were not … at the time, almost no one—crowd, competitors or press—thought there was an Olympic Games going on at all."[4]

Into this kind of chaos, women could certainly be admitted to casually scheduled events, only designated after the fact as "Olympic." The official poster for the Games is particularly curious in this vein, since it sports a buxom female fencer brandishing fencing weapons. Women weren't admitted to the 1900 fencing program, but that's never stopped advertisers. Such a poster might explain why women felt free to participate in other events.

Officially women in Paris 1900 competed in four disciplines: tennis, golf, croquet, and *chevaux de selle*. This last event was on horseback, a contest known in English as Hacks and Hunter Combined, a cross between dressage and show-jumping. Riders were judged by how pleasing their horses looked while going over obstacles. Picture, perhaps, the Miss America contestants in their swimsuit competition doing the backstroke. Italy's Elvira Guerra competed in *chevaux de selle* along with an estimated fifty men, making Ms. Guerra officially the first woman to compete in the Olympic Games.

Wimbledon had inaugurated a ladies' tennis competition twenty years earlier,[5] so it was logical for tennis to be added to the Games. By 1900, Britain's Charlotte Cooper had already won three titles, which made her a natural favorite. Only a week after losing the Wimbledon final in London, Cooper beat France's Hélène Yvonne Prévost in Paris, landing her the designation as the first female Olympic champion.

The men's champion, Laurie Doherty, was helped when his older brother, Reginald, forfeited their scheduled Olympic semifinal. Reggie himself had just won

Wimbledon, so he gallantly let his little brother advance to the Olympic final and first place, while Reggie took third. The two Doherty brothers would eventually win seven of the nine Wimbledon singles finals between 1897 and 1906, so their Paris success was no surprise.

To round it off in Paris, Wimbledon female winner Cooper and male winner Reggie Doherty took first in Olympic Mixed Doubles, too. Thus, Wimbledon cast a long shadow on Olympic tennis for the twenty years that both took place.[6] But so did aristocratic friends and families. While the Doherty brothers took tennis, the Abbotts took women's golf.

The Abbotts were a mother and daughter pair traveling the continent, which is what Americans with money did in the summers. Margaret was studying art in Paris, while her mother acted as chaperone and toured the Champs-Élysées. The duo signed up to play golf in the World's Fair on a whim. Miss Abbott won the tournament, while Mrs. Mary Abbott tied for seventh.

Fig.4. Official poster for the Games of the II Olympiad, Paris 1900, designed by Jean de Paleologu. Women were allowed to compete in a few events, though not in fencing, despite the attractive female prominently displayed. Women's foil would not debut until Paris 1924 (Wikimedia Commons).

Margaret's success came, she said, because "all the French girls apparently misunderstood the nature of the game scheduled for that day and turned up to play in high heels and tight skirts." She received a gilded porcelain bowl from the fair, though no one told her it was for the Olympics. She died in 1955 without even knowing that she was the first American female golf champion.[7]

Crossing families and crossing sports, these were athletes of means, whether American or European. At home, they had access to country clubs and estate lawns. (Cue the champagne glasses on the hurdles!) The winning male golfer, American Charles Sand, also competed in tennis. Marcel Haëntjens took fourth in the Hacks and Hunter, but he also competed in another lawn game with most of his family. It was the only other available sport open to women: croquet.[8]

Like the equestrian contests, croquet was played as a mixed-gender sport, with men and women together, just as they played on their expansive lawns. Jeanne Filleaul-Brohy, who finished fifth, was Haëntjens's sister. Brohy was the cousin of Jacques Sautereau and of Marie Ohier, who also competed. Overall, croquet seemed less like a serious competition and more as if an extended family had wandered by the lawn on Croquet Day, as people might at Epcot or Six Flags. *Here, hold my ice cream while I try this Olympics thing....*

Fifth place went to a Mme. Després, who happened to be the wife of Andre Després, president of the French Croquet Federation. Perhaps Andre thought it unseemly to compete in his own sport in his own country. Not so for his wife. All the croquet players were French. The gentlemen who played and won in Mixed Singles, One Ball, also played and won, in a slightly different order, in Mixed Singles, Two Balls. In Mixed Doubles, France played against France. France won.

Thus, all the 1900 events permitting women included families, passers-by, or friends of the organizers, with the exception of tennis. Charlotte Cooper at least had played tennis in other tournaments and was aware that she had "won" an Olympic distinction. That put her one up on Margaret Abbott.

In the third Olympiad, the 1904 St. Louis World Fair & Olympics extravaganza, women's events were trimmed back from four to only one. Given what happened, this was probably just as well.

The Dubious Olympics of 1904

If it's possible for an international sporting tournament to be less impressive than the one in Paris, the St. Louis Games succeeded. On America's first foray into hosting the Olympics, the organizers in Missouri made a very poor international impression.

To begin with, St. Louis was the IOC's second choice for the Games. Chicago was their first choice. However, St. Louis had planned a World's Fair for 1903, to celebrate the centennial for the Louisiana Purchase. Delays caused them to bump the fair to 1904, and they complained that the Chicago Olympics would conflict with their extravaganza. The IOC's solution was to simply substitute one Midwestern American city for another and move the Games from Chicago to St. Louis. Chicago was none too happy about it.

As with the Paris Fair, the St. Louis competitions lasted for months, from spring through fall. As with Paris, the IOC had little input on what events were staged. This time, they didn't even produce an official report. An opening ceremony was held in May, but the marquee sporting events didn't start until July.

Neither Britain nor France, the two strongest countries besides the United States, sent athletic contingents. It's not surprising that the Americans won 85 percent of the medals. With almost no competition, American chroniclers still gleefully celebrated while grousing about the ingratitude of other countries: "It is doubtful, indeed, if a single Frenchman could have finished even fourth in any of the events."[9]

At the same time, historians have pointed out that many of the "American" competitors were immigrants who had not been granted citizenship yet when they competed. They were not technically Americans at the time. The U.S. included them in the U.S. medal count anyway. Citizenship would remain a flexible and fractious issue whenever medals might be at stake.

The marathon was particularly bizarre. Oppressive heat forced more than half the runners off the course, especially when they weren't allowed to drink water. One runner was dosed with strychnine and brandy over the last few miles. It must have worked, since he won. A South African athlete was chased off the track by a pack of dogs. Afterward, race organizers declared that the marathon simply shouldn't be run ever again.

Somehow, the Games got even weirder.

The most notorious portion of the sports competition was "Anthropology Days." It was the combined brainchild of anthropology Professor William J. McGee and James E. Sullivan, head of the Amateur Athletic Union (AAU). McGee had designed a set of ethnological exhibits from around the world, populated with indigenous people to occupy the sites for the duration of the fair. Such exhibits were popular at the turn of the century, and people flocked to see the "human zoos."

McGee and Sullivan decided to combine the exhibits with the Olympics, as both experiment and publicity stunt to attract more people to the sports competitions. McGee also wanted to test his theory of "romantic athletic primitivism." While he believed in the superiority of civilized whites over the backwardness of non-white "savages," he thought the brute strength of uneducated "natives" would be demonstrated through athletic contests. Sullivan, in contrast, simply thought them inferior in every way. The two decided to test their competing hypotheses.

McGee had the indigenous fellows attempt the shot put, high jump, and sprints. Whether because they did not speak the language that explained the rules or because they found the requests silly, the "athletes" did not perform up to McGee's standards. For instance, in the 100 m sprint, they didn't respond when the starting pistol was fired. Once they started, the leader waited for others to catch up, and none of them understood why they needed to break a perfectly good line of string at the finish.

More "primitive" contests were added: tree-climbing, archery, and mud-throwing. These also had predictably dismal outcomes. Strangely enough, the organizers even considered water polo, until they realized most of the men couldn't swim. Overall, Anthropology Days was considered a colossal failure by the audience and a historical blemish on anthropology by future scientists. McGee, though, deemed it a success because it proved something "scientific." Romantic primitivism was wrong, he concluded: "the savage is not the natural athlete we have been led to believe."[10]

Co-organizer Sullivan himself held strong biases against more than just non-white athletes. He was also dead set against women competitors. Sullivan was busy consolidating the power of the AAU at the time. While he was in charge, American women would have no place on any athletic field. Thus, in St. Louis, golf and tennis were made off-limits to females, croquet was canceled, and the only sport left on the bill for women was archery. After all, anyone could stand and shoot, no matter how restrictive their clothing.

With no official report, whether archery was even an Olympic event is still debated. The competition appears to have been formally named the American National Championship. Still, a St. Louis 1904 "sports almanac" listed the archery results next to the other Olympic winners.

Olympic or not, the winner in the Double National Round was Mrs. M. C. Howell.[11] Later histories noted that her full name was Matilda Scott Howell, although with the memory of Anthropology Days still lingering, Mrs. Howell might have been satisfied with less notoriety. Plus, if women were going to make further inroads into sports, they might need to move around, at least a little.

Pleasing Figures

Women did increase their participation in the Games in 1908 and 1912, although one event in St. Louis was a pretty low bar to surpass. The sports of gymnastics, swimming, and figure skating brought new opportunities in contests that at least allowed some movement. The IOC remained determined to draw a line in the sand at track and field to keep the sacred "athletics" restricted to men only. The London organizing committee had their hands full, anyway.

Even without venues full of mud or exhibitions full of racist stereotypes, the 1908 Olympics had plenty of controversy. Several countries—the U.S., Sweden, and Finland—weren't given flags for the opening ceremony. When the Americans did find one, their standard bearer reportedly refused to dip the flag when walking before the royal box. Accusations flew after the Tug of War, with the Americans claiming the Londoners unfairly used hobnailed boots. Lastly, the marathon concluded with one of the most embarrassing endings possible, where judges interfered to help Italian Dorando Pietri across the finish line.[12]

Still, though the 1908 Games had its share of less-than-stellar moments, the London Olympics finally got right what had been missing from the prior three Olympiads. Twenty-two nations participated, as the host city realized that a win for the host nation only mattered when other countries showed up. Thus, there was a modest move toward inclusivity and more participation, which meant women were allowed into four events, including two new ones.

For the most part, these were still country club and estate sports. Archery and tennis stayed on the program, but yachting[13] was added, a word that dripped with even more privilege. Sailing events allowed both genders on the boats, and at least three women helped to crew in London.[14] These included the Duchess of Westminster and Mrs. John Marshall Gorman, who, like Mme. Després and Mrs. Howell, were only reported by title or as adjunct to their husbands.

The big change in London, however, was the addition of a new sport with its own women's division: figure skating. In 1908, the Olympics were not yet called the Summer Olympics. The formal idea of a Winter Games was still decades away (to be covered in a later chapter). While the majority of London's sports took place in July, several events were held in the fall. Boxing, wrestling, lacrosse, and field hockey all took place in September and October. Adding ice skating wasn't much of a stretch.

Competitive figure skating, as distinct from speed skating, was another recently discovered pastime growing in popularity. The International Skating Union (ISU) itself had just formed in 1892, with its first world competition held in 1896. During the 1902 championships in London, Britain's Madge Syers entered and took a surprising second place. Surprising, because the ISU had intended skating to be limited to men. They had just never explicitly codified it in the rules. While the ISU officials were flipping through the rule books, looking for a way to get Syers off the ice, the judges enjoyed her work enough to award her second place.[15]

The ISU met again and solved the problem by establishing separate "ISU Championships"—for ladies only—not to be confused with the "World Championships." The technical reason they gave for not allowing men and women to compete against each other was that women's long dresses made it difficult to see their feet.[16] Rather than suggest that women wear shorter dresses that allowed movement and visibility of the skates, the ISU instead suggested they not compete. Or somehow not compete against the men, only against each other.

Curiously enough, the British Figure Skating Union had no such qualms, and Syers competed against men in the National Championships for several more years. She won in 1903 and 1904, even against her husband. Madge and Edgar Syers also competed in pairs, when they were allowed. Some countries considered competitive pairs skating too licentious to be viewed in public.

By the London Games, then, Madge Syers had become something of a living legend for Great Britain. Why not include skating as a women's event when there was already a local champion? The men also figure skated, and Sweden swept the three spots in Men's Singles, so the London organizers could claim they were free of bias. When Syers won the Olympic Ladies Singles event, the judges described her as "in a class by herself."[17]

Figure skating was not the first event to be scored subjectively, based on appearance. Equestrian events had already judged horse and rider based on the "quality of the routine." Diving and gymnastics were both evaluated based on measurement to a standard. As the vast majority of athletes were men, it was men being judged on appearance.

Hence, the idea of beauty in sporting forms was not originally linked to women. Part of the original Greek ideal, after all, was represented by athletes memorialized in statues and on urns. Coubertin himself had pressed for art competitions alongside sports. Aesthetics had always been part of the package.

For many viewers and judges, it was easy in 1908 to accept women into contests which were based on form and appearance. Diving and gymnastics for women were added as demonstration sports in London as well. Arguments still raged about whether it was unsightly for women to show strain when running or to display muscles for throwing, but audiences were happy to enjoy a pleasing figure in sports. Skating, gymnastics, diving, and even archery allowed women to appear graceful within the standard of femininity.

In London, an exhibition troupe of Danish women gymnasts, dressed in long-sleeved blouses and just-below-the-knee culottes, performed in the opening ceremony. The appearance of Danish ankles, even swathed in thick leggings, attracted a great deal of attention. Salacious or not as the performance was, organizers wanted attendees, and a dozen Scandinavian bodies moving in rhythm could help pay for stadiums. The newspapers prominently covered this part of the Olympics, praising "the graceful proportions of their nether limbs."[18]

For instance, the front page of the London *Daily Mirror*[19] featured a huge photo of the gymnasts, next to pictures of the king and the procession of the athletes. The *London News* went with a full eleven pages on the "Danish Dianas":

> At the Olympic Games, the most beautiful exhibition of gymnastics was given by the team of Danish girl athletes, who among all the competitors in the Stadium, were unsurpassed for splendid physical development and grace of movement. The prettiness of their "ensemble" was increased by their charming costume, which was of cream colour with amber stockings.[20]

Thus launched the Olympic love/hate affair with aesthetic sports. Athletes and sportswriters, both men and women, would complain—and still do—that this detracted from the "real" sports, even though beauty in form had been there since the Greeks. Women who were not allowed to run in 1908 complained about being shunted into sports that emphasized form and beauty and were subject to (male) judgment.

Still, though the Danish gymnasts performing in London didn't directly help the sprinters and jumpers, their exercise did open the door a crack. Not only was women's gymnastics added to the next Games in Stockholm, but diving was as well. Along with diving, the next logical sport was swimming.

The introduction of swimming in the 1912 Games involved vigorous behind-the-scenes debate. The Official Report from Sweden documents how the issue of ladies' swimming events came up in the planning meetings, was tabled, was "proposed again from several quarters," was agreed to for one event, and was tabled again when more events were requested.

Coubertin, then president of the IOC, continued his objection to women's participation in any form. However, he was also pushing for support of two new brainchild ideas: the modern pentathlon and an arts competition. The ancient Greeks had awarded prizes for poetry along with racing and discus-throwing. Coubertin had long lobbied for this type of expansion and Stockholm was the ideal venue for it, as a song festival was already scheduled in parallel. The baron didn't want to make room for more women, but compromise was in the air, and he likely traded votes to obtain his other aims. Ultimately, the IOC voted in favor of two women's swimming events: a 100 m race and a 4 × 100 m relay. They also added the pentathlon and the arts competition.

Even only two swimming events was a great leap forward. Finally, swimmers were able to wear suits that allowed their arms and legs to move freely. While there was a lot more cloth in their suits than in 21st-century Speedos, the 1912 suits were not long-sleeved with long skirts. Suits not only bared forearms and shins, but were so transparent that bikinis were required underneath as well.

Not everyone was happy with the proposed Olympic swimming plan. The

Australian club, the New South Wales Ladies Amateur Swimming Association, banned their female members from swimming in front of men. When swimmers Fanny Durack and Mina Wylie qualified to travel to London, the club softened enough to allow them to compete. But the club refused to pay for travel, and Durack and Wylie had to raise the funds on their own. After the two women came in first and second in the 100 m sprint, though, the New South Wales Ladies Amateur Swimming Association then loudly proclaimed the women two of their own.

Meanwhile in the United States, Sullivan and the AAU effectively barred women from swimming. They didn't decree the sport off-limits, but they required women to wear long skirts when competing—even when swimming.

As a result, in 1908, the British and Australian swimmers started a friendly rivalry, the Swedes dominated the new diving events, and the Americans were nowhere to be found. But swimming remained one of the first events that allowed women to move freely and quickly enough to be out of breath.[21] Track and field events might have been close behind.

However, before the organizing committees could seriously consider the next logical step, a bullet in Sarajevo intervened. The 1916 Games were canceled as World War I broke out.

When the post-war Olympics reconvened in Antwerp 1920, they were part

Fig.5. The Women's 100 m in 1912 finally allowed bare legs in women's Olympic sport. But no U.S. swimmers, as the American Amateur Athletic Union still required athletes to wear skirts. Heat 2, left-right: Jenni Fletcher (GBR); Berta Zahourek (AUT); Josefa Kellner (AUT); Karin Lundgren (SWE) (Wikimedia Commons).

memorial to the fallen and part renewal of the Olympic ideal—as it originally had been. The expansion of participation for women was put on the agenda, but the IOC ignored the request and approved no changes.

For women, Antwerp was a definite push backward. Women's gymnastics and archery were jettisoned as the IOC complained that it could not keep expanding events. However, they kept men's archery and gymnastics while adding more men's disciplines. Women's diving and swimming events stayed, but as far as track and field was concerned, women were going nowhere. The wall erected between women athletes and the hallowed Olympic running and throwing sports seemed to be getting taller.

The Open Landscape of Women's Track and Field

The idea of an ancient track legacy that the IOC was trying to safeguard was really more myth than reality. Looking at the history of track and field reveals that these "core" Olympic sports came from the minds of organizers overcome with nostalgia for the classics rather than from sports at the time. Organized track and field was itself only a few decades old, and women's participation in it not much younger than that.

At the time of the 1896 Olympics, track organizations had barely been in place for ten years. Although the New York Athletic Club had formed back in 1868, most American track clubs were founded after 1880. The oldest intercollegiate meet, the Penn Relays, began in 1895. Sullivan had formed the AAU just in 1888, only a handful of years after he joined the brand-spanking-new Pastime Athletic Club of Syracuse.

The same was true in Europe. One of the earliest running competitions in France, the Racing Club de France, was created in 1882. Its athletes were primarily high school students from Lycées Monge, Rollin, and Condorcet.[22] Compare that with Wimbledon, which had begun holding men's singles championships back in 1877, carrying an older pedigree than all of the others.

In the early days, nothing was standardized—not the rules, not the equipment, not the participants. Race lengths differed based on location because of differing national measurement systems. The metric system, created in France, was adopted across continental Europe, but the U.S. and Great Britain still used yards and miles. Hence, American athletes like Princeton's Luther Cary, who holds the oldest 100 m ever recorded, might run either yards or meters, depending on where the meet took place. Even in the decathlon, race lengths were sometimes in yards, as in the 1904 Games in St. Louis.

Track substances also varied widely. Cinder tracks—flattened pieces of burned wood or coal—offered great traction and drainage but weren't universal. Often, meets still took place on grass or dirt, which could be muddy for a large part of the year. At the Paris Games, events took place on an uneven field, littered with trees, without a separate track at all. Eventually, the International Amateur Athletic Federation (IAAF) would standardize track surfaces, but the IAAF wasn't founded until after the 1912 Games.

Thus, the early days of track and field were an open landscape—literally—over which men were running. Women started running, too, despite resistance from the organized men's clubs. Female athletes ran both in high school and college, notably at private women's colleges like the Seven Sisters. Vassar, for example, started a robust athletic program with calisthenics but quickly adopted basketball, archery, tennis, and track. Vassar's records for the 60 yd. and 220 yd. dash date back to 1903.

High school girls often didn't run at school. Teenage girls did run—often faster than their college-age counterparts—but in meets sponsored by a local businesses or newspapers. The physical education teachers at school, often women, were against girls and women participating in competitions.

The stance held by the American Physical Education Association at the turn of the century was that girls should not be motivated to compete. Their reasoning was not that women were unable to compete or that physical exercise was bad, but they viewed men's competition as toxic, pointing to examples of gambling and cheating as proof. The APEA stance was to promote individual over team sports and to encourage participation in "play days," intramural-type competitions where there were no prizes for winners.

This paternalistic attitude from the women's divisions within the AAU and APEA would remain strong for decades, into the 1990s, even after the passage of Title IX. As a result, there was little opportunity for girls to run track in school. They ran anyway, as they had since the Games of Hera, at picnics and unofficial meets. American women formed track clubs attached to their employers rather than their colleges.

European cities also staged their own informal meets. Paris, for instance, hosted a unique footrace in October 1903. Some 2,500 "shop girls" ran a 12 k (7.5 miles), as reported in *Outing* magazine,[23] a kind of *Sports Illustrated* for *la belle epoque*. The winner finished in an hour and ten minutes. In keeping with the "shop girl" theme, she won a new set of bedroom furniture and the equivalent of sixty dollars. The young women ran in their work clothes, wearing skirts of varying lengths and long-sleeved blouses. Few were experienced runners. Yet, they did run, and their mixed audience of well-wishers and curious media pronounced it splendid rather than scandalous.

The *Outing* correspondent went so far as to argue that the race heralded a new era of interest in running, not just by shop girls of the working classes, but by the "château set" as well: "the fashionable, bored, country-seated class that is either tired of hunting or doesn't know how, or is looking for something new."[24]

Not to be outdone by the French, the Germans also organized large-scale races. In 1904, 70 young women ran in Berlin, first in several 400 m heats, then in a 500 m final. The crowd loved it, although some in the newspapers complained about indecency. This would be a continuing theme, this alternating adulation mixed with criticism.

For example, one female journalist in an 1894 *Fortnightly Review* eagerly rejoiced that women were no longer simply living on "candy and novels," which might turn them into "nervous invalid[s] before … thirty." Instead, as sportswomen, these Americans were "of strong active physique, erect carriage and energetic spirit … aglow with the ruddy color of physical health and energy."[25]

On the other hand, the more prudish Miss T. R. Coombs wondered, "How can we admire a girl, however beautiful she may be, whose face is as red as a lobster, and streaming with perspiration, whose hair is hanging in a mop about her ears whose hairpins are strewn along the race-course, and whose general appearance is dusty, untidy, and unwomanly?"[26]

While the general public couldn't decide whether they loved or hated the spectacle of women racing, promoters were happy to attract crowds in whatever fashion possible. Bernarr Macfadden, founder of a growing publishing empire built around *Physical Culture* magazine, planned a show in Madison Square Garden in 1905. Macfadden himself was a mix of Jack LaLanne, Dr. Oz, and Donald Trump from the Miss America years, both health nut and ardent capitalist. Local authorities arrested Macfadden for public indecency for putting on shows with scantily clad athletes. However, the arrest just boosted event publicity. Crowds flocked to see the "lewd display of carnality,"[27] though they may have been disappointed to see union suits rather than bare flesh. The whole shebang was a strange mix, a pageant-type parade of "shapely young women" followed by a series of challenges for the contestants like weight lifting, the high jump, and races over multiple distances.[28]

By the time of the 1920 Olympics, therefore, it was neither unusual nor socially unacceptable for women to compete in track and field events. While some on influential committees like the IOC, AAU, or APEA were against females competing, others saw races as healthy and entertaining.

Still, women's patience was running out as international meet organizers continued to put them off. They had run out of patience before, waiting to be "given" the vote. A few decades earlier, they had marched on the streets until they received universal suffrage. In like fashion, they began to exert pressure—no longer just ask permission—on the IOC for expansion.

Besides, if they couldn't get all the way into the events, they had another option. They could host a Games of their own.

Three

The Road from Alice to Amsterdam (1912–1928)

> "Since everyone agreed that track-and-field competitions were the core of the Olympic Games, the inclusion of women as runners, jumpers, and throwers was fiercely resisted."[1]—Alan Guttmann

In Antwerp 1920, the first Olympics after the war to end all wars, the world was happy to view sporting contests as a return to normality. There were more participants than ever—2668. Only 77 of those were women, 3 percent of the athletes, cloistered in figure skating, aquatics, and tennis. The 97 percent who welcomed those women to their 8 events (out of 154) couldn't understand why they were complaining rather than celebrating.

After marching for years, suffragettes had won the long-fought battle to vote in dozens of countries by August of 1920. Women were shortening skirts, cutting hair, smoking, drinking, and working outside the home. They knew how to push for more freedom. They were not going to settle for playing croquet in ankle-length skirts.

For female athletes to make it from the stately lawn sports of Paris onto the cinder tracks of Amsterdam would require a push by another French intellectual, another rower and proponent of physical education very much like Baron de Coubertin. Also like Coubertin, she didn't take no for an answer.

The movement to expand sports further for women needed a strong leader to get them organized. They got one.

Her name was Alice Milliat.

Milliat Gets Organized

Alice Milliat was born Alice Million in 1887 in Nantes, a medium-sized city in northwest France. Her parents were employed and middle class, her father a businessman and mother a seamstress. As a teenager, she traveled to England—"ran away," one biography suggests—to see a different part of the world. She ended up meeting her future husband there, Joseph Milliat, a man from her hometown. After persuading Alice to return home with him to France, Joseph died only four years later. It left Mme. Milliat in Paris, as one narrative says, "widowed and childless."[2]

Or, as another might put it, 21 years old and free to live independently and pursue her own interests without pressure of marriage.

Scant details of Milliat's early days are known,[3] but she worked as a translator, reflecting both a good education and an interest in other cultures. After her husband's death, she traveled to the United States, England, and Scandinavia, building a network of contacts. The exposure to many cultures also added to her favorite pastimes. What she loved most of all was sports.

In England once more, she fell in love with rowing, a sport not especially popular in France. Her rowing passion was so strong that she became the first woman to earn an Audax[4] certificate, finishing a race that lasted 50 km. She enjoyed other sports, too, and felt keenly that sports "develops personalities, gives confidence and courage, generates a resourceful spirit."[5]

Milliat's words about sports were shared by many French contemporaries, even Coubertin himself. However, she quickly ran into the problem that women faced in practicing their sports. All the athletic clubs were men-only.

The lack of access to fields or equipment was a big obstacle for women. Some men were sympathetic allies and saw opportunity. The first women's sports club was started in France by Pierre Payseé, a gymnast who had competed at the 1900 Paris and 1906 Intercalated Games. The club he opened in 1911, Fémina Sport, combined gymnastics and dance with sports. At the beginning, members had to take classes based on the ideas of Isadora Duncan.

Another French club, Academia, faced off against Fémina Sport in one of the

Fig.6. Alice Milliat in 1913. Like Coubertin, she was an avid rower, once finishing a 50k race (Wikimedia Commons).

first known European women's meets (1915). By then, Fémina Sport had brought in Milliat as president, and she was good at running organizations. This would be the first of many.

Other influential organizations were forming as well. Following the Stockholm Games, men's track and field was pulled under a new international track and field group, the International Amateur Athletics Federation (IAAF). Sweden's Sigfrid Edström, who had organized the 1912 Olympics, was elected its first president. Up until then, the IOC had governed track and field, but they preferred the IAAF to address changes, standardize rules, collect records, and manage competitions.

The creation of the IAAF put a buffer between the IOC and groups lobbying for more inclusion, notably women. Coubertin, still president of the IOC, remained stubbornly resistant to adding women's events. Edström of the IAAF was less rigid about women competing, but at Stockholm there were no women's track events, and he seemed ready to keep it that way. American James Sullivan had died in 1916, removing one of the loudest American voices against female athletics, but the AAU was still ambivalent. When the 1916 Games planned for Berlin were canceled, what to do about the pesky women was blissfully put off.

During the war, meanwhile, while many European male athletes were on the battlefield, the females continued competing, in between working in factories and supporting the war effort at home. People at home appreciated the chance to take their mind off the news, even to watch women. In Britain, female soccer teams flourished, until over 150 teams were playing by 1917, sometimes in stadiums with tens of thousands of fans.

Fémina Sport and other clubs could also entertain fans with track meets. Hence, the first French women's athletics championship took place in 1917, while in April 1918 the first French cross-country championship was held. The increased number of intra-country meets highlighted the need for an organization at the national level. Pierre Payseé of Fémina Sport and Albert Pelan thus created the *Fédération des Sociétés Féminines Sportives de France* (FSFSF)

This new national group, FSFSF, gave Milliat another opportunity for leadership. She had done this before, starting as a cashier for the inter-club meets and Fémina Sport, then running for and winning the top office. She began as treasurer of FSFSF, but by 1919 had been elected general secretary.

Some biographers give her complete credit for organizing the federations, while others relegate her to a behind-the-scenes role. The truth was somewhere in the middle. Milliat had certainly proved herself capable. She understood money and resources; she knew how to network and how to handle negotiations. She clearly wasn't afraid of being the only woman in the room, despite not coming from an aristocratic background.

By 1919, the FSFSF was launching nationwide women's championships in France in rugby, basketball, swimming, and field hockey. Other countries were fast followers, and soon national championships were held: Austria (1918), Germany (1920), Great Britain (1922), and the U.S. (1923).

With women organizing across multiple countries, it was time to go back to the IOC. Milliat and others petitioned the IOC to add track and field to the 1920 Games, now that they had a multi-year history of fielding championships behind them. They met a "solid wall of refusal."[6] The 1920 Games passed with its handful of women's events.

While success had happened in so many venues, women couldn't seem to make inroads into the IOC. The upcoming Paris Games for 1924, proudly shepherded by the IOC's Coubertin, also promised little or no change. Milliat needed a stronger organization and stronger bargaining power. Events in 1921 would create the clout that she needed.

The Women's Olympics

The ultimate path to the Olympics for women's track and field started in tiny Monte Carlo. Accounts differ a little on who did what. Some suggest that Alice Milliat organized what became the first international women's championship, while others credit the mayor of Monte Carlo, Camille Blanc. Blanc, according to Olympic sports historian Alan Guttmann, "realized that the tiny principality on the Riviera was an ideal place [for an event], … set up an eight-man organizing committee," and *voi-la*, all the women came magically and mysteriously to Blanc's beck and call.

This seems unlikely. Would the men of Monte Carlo be able to persuade the best French, English, and Scandinavian women runners to compete on their own? Blanc *was* the president of the Monaco International Sports Club, and Monte Carlo *did* know how to throw a party. But he and his organizing committee hadn't run international track meets before.

At the same time, Milliat could not have organized such an event on her own and would have needed a city happy to bring in activities that the Olympics had shunned. Monte Carlo was a good starting place. As a result of this happy collaboration, the first women's international track and field competition—*Ier Meeting International d'Education Physique Feminine de Sports Athletiques*—was held in the garden of the Monte Carlo Casino. For one week in August 1921, a Monte Carlo field normally reserved for clay pigeon shooting became the center of the world for women's track and field.

Competitions for track and field included six running distances: 60 m, 250 m, 800 m, 4 × 75 m, 4 × 175 m, and the 65 m hurdles. Women also competed in the long jump, high jump, javelin, and the shot put—ten separate events in all. They rounded out the events with a basketball tournament, a pushball[7] tournament, and a gymnastic/dance exhibition.

Although this was only the first international women's meet of its kind, the event was a huge success. Over 300 women attended from several European countries: Great Britain, France, Italy, Norway, and Sweden. The fastest woman in the world at the time, Britain's Mary Lines, was a headliner, showing off the flaming speed that could whiz 100 yards in 11.8 seconds. Monte Carlo loved it and planned to do it again the next year.

Milliat planned bigger. She took the French organization one step higher. She founded the *Fédération Sportive Feminine Internationale* (FSFI) and now ran both a national and an international women's sports organization.

Monte Carlo held a second women's track event in the spring of 1922, but Milliat and the FSFI initiated the *Jeux Internationaux* in Paris in the fall of that year. This time, the program included a full set of track and field events, with athletes from more countries, including the Americans. Finally, the star women athletes from the big three countries—France, Great Britain, and the United States—could face off. Twenty thousand spectators gathered in Paris's Pershing Stadium to watch the Women's Olympics.

Two world records were set. Speedster Lines of Britain lived up to her reputation and won three golds, a silver, and a bronze. The media reported results "with the same mixture of respect, admiration, and mystic fervor as the 'real' (i.e., male) Olympics."[8]

The reaction by the IOC was to pretend the Women's Olympics never took place. They ignored the success of the event and acted unconcerned at the use of the word "Olympic." This was years before they had learned to drop the hammer on their intellectual property and decades before they would sue anyone using their sacred word or images of the rings.

It's not that the IOC didn't notice that women were gaining ground. They were, in fact, concerned that the "abuses and excesses"[9] of suffragettes had now taken over women's sports. They were just unsure of what to do about it. Eventually, they chose to shift responsibility to the IAAF.

The following spring, the IOC told the IAAF to "draw up rules for taking control of women's track and field."[10] Edström agreed. The IAAF committee—all men—then voted to run women's track and field, without negotiating with Milliat and despite never having sponsored any women's events. The IAAF next took up the question of whether to allow athletics for women in the upcoming 1924 Games. They voted against it.

The federation recommended the "status quo" of women's events for the 1924 Games. As a result, the IOC only added a single woman's fencing event—the foil—to the small program of diving, swimming, and tennis. They could claim they were open to expanding events but only the right events. Besides, the French just liked fencing, even if it had to be women.

After thirty years steering the Olympic ship, Coubertin stepped down in 1925. He handed the reins of the IOC over to Belgian Henri de Baillet-Latour, one of the organizers from Antwerp. Baillet-Latour had no interest in innovation, either. He held the same staunch objections to female athletes as his predecessor, although his criticisms came across quite differently: "I can only hope one thing: that the day may come soon that women liberate themselves completely from men's custody, that they organize the Women's World Games (*Jeux Mondiaux Feminins*), which would allow us to exclude them entirely from the Olympic Games."[11]

Fair enough, said Milliat and the FSFI. The 1926 women's competition would continue to be called the Women's Olympics. This one would take place in Gothenburg, Sweden, in Edström's backyard. This time there would be ten nations, with a "spectacular" opening ceremony attended by the Swedish royal family. The FSFI was gaining prestige and momentum.

The IAAF tried again, more urgently, to wrest control away. Edström wanted the FSFI to stop using the word "Olympics." Milliat was a strong bargainer. She, in turn, wanted a full slate of women's track and field in the upcoming Amsterdam Olympics, as well as control over their own Games, women's records formally recognized, and the ability to make changes to events as needed.

Edström was no feminist, but he did put Milliat's proposals in front of the IAAF. Many IAAF members were still too conservative. For instance, Lauri Pikhala, a Finnish delegate well acquainted with long-distance running, felt that women lacked endurance, a critical part of track events.[12] Another member griped that women were troublesome, mentioning those suffragettes again. Despite the potential success of the Gothenburg Women's Games, the old guard still resisted.

The IAAF as a whole balked, then agreed to only five of the Olympic women's track events, and only as "an experiment."[13] This limited schedule was taken to the IOC without agreement by Milliat and the FSFI. The IOC accepted the shortened list. When she heard of it, Milliat was incensed: "Women's participation in the Olympic Games can only make sense if it is total, since women's athletics has proved itself and does not want to serve as an experiment for the Olympic committee."[14]

However, Milliat decided to accept something rather than nothing. The FSFI agreed to five track events for the upcoming Olympics and to drop the offending word from their competition in Gothenburg. As anticipated, the 1926 Women's World Games were a big success, and Milliat was thrilled with the turnout: "People

Fig.7. The highly successful Second Women's World Games held Olympic-style ceremonies, including an athlete's parade of nations before 20,000 spectators and dignitaries, such as the king and wife of a former Prime Minister (Wikimedia Commons).

are interested in the Women's Olympic Games; during the last games in Gothenburg, all foreign diplomats spent a night traveling from Stockholm to watch the athletic events. Is that not proof itself?"[15]

Another Women's Games was planned for 1930, with hope that a strong showing in Amsterdam would support further expansion of events. Still, not everyone was thrilled with the Amsterdam Olympic plan. The British women's track and field team, best in the world at the time, was incensed that their events had been limited to less than half the number in the 1926 Women's World Games. They refused to participate in the 1928 Olympics.

Milliat was given credentials for the Games in Amsterdam as a "technical official." She would help oversee the five events that had been approved: the high jump, discus, 100 m, 4 × 100 m relay, and 800 m. From individual sports clubs to national groups to an international organization, women's athletics was finally recognized. Track and field for women, after a torturous two decades of negotiations and growth, was at last on the schedule.

Running for a Train, Running on a Dare

The first Olympic contest for the world's fastest woman would be without British superstar Mary Lines. However, it would feature two other sprinting powerhouses, the U.S. and Canada, and their two talented runners, Betty Robinson and Bobbie Rosenfeld. The 4 × 100 relay would also miss the British team that had dominated in Gothenburg. Yet, the Canadian team, which would come to be called the "matchless six," had its speedsters. Even without the Brits, there would be plenty of talent, and the 100 m sprint would turn into a showdown between a teenager and the future Canadian athlete of the half century.

These two 100 m finalists were virtual unknowns when each burst on the scene to beat a national champion. Both wore short, bobbed hair in the fashion of the twenties. One had a little more experience. By early 1928, Canada's Rosenfeld had at least tied the world record for the 100 yd. dash. American Betty Robinson came out of nowhere.

Robinson's story sounds like something out of a 1950s movie, like Lana Turner being discovered in a malt shop. Robinson was a 16-year-old junior in high school, late for a train one day in March 1928. She put on a bit of extra speed to make the train and just happened to do it in front of the high school track coach. Even without a stopwatch, Coach Charles Price suspected it was unusually fast.

When Price got out the watch and timed her running down the halls of Thornton Township High School in Harvey, Illinois, he confirmed his guess. She was wild, had terrible form, and was wearing the wrong shoes. But her 6.2 seconds over 50 yards was near the U.S. indoor record.

American high school track was rising in popularity in 1928, trying to elbow its way in next to football and basketball. Like most high schools, Thornton didn't even have a girls' track team. But Price knew how to spot talent, and Robinson was the real deal.

The talented Elizabeth Robinson was born and raised in Riverdale, a small suburb south of Chicago. While Riverdale and nearby Harvey are upscale communities today with nature preserves and country clubs, in the early 1920s the area was bustling with factories and brickyards.

Betty's dad, Harry, was an immigrant from Ireland, who worked his way up to become the manager of the local bank in the growing community. This provided the means for the family to indulge their third daughter, the baby of the family, in plenty of extracurricular activities. A century earlier, Robinson at 16 might have been working or married, but in 1928 she was still in high school and flitting from one club to another.

Both energetic and extroverted, Robinson performed in dance and piano recitals, even playing on local radio stations. Her days were a whirlwind of activity: ballet practice, hunting with dad, studying, or socializing in Latin and French Club. Running for Coach Price was one more activity added among many. But Robinson liked to compete. As a kid, running through the neighbors' backyards or racing for ribbons at church picnics and her father's Masonic meetings, she enjoyed the dizzying feeling of speed.

Her first official race came only a few weeks later after she began working with Coach Price. It was an indoor meet, sponsored by the Institute Banking Society. Chicago, as it happens, was ground central for women's track. The Illinois Women's Athletic Club (IWAC) was one of the most prestigious in the country. On March 30, 1928, Robinson was about to meet the toast of Chicago, the multi-talented, multi-sport athlete, Helen Filkey.

Filkey herself already had world records in the 70 and 100 yd. dashes by age 20. She was the AAU champion in the 60 yd. hurdles, her specialty, and also routinely won the long jump. She would have been a natural for the heptathlon, if such a multiple-event opportunity existed, but it did not. Men had the pentathlon and the decathlon. Women were happy to be on the track at all.

Still, a California newspaper had called her "the greatest woman athlete in the world."[16] By the time she moved to Chicago from the West Coast and began fronting the IWAC in championships of the mid–1920s, the Chicago newspapers were featuring pictures of Filkey often, sometimes next to a photos of a greyhound.

Robinson hadn't raced much against women like Filkey. She was still learning the basics, mostly running with the boys' track team. She was a fierce competitor, between the piano recitals and the singing competitions. But this was *the* Helen Filkey, and 60 yards was a short distance, indeed.

When they called the 60 yd. dash, the crowd began shouting for Filkey. Robinson went inside to the starting line and mimicked what she had practiced, crouching and digging in the toes of her brand-new track shoes, which were heavy and hot. Likely she was just hoping not to fall down.

The start was fair. Eight seconds lasts only a few breaths. Filkey led all the way, but Robinson had been gaining ground near the end. Twenty-year-old Filkey clipped another chunk off the world indoor record in order to stay in front of a teenager who had just run her first big race.

Betty Robinson wasn't the only natural runner who would attract attention by taking on a national record holder. Up over the Canadian border, a day's drive away, Toronto had become the hotbed of Canadian women's track and field just like Chicago in the U.S. Bobbie Rosenfeld, like Helen Filkey, was good at practically every sport. Like Robinson, she had started running almost by accident.

Rosenfeld, a teenager herself back in the summer of 1923, had been playing in an Ontario picnic softball tournament. Between games, someone dared her to run in the 100 yd. dash. She was already a star at softball, hockey, and basketball but never turned down a challenge. Sprinkled among the other young ladies in shorts was Rosa Grosse, the Canadian national sprint champion at the time. Rosenfeld didn't recognize her name and hadn't paid any attention to track, until now.

By the time the picnic race was over, Rosenfeld had beat Grosse and set a new national record. Not bad for a dare. In addition, she had caught the attention of track scout and organizer Walter Knox. Rosenfeld, at 18, had talent coming out of her ears.

Nicknamed "Bobbie" for the short haircut that so many young women had adopted in the 1920s, Fanny Rosenfeld had been born in the Ukraine, but was brought by her Jewish parents to Canada as they fled the Russian pogroms of 1905. The Rosenfelds were indifferent to their daughter's physical pursuits as long as she did her other work. She was already employed at a local chocolate factory by the time she was a teenager. But she played sports on the weekend, year-round.

In the spring, Rosenfeld was a star center on the Young Women's Hebrew Association (YWHA) basketball team, Ontario champs. In the winter, she helped her company-sponsored women's hockey team, the Toronto Patterson Pats, win two championships. A few months after Rosenfeld took up tennis, she won the Toronto Ladies Lawn Tennis Championship.

At one point, Knox brought Rosenfeld and other protégés to the Canadian National Exhibition in Toronto for a sports day in 1923. The marquee event was a race against the biggest stars in their hemisphere, the Chicago Flyers, which included "Greyhound" Filkey. The Flyers came dressed in matching shorts and clinging sweaters. The Canadians managed bloomers and midi skirts. Rosenfeld herself didn't even have that. She wore her brother's swim trunks, her Hinde and Dauch company softball sweater, and her dad's wool hockey socks.[17]

Rosa Grosse was also there, along with future Canadian speedster Myrtle Cook. At the finish line of the 100 yd. dash, much to the surprise of the better-known Americans, Rosenfeld and Grosse placed first and second, beating world-record holder Filkey. Next, the relay team of Rosenfeld, Grosse, Cook, and Grace Conacher—a foursome that had never competed before—also edged the Flyers.

Rosenfeld and Grosse would go on to trade wins and records, back and forth, for two more years. Filkey would also redouble her efforts and return to prominence. Despite losing races to teams across the border, Filkey again became the one to beat.

As the summer of 1928 approached, runners and coaches began thinking about the Olympic Games. In June 1928, the IWAC quarters in Chicago was full of hopeful women training to catch a ticket to Amsterdam, and Betty Robinson was among them. With biology finals over and high school yearbooks signed, Robinson was looking forward to a summer free from studying. She was considering college, but not sure yet. Maybe a job waitressing or at the five-and-dime? Maybe she could meet some boys? Latin and French Club were over for now, but she was still part of this running club, and a big meet was coming up. She might even get to travel!

The 1928 U.S. Central AAU Meet would be in Chicago's Soldier's Field, a stadium just built. It was massive, big enough to hold tens of thousands of fans. The AAU track meet, however, only attracted a modest group of spectators on a chilly night in the Windy City. The officials kept their eyes on the wind gauges. There probably would be no records set because of the breeze, and that might have dampened fan enthusiasm.

Robinson faced off against Filkey and several other elite runners. While she still lacked experience, her raw speed and youthful exuberance were a potent combination. Hunting with her dad had taught her how to time the squeeze of the starter's pistol, especially if she peeked. This pistol moved, and Robinson took off.

Twelve seconds later, Betty Robinson had beaten Helen Filkey. Due to the wind speed, it was not a record, but Robinson didn't care. She just enjoyed standing atop the podium. She had been reading a little more about this Olympics thing. Maybe there would be something else for her to do this summer.

Golden Feet

The U.S. Olympic Trials for the Games in Amsterdam took place in New Jersey on July 4, 1928. Like most eastern seaboard cities in summer, Newark was a sweltering 90 degrees in the shade. On the field and in the humidity, it felt even hotter. Chicago could be humid and muggy, but it had a breeze off the lake. In Newark, even after an afternoon thunderstorm, the air was like breathing in a steam room.

The Chicago women had come in by train a couple days before, with their IWAC chaperones. Robinson was joined by Filkey and Nellie Todd, a runner and record holder in the long jump. Unfortunately for Todd, the long jump was not one of the five events selected for Amsterdam, so her only shot was in the sprints, and Todd didn't have Robinson-like speed.

Filkey had a good shot at both the 100 m sprint, if Robinson were to edge her again, and the relay team. At least there would be something! She, too, was disappointed that her specialty, the 60 yd. hurdles, was left out of the women's events. With only a handful of options, all the multi-talented athletes were clamoring for the same few spots.

Because the trials were on a national holiday, only a small crowd braved the muggy heat inside the stadium. Most people had headed for a nearby beach to celebrate the Fourth of July. It also was a long, repetitive afternoon of preliminaries. The athletes would come up to the starting line, dig a spot for their start, explode onto the track, strain for the tape, then wait for the official announcement of who had advanced. Crouch, fly, turn to look at the officials. Lather, rinse, repeat.

In the middle of the sleepy, interminable heats, the unthinkable happened for Helen Filkey. She had easily won the hurdles but was nervous about the sprint. The competition was fierce. The team from California had brought in extraordinary runners who were blazing up the track. Filkey had made it to her sprint semifinal, but races were close.

Maybe she was thinking too far ahead to the finals. Maybe the wet track was more slippery than she had expected. Whatever the reason, Filkey got a good start and was streaming down the track when she stumbled. She lost her stride and ended third. She was a world record holder, but one mistimed step and she was out: out of the finals, out of the relay team, out of the Olympics, and, effectively, out of the headlines of women's track history.[18]

Robinson was surprised that Filkey was not in the finals. She had wanted to beat her Chicago rival, perhaps set a record without interference from the wind. Two of the Californians, Elta Cartwright and Anne Vrana, ended in the finals. Cartwright, a 21-year-old college student at Humboldt State in northern California, was aptly nicknamed "Cinder-elta" because she was a demon on the cinder track.

Cartwright lived up to her nickname. Despite the steamy air and the lengthy afternoon of running, the women all popped out of the blocks as if it were the first race of the day. The Californian leaned just a little harder and sooner, and her time of 12.4 seconds was a new record. Robinson's time of 12.5 matched the one Cinder-elta had just eclipsed. Robinson, the Californians, and three other young Americans would represent the U.S. in the 100 m sprints and on the relay team. The U.S. Olympic team was set. Helen Filkey was not on it.

Another disappointed young woman, just edged out in her semifinal, was teenager Stella Walsh of Cleveland, Ohio. Filkey would never get to the Olympics. Walsh would show up a few years later, but under very different circumstances, and her story will be highlighted in Chapter Five.

The Canadian Olympic Trials also took place in early July on the East Coast of North America, though in Halifax, much further north and much cooler than Newark. Bobbie Rosenfeld had a banner day. She set records in the running and standing long jump as well as the discus. She was another natural for the heptathlon, an event still decades away. But she could run, and, at the 1928 trials, her 100 m sprint was less than a second off the world record.

Rosenfeld would run the 100 m in Amsterdam. She might have thrown the discus as well, except that scheduling conflicts prevented her from doing both on the same day. Women only had five track events, yet the organizers couldn't even spread those across the existing multiple days of men's track events.

Rosenfeld's Canadian relay teammates would be Myrtle Cook, Ethel Smith, and Jane Bell. Rounding out the Canadian team were high jumper Ethel Catherwood and middle-distance runner Jean Thompson, a strong group full of multi-sport athletes. With the international superstars from Great Britain out, Canada's chance for medals was high.

A week after the U.S. Trials, the American team sailed for Amsterdam on the S.S. *Roosevelt*, a chartered ocean liner chaperoned by General Douglas MacArthur. While the ship was big enough for the 280 American athletes plus coaches and staff, it felt cramped for young people accustomed to moving around several hours a day in wide-open spaces. Runners would take turns doing laps on deck, but they had to time their jogging with the rolling waves of the Atlantic. Swimmer

Johnny Weissmuller used a special pool but had to tie himself aboard for extra safety.

Then, there was the problem with the food; it was too good and too plentiful. This would be the bane of American coaches for every meet across the Atlantic, before plane travel and nutritionists became commonplace. Athletes unused to eating much were treated to second helpings of breakfast and daily ice cream. Nine days later, they would arrive in the Netherlands (or Paris or Berlin) bloated and sluggish.

As the *Evening Standard* wrote upon the U.S. team's arrival: "A good cargo of ice cream may perhaps act as ballast for a man whose business is to put the shot. But it must be a heavy burden to carry in a sprint."[19]

Once in Amsterdam, the team then had to stay housed on the ship. They could get off to practice, but the fields were not made for running. Summer in the Low Countries produced moist soil conditions for growing tulips. Not so great for a high jumper. Athletes complained it was like trying to run through a plowed field.[20]

The track in the Olympic stadium was little better. The new complex had been built on springy dirt as a way to keep the walls from sinking, a nuisance for Dutch engineers for centuries. While good for the walls, this was a poor choice as a running surface, and days of rain had turned the track to slush. Plus, the oval wasn't even finished when the ship arrived, so the athletes couldn't practice anyway.

The men lost early races—the 400 m hurdles to Lord Burghley of Great Britain and the 100 m men's sprint to Canada. The U.S. coaches complained about the conditions being a "sandbox,"[21] but it sounded like sour grapes. After all, it was a muddy sandbox for everybody.

For the women, the day that had taken 32 years finally came on July 30: the first preliminary heats for the women's 100 m race. For such a momentous day, the day dawned gray, with a soft and steady drizzle. Still, the women from Chicago, Ontario, and Germany were used to such miserable weather, and, after so long a wait, they would have run in a hurricane.

Yet the preliminaries took their toll. Whether from slushy conditions, nerves, or the tough competition, many of the hopefuls washed out early. The Americans lost three of their four runners: Vrana eliminated in the first race; Cartwright, still feeling the effects of seasickness, in the second. Robinson became the only American woman who advanced steadily, race by race, trying not to expend too much energy while placing high enough to advance.

The Canadians fared slightly better. The fastest two women, Rosenfeld and Cook, made it to the finals, along with Ethel Smith, who always seemed to place right behind her two Ontario rivals. Rosenfeld edged Robinson in an early heat, so they had faced each other at least once. Then, in separate semifinals, each ran 12.4, which became the first official Women's 100 m Olympic Record. The final would take place the next day. One more day to let the butterflies collect.

On Tuesday, July 31, 1928, the 100 m finalists gathered in the locker room. The semis had produced a field of six: three Canadians, Bobbie Rosenfeld, Ethel Smith, and Myrtle Cook; two Germans, Erna Steinberg and Leni Schmidt; and the lone American, Betty Robinson. The Germans were a mystery to the Americans and Canadians. Leni Schmidt was another woman who had set 100 m world records in 1925 and 1926.

Robinson, however, was in a panic. She had packed two left shoes in her excitement. One of the coaches hurriedly sent a runner back to the ship to retrieve the correct shoe, the runner returning out of breath and just in time. Robinson hurried out to the track with barely a moment to jog around and size up the competition. Immediately, the women were called to the line, and the runners began to dig out starting holes in the wet cinders.

Each finalist got into their crouch, fingers touching down just for balance, both knees bent at those peculiar angles, in the days before starting blocks. As they all waited for the gun, Cook took off early. It was a false start, but one was okay. It cleaned the butterflies out a little. But only one, as a second false start meant disqualification. They all crouched again, Robinson probably trying her pistol-peeking trick.

Once again, Cook took off early. On paper, she had one of the fastest times, but she was now out. She left the track in tears. Then, Leni Schmidt also false-started, twice. Dreams of being the first Olympic women's track champion gone. Schmidt stood and argued in German until the officials pushed her off the track, still shaking her fist at the judge.

The remaining four runners returned to the start, now oddly spaced out across the lanes. Rosenfeld and Robinson were next to each other on the right, with the other German, Steinberg, in the middle. Bespectacled Ethel Smith was on the far left. Three of these runners would get medals. One would win. One would get nothing.

Crouch and start. This time, the start was legal. Steinberg in the center jumped out to an early lead in the first 50 meters. Robinson, right behind her, slowly ate up the distance, edging up as the tape rushed toward them. Rosenfeld, on Robinson's back shoulder, tried to do the same, gaining on the American, then surging toward the front.

At the line, two women threw their hands up: *I won!* Robinson broke into a smile, while Rosenfeld bared her teeth in a grimace, but triumphant. They had both been close enough to feel the tape break.

There was no photo finish and no video replay to review. The Canadians and Americans were both celebrating as the officials huddled together. The crowd was roaring, but the sound was just a blur to the panting finalists. One judge declared for Robinson, another for Rosenfeld. After several minutes, Betty Robinson was declared the winner, the first Olympic gold medalist in women's track and field.

The Canadian team lodged a protest that eventually was denied. There was nothing to review. Rosenfeld and teammate Smith took second and third, so at least the women from Toronto could be pleased with having two medals.

A rematch came a few days later in the relay. Here, the Chicago runners would have a second chance. Here, Myrtle Cook would not false start. The four Canadians had run relays more than a few times. The Americans had practiced but were not very experienced with each other. A bit more experience would make a big difference here. The Canadian foursome had already logged a world record in their first heat.

The Americans did grab an early lead, but their handoff was slow, and they were tied after the first exchange. Robinson was set to run the anchor leg against

Jean Thompson, and the crowd hoped to see another close finish. However, Cook's third Canadian leg made up for her false starts. She handed the Canadians a sizable lead for the final baton pass. Robinson tried to catch up, but Thompson was able to fend her off. The Canadians took gold, the Americans silver. Germany did get their medal, this time bronze.

American Lillian Copeland was happy to add a silver for the U.S. in the discus, behind gold medalist Halina Konopacka of Poland. Canada was unhappy that Rosenfeld had been unable to try for the discus, since the competition occurred simultaneous with the races. Still, they were thrilled with the gold medal by Ethel Catherwood in the high jump. Catherwood, nicknamed the "Saskatoon Lily," had set a new world record at 1.6 m.[22]

The final event, the "long distance" race of two laps around the track, took place on August 2. Women had run longer distances elsewhere, a 1,500 m in Russia and the 1000 m at the Women's World Games. Europeans regularly ran cross-country distance races often—like the thousands of shop girls in Paris in 1903 who managed a 12 k. Two laps on the track would be a walk in the park for those who ran cross country. Certainly, running at full speed was different from doing practice laps, but none of the competitors were concerned about the distance.

It was the hottest day of the track events. The athletes were finally glad to get a break from the rain, but the humidity was oppressive—shades of Newark. Running jerseys were already clinging to the skin as athletes climbed off the transport from the ships. Similar conditions for the men had occurred a few days earlier. Organizers, as was customary, stood by with smelling salts and water, perhaps a little less free with the strychnine compared with the early marathon days.

The biggest concern for the Canadians was the status of Jean Thompson, who was recovering from an injury and nervous about the race. Rosenfeld would be running with her, despite the 800 m not being her specialty. Rosenfeld hadn't even trained for it, but her ability to take on any sport made her confident enough. She was just always fast—fast chasing down a fly ball, fast skating with the puck toward a goal, and fast flying on the track.

Thompson had won her 800 m heat with a quick time, and Germans Marie Dollinger and Lina Radke also won their semis. A pack of nine women in total ended in the finals, including Florence McDonald from the U.S., Hitomi Kinue from Japan, and Inga Gentzel from Sweden.

Thompson went out quickly in the first lap. By the back stretch, though, she was overtaken by Sweden's Gentzel and Radke. Rosenfeld had been hanging back but moved up to run with her colleague for the second lap.

As usual, the race for the three top spots in the 800 m started heating up on the final back stretch as Hitomi also moved up and the passing started. The four behind the Canadians seemed to slow as the five in front all started accelerating.

On the final curve, where elite runners today use their kick, both Radke and Hitomi passed Gentzel, who had been leading. The German stayed in front, glancing back. Looking back lost time, but Radke by then was several strides ahead. Hitomi started to pump her arms mechanically as if to gain speed, although she stayed in second place, also glancing back.

Three. The Road from Alice to Amsterdam (1912–1928)

The race was over with 10 m to go. Radke grinned at the tape, and Hitomi behind her passed the finish, then walked to the grass, breathing heavily in the heat. Radke had set a new world record. Gentzel took the bronze, echoing the great legacy of many of her nation's male contemporary distance runners.

Thompson and Rosenfeld finished fourth and fifth. Later reports suggested Rosenfeld might have had enough in the tank to edge past her teammate, but medals were no longer at stake. She slowed down, and Thompson crossed ahead of her. Canadian writers were thrilled at the display of what they termed good sportsmanship, one remarking: "In the annals of women's athletics, there is no finer deed than this."[23]

All nine of the runners finished, although several were panting. One fell right at the finish, although it was later shown that she was leaning as runners are taught and lost her balance. An official helped her up. The others walked about the track, bending over and catching their breath.

Fig.8. Hitomi Kinue (JPN, left) and Lina Radke (GER, right) calmly battled it out in the 800 m, after both passed Inga Gentzel (SWE, back). Radke, Hitomi, and Gentzel medaled without collapsing. False reports later of fainting runners mystified them all (Japanese Olympic Committee, Wikimedia Commons).

Linda Radke, in a near replica of the pose Betty Robinson had taken two days earlier, went over to the photographers for the requisite media shoot, a smiling winner. Somehow, though, that wasn't the picture that the world saw.

A Pitiful Spectacle

> "Below us on the cinder path were 11 wretched women, 5 of whom dropped out before the finish, while 5 collapsed after reaching the tape."—John R. Tunis[24]

In the distorted mirror of media, journalists afterward described a completely different race. Tunis, author of the "acme of absurdity" quote referenced in the Introduction, wrote as if all the 800 m racers were scattered about the track in exhaustion. The *Times* of London described a "half dozen prostrated and obviously distressed forms lying in the grass at the side of the track after the race." The *Chicago Tribune* wrote of the "picture ... of eight girls who finished, six of them fainted exhausted—a pitiful spectacle and a reproach to anyone who had anything to with putting on a race of this kind."[25]

Once a few reporters added some drama to the story, others went into a *can-you-top-this* mode. The *New York Times* writer suggested: "the gals dropped in swooning heaps as if riddled by machine-gun fire."[26] *De Maasbode* of Rotterdam said they "tumble[d] down after the finish like dead sparrows."[27] Rather than mentioning the world-record finish, a different result entirely was injected into the public consciousness. There were only eight finishers ... no six ... no eleven. Half didn't finish! Half collapsed!

The exaggeration was mystifying, though widespread. Where on earth were they getting this from? Perhaps the distortions shouldn't have come as a surprise. The IOC had deemed the women's track events to be an experiment. Medical professionals beforehand had said that women would find it too taxing. They saw what they expected to see.

The reality of the Amsterdam Olympics was that, despite the rain, junk food, and horrid condition of the track, the athletes had thrived. Five world records had been set in the five women's track events.

The American press *was* thrilled with Betty Robinson's "star" appearance and judged her gold and silver medals to have redeemed the dismal showing on the men's side. The Associated Press crowed: "Where the American men had been failing dismally, Miss Robinson, the only Yankee to reach the women's sprint final, ran a beautiful race ... flashing a great closing spirit to best the Canadian favorite, Fanny Rosenfeld, by two feet."[28] That the race was won by two inches, rather than two feet, might have been the first sign that exaggeration was the order of the day.

Robinson, gold medalist and expert in running very short races, was asked her opinion about the longer race. It's not clear whether she, in fact, had seen the race. Sixteen-year-old Betty Robinson, a senior in high school, declared, "I believe that the 220-yard dash is long enough for any girl to run. Any distance beyond that taxes the strength of a girl ... the laws of nature never provided a girl with the physical equipment to withstand the grueling pace of such a grind."[29] It added unfortunate fuel to the fire.

In the aftermath of the 800 m, the IOC voted to drop all track and field events from the women's program in the next Games. Despite photographic evidence that the reports of women collapsing were greatly exaggerated, the IOC produced descriptions from the press as evidence. Never mind that writers who weren't even there didn't know how many women had started or finished. The IOC had its facts to end their "experiment."

The FSFI and Alice Milliat didn't take this well. They went ahead with the third Women's World Games in 1930, this time in Prague. Milliat also tried to persuade her FSFI colleagues that women would be better off holding their own games and abandoning the Olympics. The FSFI thought it better to go back to the IOC.

The reaction from some was more supportive. Gustavus Kirby, the new American president of the AAU, was a man much more open-minded toward women athletes than his predecessor, James Sullivan. After seeing women compete, Kirby could find nothing wrong with it. "I personally saw groups of young girls ... trotting around the fields ... and hopping about in all kinds of athletic and gymnastic movements; and ... it was good for them."[30]

Kirby and the AAU wanted to include women in the upcoming games, at home in Los Angeles. He responded to the IOC's proposal by threatening to pull the American men out of track and field as well, which would have been a devastating blow to the Olympic movement.

Grumbling, the IOC partially restored women's track and field events for the 1932 program. They put back the 100 m sprint, discus, high jump, and the 4 × 100 relay and even added the 80 m hurdles and javelin throw. But not the 800 m. Distance running was out of the question and would stay out for decades.

Despite the hue and cry over eliminating women's track and field, the 1932 and 1936 Olympics would both end up with more events for women than were held in 1928. But eliminating the 800 m was a bitter pill, after the gains made by the FSFI and the Women's World Games. Milliat was still not happy. She once more made her case to the IAAF that either (a) women's track and field should include all events or (b) women should be free to host their own games. But control, once ceded to the IAAF, would not be returned.

Instead, the IAAF agreed to recognize women's world records and proposed that the planned 1938 Women's World Games become the first European Championships, run by the IAAF. Its program would expand to nine events.

All in all, women's track and field *had* gained some of the respect it desired, even if certain events were still considered off-limits. The FSFI *had* moved the goalposts, so to speak, from "no events allowed" to "these events allowed; those events forbidden." Beyond that, the FSFI had no more leverage left. After twenty years, Milliat was also ready to pass on the responsibility to others and rest on her laurels.

The best "praise" of Milliat's efforts might ultimately have come from Avery Brundage, the American decathlete who would preside over the Olympics for a good part of his life. A member of the AAU and later president of the USOC and the IOC, Brundage had locked horns with Milliat repeatedly on committees. He described her as always demanding more and more. "She made quite a nuisance of herself."[31]

Alice Milliat eventually died in 1957, after four more sets of Olympic Games. During her lifetime, she survived two world wars—in France no less—saw the fall of empire, the rise of communism, and the rise and fall and rise of feminism. She also saw the rise and fall and rise once more of women's athletics. She passed away at age 73 in relative obscurity, though there are plans for a Milliat monument to be erected in time for the Paris Olympics of 2024.

Her advocacy of women in sports paved the way for women like Bobbie Rosenfeld and Betty Robinson. Their duel on the mushy track of Amsterdam was a watershed moment in women's track and a high point in both their careers, though not the end of their stories.

After being heralded as the Golden Girl of the Games, Robinson began training for the Los Angeles Olympics. However, a year before their start, Robinson was accompanying a pilot friend in his airplane, a practice she had enjoyed several times before. The plane crashed and rescuers who discovered Robinson's body among the wreckage initially took her for dead. Fortunately, she was alive, though badly hurt. The doctors thought it unlikely that she would walk again, but she proved them wrong. Five years later, she would return to the Games to compete with the American relay team in Berlin, a testament to endurance beyond what the IOC could ever have imagined.

Bobbie Rosenfeld and her Canadian companions returned home to Toronto from Amsterdam lauded as national heroes. Rosenfeld, with a first, second, and fifth place finish in Amsterdam, was called the star of the games, at least in the Canadian newspapers. The six medalists proudly paraded before 200,000 fans, forever after referred to as "The Matchless Six."

A year later, though, Rosenfeld was felled by an attack of rheumatoid arthritis, enough to put her on crutches. Though she recovered to play ball and other sports for a while, the arthritis would persist and effectively ended her track career. She would go on to become a sports journalist, eventually becoming one of the most beloved stars of Canadian sports media in the 20th century. She was named the Canadian Female Athlete of the Half Century—half only because her Olympic career was cut so short.

As a writer, she became known for her colorful turns of phrase, and her own clarion call to women of sports would echo down the ages:

> Athletic maids to arms! … We are taking up the sword, and high time it is, in defense of our so-called athletic bodies to give the lie to those pen flourishers who depict us not as paragons of feminine physique, beauty and health, but rather as Amazons and ugly ducklings, all because we have become sports-minded.[32]

Many maids to arms would take up Rosenfeld's call, now that they could. Milliat and others had further showed that activities like organizing, lobbying, and becoming a nuisance were all also part of the game.

Women had gotten in. Now, they wanted to do everything. One woman, in particular, would show the world that sometimes women could do everything—or at least try. As the 1930s approached, this multi-talented athlete took up the challenge. She would become another Female Athlete of the Century. With track and field back on the menu in 1932, the time was ripe for Babe Didrikson.

Part II

Taking Aim

Four

Let 'Er Fly

Babe Didrikson and Exceptionalism (1930–1932)

The rainy fields of northern Europe gave way to the sunny beaches of the Pacific, but the bold flappers of the 1920s turned into the unemployed and hungry of the 1930s. In such a time of contradiction, just after women's track events survived another call for elimination, the Los Angeles Olympics might give rise to the World's Greatest Woman Athlete.

The Greatest of All Time was not a title that had been bestowed on Bobbie Rosenfeld, the double medalist of 1928 who also held championship trophies in basketball, baseball, and hockey. Nor did the designation of "greatest" land on Helene Madison, the sensational 1932 Olympic swimmer who became the first woman to win three gold medals. The title went to Babe Didrikson, who ushered in a new era of superstar celebrity athletes.

Didrikson was labeled "a new feminine athletic marvel" before she ever appeared in the Olympics, even before the track meet that would make her a star. Her actual Olympic performance of two golds and a silver—fewer medals than teammate Madison and two of the medals controversial—still led sportswriters to vote her Athlete of the Year.

The 1930s were especially fertile ground for putting Didrikson up on the highest pedestal, for two specific reasons. First, people were eager for news that would distract them from the breadlines of the Depression. Stories of heroes or villains on the athletic field were perfect accompaniments to other therapeutic diversions like gangster movies and Busby Berkeley extravaganzas.

Secondly, the Games of Los Angeles and Berlin were, as historian David Goldblatt labels them, "The Olympics of Spectacle."[1] With Hollywood palm trees and film stars as a backdrop, the 1932 Games were the perfect place to turn swimmers and runners into celebrities. Johnny Weissmuller was already launching his film career as Tarzan, following his five gold medals in Paris and Amsterdam.

Berlin in 1936 took the idea of spectacle up a notch. Athletes literally became the stars of Leni Riefenstahl's *Olympia*, a documentary mainly intended to showcase the superhuman exploits of the "master race." Even today, a great number of bestselling Olympic books focus on U.S. athletes competing at the "Nazi Games,"[2] as if those contests had more significance than all the others.

Whether putting women on pedestals was to sell American newspapers or to provide proof of Aryan super-stardom, the trend in the 1930s was to treat certain athletes as almost other-worldly.

Women had seen this treatment before. Many women were described as if they were the only ones capable of such achievements. When Gertrude Ederly swam the English Channel, she became Queen of the Waves. When tennis greats Helen Wills Moody and Suzanne Lenglen met, it was the Match of the Century—in 1926, barely three decades into the century.

Didrikson wasn't the only one crowned with superlatives. Sportswriters liked to give nicknames to everybody. They still do. In the 1920s, they named one the "New York Thunderbolt" (American sprinter Jackson Scholz) and another the "Saskatoon Lily" (Canadian high jumper Ethel Catherwood), just like they called Reggie Jackson "Mr. October" decades later. Yet somehow Didrikson went from the moniker "Texas Tornado" to "Greatest Woman Athlete." Crowning her athletic royalty emphasized how unusual it was to be athletic and female. After all, there's only room at the top for one.

Which One of You Will Take Second?

"Loosen your girdle and let 'er fly!"—Babe Didrikson[3]

Mildred Ella Didrikson was a legend in her own time, a legend before she had even accomplished the things that would make her a legend. She was not necessarily a pioneer. She was a versatile athlete in a world filled with Bobbie Rosenfelds, Helen Filkeys, and other multi-event, multi-sport talents.

Didrikson was similarly talented, but she could also spin a Texas yarn bigger than a house. While her peers were taught to be demure, to say they were "just happy to be here," Didrikson boasted openly of her exploits. In this way, she was far more like Usain Bolt than Betty Robinson.

Like her alleged namesake, Babe Ruth—and even that "alleged" was probably an exaggeration—she attracted attention, then performed with the photographers crowded around her. After all, Babe Ruth was not unique for hitting home runs. He was unique for pointing before he hit them.

The sixth child of seven, Didrikson was born in June 1911, three months before gold medalist Robinson. The tiny Texas towns of Port Arthur and Beaumont, however, were not the hotbeds of track and field that Chicago was. As fierce a competitor as Didrikson was, and as much as sports was a part of her life, she came to track and field much later than some of her rivals.

Her mother called her "Min Bebe." Later in life, she told the sportswriters that the boys called her "Babe" because she hit home runs in their sandlot games. Either reason or both could have led to her lifelong nickname.

Port Arthur was where her Norwegian immigrant parents settled to raise their family, as her father was a shipbuilder by trade. However, when a hurricane big enough to make national news hit the coastal town four years later, the family moved inland to Beaumont, a town filled with oily smoke from a neighborhood refinery. While some men got rich from what was extracted from the ground, Ole and his family just scraped by. There were no ships here; the only work he could find was as a cabinetmaker, which barely covered basic needs. Mama Hannah took in washing to add to their meager earnings.

The children were kept busy with chores, helping with the laundry, washing windows, and mopping floors. Young Babe did her part, sometimes vigorously and other times carelessly. One day she might strap brushes to her feet to "skate-mop." The next, she'd leave the groceries forgotten on the ground while she stopped for a baseball game, arriving home chagrined that a dog had eaten the family dinner. Afterward, she was remorseful enough to take on factory jobs, cleaning figs and sewing potato gunnysacks. By all reports, she was a whiz with a needle.

The Didriksons went to school, though none of the children was particularly studious. Mostly, they were full of energy, and there were seven of them. Papa Ole installed an exercise field in the backyard with an obstacle course, gymnastic equipment, and weights. The four boys and three girls competed against each other in mock battles.

Ole and Hannah were not overly preoccupied with their daughters' femininity. Babe and sister Lillie both ran a little wild, but together. Both discovered how to hurdle the neighbor's hedges. One story said they once knocked on his door to inform him that they needed clipping. Both traveled briefly to California with a circus. It might not have seemed so obvious at the time that "Min Bebe" would become Athlete of the Century.

Certainly, Didrikson was sports-obsessed and pugnacious about it. She wanted to play with the boys and pushed her way into their games. As one said, "once you saw her play, you didn't mind having her around."[4] When teased by the boys, she didn't cry as other girls might but would respond with an insult or a practical joke in turn. She played the harmonica, goofed around, and never said no to a challenge. Her honesty and fearlessness made it easy for the boys to accept her.

The girls felt differently. They were dismayed by her aggression and found her hard to like. Susan Cayleff, author of a Pulitzer-nominated biography on Didrikson, describes how Didrikson's competitiveness separated her from others of her gender:

> Boys were also taught that they had a choice: either play only with your best friend, or play football. Girls played by themselves or with just a single friend. … They played small sports, skating, swimming. … Being competitive wasn't being a Good Girl…. Babe would walk into the women's locker room and say… "All right, which one of you will take second?"[5]

Texas, as with most places in 1920s America, did not offer track and field in high school for girls. Didrikson *was* a high school sports phenom, but in the game that girls were allowed to play in the dusty, oil-reeking towns of East Texas. She played basketball.

Didrikson was a little older than others in her high school class, having had to repeat a grade due to her circus exploits. At only 5'6" she was small for basketball, and Coach Beatrice Lyle of the Beaumont High Royal Purples was initially skeptical. However, Coach quickly discovered that the smallish Didrikson was fast, had good hands, and shot well and often. It didn't take long for the freshman to make varsity and to start setting school scoring records.

Four. Let 'Er Fly

In early spring 1930, 18-year-old Babe had just had one of those games where no one could stop her scoring, when a tall gentleman with a military bearing stopped her afterward for a chat. His name was Colonel Melvirne Johnson McCombs, and he wanted her to play basketball for his Employers Casualty Golden Cyclones. They had lost the league championship to the Sunoco Oilers the previous year, and he needed a ringer on the company team. He had found one.

Didrikson joined Employers Casualty as a stenographer because she could not technically be paid for basketball. Women's basketball was governed by the AAU, which still compelled adherence to the notion of "amateur." Except that Didrikson could neither type nor spell. She did once claim she could type 180 wpm, but she didn't clarify whether it was actual words.

Occasionally, she would be photographed at a desk. Yet the reality was that she joined Employers Casualty for the basketball. At the time, college teams were extremely rare, especially for women,[6] but company basketball teams were plentiful and popular.

The new Employers Casualty hire had the big impact on games that McCombs had in mind. Exactly how much is a little suspect. Didrikson had befriended a sportswriter back home, "Tiny" Scurlock of the *Beaumont Journal*, and he tended to exaggerate as much as she did. He would write that she scored 210 points over five games, or 195, or whatever number came to mind. He later confessed that the numbers were more aspirational than real. She did once score as much as 106 points in five games, an impressive number for a woman, but only half the number to make it to print.

Didrikson was notably not a good team player. She felt she was the star and behaved accordingly. The other young women hated when journalists referred to them as "Babe and her Employers Casualty girls." Didrikson didn't much care any more than she did at Beaumont High or playing sandlot ball with the neighborhood boys.

In the 1930 basketball championship tournament, Employers Casualty again met Sunoco in a game that went down to the last point. Didrikson was chosen to make a game-winning free throw. She missed. It stuck in her craw and motivated her to stay on with basketball for a few more seasons, to win the championships that McCombs had promised.

However, McCombs was thrilled with the performance of his young star. He added her to the company baseball team when the season transitioned. Even then, he knew she had energy to burn, and he didn't want her becoming distracted by other pastimes, by offers from other companies, or—heaven forbid—by dating. In the summer of 1930, McCombs took her to a track meet at Lakeside Park in Dallas, and her eyes lit up.

As the colonel explained how the events worked, how an athlete had to be skilled in different ways to win both in track and field, Didrikson was intrigued. It was like Papa Ole's obstacle course again. So many fun events to try and master! There was also no one to pass the ball to or complain that she was hogging the spotlight. On the track, Didrikson could shine as an individual. It was a match made in heaven.

A heavy stick was lying on the ground—the men's javelin—and she picked it up to give it a heave. She stabbed herself in the back, trying to throw it that first time. A challenge! She was hooked. A world of possibilities opened up. Didrikson had been interested in track ever since 1928, when her family had huddled around the radio to listen to the Olympic exploits from Amsterdam.

The baseball throw was also something she knew well, and she could adapt that style to the javelin. She also learned the ropes of the high jump and broad jump and began practicing with the discus and shot put. She told McCombs that she would train to win every event. It was a ridiculous claim. After all, women were still limited to competing in three events. But she'd figure a way around that.

The first opportunity to compete came just a few months later, when the 1930 national championships came to Dallas. Didrikson watched and admired one dark-haired speedster who effortlessly flew ahead of the others in the sprints. She knew the feeling of being way out in front and saw the same woman float through the air at the broad jump. This was her first look at another multi-talented athlete, Stella Walsh.

Fig.9. In the earliest days, Babe Didrikson (USA) was likened to Stella Walsh of Cleveland, before Walsh became a pariah (Chapter 5). Their first meeting in 1931 produced an epic long jump battle, with Walsh edging Didrikson on the final leap. Cartoon by Jack Burnley, King Features (courtesy of the *Coriscan Daily Sun*).

Walsh was known as a sprinter, but she competed against Didrikson in the broad jump, each one pushing the other on successive leaps. Didrikson broke the record five times; Walsh broke it six times to win.

Didrikson then set records in the javelin and the baseball throw. She ended with a plan to ramp up her training in all of her non-basketball spare time. She wanted to beat everyone in everything.

The Golden Cyclones finally did take the basketball title in the spring of 1931. They returned to the finals again in 1932 and 1933, although they didn't take the title. By then, Didrikson had begun working on track events with a devotion near fanaticism. The only problem was that pesky event limitation still in effect. Didrikson, like all participants before her, could only enter three events. Like so many champions before her, she didn't like it.

The national track and field

championships of 1931 took place at Pershing Field in New Jersey. Didrikson and McCombs chose her three events: the hurdles, baseball throw, and broad jump. If there were to be only three, then she wanted to win across disciplines. She promptly set a world record in the hurdles and an American record in the baseball throw.

In the broad jump this time, Didrikson beat Walsh, who fouled out trying to find a few extra inches. In the hurdles, Evelyn Hall came in close behind Didrikson. High jumper Jean Shiley, the fourth-place finisher from Amsterdam, took first with a much improved form. Lillian Copeland, a talented law student from southern California, won the javelin and the shot put. All of these women would compete against Didrikson multiple times. Track and field was a pretty small world.

Overall, the meet was won by the Illinois Women's Athletic Club (IWAC), as it had been many times before. With Didrikson limited to a few events, Employers Casualty could not beat the powerhouse from Chicago.

In the *New York Times* write-up of the meet, Arthur Daley devoted the first 10 of his 22 paragraphs solely to Didrikson. He coined the phrase "new feminine marvel" at her winning three events, though she was not the first and would not be the last to do so. Daley listed Didrikson's age as 19, although she was actually 20 at the time. It was another Didrikson exaggeration. She liked to misstate her age because she thought it sounded more impressive.

Overall, Didrikson was both pleased with her performance but frustrated that she couldn't do more. She threatened to quit. McCombs considered letting her. He later described her as "the easiest girl to coach and the hardest to handle."[7] However, McCombs enticed her back with one more promise. Next summer, at the national championships—the ones that would double as the Olympic Trials—he would let her become a "one-girl" team.

The "One-Girl" Team

> "It came time to announce my 'team.' I spurted out there all alone, waving my arms, and you never heard such a roar."
> —Didrikson at the 1932 U.S. Olympic Trials[8]

The display that Babe Didrikson put on in two and a half hours on July 16, 1932, was one for the ages. It was the one that most justified all the hype, the one that showed off the "new feminine marvel." In the heart of Illinois, at the Olympic Trials in Northwestern's Dyche Stadium, the eleven women's events took place in less than three hours, making it virtually impossible for athletes to cross multiple events. Didrikson did it—and won.

The plan that McCombs had developed was for Didrikson to compete in eight of the scheduled events: all three throwing events, two jumping events, and two of the four running events. McCombs recommended skipping the two running events that were not on the Olympic schedule, and, obviously, his single athlete would have to skip the relay. But first, he had to persuade the AAU to relax the three-event rule.

The current overseer of the AAU women's championships, Fred Steers, was a stickler for regulations. He believed that the maximum event rule was necessary to safeguard women's health. Everyone remembered all those women collapsing in the 800 m in 1928, and Steers was determined to be on the side of women's safety.

Many athletes, not just Didrikson but Lillian Copeland and Stella Walsh as well, would have competed in more than three events, given the chance. They all would have welcomed a multi-discipline event, like the decathlon on the men's schedule. Women had lobbied for years for more events, but their arguments had fallen on deaf ears.

McCombs, in true Texas businessman style, decided to try an end run around the rules. He announced to the press a few weeks earlier that Didrikson would represent his team alone with his full confidence. He then went to the Texas AAU and hinted that if they didn't allow his athlete to compete in all the events for Employers Casualty, he would withdraw his team *and* their financial sponsorship. The AAU officials grumbled and said it would be entirely left up to Steers. Besides, rules were rules.

Steers himself did not openly object to the plan, although he was furious that McCombs had made some sort of separate agreement with the Texas AAU locals. Even worse, Steers's boss Avery Brundage, now president of the AAU, personally greeted Didrikson's train coming from Texas as if she were a visiting dignitary. The newspaper next day featured a huge photo of Brundage shaking hands with her—and only her.

Nevertheless, Steers told McCombs and Didrikson that she would have to choose which three events she planned to enter. He informed her that she must tell him before the competition started the next day. Didrikson went to sleep with her stomach in such knots that the hotel doctor had to be called for fear it was appendicitis. It turned out to be a whopping case of nerves.

The day of the Trials, after first oversleeping, then getting stuck in heavy Chicago traffic, Didrikson arrived late to the stadium. Her chaperone even had to help her put on her track uniform in the taxicab. They arrived at the field barely in time for Didrikson to line up for the big parade.

For these ninth annual women's AAU track and field championships, five thousand spectators packed the stands in Evanston to root for their hometown IWAC team. As other groups paraded in with 15 to 20 members, Didrikson came in representing Employers Casualty alone. The crowd erupted in cheers when they saw a one-woman team.

Immediately after the parade, she ran off to start preparing, before Steers could track her down. Whether due to the confusion, the crowd's enthusiasm, or the press watching every move, Steers decided to let Didrikson compete as she wished. Perhaps he thought she would fail and thus "prove" that such multi-event shenanigans should be banned in the future. Perhaps he believed what the medical practitioners argued, that no woman would have the stamina.

The schedule did seem artificially squeezed. Didrikson would have to complete all of her qualifiers and events in a time frame that required one event every six minutes. Why were so many different contests shoved into two and a half hours?

Such passive-aggressive tactics had been used before, where organizers didn't ban women outright but made competing impossible with circular rules. Women couldn't enter the first marathon without being blessed, yet the priest only blessed people who had been officially entered. Female figure skaters couldn't compete because the judges couldn't see their feet, due to the long skirts that were mandatory for women. Here, an athlete would find it impossible to compete in multiple events because they were scheduled so tightly together. *Not up to me, it's the schedule!* the scheduler might shrug. *Nothing I can do....*

Didrikson had to perform in heats and finals that nearly overlapped each other. To make matters worse, a large crowd of photographers followed her everywhere, asking her to pose as she competed. The other athletes had to wait or limit their warm-ups in order for Didrikson to get hers in, and morale among the women was awful: "That reporters treated the rest of the team as merely a supporting cast created resentment ... [plus a] sense that she had unfairly eliminated athletes who had trained just as hard for the Olympics by entering so many events."[9]

When the day was over, the press dubbed the one-woman track team "the heroine of the meet." Of her eight events, she won five outright and tied for first in a sixth. She was disappointed that she came fourth in the discus, which meant that she did not qualify for the Olympic team in that event. She also did not seriously challenge the experienced sprinters in the 100 yd. dash. While she had once claimed she could run the distance in 11 seconds, that turned out to be another exaggeration.

Two of her wins and the tie were Olympic events, while three were not. Still, she immediately began telling reporters that she wanted to do a "grand slam" of four Olympic events, something "no girl had ever done." Of course, no woman had done it because none had been allowed, but Didrikson's boast still suggested she was capable of something unique. However, not only were Olympic women's track events limited to three, she had only qualified for three in any case. On the other hand, she *had* set three world records.

Her tie for first was with Amsterdam Olympian Jean Shiley in the high jump. The results foreshadowed a scenario that would repeat in the Olympics. There was controversy over whether Didrikson's jumps were legal.

High jumping forbade diving, for both men and women. Landing headfirst was dangerous. The rules explicitly stated that an athlete's leg had to proceed any upper part of the body over the bar. Most high jumpers, including most of the women, used the "scissors-kick" style. The jumper ran toward the bar and lifted off with their back leg, slicing the front leg up and over the bar first. It was hard to jump high with a scissors-kick but unlikely to foul.

Didrikson favored using a new style called "the Western roll." With the roll, the jumper approached the bar from an extra-sharp angle and launched with their front leg so that their back leg and shoulder would "roll over the bar." It's hard to describe and visualize and even harder to execute. The motion is awkward and getting the back leg to precede the head was very difficult. The style was risky because it was easy to commit a foul.[10] Judges raised the red flag frequently.

Observers at the 1932 Trials later said that Didrikson had been fouling on nearly every one of her "roll" jumps, but the judges weren't calling them foul. In later interviews, Shiley said that her coach was livid about the violations. However, she preferred to focus on her own jumping rather than worry about other athletes. In the end, Shiley was happy when both women reached 1.61 m. It was called a tie, and they were both credited with a new world's record.

There was more drama in the hurdles. Didrikson and longtime rival Evelyn Hall, running in lanes on opposite ends, approached the finish line simultaneously. Didrikson was coming from behind after her typically slow start. The two judges in charge of calling the winner judged it to be Hall. The two judges in charge of second also called it for Hall.

In conference, they discussed who would have won if Hall came second, and the answer was Didrikson, obviously. Together, they agreed to award the victory to Didrikson. Hall felt she had won but was too shy to argue, while Didrikson was already taking congratulations as if there had been no contest.

Years later, Didrikson commented that she had learned several "tricks" that runners did to press for a win. They could lean aggressively right at the end or break the tape outright, even if another runner had already stretched the finish line. Most importantly, they should wave their hands and smile, whether they won or not. Betty Robinson had turned that technique into an Olympic gold medal. Didrikson told reporters, "All you have to do to win if it's close is to throw your arms just before the finish."[11] Photo finishes had been theoretically possible since 1912 but really close races couldn't be distinguished yet.

The Employers Casualty team of one ended up with 30 points. IWAC came in second, 8 points behind, even after winning the relay. However, the American Olympic team would consist of more than one person. Going to Los Angeles along with Didrikson would be rivals Copeland, Hall, and Shiley.

Something No Girl Has Ever Done

Didrikson and McCombs immediately started publicly lobbying for more events and for a relaxation of the event limits in the Olympics, so that Didrikson could complete her "Grand Slam." "What I want to do most of all in the Olympics is to win four firsts.... If they will let me enter the discus, I think I can do it."[12]

She seemed to forget that she hadn't actually earned a spot in the discus. The press conveniently forgot that only four years earlier was the first time women had been allowed in Olympic track events at all.

Lillian Copeland, who *had* earned a spot in the discus, could barely contain herself. In an interview with the *Los Angeles Times*, she openly criticized the AAU for not enforcing the three-event rule in Evanston. Copeland was a multi-discipline athlete, an expert in throwing, but also a solid runner and jumper. In addition, she played baseball, basketball, field hockey, and tennis at the varsity level. On the "side," she was also studying law at USC and presided over the Women's Athletic Association, thus multi-talented outside the stadium, too.

She feared that the AAU would turn the clock backward for women athletes, if pressed too hard. Another new group, the Women's Division of the National Amateur Athletic Foundation (NAAF), presided over by first lady Lou Hoover, had already joined those lobbying the IOC to pull women's track and field back out of the Olympics. They argued that the rising level of competition would create a negative environment which would "derail [a woman] from her true path: marriage and motherhood."[13]

Copeland worried that Didrikson's antics would add gasoline to the fire in these discussions, and that more restrictive rules than ever would be imposed. Didrikson dismissed the comments as jealousy. Years later, an article in the *Los Angeles Times Sunday Magazine* claimed the two agreed to resolve their differences with a discus throw-off. In private at a Los Angeles practice field, a few days before the Games, Copeland reportedly beat Didrikson. Whatever happened, Didrikson stopped pressing—at least for a while—for a "grand slam" of four events.

Risking injury from an unsanctioned match right before the competition might seem childish now, but, for Copeland, it had been a week-long frustrating train ride to California from Illinois. Didrikson had made the team miserable by running up and down the corridors, playing the harmonica, and stealing pillows. Some accounts even suggested that she particularly harassed the two Black women on the U.S. team, Tidye Pickett and Louise Stokes, both by hurling racial slurs at them and throwing ice water on them when they were trying to sleep.

Upon arrival, Didrikson kept up the boasting in the lobby of the Olympic hotel. She would loudly claim to reporters that she could out-swim American swimmer Helen Madison or out-dive Georgia Coleman, if they'd only let her. Meanwhile, her ID tag again listed her age as 19. Apparently, among other superhuman feats, she never aged.

At last, on Sunday, July 31, 1932, the women's Olympic events began in earnest. Cleveland's Stella Walsh, running for Poland under her birth name, Stanisława Walasiewicz—a story for the next chapter—won the 100 m sprint. Canadian Hilda Strike and American Billie von Bremen took silver and bronze.

Next, it was time for Didrikson's first competition in the javelin. Ellen Braumüller and Tilly Fleischer, outstanding throwers from Germany, were in great form. Both were record holders, though one of Braumüller's records was curiously listed in the *Official Programme* as an "Olympic record." Since this was the first Olympics where women threw the javelin, no one could have set such a record before. Braumüller's previous best was nevertheless used as the benchmark for measurement by the officials, so perhaps that made it—temporarily—an Olympic record.

As luck would have it, Didrikson was randomly chosen to throw first. She had come a long way in her javelin form since that first day in that Dallas park when she hit herself in the back. She gripped the rope-covered section and began her run-up. Midway in her dozen steps, however, her hand slipped. The heave was forceful, but she lost something on the throw, and it didn't arc as it should have. Instead, it flew straight, she said, like "a catcher's peg, from home to second."[14] Still, it flew far past the marker in the field that had been printed in the program.

The javelin landed at 43.68 m, which would indeed be a new Olympic record.[15] It was more than a meter further than Didrikson had thrown at the Trials just two weeks earlier. Fred Steers, who was coaching the U.S. track team for the Games, said that if her hand hadn't slipped, the throw might have set a mark that would have lasted decades. Braumüller and Fleischer followed with tosses both past the old mark, too, but they couldn't beat Didrikson's first throw.

Neither could Didrikson herself. In that first giant, slippery toss, something twisted in her shoulder. Her second and third throws were anemic, and the crowd grumbled, thinking she was saving her strength and depriving them of another amazing throw. In reality, she had torn cartilage, and her shoulder was on fire.

For years afterward, she continued to complain that she wish she had "been allowed" to throw the discus. She even participated in a post–Olympic competition where she took second in the discus and pointed out to the press that it would have earned a medal if she'd done it in Los Angeles. Yet, it's hard to imagine how she would have thrown a discus with a major shoulder injury. Copeland, who may or may not have beaten Didrikson in a bragging-rights throw-off, did win the gold in the discus. And with a new world's record.

Five days later, it was time for the 80 m hurdles. In an early heat, Didrikson set a record (11.8 seconds) edging out her U.S. teammate Simone Schaller. Evelyn Hall, in her own heat, matched a previous record (12 seconds). Shoulder injury or not, Didrikson could still burn down the track.

As the women approached the starting line for the finals, Hall was a little startled to see that someone had already dug her holes. She was assigned lane one, right next to Didrikson, and wondered if it was another little Texas mind game. She hurriedly fixed them before the starter called them to be ready.

Before the official's pistol sounded, though, Didrikson took off: a false start. It was quite common in races, but there were so many horror stories of runners false-starting out of their race. Myrtle Cook and Leni Schmidt had done just that in 1928. Didrikson settled back into her blocks, taking extra care.

But she was always a slow starter. Didrikson's special talent was the technique between the hurdles, courtesy of the crooked-leg style that she'd developed on the neighbor's hedges. After an even slower start than usual, Didrikson was surging past Hall by the sixth hurdle. She pushed into the lead. Then it was Hall's turn to come from behind.

As they both hit the yarn that had been strung to mark the finish line, Didrikson shoved her shoulder forward in one of those favorite running tricks. Hall caught the yarn on her neck, hitting it so hard that it raised a red welt. The Texas phenom then finished with her other favorite trick, waving her arms and smiling with victory. Hall, in response, chewed her lip. The U.S. team, crowded in a nearby stadium tunnel, was on Hall's side, and they waved one finger in the air at her. She wasn't so sure and waved two fingers back.

The judges' deliberations took a half hour. To her dying breath, Hall insisted that she had won or at least tied with Didrikson. The officials saw her two fingers, she thought, and decided that she "knew" she hadn't won. There was newfangled photography equipment, a state-of-the-art Kirby camera, but the race was still too close for the photo to confirm the winner. Updated timing mechanisms still only went to the tenth of a second, and those stopwatches listed both women at 11.7.

The officials could have given them both a tie. They awarded both of them a new world record of 11.7. Had Hall been from another country, her team might have lodged a protest that it was an actual tie, but no one on the U.S. Olympic staff protested on behalf of her against her more celebrated teammate. Team USA was happy the winner was from Team USA.

The judges awarded the race to Didrikson, who, as always, was shaking hands and accepting congratulations before the ruling had concluded. Whether Didrikson won by the reported "eyelash," or actually did tie with Evelyn Hall, she was awarded her second gold medal.

With two wins of three in the books, Didrikson approached the high jump, her last event, outwardly confident and inwardly nervous. She told reporters, "I don't know who my opponent is."[16] It seems unlikely that she didn't remember facing off against Shiley at the Trials—Shiley who already had one Olympics under her belt.

The event started as expected. The Canadian and Dutch jumpers excelled with the scissors-kick style, as did Shiley. Didrikson, using her Western roll, pressed Shiley hard.

Both passed 1.65 m (about 5'5"), another world record, which left them alone in the top two spots. They both attempted 1.67. Shiley missed. Didrikson rolled over the bar cleanly, but, in the pit, her foot kicked one of the stanchions, and the bar popped off.

Fig.10. Babe Didrikson (far right) won her 1932 Olympic heat in world record time against Simone Schaller (USA, left) and Nakanishi Michi (JPN, middle). Didrikson might have beat Evelyn Hall in the finals ... or not. Tie goes to the confident (Library of Congress, Prints and Photographs Division, NYWT&S Collection, LC-USZ62-113281).

Throughout the high jump contest, Didrikson had not been assessed a single foul for rolling over the bar shoulder first. Behind the scenes, though, the Canadian and Dutch coaches had been pulling the judges aside and complaining constantly. Had the judges called a foul early on, Didrikson might have corrected her technique. Or, Shiley might have already won. But, just as Fred Steers didn't intervene at the U.S. Trials, the Olympic officials decided to take a passive approach to the rules for most of the match, until the jump-off.

The bar was reset to 1.67 m, and both Shiley and Didrikson jumped. Shiley passed. Didrikson jumped and cleared the bar, in the same manner that she had all day. The judges huddled, however, and emerged to declare that Didrikson had fouled. Shiley was awarded the gold and Didrikson the silver.

Didrikson was peeved. She pointed out that she had been jumping like that all day, oblivious that the judges could have disqualified her entirely, if that was the case. Had she been forced to use a scissors kick as everyone else did, she might not even have earned a medal. Still, she pouted afterward: "The collection is spoiled now. That silver medal for the high jump spoiled it."[17]

Nevertheless, the press crowned her officially—as they had been planning for days—as the "undisputed athletic star" of the meet, with her three medals, one silver. Helen Madison's three golds was deemed a lesser achievement, as was Romeo Neri's three medals in men's gymnastics. Medals are medals are medals, but some medals are more equal than others.

Didrikson flew home on a plane chartered by Employers Casualty and was met at the airport by a crowd of cheering fans. Jean Shiley endured a multi-day bus ride home from southern California to Illinois. Evelyn Hall drove home alone in her old car, which was repossessed by creditors within a few months after the Games.

Only the one-woman team from Texas ended up with earnings from her "stenographer's job" that could afford a new car. Didrikson decided to splurge and buy herself a red Dodge Coupe after the Games. When she told the Dodge dealer how much she loved it, he decided without her permission to put her positive comments into an advertisement. Avery Brundage, always on the prowl for athletes who violated their amateur status, immediately suspended her from any further AAU competition.

Didrikson argued that the "endorsement" was inadvertent. She petitioned for reinstatement, although not especially vigorously. She might have been tired of training or simply looking for a new adventure. As the AAU was evaluating her petition, she arranged to appear in another Dodge ad, for which she was paid. Take that, AAU!

After the sportswriters voted Didrikson Athlete of the Year for 1932, she launched a whole new career in entertainment. First, she appeared in a vaudeville act built around her unique talents. She would walk down the aisle in high heels, then kick them off to don track shoes and run on a treadmill. Afterward, she played the harmonica and sang.

In another professional sporting "act," she joined a Jewish men's baseball team, the House of David, which sported Orthodox rabbi-style beards. For some of the games, they played while riding donkeys. The money was great, considering the awful state of the economy, but Didrikson was growing bored. She started looking around for a new sport to master, something that didn't involve a team or pesky Olympic judges.

In 1935, she loosened her girdle and decided to take up golf.

Exceptionalism Defined

Without question, Babe Didrikson was a multi-talented, versatile athlete capable of exceptional achievement. She was also given opportunities that peers were not, including favorable press unlike what others received. She trained long and hard, but so did her biggest competitors. She had a paying job in one of the worst economies in history, without having to support or care for a husband or children.[18] She was promoted early on by a larger-than-life front man, Colonel McCombs, who helped eliminate obstacles in her way.

The public granted her what has been called "individual exceptionalism," where a person is held up as a shining—and single—example of a group far above others. Exceptionalism has often been bestowed on minority athletes, Jesse Owens being the most famous example. The talented Owens won four gold medals in Berlin, overcoming long-held attitudes that Blacks were inferior. Many labeled Owens a "credit to his race," suggesting that his exploits were highly unusual for a Black athlete. The press created an "Owens vs. The Nazis" narrative which turned Owens into a superhero.

In contrast, far less attention was given to the other seventeen Black athletes who also competed successfully on the 1936 American team. Filmmaker Deborah Riley Draper wrote a film and book about those other minority athletes, *Olympic Pride, American Prejudice: The Untold Story of 18 African Americans Who Defied Jim Crow and Adolf Hitler to Compete in the 1936 Berlin Olympics*. Draper described why the exceptionalism narrative prevailed: "It was easier to explain this one athlete against Hitler than, at a time when Jim Crow was prevalent, to say that there were 18 exceptional black people. That's not a story anyone wants to hear. One exceptional black person is digestible; 18, way too much."[19]

Because of Didrikson's pushy coach/publicist and the favorable media, she was able to break through the three-event barrier. But allowing her to compete as a one-woman team took spots away from other athletes. Crowning her as the de facto winner before she even competed made it more difficult for other women athletes to be taken seriously. Sure, let one unique female athlete try all the events and proclaim her skills a wonder as all others are barred from doing the same. When a woman medalist is treated as an exception to the rule, then the rules stay in place.

Not all the press that Didrikson received was positive. Even in this, there seemed to be no neutral opinions. Two of the most highly regarded sportswriters at the time, Paul Gallico and Grantland Rice, stood on opposite sides of the "Babe" question. Gallico barked his thoughts about Didrikson (and any other woman track athlete) loud and clear. He mockingly called her a "Muscle Moll" and further, "openly speculated whether she was a lesbian or even a member of a 'third sex' that is neither male nor female … [saying he] was as curious about her as he was about 'the bearded lady' and the albino girl at the circus sideshow."[20] Gallico's viewpoint will be further explored in Chapter Fifteen.

Didrikson didn't enjoy the muscle moll designation or speculations about her love life: "People are always asking me, 'Are you going to get married, Babe?' and it gets to my goat."[21]

When Didrikson did marry professional wrestler George Zaharias, whom she met on the golf course, headlines trumpeted: "Babe is a Lady now."[22] Gallico's criticisms after Didrikson's marriage transformed into a chorus of unlimited praise: "if some yet unborn games queen matches her talent, versatility, skill, patience and will to practice … the Babe must be listed with the champions of all times."[23]

On the other hand, writer Grantland Rice had been on Didrikson's side from the time he first saw her in 1931. After the Trials, he described her as achieving what no other woman could attain: "She is an incredible human being. She is beyond all belief until you see her perform. Then you fully understand that you are looking at the most flawless section of muscle harmony, of complete mental and physical coordination the world of sport has ever known."[24]

When Arthur Daley and Grantland Rice extolled her talents as if she achieved the impossible, she was not only the one to beat but also the only worthy on the track. This, in turn, influenced the judges, who made very close calls in the hurdles and the high jump contests (in her favor), both in the Olympic Trials and the Games themselves.

Her treatment as an exception was also noticeable in the handling of her amateur status. Jim Thorpe had his Olympic medals stripped for playing a few games of semi-pro baseball, a sport completely unrelated to his Olympic exploits. Eleanor Holm told the press she was interested in offers from the movie studios, but that she would not be able to take a dime for work because of her fame as a swimmer, until after her Olympic career was officially over.

Yet Didrikson was able to work for Employers Casualty, to be on the payroll for a job for which she was highly unqualified, to play on their sports teams and represent them on the track, without her amateur status being questioned. She literally had to appear in an ad with her name saying "Track star endorses our product" for her amateur status to be stripped.

For a person whose exploits were "beyond belief," everyone would bend over backward. When officials wanted to go the other way—to exclude or include people, based on whatever criteria came to mind at the time—they could do that as well. Women who were not the new feminine marvels were expected to comport themselves in a certain manner.

Those that strayed from the model image would be given no such leeway.

Five

Pariahs (1932–1936)

Babe Didrikson's leap into the sporting world did not lead to a general loosening of standards or rules. Far from it. Three other Olympic athletes became as notable for their negative press as for their successes. Criticism was heaped on them because of their failure to meet standards of feminine behavior.

Swimmer Eleanor Holm dominated in the backstroke in 1932, but, on the trip overseas to defend her Olympic title, she was kicked off the team for conduct unbecoming of women. Stella Walsh, a Polish immigrant from Cleveland, won two Olympic medals. However, while fair-haired teenage Betty Robinson was praised for her speed, square-jawed Walsh was vilified. Finally, Helene Mayer won a gold medal fencing for Germany in 1928, yet returned to compete in Berlin and was broadly characterized as a turncoat, traitor, and token.

Why did Didrikson earn such special accolades when other multi-discipline athletes of her era did not? Why were such harsh criticisms lobbed at Walsh and Holm? How did Mayer get stuck in an untenable situation?

What these women had in common was encountering a new type of barrier. Over the decades, female athletes had finally earned their place in competition, and the number of events had expanded, from six in 1908 to fifteen by 1936.[1] However, female athletes were now challenged by something else: their character.

The debate no longer centered around whether women could be athletes.[2] Now the question was whether *this* woman, given her appearance or attitude, *should* compete. The questions were not "what was her race time" or "how many points did she score," but "is she a real woman" or "is she an appropriate role model?" Athletes were evaluated based on their femininity, deportment, and patriotism. Navigating that set of expectations created a new set of challenges.

Men also had to navigate the treacherous waters of the press, yet they weren't held to the same standards of physical appearance. They weren't told that, when they run, "the upper part of their legs go in at the wrong places" or that their faces during competition were "twisted and contorted."[3] Instead, they were encouraged to exercise because "Weakness is a crime. Don't be a criminal."[4] For men, the standard was victory. Losers were criticized. Men only needed to win to receive praise. They didn't need to look a certain way while they were doing it.

Women who passed scrutiny became Vikings, mermaids, or queens. Women who did not fit the mold of grace and loveliness, who were insufficiently feminine or modest, were punished in a variety of ways. Women were made examples of, for better or worse.

Training on Champagne and Cigarettes

Eleanor Holm—also known as Eleanor Holm Jarrett or Eleanor Holm Jarrett Rose Whalen—was a two-time Olympian who ran afoul of the chauvinism of the man who ran Team USA. Like Didrikson, Holm was raised in a large family and was a teenage sports prodigy. The resemblance stopped there.

The Holms were affluent socialites of New York, parents who summered on Long Island. Eleanor grew up enjoying shopping on Fifth Avenue and parties after a day of swimming at the club. She loved being described as "glamorous Eleanor Holm" or "the New Yorker Miss Holm," and told reporters, "If I had to choose between swimming cups and honors, and the loss of looks … I'd give up the championship."[5] She saw the competitions as a means to an end, a way to break into entertainment or at the very least marry into it. But she still liked to win.

Holm was part of the U.S. Swim Team when she headed for Amsterdam as a 14-year-old ingénue. One story about that 1928 team, waiting on the ship for the competitions to begin, says that the swimmers got bored and ditched General Douglas MacArthur, their Olympic chaperone, for a shopping expedition in Paris. It's not hard to imagine Holm as one of the instigators, coming as she did from a culture as familiar with haute couture as with swim lanes. Still, in the pool, she was all business. She won her 1928 Olympic heat, although she only tied for fourth in the finals. She knew she would be back.

At the 1932 Los Angeles Olympics, she dominated in her single event: the 100 m backstroke. Yet she was careful to maintain her amateur status even while the Hollywood agents were pressing business cards into her hand. She swam for four more years, going unbeaten in the backstroke all the way through the 1936 Olympic Trials. As world-wise as she was, she wanted to compete and win. Her dream was to crown her career with a second gold medal in Berlin. The ocean voyage would be fun, too, and Berlin was notorious for its nightlife. She couldn't wait to board the SS *Manhattan* in July 1936, bound for Hamburg.

However, she was no longer a wide-eyed teenager. Two years earlier, age 20, she had married band leader Art Jarrett. She loved the night life, and singing with the band was a fringe benefit. Dressed in a cowboy hat and a bathing suit, her rendition of "I'm an Old Cowhand" brought the house down.

When Holm left the band to board the ship for the Games, she expected to buy a first-class ticket so she could party with A-listers on the upper decks. Instead, she was told she had to bunk with the team down in steerage. So, she would frequently sneak out of the athlete quarters to go upstairs. She wasn't the only one.

There are conflicting stories of what happened, one night early into the cross-Atlantic trip. One account says that Holm passed out drinking and was spotted by the chaperone being helped down the stairs by two men not known to the Olympic staff. The chaperone allegedly called the team doctor, who diagnosed Holm with "acute alcoholism."

Holm's story is slightly different. She claims she was at a party when the chaperone told her it was curfew. They were days away from Germany, but supposedly Olympians needed their sleep. Her response:

God, it was about 9 o'clock, and who wanted to go down in that basement to sleep anyway? So I said to her: "Oh, is it really bedtime? Did you make the Olympic team or did I?" I had had a few glasses of Champagne. So she went to Brundage and complained that I was setting a bad example for the team, and they got together and.... I was fired.... I was heartbroken.[6]

Holm argued that the regulations said she had to continue her normal athletic training routine throughout the trip. For her, that was a glass of champagne after a workout. Or two. Or three. She told the sportswriters that she "train[ed] on champagne and cigarettes."[7]

Whichever version triggered the meeting the next day—midday probably—the new president of the American Olympic Committee (AOC), Avery Brundage, summoned her to his room and banned her from the Olympics. According to Holm, he propositioned her, and she turned him down. It is hard to know where the truth is, but it's possible that both of them used frank language. He might have commented on her behavior in a suggestive way.

Brundage, over his lifetime, had multiple affairs and fathered at least two children out of wedlock. However, he had no trouble enforcing strict double standards on female athletes, whom he barely tolerated in competition.[8] Female athletes, most especially his American female athletes, were supposed to act with grace and decorum. Male track athletes were known to partake of brandy or a few beers before a race, but drinking was considered wrong for women, and late-night partying right out.

Holm noted later that Australian swimmer Dawn Fraser became infamous in the 1960s for a drunken swim across a Tokyo moat to steal a flag. This was a double standard, in her eyes. But that was years after, and not under the watchful eye of Brundage, who unceremoniously kicked the "glamorous New Yorker" off the Berlin Olympic team. (Technically, Brundage obtained the full vote of the AOC, but they followed the recommendation of their chair.)

Holm's American teammates petitioned by the dozens to reinstate her, but their pleas were ignored. Brundage was pilloried in the press for his unfairness, but the more criticism was heaped on him, the more he dug in his heels. The AOC president never changed his mind.

Free from team restrictions in Berlin, Holm continued to party. The Associated Press hired her as a reporter, and she attended everything with a press pass, mingling with American and German celebrities in the same room with Brundage. The Europeans didn't understand the punishment at all, according to her. "I was drinking *champagne*. If it had been whiskey or *gin*, well, all right. But they drank wine at their training tables, so they couldn't figure out *what* was the matter."[9]

More stories surfaced of Holm frolicking in Germany. She was seen swimming naked in a pool. She fraternized with the Nazis, commenting that Hermann Göring was "fun." He gave her a silver swastika; as soon as she got home, she mounted a huge diamond-studded Star of David over it.

In the Berlin Olympic swimming competition, the Dutch team easily dispatched the Americans, cheered on by the fans who had made the trek from Amsterdam. Dina Senff and Rie Mastenbrook took gold and silver in the backstroke, and Holm grumbled that she could have beaten Senff's 1:18.9 "with a champagne bottle in either hand."[10] But her swimming days were over.

Between censuring Babe Didrikson for a car ad and kicking Eleanor Holm off the team for a few glasses of champagne, Brundage cemented his image as an old-world stick in the mud. It never changed his opinion. Yet, in attempting to punish her for her lack of femininity, he turned Holm into an even bigger star. According to her: "I was everything Avery Brundage hated. I had a few dollars, and athletes were supposed to be poor. I worked in nightclubs, and athletes shouldn't do that. I was married. ... It didn't matter to him that I held the world record.... He did make me famous. I would have been just another female backstroke swimmer without Brundage."[11]

However, though Brundage was criticized for his actions in the court of public opinion, Holm's tale still remained a cautionary one. Free spirits might be entertaining, but athletes must be tamed. Women who wanted to compete in sports were limited in what they were allowed to say and do, even off the field. No matter what happened afterward, Holm lost an opportunity because she was a woman.

Fig.11. The always-smiling Eleanor Holm (USA), 1932 backstroke gold medalist, before being booted off the 1936 team for alleged drunkenness, partying with the press and the Nazis, swimming in Billy Rose's Aquacade, and going through several husbands (Courtesy of the Boston Public Library, Leslie Jones Collection).

Maybe she got the last laugh. Laughing was a key component of what the public wanted to see. They hated to see strain on women's faces, which may be why Holm's smiling pinup shots and Didrikson's clownish boasting made them so popular. Those who could win and smile were held up in the highest esteem, at least in the court of public opinion, if not by Olympic officials. Not smiling was counted as a strike against a woman athlete. It wasn't the only thing.

Stella Walsh, American Girl

For a few moments in 1930, Polish-American runner Stella Walsh earned the accolade the "World's Greatest Woman Athlete" after earning wins in four events at an international track meet. But it was only once, and, when Didrikson and others came along who were more likable, the memories of Walsh's exploits quickly dimmed.

Her reputation today in her hometown Cleveland is as a beloved champion, but much of the world has turned its back on her. Her legacy also carries an asterisk for something that happened decades later. However, part of the controversy came because even when she competed, she was guilty in the public eye of two unpardonable sins: she was an immigrant and she never smiled.

While this section will focus on Walsh's achievements in the 1930s, it's necessary to address the asterisk up front. Although it was not publicly known at the time she was competing, Walsh was born intersex. Her chromosomes expressed both male and female genders. Tabloid writers today have reduced this to her being "mostly male," but the truth was more complex. The final chapter will place her in context of the Olympic history of gender testing.

Still, it's important to clarify at the outset that Walsh was not a man masquerading as a woman. She was not a boy in girl's clothing. Her body was between genders, as if she were on the threshold between two different worlds. In 1932, that might have disqualified her as an Olympian, but, in our current culture, she would be allowed to compete. For now, assume she competed in track and field as a female. That is what she assumed.

Walsh was born Stanisława Stefania Walasiewicz in 1911, the same year as Betty Robinson and Babe Didrikson, as it happens. Her 18-year-old mother gave birth at home in Poland, in a tiny hamlet called Wierzchownia. Neither a doctor nor her father were present, and the midwife declared her a girl. Stanisława was listed as female on her birth certificate and always behaved accordingly.

However, she was also born with the broad shoulders and strong torso of her Polish ancestors, who had eked out a meager living in the tough Eastern European soil. She had the long hooked nose of her grandparents, coupled with the square face and wiry hair of her father. Some would call the look masculine, but what she really appeared to be was Eastern European, at a time when distrust against foreigners was high.

The distrust was specific to Polish Americans, too, ever since a disgruntled Polish American anarchist shot President McKinley in 1901. Not that the Irish, Italians, or Germans fared better, but there was a little extra venom aimed at Poles, an increase in "Polack" jokes and negative stereotyping in the decades following the assassination. Woodrow Wilson, for example, at one point referred to Poles and Hungarians as "men of the meaner sort" who possessed "neither skill nor energy nor any initiative of quick intelligence."[12] Being Polish and looking Polish was a cause for suspicion in 1920.

Stanisława learned to speak and write perfect English at Catholic elementary school, even though her parents only spoke Polish at home. In high school, the teachers changed her name to Stella Walsh because they couldn't pronounce the other one. By all accounts, she didn't mind Stella, but it was one more thing about her that people wanted to change.

She also quickly shot up to 5'6", the same height as other female athletes of her day, although she towered over her smaller parents and classmates. Had she been blond or dimpled, they might have called her "lanky." Instead, she was described as "hulking."

The girls teased her for her indelicate looks, so she went to play with the boys. The boys were worse. They called her "Bull Montana," the stage name of a celebrity pro wrestler. She became determined to beat them at their own games and ended up a star basketball and baseball player on the varsity boys' teams. She also found out she was fast.

Did she run fast because she was chased? Because they yelled names or threw things at her? Or did she just want to be the best at something? However it started, Walsh lucked out that Cleveland had a Polish *sokol*.

The sokols, or athletic clubs, were imports from the old country. As will be noted later, they were instrumental in spreading gymnastics through Eastern Europe. In the U.S., however, the sokols were more successful promoting track than gymnastics. The clubs combined sports with religion and a military-like regimen, not unlike Asian dojos, although the sokols focused on sports rather than martial arts. In America, the clubs were also social gatherings of people who spoke the language of the old country while learning new racing techniques.

With training from the sokol, 16-year-old Walsh won the 50 and 70 yd. dashes at a citywide Cleveland Junior Olympics, along with the baseball throw and the standing broad jump, displaying the kind of versatility that was so admired for others. In her first meet outside of Cleveland, at a New York gathering of nationwide Polish sokols (a *zlot*), she won an "all-around title." The AAU didn't sponsor such contests of versatility, but local clubs could for a Walsh or a Didrikson.

These successes propelled her on to New Jersey, in that sweltering July of 1928, for the U.S. Olympic Trials. At the time, all eyes were on sprinters Helen Filkey and Betty Robinson. Despite being a few months older than Robinson, Walsh's sokol training and raw speed didn't make up for inexperience. Chicago coaches were, after all, world-class.

Although Walsh tied for first in her early heat, she was edged out in the semifinal. Even so, the American Olympic organizers wanted to put her on the 4 × 100 relay as an alternate, which would have been a dream come true. They were measuring her for a uniform when they looked at the birthplace listed on her form. She hadn't thought to lie, but she was not a U.S. citizen. European-born young immigrants could not apply for citizenship until age 21, and that was four years away. She was turned away, her first Olympic disappointment.

For the next two years, she competed locally and internationally. They knew her by name in Warsaw, when she took five firsts in 1929. They learned her name in Madison Square Garden at the 1930 Millrose Games, dubbed the "American Olympics" by those in the track community. There, Stella ran against three Canadians and, for once, was treated as American as apple pie when she broke the world's record.

The *Cleveland Plain Dealer* wasn't concerned about what it said on her birth certificate. They wrote that "she was bound to win—because she was Stella Walsh, American girl."[13] Walsh herself gushed at the pride of bringing the prize back home. Citizenship didn't seem important to her or to others at the Millrose Games. "I didn't just feel like Stella Walsh then, but as if I was part of every girl in the United States.... I was just one American girl against these aliens.... I was the one chosen to run this race. That was the thrill."[14]

A few days later in Philadelphia, Walsh did something besides just win. As Walsh broke the record for the 220 yd. dash, she turned around to see where the runners were behind her—twice. Many athletes were confident. Didrikson was infamous for boasting, and even Betty Robinson would cock her head and smile right after crushing her rivals. This look-back, though, was described as "gloating," and some wrote that it reduced her rivals to tears. The *New York Times* referred to it as "startling."[15] The *Plain Dealer* called her a "whirlwind."[16] No one called her a "feminine marvel."

The 1930 AAU national championship was where Walsh met Didrikson in that broad jump for the ages. During the meet, she broke world records in the 100 m and the 200 m, in addition to the broad jump. One writer nicknamed her the "Cleveland Flyer." She won three medals, but only gained a nickname, nothing like a "performance for the ages." A year later, when Didrikson won track *and* field events, the *Times* wrote as if no one had ever displayed versatility before.

By 1930, Walsh was also working for a new employer, the New York Central Railroad, as a clerk in their Cleveland office. She did know how to file and spell, with her nun-taught English. She proudly wore the track uniform of the New York Central RR Athletic Association.

In a strange turn of events, she wore that uniform at the Women's World Games in Prague, despite competing under the Polish flag. The issue was that the Americans opted not to send a team, either irritated with Alice Milliat or just uninterested in non–IOC-sanctioned events. However, Walsh wanted to compete and asked the AAU to grant her an exception to compete for another country. The AAU said yes.

No one objected at the time that the American girl apparently had her foot in the citizenship of another land. She won the 60, 100, and 200 and helped Poland to a bronze in the team relay. For one brief moment, a journalist called Walsh the "World's Greatest Woman Athlete."[17]

Perhaps her decision to move between countries didn't seem odd to someone who spoke two languages and who was fluid in other senses. Walsh thought it demonstrated that organizing committees might be flexible or sympathetic. She was mistaken.

In July 1931, a year after her "startling" performance, Walsh defended her multiple wins in a New Jersey meet against Didrikson and others. However, the meet went wrong nearly from the beginning. Warming up for the discus, she misjudged a practice throw and hit a spectator who was crowding the track. She fractured his skull, and the park commissioner took the unusual step of arresting her, though he agreed to let her finish competing. Distracted and mortified, she fouled on the broad jump and lost the 100 m, although she did win the 220 yd. dash, before the police detained her.

The matter was dropped, but holding her accountable was a peculiar choice. Bystanders were often hit by flying objects at meets. Even as late as the 1990s, the javelin had to be redesigned because audience members were being impaled up in the stadium seats. However, no one was ever arrested. Yet neither the AAU nor the Athletic Club seemed willing to prevent Walsh from being charged.

Whether to make amends for the discus throw or to help improve her reputation, Walsh next decided to try a different kind of contest. Cleveland held a "Miss Stadium" beauty contest in August 1931, as part of their 135th anniversary celebration. When Walsh entered, one writer scoffed, "Girls with lots of dimples and personality usually becomes queens in this sort of thing,"[18] implying that this was not what Walsh had to offer.

However, she canvassed votes and sold tickets in her neighborhood with the same intensity as when she raced. When the final tally was counted, Walsh had received 50 percent more votes than the next person, an attractive, dimpled pianist. She happily accepted the robe and crown of "Miss Stadium."

The Los Angeles Olympics finally approached, along with her 21st birthday. Walsh began applying for citizenship, so she could add a gold medal for America to the pageant crown and slew of world records.

A new challenge emerged. A few weeks before the meet, the railroad eliminated her job, at the height of the Depression. Her father's factory hours had also been cut back, and the family faced severe financial straits. Walsh pleaded publicly for support or another job, but the only one offered was from the Cleveland Recreation Department, a job which would have ruined her amateur status. Running on the athletic club for the New York Central Railroad or for Employers Casualty was for amateurs; running on the athletic club of the recreation department made her a professional. Those were the rules.

The Polish embassy jumped in with an offer to pay for her training and travel expenses as well as for her education if she ran under the Polish flag. She had run for them before, although not in the Olympics. It was an agonizing decision, and she asked the media, "If a big company like the New York Central can't give me a job, where can I get one?"[19]

The silence was deafening. Employers Casualty already had their athlete. No one else stepped up to raise funds on her behalf. Four days later, Walsh accepted Poland's offer.

It may have crossed her mind that people in Poland, who looked more like her, would not call her Bull Montana. She planned to move to Poland after the Games, finish her schooling, and accept the appreciation from kindred spirits.

The newspapers were livid. The *Los Angeles Times* headline screamed "STELLA WALSH SHOULD BE BARRED FROM THE OLYMPICS." The *Washington Post* opined that she would be "running for herself and not for any patriotic inspiration,"[20] completely ignoring the ideals of Olympism which imagined sports to be above country.

America had not allowed her to be a citizen when she wanted to run for them. The AOC had happily let her run under the Polish flag more than once. But now, Walsh was the villain, turning her back on "her" country. It was as if the pageant, the triumphant race against the Canadians, and all the world records were wiped away. Bad enough that Stella had dark features and a square jaw, that she was an unsmiling girl with no dimples or personality. Her worst offense was out in the open: she was un–American.

Five. Pariahs (1932–1936) 81

On July 31, 1932, the day Didrikson won gold in the javelin, Walsh competed in the Olympic 100 m as Stanisława Walasiewicz. She won.

Some speculated she might have even broken a record if she hadn't been wearing a beret. Walsh's 11.9 seconds, a significant improvement over Betty Robinson's previous Olympic record, had one writer say that she ran "with a fury no other girl sprinter has ever known."[21]

Other comments were less charitable. Writer Gaston Meyer of the French newspaper *L'Equipe* called her a "large brunette, of whom it is said that she shaves every day."[22] Even back home, the Cleveland *Polish Daily Monitor* said, "We are glad to see Walsh win, of course, but we would have been more glad if she had finished her naturalization and won as an American. We are Americans."[23]

She did move to Poland but, within a year, had fallen out of love with her new country. A bad ankle injury was treated with substandard medical care. Her Polish neighbors couldn't care less about her medals. By summer's end, she was back in Cleveland, still winning races and still the world's top sprinter. But still not an American citizen.

Three years later, Walsh was still running, perhaps chasing something or being chased. She was certainly trying to outrun time and the battle against her 24-year-old body. Maybe she hoped another Olympic gold medal could improve her reputation. But in March 1935, it finally happened. At an indoor AAU meet, she found herself passed by a "tall, lanky, sun-burned country girl from Missouri."[24]

The press rushed by Walsh at the finish line to interview this new phenom, Helen Stephens. The "Fulton Flash," the nickname bestowed on Stephens by the Missouri papers, had just beaten the unbeatable. The enthusiasm from sportswriters was partly because Stephens was new, but there seemed to be extra exultation in the comments: "Spectators went wild. Sportswriters went crazy, bolting onto the track, passing by the former titleholder, pushing toward the kid who had just stomped Stella."[25]

Fig.12. Multi-talented Stella Walsh (Stanisława Walasiewicz) displaying her trophies and medals, wearing her New York Central Railroad shirt, when she still hoped to compete for the U.S. in Los Angeles. It didn't work out that way (Polish National Digital Archives).

This was the public approving the light over dark, the smiling over the dour, the all-American over the perpetual foreigner.

At the 1936 Berlin Olympics, in Walsh's last opportunity for some sort of redemption, she fell short. A UPI correspondent was almost gleeful as he wrote about Walsh's grim expression: "It's written all over her face as she digs her starting holes with a shovel. Next to her is the girl who displaced her as the fastest femme—Helen Stephens, the country girl from Missouri. Helen laughs as she readies herself for the run down the straightaway. She knows she is tops."[26]

The writer's word choice of "laugh" is a dead giveaway. It is as if Stephens wins because she is laughing. The race wasn't especially close.

After the race, the truly bizarre occurred. A Polish newspaper printed an accusation that Stephens was a man in disguise. At the time, Walsh was rumored to be partly behind the accusation. Given Walsh's own secret, it seems unfathomable that she would want either one of them spotlighted for such a reason. The IOC required Stephens to submit to a full gynecological exam. They could have asked both racers, but they didn't. The humiliating experience for Stephens quashed the accusation. It was an absurd and ironic end to Walsh's great career.

The last Olympic photo of Stella Walsh is of her shaking hands with Helen Stephens, who was three inches taller, but somehow was never described as "towering," "husky," or "big and aggressive." Stephens is grinning from ear to ear. Walsh, who had just earned a silver medal, looks haunted.

As Babe Didrikson said of Walsh years earlier, "you would not think she gets much pleasure in running." There wasn't pleasure in losing. It never seemed to be fun to win either. It wasn't fun to be shut out of the country she truly loved. That was Stella Walsh's ultimate downfall.

The Token

> "Once you've been to the games, you would understand."
> —Helene Mayer[27]

At the tender age of 17, Helene Mayer received the glowing accolades from her countrymen that were denied Stella Walsh. The country in this case was Germany and the sport, fencing. By 25, Mayer was desperate to hear the cheers again, willing to do almost anything for a repeat.

As much as these three women, Holm, Walsh, and Mayer, wanted to be evaluated solely based on the quality of their competition, Mayer showed most of all that women could not simply be athletes. They were always symbols of something else—femininity, versatility, glamor, or homespun innocence. Or even what it's like to be a pawn between nations. Helene Mayer fenced for Germany in Berlin, 1936. She was the only one—not the only fencer, or woman, or even the only German woman fencer, but the only Jew allowed—on the German team.

Forty years had passed since 1896, but the Games had long abandoned the pretense that it was one big, happy, international family of athletes competing without

Five. Pariahs (1932–1936)

regard to national borders. That notion of the Olympics had ended in a cloud of after-dinner cigar smoke. From the time that Major Papadiamantopoulos galloped into Panathenaic Stadium at the end of the 1896 marathon, shouting, "A Greek! A Greek!" the Olympics would let nations drive behavior, rather than the athletes. After all, nations were paying the bills.

Having won the gold in Women's Foil in Amsterdam in 1928, Mayer was intoxicated by the idea of winning another medal for her country. The problem, of course, was that countries come with political structures and leaders who are willing to use a citizen's patriotic impulses for their own purposes. Mayer wanted to win for Germany, not for the Nazis, but the two became inseparable. As one of the best fencers in the world, Mayer was more important as a symbol than as an athlete. Women had risen in stature enough to be used.

Fencing has a long history, although it rose as a sport much later than its practical origins. Though Egyptian hieroglyphics show armies with swords, most combat fighting involved hacking and slashing rather than the thrust and parry. Dueling, which involved technique and footwork, developed more slowly as an offshoot of medieval jousting. The art of fencing really took off in the 16th century, when newly printed books allowed masters to describe their technique in guidebooks.

Those masters of fencing came from Central Europe, mostly Italy, France, and Hungary. Other countries like Germany, Russia, and England developed their passion and practice by importing Italian and French instructors. The sport was primarily male, but talented women might be occasionally taught to excel. For every D'Artagnan, there might be a Julie d'Aubigny, a fictional female fencer nicknamed "La Maupin," who entranced 17th-century French novel readers eager for dashing exploits.

Since the sport of fencing was concentrated among gentleman, rather than the lower classes, it was a perfect fit for an athletic competition invented for gentleman athletes. Paris was thrilled to include it in the II Olympiad, as their poster suggested. But despite the woman in the advertising, women would have to wait until the Games of Paris 1924.

Like archery, fencing was considered quasi-acceptable for women once rifles had replaced bows and swords in military combat. Fencing footwork also closely mimicked dancing, so it was an easy translation for those who had ballet training. Women were allowed to fence in the Olympics even before they were admitted to track and field.

They did not compete with all the blades used by the men, however. The long, heavy épeé and flat-bladed pirate sabre were considered off-limits. It would be a half century before women were allowed access to those weapons. But fencing with the light, short foil relied on quick feet and flexibility. When ballet-trained Helene Mayer fenced, it was not unusual for an expert to comment: "Her technique is spectacular. Her footwork is just how they teach you."[28]

Nor was it considered odd that one of Mayer's biggest adversaries, Austrian Ellen Preis, left Berlin and her German citizenship solely to attend fencing school in Vienna. Preis chose to fence for Austria because Germany rejected her. They had too many good female athletes, like Mayer. This added to the rivalry between Mayer and

Preis when they met in Los Angeles for the 1932 competition, as Mayer sought her second gold medal.

In 1932, Mayer was at the top of her game, having won the world championship the year before and six German national championships in a row. Unfortunately, personal tragedy overwhelmed her right before the Olympics. A few days before the matches began, Mayer's beloved, Alexander Gaihardt, died in a naval training accident. The reigning medalist fenced, but many described her as distracted and ill.

A few observers even had heard the Austrian cheering section taunting Mayer about her late boyfriend. Such audience behavior would have been unsporting, but not unusual. Preis herself wrote in her memoirs that it was sad to see Mayer crumble in the later rounds. Perhaps the jeering wasn't at Preis's behest.

Mayer's losses were by small margins—three by a single point. But she didn't even reach the semifinals. There would be no repeat medal for Germany.

The final match between Preis and Great Britain's Judy Guinness was dramatic for other reasons. Guinness pointed out to the judges two touches that they had missed for her opponent. It cost her the match. Preis took gold, while Mayer came in fifth, heartbroken and disappointed.

Too distraught to return home, she stayed in southern California to attend college as a German exchange student. The following March, Hitler was elected chancellor. Germany began to change.

The Nazis started cutting off opportunities for Jews. They canceled Mayer's membership in her hometown Offenbach fencing club as well as her exchange program with the American Scripps College "on racial grounds."[29] Though Mayer was tall and blond, as Aryan-appearing as could be, her father was Jewish. This made her entirely Jewish as far as Germany was concerned.

She complained that she did not perceive herself as Jewish; she did not practice the religion and had been brought up in a secular household by her mother. Plenty of Jews in Germany felt the same way. It didn't stop Nazi sympathizers from burning down their businesses or confiscating their belongings.

Mayer finished her American degree and acquired a position teaching German and fencing at a small prestigious women's college in northern California. She wanted to return home but thought it too dangerous. Non-Americans were allowed to compete in the U.S. national championships, so she fenced and won. It would not be her last American championship.

Meanwhile, her dance with Germany continued. She declared publicly that she would be happy to represent Germany in international competition or in the 1936 Olympics. Her dreams of retaking her gold medal apparently overshadowed any concerns about her status as a Jew or whether representing the Nazis might lend support to their racist attacks.

With the rise of anti–Semitism and violence in Germany, Jewish organizations began calling for a complete boycott of the Berlin Games. This led to a war of words among Germany, the Olympic organizing committees, and the international Jewish community. The Nazis barred German Jews from competing and steadfastly told the *New York Times* that they had no Jewish athletes of Olympic caliber.

The AOC and the IOC wanted to find a way to keep the Games going, worried that the Olympic movement itself would be threatened if athletes became embroiled in politics. Avery Brundage visited Germany in 1934 at Hitler's invitation and declared himself satisfied that he found no anti–Semitism in German sport. The IOC still pressed Germany to include at least one Jewish athlete on the team. They just needed one.

Mayer's position remained that she was not Jewish and simply wanted to perform as an athlete for her country. The politics, in some sense, was all beneath her. A report of the German consul about Mayer was especially revealing:

> ...she does not want to have anything to do with Jewish circles ... nor does she want to be regarded as Jewish by others ... the pressure exerted on her by the [American] press is particularly strong and she does not know how she will be able to escape this daily badgering.... Miss Mayer who has an impulsive temperament and does not always weigh her words carefully will let herself be carried away into making remarks which will do [Germany] unnecessary harm.[30]

Brundage and Mayer both donned massive sets of blinders.

Germany's solution was elegant and complete. They invited Mayer to fence on their team, as a Jew. Then, they steadfastly eliminated all other Jewish athletes, even claiming that the Jewish woman who won the German national high jump Trials was unqualified. Mayer, fair-haired, statuesque, pretzel-braided Helen Mayer, was the lone Jew—the exception—on the German team. She could continue to claim that she was not really Jewish, but the Nazis invited her rather precisely because she was Jewish.

In Berlin, the athletes contesting in the finals of the women's foil were, unsurprisingly, all Central European. The top three turned out to be Helene Mayer, Ellen Preis, and a small but deft Hungarian, Ilona Schacherer-Elek. Elek had won the European title for the past two years in Mayer's absence. All three had multiple championships behind them and more still to come, "three of the finest women fencers of all time."[31] To that end, the Olympic "process" had done its job. Incredibly, all three were also Jewish.

The final competition used a round-robin format rather than the head-to-head elimination style that would be adopted later. Those who won the most matches against the other seven fencers would win medals. Each match went to the first athlete to reach five points. Ties in the final ranking would go to the person with the lowest cumulative touches from all opponents.

As one of the tallest fencers, Mayer towered over Elek in their early bout, but Elek was small, quick, and strategic. She would wait when Mayer attacked to find the right opening. She was able to best Mayer 5–4, then beat everyone else except for one other finalist. In Mayer's rounds, she beat all her other opponents. At last, she faced Preis in the rematch so many had anticipated.

The bout between Mayer and Preis was one for the ages. It was hard-fought, two titans of the sport lunging and flying, both with something to prove. Preis wanted back-to-back medals. Plus, a lopsided win against Mayer after a loss to Elek could still pave her path to the gold. Mayer wanted redemption and to prove the storm of negative public opinion had been worth it.

The two titans were tied at 4–4. Then, Preis took one more touch to win 5–4. With two losses, Mayer would not get the gold.

When the rounds were completed, Elek remained on top at 6–1. However, there was a three-way tie for the second spot, three women with records of 5–3: Preis, Mayer, and Germany's Hedwig Haß, the woman who had beaten Elek. The judges added up the points. Touches scored against were: Haß, 23; Preis, 20; Mayer, 19. Even though Mayer had lost to Elek and Preis, she won her other matches by giving up fewer touches. Mayer took the silver medal, while Preis took the bronze. Elek took the gold, all three of them Jewish medalists.

Athletes from all nations were expected to give the Nazi salute at various times. Entering the stadium, for example, the entire French team saluted the stands where Hitler waited. Figure skaters Sonja Henie of Norway and Cecilia Colledge of Great Britain gave the Nazi salute when coming onto the ice. When the British soccer team played Poland and China, they refused to give the salute before the match, which caused a diplomatic uproar at the time. All German medal winners had tacitly agreed with their national committees that they would salute from the podium, in the same way that Americans were expected to place hand over heart when facing their flag or hearing the national anthem.

When Mayer mounted the podium with the other medalists, she apparently hesitated. But the instructions to her from the German team were clear. The photo circulated around the world is also very clear. In her spotless white German uniform, with a laurel resting atop her blond circular braids, Jewish Helene Mayer gave the Nazi salute.

Hitler had, by then, left the stands. It didn't matter. The image of Mayer on the podium would always supersede her eight national titles and her "best fencer in history" moniker. She would always be remembered for giving the Nazi salute to Hitler.

The criticism of Mayer after the Berlin Games was twice as ferocious as before. She was called "Goebbels's little heifer"³² and chastised as "a special case of race betrayal."³³ The Nazis weren't happy with her either, with SS leader Reinhold Heydrich referring to her as the "Jewish c***" who lost Germany's medal. A year later, after winning the international foil championships in Paris, she asked friends back home

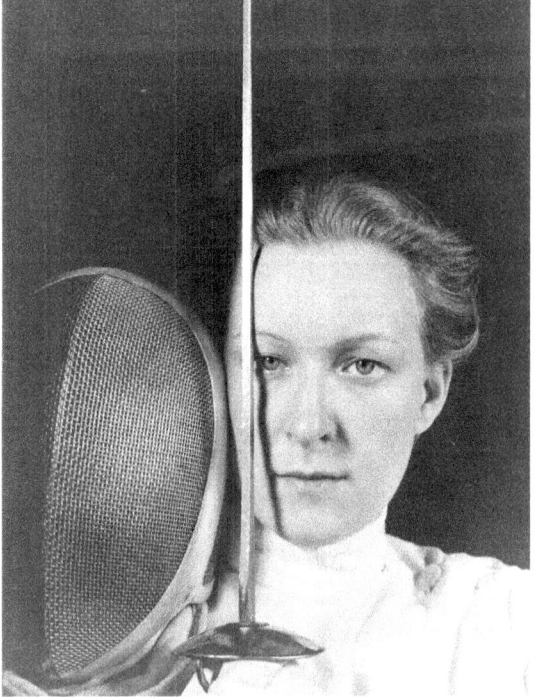

Fig.13. Helene Mayer continued to fence, winning U.S. national fencing titles until 1946. The ignominy of competing for the Nazis faded, but she remained a tragic figure, misunderstood, a sensibility captured by famed photographer Imogen Cunningham in 1935 (© 2021 Imogen Cunningham Trust).

how the German people celebrated her silver medal. The answer was with nothing. The press never even reported her win. They paid no attention to her. All they had ever wanted was their single Olympic Jew.

Despite trying to define herself as only an athlete, Mayer had struck an unholy bargain with a repugnant regime. She might have later applied for American citizenship or claimed refugee status to obtain an IOC exception to fence under a different flag. But she wanted to compete for Germany. Hence, she will always be judged and remembered for her actions as a German.

The Russian fencer and filmmaker Pinkhasov put it in perspective: "She attempted a compromise with the Nazi regime. She knew what the Nazis were about and still tried to have a compromise. To me that is a sin. She put herself above everyone else."[34]

Women had reached the ultimate stage as athletes. Just like men, they could make terrible choices. Just like men, they would have to face the consequences.

End of the 1930s, End of the Legends

Helene Mayer undoubtedly hated being treated as a symbol and a token. She wanted to fence simply for who she was, but those days were over. Individual women must be held to the standards of femininity, decorum, and patriotism. Moreover, anyone representing a country could be painted with the brush of the country.

After the Games returned to post-war London in 1948, Ilona Elek won a second gold in Women's Foil. Ellen Preis, now Ellen Müller-Preis, took another bronze, bringing her total to three medals. Five gold medals in a row had been won by Jewish women.[35]

Germany and Japan were banned from sending teams in 1948, so Mayer did not compete in the Games again. She did win the U.S. nationals six more times, the last time in 1946. In 1952, she returned to Germany and married an old friend, planning to settle down back in the land of her heart. Before a year had passed, though, and before she had reached her 43rd birthday, Mayer died of breast cancer. *Sports Illustrated* in 2000 described her as one of the top fencers of all time. But her legacy would always be "The Woman Who Saluted Hitler."

Stella Walsh's end was also tragic, although not because she was young. Walsh competed for decades more, perpetually trying to get back into the Olympics. In 1956, she even got married, apparently for the sole purpose of gaining U.S. citizenship to compete on behalf of the United States in Melbourne. She and Harry Olson split four months later, and she failed to make the finals at the U.S. Trials. Even so, at age 56, she kept winning senior circuit races and beating the pants off younger reporters who challenged her, after which she would drink them under the table.[36]

On December 4, 1980, after buying ribbons for prizes as part of her job with the Cleveland Recreation Department, Walsh was mugged in a discount store parking lot. She fought off her attackers, but one pulled a gun. She was fatally shot. Because she was a minor Cleveland celebrity, her autopsy attracted reporters.

The coroner was surprised by her ambiguous gender, and someone among the attendees leaked the information to local TV stations, who raced to top each other with salacious stories. What Walsh had feared for fifty years had finally happened. All her racing achievements became reduced to an asterisk and scholarly articles about intersexuality.

Eleanor Holm's life was full of drama early on, although it ended far more sedately. After returning from Berlin, Holm embarked on the brief movie career she had sought, even making a Tarzan film with decathlete Glenn Morris. Neither athlete could act.

She left California for New York and was offered steady work in the brand-new Aquacade. She swam 39 shows a week with fellow Olympians Johnny Weissmuller and Esther Williams. She swam, she said, until her hair turned green.

The mastermind of the show was impresario Billy Rose, at the time married to legendary Jewish comedienne Fanny Brice. Holm broke up Brice's marriage to Rose. She ultimately divorced Rose, too, in a messy, tabloid-sprawling "The War of the Roses."

Her third and final marriage was to a nightclub owner and onetime murder suspect—the stories just kept coming—Tommy Whalen. Luckily, Whalen moved to more mundane investments, finding oil property in Wyoming and uranium mines in Utah. Eleanor Whalen was last settled down with golf, tennis, and charitable causes in Miami Beach, vowing never to jump in a pool again. She lived to a ripe old age, dying in 2004 at age 90, with no regrets.

The exceptional Babe Didrikson did continue to compete and, in some ways, finally became the legend that had earned her superlatives in track. This time, it was in golf. Once she started whacking golf balls, hitting drives as hard as the men, she won 41 championships. She even helped establish the LPGA.

Like Mayer, though, she was stricken with cancer, barely after turning 41, at the height of her golf career. In 1954, after recovering from colon cancer surgery, she trained herself back into competition shape to play in the U.S. Open. She won several tournaments wearing a colostomy bag.

Perhaps the characterization of Didrikson as the greatest ever was premature in 1930. It might not have been wrong. Perhaps Paul Gallico was exaggerating when he said she would come to "be listed with the champions of all times." Or, he might simply have been a few years too early. She became a champion in the fight against the cancer that finally defeated her in 1956 at age 45. Gallico's words were perfect, and sounded more like the perfect epitaph: "For even if some yet unborn games queen matches her talent, versatility, skill, patience and will to practice … there still remains the little matter of courage and character, and in these departments the Babe must be listed with the champions of all times."[37]

There were four exceptional women that exemplified the Olympic experience of 1932 and 1936. One was brash. One was reckless. One was haunted. One was blinded. All four were among the best at their craft and wanted to be judged only by how they competed. But those days were over.

The days of pretending the Games were apolitical, or above nation, were over as well, despite the IOC's attempts to pretend otherwise. Athletes could not be separated from how they represented their country. Ironically, in the end, this would open up a whole new set of opportunities.

Six

The Cold War and the Feminine Mystique (1948–1968)

The war that swept across the world beginning in 1939 left a wake of destruction that included cancellation of the next two scheduled Olympics. There would be no truce for international sports competitions while Hitler's armies marched. When the Games returned in 1948, however, female athletes found new frontiers.

A generation of potential Olympic competitors—both men and women[1]—died during the dozen years between the Games of Berlin and those of London 1948. New athletes had been waiting in the wings. After the drought of sports, the public was eager for any form of competition. Pressure increased on the IOC to expand women's events. However, there was another reason women had more opportunities, one which would impact Olympic sports for the next forty years: the Cold War.

Soviet women helped their still-fledgling country make an immediate impact, once the USSR finally entered the Games in 1952. They excelled in disciplines that were already a strength, such as gymnastics, and in new events that Western cultures didn't consider ladylike, like the throwing events.

Meanwhile, America was still persuading women to leave their wartime jobs to focus on domestic life. They hadn't planned for women athletes to be "cold warriors." But those messages shifted to encourage fitness for women once the USSR started climbing in the medal counts.

Overall, during the 1950s and 1960s, the Cold War in sports helped create some of the greatest Olympians of all time. The Soviet Union had Larisa Latynina and the Press sisters. The United States had the Tigerbelles. All would widen the scope of how well women could compete.

Winning vs. Lipstick: The Russians Are Coming

During World War II, women stepped in to fill the empty factories and offices, finding new opportunities for work outside the home. They also gained ground in athletics, as audiences were receptive to professional leagues that filled empty stadiums. For example, the All-American Girl's Professional Baseball League (AAGPBL) was formed in 1943 with league attendance that peaked in 1948 at nearly a million spectators. Company-based women's basketball teams continued to appeal to local audiences, especially in the American South, while women's factory soccer teams attracted fans in England.

When the war was over, though, veterans returned home from the shores of Normandy and the battle cruisers of the Pacific to find women running factories and hitting home runs. The men wanted their jobs and their baseballs back.

Cultural messages, in the U.S. especially, began to emphasize the value of home and family over work, to "restore" the environment as it had been. Popular women's magazines were launched, focusing on fashion, cosmetics, cooking, and decorating. Movies increasingly contrasted happy mothers with unhappy careerists. For instance, actress Rosalind Russell, a veteran of twenty-plus films playing career women, said her post-war movie wardrobe consisted of "a tan suit, a gray suit, a beige suit, and then a negligee for the seventh reel ... when I would admit to my best friend on the telephone that what I really wanted was to become a dear little housewife."[2]

This broader social movement, which Betty Friedan labeled "The Feminine Mystique," had a widespread impact on sports, even though it was not particularly aimed at athletic pursuits. Opportunities began to dry up. The "league of their own" AAGPBL disbanded in 1954. The thriving North Carolina women's basketball circuits slowly dissolved in the 1950s.[3]

The media, for its part, also shifted focus from the exploits of the Queen of the Waves and the "Fulton Flash" to their looks. On the tennis circuit, for instance, the most popular tennis player of 1948 was Gertrude "Gussie" Moran, not from winning Wimbledon, but because she wore frilly panties peeking from under her tennis dress. "Gorgeous Gussie" had photographers following her every move. She even rated a cameo in the movie *Pat and Mike* next to golfer Babe Didrikson, despite Moran never winning a major tennis tournament.

The substitution of housewife for athlete continued. The winner of the 100 m in the 1948 Olympics, Fanny Blankers-Koen, earned the headline "FASTEST WOMAN IN THE WORLD IS AN EXPERT COOK," while silver medalist Maureen Gardner was described "as more excited about September 11 than about her record-breaking run. It is her wedding day."[4] The 1948 U.S. women's track team ended with a dismal showing after years of success. As historian Heather Dahl put it, "In 1950, most Americans preferred feminine and pretty, even if it meant Olympic losses."[5] However, just as these images of the Happy Homemaker were reaching their peak, the Soviets came to play, and conversations about the role of women shifted.

Up until 1950, the Soviet Union had not sent teams to the Olympics. The pre-revolution Russians had won medals back in 1908 and 1912, but the hammer and sickle flag had yet to make an appearance. Both Lenin and Stalin had ignored the Games, labeling them bourgeois entertainment and a capitalistic tool. The IOC considered the communist ideology to be incompatible with Olympism. During Henri Baillet-Latour's tenure at the IOC, he didn't invite them to participate, and they didn't ask.

Instead, rising socialist ideals across Eastern Europe in the 1920s spawned a series of alternate Olympics: "Worker's Olympiads" and "Spartakiads." In the same way that the Women's World Games aimed to show that women could compete, Spartakiads were staged to provide sporting contests for the working class. In Germany, Czechoslovakia, Austria, and the Soviet Union, these events emphasized the egalitarian nature of athletics—games for everyone—to contrast with the elitist Olympics.

After World War II, though, the Soviet Union saw the Olympics as a way to demonstrate cultural and physical domination over other ideologies and other countries. A 1949 Soviet Central Committee resolution outlined a plan "to spread sport to every corner of the land … [and] win world supremacy in major sports…."[6]

In 1951, the Soviets petitioned to send a team to the 1952 Games. There was some hand-wringing over the amateur question. Outgoing president Edström and incoming president Brundage were both obsessed with banning anyone even suspected of receiving payment for sports. Moscow openly published cash prizes for athletes, and the government directly funded sports training camps.

The IOC decided to look the other way in an attempt to bend over backward to be "fair" to the Soviets. The newly elected USSR representative to the IOC, Konstantin Andrianov, claimed that Soviet athletes were absolutely not professional. Brundage sniffed that the committee should "assume that Olympic rules are being followed until we learn to the contrary."[7]

Internationally, Brundage was nonchalant about the Soviets coming to Helsinki. Within the U.S., however, he was eager as anyone to show that democracy and capitalism were superior. Brundage was thrilled when Hollywood suggested helping close the USOC's[8] financial gap with a new invention, a charity-entertainment event called the telethon. During a 14-hour televised marathon, emcee Bing Crosby implored Americans to "get behind our Olympic team and send our athletes across at full strength and in the finest style possible." Partner emcee Bob Hope was more direct in aiming at the "Red Menace": "I guess Old Joe Stalin thinks he is going to show up our soft capitalistic Americans. We've got to cut him down to size."[9]

Always concerned about the medal count, the U.S. was now hyper-obsessed about the Soviets, before the team had even appeared. Bob Mathias, who had won the decathlon as a teenager in 1948, noticed the change as he planned to defend his medal in Helsinki:

> There were many more pressures on American athletes because of the Russians than in 1948. They were in a sense the real enemy. You just loved to beat 'em. You just had to beat 'em. It wasn't like beating some guys from a friendly country like Australia. This feeling was strong down through the whole team, even members in sports where the Russians didn't excel.[10]

Sportswriters jumped into the political fray as well. Months before the torch relay had begun, Arthur Daley, who had extolled Babe Didrikson's virtues so effusively, described the prevailing attitudes toward the Soviets: "the Red brothers are so devious … that their official acceptance of the Helsinki bid the other day cannot be greeted in normal fashion … the Kremlin controls muscles just as it controls thoughts."[11]

The results in Helsinki could be characterized as a flop or a triumph for the USSR, depending on the point of view. *Sports Illustrated* writer William O. Johnson, Jr., emphasized that the "Russian men did not win a single gold medal in track and field competition. In contrast, the United States picked up 14 gold medals—the most Americans had won since World War I."[12] The U.S. could also boast 18 swimming and diving medals to none for the Soviets, though Moscow wasn't exactly known for its swimming pools. Cherry-picking a sub-group of sports could create all manner of proofs of superiority.

On the other hand, in their first Olympics, the USSR earned 71 medals, second only to the U.S. Other Olympic-loving perennials like France, Great Britain, and Australia barely eked out double digits. This was the result that many had feared. Western countries began calling for more investment in fitness at home.

England's response to communism, for example, was to spruce up its parks. Sir Noel Curtis-Bennett, who championed park expansion, noted "there can be no doubt that the complete failure alike of communism and authoritarianism to make headways in Great Britain is ... [because] our people ... mingle freely in the fellowship of sports."[13]

Presidents Eisenhower and Kennedy took a more direct approach. Eisenhower created the Presidential Council on Youth Fitness, which recommended exercise and fitness testing in schools for everybody. President-elect John Kennedy wrote an article for *Sports Illustrated* about the "Soft American," claiming that "if we are to retain [our] freedom ... then we must also be willing to work for the physical toughness on which the courage and intelligence and skill of man so largely depends."[14]

Women, who were now expected to maintain the essentials of home and family, were put in charge of family fitness. The new model was that healthy mothers should raise healthy children who would become healthy soldiers. (Shades of the Spartans!) This responsibility meant women could once again pursue athletics, albeit the more feminine sports, i.e., diving, swimming, and fencing.

Brundage still insisted, "Track and field is not their sphere." If they must pursue track and field, then shorter runs were considered preferable to the "exhausting" longer ones, and, above all, they mustn't throw anything. "The shot put does nothing for them."[15]

The Soviets were less concerned about whether the medals came from men or women or which sports were the "right ones." They used talent wherever they could find it, and thus discovered that some female athletes might have a pretty open path to piles of victories. In 1952, only 11 percent of the total Olympic participants were women. But for the USSR, of the 71 medals they obtained in their first Olympics since the Russian Revolution, fully one-third (23) came from women. As it turns out, half of those were in gymnastics.

Gymnastics, Sokols, Ballerinas, and Protests

The gymnastics seen in recent Olympics is in stark contrast to the competitive version of the 1950s. Female gymnasts of yesteryear were older and larger because grace and style were valued more than speed and power. They also did handsprings on floors with no bounce and swung on wooden bars with no give. Originally, the vault didn't even have a springboard.

Six. The Cold War and the Feminine Mystique (1948–1968)

Individual exercises are ancient. Tumbling, flexibility, and strengthening exercises can be traced back to the Greeks, Egyptians, and even those ancient Minoan youths who leapt over bull's horns. The Greek idea of the *gymnasium* meant a place to exercise naked, free-form. Eventually, *gymnastic* forms inspired two different exercise systems, one Swedish and the other Prussian.

The Swedish version used exercise to improve health through calisthenics and floor workouts. The other version, developed by German-Prussian Friedrich Ludwig Jahn, used vaults, climbing ropes, and horizontal bars to enhance conditioning, notably for the military. Jahn's soldier-based exercise was unabashedly nationalistic, claiming: "the purpose of the gymnastic activity was to show to the nation that her sons were able to preserve what their fathers had obtained."[16]

Coubertin himself had been happy with the role both types had played in the history of sports and compared the two systems by saying: "To move from German gymnastics to Swedish gymnastics is to hear a pastoral symphony after a heroic symphony."[17] It makes sense that the Nazis pressed to include German-style gymnastics in their Berlin Olympic program. They then won 13 of the 27 medals. However, the single women's event allowed, the Team Exercise, was performed in unison, Swedish-style. It hearkened back to the Danish display of "pleasing figures" so popular at the 1908 London Games.

Czechoslovakian women took the silver medal in the Team event behind the Germans in Berlin, also no coincidence. The Czechs had their own gymnastic history, and their own gymnastics guru, Miroslav Tyrš. Like the Prussians, Tyrš had been fascinated with group exercise, but not for the military. He launched a series of non-political clubs where gymnastics teachers and students intermingled, working together to build sound minds and bodies in harmony with each other. Thus was born the *sokol*, the same type of club which helped shape Stella Walsh's career, although in America, the gymnastic discipline never took off.

In the European sokol, gymnasts would gather in *slets,* masses of two or three thousand people, performing calisthenics to drumbeats or simple music. Sokols were egalitarian and permitted women. Some of the best male and female gymnasts in international competition at mid-century were, therefore, German, Czech, or Hungarian.

At the post-war Olympics of 1948, with neither a German nor a Soviet team invited, Czechoslovakia won the sole gymnastic women's event, the Team Exercise. The Czech women overcame a tragedy on their way to gold, when one of their best gymnasts was stricken with polio upon arrival in London. She died in the hospital just as the gymnastics competition began. After the Czechs beat the Hungarians in the final round,[18] the women wore black armbands atop the podium, and the raised Czech flag was draped in black. It would not be the last gold medal for Czechoslovakian gymnasts.

The International Gymnastics Federation (FIG) felt the time was ripe for expansion of women's events in 1952. FIG's vision was to build events unique to each gender. Women would display different skills—not just lesser versions of the men's skills—but events "in harmony with their constitutions."[19] Up until 1950, both men and women used the same equipment: rings, parallel bars, balance beam, and vault.

FIG's 1950 proposal was to eliminate the rings and modify the bars to an uneven style for women in order to emphasized female grace and flexibility rather than brute strength.

This "separate but equal" approach was approved. Women's gymnastics gained a solid foothold by avoiding the criticisms over lack of femininity lobbed at other events. Gymnastics further provided a gateway to increased acceptance of women as athletes. When the IOC voted on the proposal in 1950, nearly the entire committee supported the expansion of gymnastics, including many members from other sporting disciplines. International support was solid, even before the Soviet Union had ever stepped foot on an Olympic mat.

In Helsinki, the USSR at last entered the Games and the gymnastic events. In their debut, the men's and women's teams took nearly half the medals, including both team events, as well as gold and silver in both individual all-around contests. This was because, like Germany and Czechoslovakia, the Soviet gymnastics legacy far predated Olympic competition.

Contrary to popular belief, Soviet gymnastics history did not start with Olga Korbut in 1972. Korbut appeared at the midpoint of a stream of sporting excellence. Her style, in fact, was a departure from that of her predecessors, though her success was part of a legacy that went back to the 19th century. Russia could trace its gymnastics history to Peter the Great, who advocated calisthenics for both the schools and the army. Peter, and later Catherine the Great, also embraced European arts and culture with such enthusiasm that an entirely new style of classical music and ballet emerged. By the 20th century, Russian dancers and choreographers were among the best in the world.

Both Lenin and Stalin disdained the Olympic Games but embraced the popularity of Russian-style sokols and mass performances of working-class athletes. In the Spartakiads, those "worker" Olympics held in Moscow, mass gymnastic displays were a highlight. Under Stalin, the displays became compulsory and included not just gymnasts but athletes from all sports, along with soldiers and entire families, groups that might reach ten thousand.[20] Take a culture where everyone learns strength and flexibility exercises in school, add in special training for classical dance, and have them perform in unison by the thousands. By 1952, Soviet gymnastics had been honed to perfection.

In the Helsinki Olympics, Victor Chukarin won six medals for the USSR across eight men's events. Maria Gorokhovskaya went one better, winning seven medals in the seven women's events. The best was yet to come. Larisa Latynina would debut in Melbourne 1956, and, by the time she was done, would set medal records that would last a half century.

Latynina grew up in the Ukraine, raised by her cleaning-lady single mother after her father was killed at the Battle of Stalingrad. Although pre-teens were not yet making international debuts, Latynina was still on the young side, only 19, when she joined the Soviet team at the world championships of 1954, sharing a team win with Gorokhovskaya and other Olympic veterans. As a 21-year-old in Melbourne 1956, she led the team to six medals, four of them gold, eclipsing her elders at the start of an Olympic career that would continue for another eight years.

Over her three Olympics, Latynina won eighteen medals, nine gold, a record which put her at the top of the all-time list until 2012. She was finally passed by Michael Phelps, although he took four Olympics to do it. Latynina won a medal in every event in which she competed but one, coming in fourth only once in the balance beam in Melbourne.

The gymnastics style that earned Latynina so many medals balanced strength and grace with an "appearance of ease." Today's routines, which earn bonuses for speed and power, make older routines seem less difficult, but such comparisons are deceptive. As Allen Guttmann puts it, "the strength necessary to appear graceful was far beyond anything possible for most of the world's men."[21]

In 1956, women mounted the uneven bars without help, swung sideways between them as if they were parallel bars, pushed up into handstands with the barest of swing, and could stand atop a bar as if it were a balance beam. Comparing today's tumbling with yesteryear's flexible poses is like comparing circus trapeze artists with the contortionist who glides up and down a drape of fabric. Both are breathtaking but for different reasons.

Additionally, the mats were also thin pads over wooden floors. Routines were accompanied by simple classical piano music, as in a ballet class. Latynina could flip almost leisurely through a series of handsprings, finishing by landing on one foot with the other outstretched perfectly, arms and fingers extended like Anna Pavlova playing a dying swan or a mourning Juliet. She was the complete package.

In 1960, the entire Soviet team had improved and took 26 of the available 43 gymnastics medals. Teams that did not excel in gymnastics complained about the Soviet dominance of the sport. Multiple IOC meetings rehashed the topic of cutting back gymnastic events. However, a reduction at this point would smack of bias, fairly so. It would be like suggesting that swimming should be cut back because of

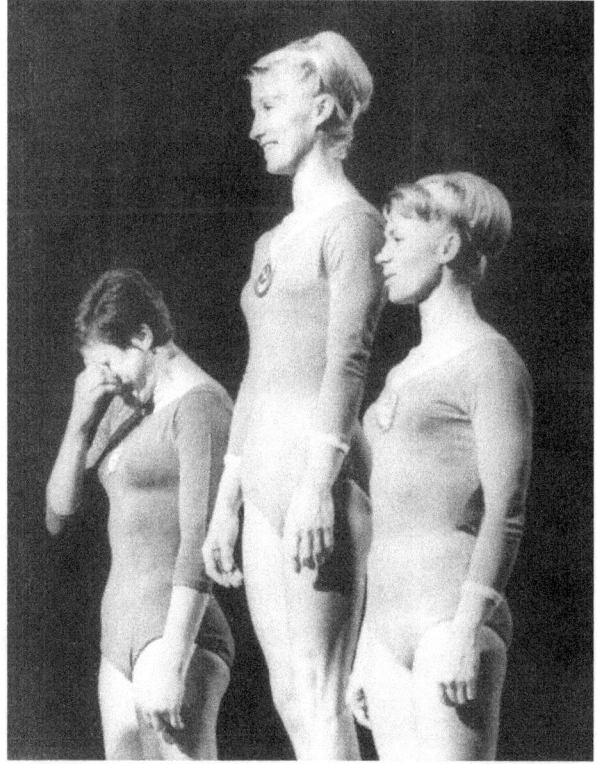

Fig.14. Larisa Latynina (URS, right) receiving a rare bronze among her record-setting 18 Olympic medals in gymnastics. Teammate Polina Astakhova (URS, center) took gold in the 1964 Parallel Bars, while Katalin Makray (HUN, left) accepted silver with emotion (Wikimedia Commons).

all the winning by the U.S. and Australia.[22] Brundage noted at one point that "if one man can win eight medals … the events must be altogether too simple."[23] However, the IOC could not muster the votes to reduce the number of events, only pressing to reduce the size of the teams.

In Tokyo 1964, on her way to seeking a third gold medal in the all-around, Latynina ran into stiff competition. Where else could it come from but Czechoslovakia? The new rising star was Věra Čáslavská.

Čáslavská was a former figure skater who also had debuted in gymnastics as a teenager at the world championships, four years after Latynina had done so. Čáslavská won a team silver medal in Rome as an 18-year-old and finished eighth in the all-around, among a host of stellar Soviet women. At the 1962 world championships, she took Latynina on full bore, barely losing by less than a half point. The rematch in Tokyo promised to be epic.

It was a promise fulfilled. Latynina started the all-around with a high score on the floor exercise, leaving Čáslavská to play catch-up. The Czech gymnast then beat the Soviet veteran on the vault and maintained her slight lead in uneven bars. Čáslavská sealed the deal with a slightly better balance beam routine, taking the gold in an upset. The remaining individual medals were then sprinkled between the two superstars, 29-year-old Latynina and 22-year-old Čáslavská.

Čáslavská's history then took a significant turn. Three months before the 1968 Games opened in Mexico City, the Soviet Union invaded Czechoslovakia to re-assert control over a country pushing for liberalization, teeming with student protests. The Soviets had done this before: Hungary was occupied during the Melbourne Olympics, leading to the infamous "Blood in the Water" water polo match between Hungary and the USSR

Čáslavská publicly criticized the newly installed Soviet-supported regime. She signed a protest manifesto in the spring of 1968, so her name was put on a list of "enemies of the state." She went into hiding to finish her Olympic training and traveled to Mexico City in secret.

At the Olympics, she pleased the local crowd with a tumbling routine to the "Mexican Hat Dance." The judges liked it, too. With Latynina retired and out of the picture, it looked as if Čáslavská would sweep the events easily. She did win the all-around and led her team to a silver medal.

But controversy was still to come. Although Čáslavská scored well enough at first to win the gold outright in the floor exercise, a Soviet judge changed the score for Soviet gymnast Larisa Petrik *after* all the routines were scored. Petrik thus tied for the gold medal with Čáslavská.[24]

Another scoring decision by a Soviet-bloc judge gave Čáslavská a surprisingly low score on the balance beam, costing her another gold. After the score was announced, the crowd howled in protest for ten minutes. On the podium, as the Soviet flag was raised, Čáslavská turned her head away, both a protest of the scoring and against the invasion of her country. After the anthem finished, she shook hands with Petrik, leaning in for a quick comment, later reported as "Congratulations for your success as a gymnast, but not for what your country has done to my country."[25]

When Čáslavská returned home, instead of being heralded for her medals, she was blacklisted by the new regime. She was forbidden from talking to the media, traveling, or working as a coach until the fall of communism in 1989. Yet, her quiet protest, though overshadowed by others[26] at the Mexico City Games, eventually brought her folk hero status around the world.

After Latynina earned her eighteenth medal, she hung up her leotard and became a coach for the USSR, helping the team to another five team gold medals. By the time the Soviet Union disbanded, the women's team could claim they had never lost a team medal.

Meanwhile, the USSR found another way to achieve medals among the women's events, by focusing on a different kind of specialization. Their petite, graceful women had carved out a path of dominance on the gymnastics mat. Their muscular women could have a different impact in track and field. While the Soviets couldn't make inroads among the highly competitive sprinters that Western countries lavished attention on, they found events that led to success, especially since the U.S. had such hang-ups over strong women who liked to throw things.

Fig.15. Czech gymnast Věra Čáslavská (TCH) quietly scooped up 11 medals (7 gold) in her two Olympics competitions before becoming an outcast at home for her protests. Her 1968 Beam and Floor Exercises earned gold until a judge altered scores in favor of her Soviet rival. Photograph by Ron Kroon (Dutch National Archives).

Rocket Launchers

"If I had my way, there'd be no women shot putters or their like in the competition. To my way of thinking, they just don't belong in it."
—Avery Brundage, 1960

The Greeks had their gymnasium exercise, but they also competed in the discus and javelin, two of the oldest Olympic events, practically sacred to the Olympic revivalists. Naturally, the discus was included in the 1896 Games along with the shot put, while the javelin was added in 1908 along with the hammer. However, hurling objects was still relegated to men only, for decades. The activity that critics seemed to hate the most was women throwing things.

At first women were thought too fragile to toss objects for sports, even though for years women had swept, scrubbed, stirred, milked, and carried water buckets, firewood, groceries, children, etc., as a regular part of their housework. Female athletes could swim, dive, fence, jump over a bar, or dance atop a four-inch beam, but once they started tossing heavy objects, sportswriters recoiled in horror. Suddenly, women became "big-limbed, hard-faced girls, with legs and biceps of an all-America fullback."[27]

Nevertheless, the throwing events slowly made their way into the women's program. The discus and javelin were added first, as they were believed to acquire more skill than strength. Didrikson's shoulder-torqueing javelin throw had impressed the crowd, while Lillian Copeland's discus toss had earned her a second Olympic medal, both to the delight of American fans. Yet organizers continued to stumble over letting women throw the shot put.

Putting the shot had its own vaunted history. Rocks were hurled as weapons in Greek epics. The Scots had turned the shot put into a sport, throwing cannonballs as a test of manhood and sometimes when choosing a clan chieftain.[28] At 16 pounds for men and 8.8 pounds for women, the Olympic shot required technique but it also needed muscles.

Still, women had been putting the shot since the Alice Milliat era. The 1922 Women's World Games included a rip-roaring competition between two Americans and a Frenchwoman. In those early days, athletes threw twice, once with each hand, and the final score was the total of the two throws. When the sport was at last included for women in the 1948 Olympics, they were happy to throw only once, with their preferred hand.

The first winner of the women's shot put, in fact, was relatively less famous for her Olympic medals than for her post–Olympic career. France's Micheline Ostermeyer threw the shot 13.14 m for the first Olympic record. Ostermeyer took the gold as well as a silver in the discus and a bronze in the high jump, a triple-medal performance worthy of a Didrikson-wannabe.

However, it was Ostermeyer's later career as a concert pianist that made her the real celebrity. Her ability to move from throwing objects to playing classical music was the real proof which "made an eloquent statement about the future of women's sports."[29] To some sportswriters, this reassured parents that their strong and swift daughters would grow up to become sensitive artists, not muscle molls.

Ostermeyer herself claimed superiority for another reason. Not only did she win this first shot put contest, but she thought herself better-looking while doing it: "The training now is too much for women ... the weight throwers—they are fat, too gross, too big, too much like great whales.... It must be horrible for a woman to look as fat as that."[30]

Sportswriters agreed, as only two years later they compared Soviet shot putter Anna Andreyeva, a "husky Moscow student in her mid-twenties" to "pretty, young" Ostermeyer. "Young" clearly had more to do with the face than the body.

The Frenchwoman at the time was 28, while Andreeva was actually 33. Ostermeyer, at 5'10", could herself have been described as "hulking," but she offset her height with stylishly curled black hair, lipstick, and designer sunglasses, even when competing.

For Americans, even though they donated money to help Olympic athletes show Joe Stalin a thing or two, women should not look strong, fat, or husky. Even though a European—not a Soviet—had earned those two throwing medals, Americans were reluctant to invest in strength training for women, fearful of putting "muscles in what Slenderette would call the wrong places."[31] The USSR had no such reluctance.

The Soviets saw a clear opportunity to gain medals in women's field events where Westerners weren't interested. Team USSR entered men in field contests, but they knew that American men had won two or three shot put medals in nearly every Olympics. It would be harder to break through on the men's side than on the women's.

In theory, the advantages in technique gained by the men ought to have given U.S. women a leg up in throwing events. Instead of passing on the training to women, though, the U.S. responded to the Soviets' approach with insults. The media decreed that U.S. women be considered the real winners because of their superior body measurements.

Sportswriter Bill Jaus, for example, thought it important to note that the American women's discus qualifier for the Helsinki Olympics, Pamela Kurrell, weighed only 129 pounds and was 5'2". More importantly, she was "feminine-looking," with her blond pony-tail, in stark contrast to Soviet Nina Ponmareva and her 210 pounds. Their actual 1952 Olympic performances—where Kurrell didn't even qualify for the finals and where Ponmareva threw the discus 10 m farther than Ostermeyer's previous Olympic record—weren't worth mentioning.

The solution, then, was to cede all the women's throwing events to the USSR and claim it was because the Soviet women were "miners, ditch diggers, stevedores."[32] The same writers then complained that the Soviet system included sports academies where women were trained for free, with jobs that paid athletes to set records and win competitions. Busy women, to be both stevedores and full-time student-athletes!

The Soviets could easily ignore the insults, if it meant winning with less competition. After all, their slim ballerinas were already proving their gymnastics mettle on the balance beam and vault. Their strong women who threw heavy objects might be called fat, but so what? When Americans published medal counts, they didn't create separate columns for thin athletes and husky ones.

Not only did Western media claim that Soviet women were too muscular, but they routinely suggested they were men in disguise. For example, the shot put gold medalist in the 1952 Olympics, Galina Zybina, was characterized as "tall with disproportionately large and masculine hands."[33] In fact, Zybina was 5'6", the same height as Babe Didrikson.

Like American discus thrower Kurrell, Zybina had blond hair, but she had no interest in posing like a fashion model. Her Ukrainian features featured narrow eyes and a hooked nose, and she sported an uncorrected overbite. However, she set shot put records for seven consecutive years, winning three medals across four Olympics between 1952 and 1964. Her response to criticism of being too masculine was that

American women were too "fragile." She didn't medal in 1960, according to one bio, because she gave birth to a son, so she was certainly no man in disguise. Even then, as a mother of a young child, she competed in Rome and then again in Tokyo, winning a bronze medal at age 33.

The next generation of rocket-launching women would again be accused of being overly masculine. They also were highly successful. Tamara and Irina Press were the only siblings to win track and field medals in the same Games, earning six medals in 1960 and 1964, five of them gold. Tamara took the gold in the shot put and silver in discus in 1960, then followed with a double gold in 1964.

The Press sisters were Ukrainian Jews, with dark hair, broad faces, and gap-toothed smiles. Tamara at 5'11" weighed 225 pounds;[34] one writer called her a "big strapping gal ... built along the lines of a 10-ton truck."[35]

Irina was smaller, at 5'6" and 165 pounds, but she also threw the shot put and was a multi-event specialist, like a Didrikson or Rosenfeld. Irina ran the hurdles and also competed in both the high jump and long jump. She won gold in the 80 m hurdles in Rome but finished just out of the medals in Tokyo—a disappointing fourth place—in both shot put and hurdles.

However, in 1964 women were finally allowed to compete in multi-event contests, as the men had done since 1896. Irina Press won the first women's pentathlon gold, a combination of shot put, hurdles, high jump, long jump, and 200 m sprint. Her pentathlon shot put throw was long enough to have won the silver medal four years earlier, behind her sister's gold. It's easy to imagine the sisters trying to out-throw each other in training practice.

When the Press sisters burst onto the Olympic scene in the early 1960s—Irina, dark-haired and swarthy, and Tamara, massive and broad-faced—the media came to a swift conclusion. Sportswriters baldly said they were men in disguise and called them "the Press Brothers." Both competed, setting one world record after another, and the rumors grew louder.

Fig.16. Galina Zybina (URS) won the shot put gold in 1952, followed with silver in 1956 and bronze in 1964. Despite being a mother and more lithe than muscular, she was still criticized for being too masculine (Dutch National Archives).

Six. The Cold War and the Feminine Mystique (1948–1968)   101

Gender verification did exist, but it was monitored by each country. By then, Eastern bloc countries were increasingly treated with suspicion, and the final chapter will describe how this led to the IAAF instituting mass international gender testing in 1966. Shortly after this happened, both sisters opted to retire, abruptly according to some, or after long, distinguished careers, according to others, as Chapter Sixteen will review in more detail.

After retirement, Tamara returned to college, earned a doctorate in pedagogy, and wrote multiple books on railway engineering, sports, and economics. She was awarded several honors and singled out on her 75th birthday by the Russian government. Irina worked as a Border Guard in the KGB for a time but eventually moved into coaching and ended up chairing the Moscow Committee of Physical Culture and Sports. She died in 2004. Tamara lasted through COVID only to pass away in 2021, right before her 84th birthday.

Meanwhile, despite the campaign of insults and accusations lobbed at Soviet women athletes, the U.S. still burned to increase their own medal count, as their attempts to promote fitness and healthy mothers were falling short. The push for more women athletes ran up against the physical educators, like at Vassar and Wellesley, where there was still resistance to athletics as an end goal.

Fig.17. Tamara Press (USR) hurling the discus in Tokyo, 1964. Her multiple golds in shot put and discus caused western media to harp on her size, although at 5'11" and 225 lbs., she would be dwarfed by 21st century female basketball players and shot putters (courtesy of the International Olympic Committee).

But other colleges were happy to let women pursue athletics. These were not the kind of college girls many in the U.S. envisioned. These were Black female athletes, long neglected but perfectly able. They were about to help America improve its athletic fortunes, not just in track but also on the field.

La Gazelle and the Beautician

Coach Ed Temple was a good judge of potential. The track at Tennessee State Agricultural and Industrial School was only 75 percent complete when he arrived to attend on an athletic scholarship. The unfinished oval was still U-shaped and ended in a dump. But he imagined much more and had visions of training women in speed and power. When he was made coach of the 1950 women's team at Tennessee State, a historically Black university, he had no money for scholarships or recruiting. But he had ideas. He would call his athletes Tigerbelles.

By the time Temple would finish his forty-plus years of coaching, the Tigerbelles would collect 34 national titles, 23 Olympic medals, and 13 Olympic golds. Eight of his athletes would be inducted into the Track and Field Hall of Fame, including speed superstars like Wyomia Tyus and Chandra Cheeseborough. Up until 1950, the AAU had barely acknowledged that it had a huge pool of talented Black American athletes, just waiting to be discovered. Temple thought it was time they noticed.

The Tennessee State Tigerbelles weren't the "firsts," by any means. The roll call of distinguished Black American Olympians started with George Poage in 1904 and John Taylor in 1908. Chicagoan Tidye Pickett was the first Black American woman to compete in the Olympics, placing second in the 80 m hurdles at the U.S. Trials in 1936. It was a redemption of sorts, after she and Louise Stokes were bumped from the 4 × 100 m relay team for white athletes who were less qualified.

Jesse Owens, of course, won multiple events at the "Nazi Games," sticking a thumb in the eye of white supremacists in 1936. But it wasn't until 1948, when Alice Coachman took first in the high jump, that a Black woman won the first gold medal. It didn't set an immediate trend.

Despite high hopes from Coachman's performance, American women's track in the next Games faltered. While 31 track medals were awarded to the U.S. in Helsinki, only one went to women, to the 4 × 100 relay team. That relay win was even considered an upset of American unknowns over the Australians, who by then had become the best sprinters in the world but had a poor baton pass in the relay. All four of the American runners were Black; two were from Tennessee State.

Many women left the track once the Feminine Mystique was in full bloom, spreading its cultural ideas that women ought to focus on being housewives. Yet many have noted that those messages were mainly aimed at affluent white women. Women of color did not necessarily see themselves in the fashion magazines or advertisements, nor did they have the "luxury" of only focusing on their own family.

Of course, Black women encountered other barriers. They faced more direct discrimination, from slammed doors to burning crosses. Pickett's and Stokes's experience, where they were overtly snubbed, was all too common. By 1956, Black women

Six. The Cold War and the Feminine Mystique (1948–1968)

had found some opportunity through the college programs offered by Tennessee State and the Tuskegee Institute. Times had changed, a little.

For Temple, athletic progress was slow. At the 1956 Melbourne Games, only three track medals went to American women. The Soviets won the throwing events and the Australians won most of the sprints. The U.S. women's relay team only managed a bronze, as Australians Betty Cuthbert and Shirley Strickland outclassed the racing field, this time propelling their team to a gold in the relay. Still, the entire American relay team was full of Tigerbelles, and they had run faster than four years earlier.

Tucked in among the bleak American results in Melbourne, though, were a few other bright notes. While Soviets Tamara Tyskevich and Galina Zybina took gold and silver in the shot put, an American elbowed her way into sixth place. Another American flag also popped up fourth in the discus, just a half meter short of a medal. The shot putter and discuss thrower was affiliated with the Tigerbelles.

The biggest name-about-to-be, the 16-year-old junior anchor leg of the Melbourne bronze-medal relay team, was Wilma Rudolph. The lesser-known name, the one making a credible showing with the rocket launchers, was her teammate, Earlene Brown. The two women were close companions, united in friendship and athletic success. Together, they would cement the Tigerbelle legacy in 1960.

Rudolph's story has been well-chronicled, deservedly so. She was born prematurely, the 20th of 22 children. She survived childhood polio and bouts with pneumonia and scarlet fever. Therapy at the nearest segregated hospital improved her strength until her leg braces came off. When she entered high school, she excelled in basketball first before starting in track, but, within two years, scout Ed Temple had her training with the Tigerbelles before she graduated.

After squeaking out that bronze medal in the relay in Melbourne, Rudolph was ready for more. However, a ripple in the plan cropped up in her senior year of high school. She became pregnant and bore a child out of wedlock, in 1958, a baby passed off for years as her niece. She returned to training, determined to make up for her "lapse" with strong performances.

At the 1960 Rome Olympics, Rudolph's combination of speed and poise caught the imagination of the world. She was soft-spoken but determined, and her childhood-invalid-turned-superstar story resonated with the public. The Italians fell in love with her, calling her *La Gazella Nera* (the black gazelle), while the French labeled her *La Perle Noire* (the black pearl).

Temple had trained his athletes to appear composed and to wear makeup in public, counseling that they should appear explicitly feminine to minimize criticism. The coach always considered looks when he recruited his athletes, famously saying: "I had a motto. I said, I don't want oxes, I want foxes. I want nice-looking girls."[36] Rudolph captivated the cameras and crowds with her grace and beauty. She was also about to fulfill the hype.

On September 12, 1960, six women lined up for the finals of the women's 100 m. Towering a little over the white Europeans next to her, Rudolph was in a middle lane. She got a slow start, with the Soviet runner on her left bursting to the front. But Rudolph's strong kick steadily helped her pull away from the others by race's end.

The final was not close, though the wind speed eliminated the possibility of records. Rudolph went on to win the 200 m, setting an Olympic record in the heats. Anchoring the 4 × 100 m relay, she became the first American woman to win three gold medals on the track.[37]

After the 100 m final, Rudolph needed to prepare for the public medal ceremony. The first person she turned to for a spruce-up was her shot putter friend, who had a comb and a towel handy. The multi-talented Earlene Brown also happened to be a beautician, with her own circuitous path to the Games.

Brown's story is often downplayed in recaps of the 1960 team, given that long list of distinguished Tigerbelle sprinters. Still, considering how difficult it was to be a strong woman in American track, how difficult to train for the shot put or javelin, Brown's accomplishments deserve more attention. She was the first U.S. woman to earn a shot put medal and the only such woman to medal in the event for nearly sixty years. Somehow, she made it past Temple's admonition against "oxes" and, in doing so, was uniquely positioned to take on the international competitors, especially those from the USSR.

Like Rudolph, Brown was also born in the South, in the tiny Texas town of Latexo (pop. 322). Her father played semi-pro baseball in the Negro Leagues, though he was out of the picture by the time Brown moved with her mother to Compton, in southern California. Brown grew up big-boned and tall, a heavy girl and teased about it.

She was large but also quick on her feet, with a strong back and arms. She excelled in high school athletics when called upon to throw basketballs, baseballs, the shot put, or the discus. Unlike her Soviet counterparts, though, she was not interested in sports and spent little time training. Occasionally, U.S. track officials would stop by the high school, trying at one point to recruit her for Helsinki, but she shrugged them off. She preferred going to dances and looking for a husband.

She found one in Henry Brown, a bricklayer, and was married by age 20. She began raising their son Reggie and working part-time in a plastic-cutting factory. Yet, once she had reached her goal of marriage and family, she wanted more. When the USOC came knocking on her door again in 1956 to ask about Melbourne, she said yes. At the time, she had no money, and Henry didn't like the idea.

> Hey, I didn't know you got to travel overseas. I want to see the world! Wait 'till I tell my husband…. To start off with, I asked him if I could go. That was a mistake, because I gave him the authority to tell me whether or not I could go. He ordered me not to go.[38]

Although Brown was known as easygoing, she had a stubborn streak. Forbidding her to go did not work out for Henry. Soon, toddler Reggie was staying with Grandma while the track star was off to Melbourne, the beginning of the end of her marriage. Stories of her lack of funding found a sympathetic ear in a local California businessman, Brad Pye, Jr., who helped raise the money for her trip.

Brown's results in Melbourne were respectable, considering her lack of training and the Soviet talent she confronted. Her sixth place in the shot put wasn't close to a medal, but the finish was the best for an American woman since the debut of the event. Her fourth in the discus was a whisper shy of a medal. She set the American record in both events, despite not medaling. After the Melbourne Games, she started working with American javelin coach Steve Seymour and with Ed Temple's Tigerbelles, though Brown was never technically a Tennessee State athlete.

She continued traveling to international meets, to places even more exotic than Melbourne, like Moscow and Warsaw. At a meet in Athens, Brown threw the discus into the stadium seats and nearly hit a spectator. Unlike some of her predecessors, she wasn't arrested. She still climbed up into the stands and apologized. The spectator was surprised but thrilled to accept a hug and an autograph.

With the Rome Olympics more than a year away, Brown was in better form than before but again lacked funding. The community was willing to pitch in, but she needed more money than what she earned as a housekeeper. She enrolled in Henrietta's Beauty College. Hairdressing paid better than housecleaning, but the hours were long, and the fumes left her worn out at the end of the day, without the time or energy to train. She threw the shot put in a nearby park on her lunch hour. The locals probably saw her coming every day in her pink beautician's coat, one hand on a sack lunch and the other on a bowling bag with her shot put. *Clear the field! Earlene's gotta practice!*

All the training paid off. In Rome, on September 2, 1960, she threw the shot farthest of the qualifiers in the preliminary round. In the final round, Tamara Press began by setting a new Olympic record, which put the gold medal out of reach. Before her last throw, Brown found herself in fourth place just about to miss a medal—again! New Zealand's Valerie Sloper was in third as Brown stepped into the circle for her last attempt of the competition.

The launch was Brown's strongest of the day. She squeaked by Sloper to take the bronze medal,[39] the lone American on the podium between Soviets Zybina and Press. It would be the last shot put medal earned by an American woman until 2016.

Brown stayed in shape, working out with the Tennessee State team, looking forward to Tokyo. But she was approaching thirty. In the 1964 Olympics, on the night of the finals, the steady rain and mud in the throwing circle made it hard for her to see and plant her feet correctly. Shot putters have to contend with weather like any other athlete, but it was especially hard for the nearsighted Brown, who could hardly see, let alone find her form. Although she made the finals, she came in last of the group.

Even then, Brown became the only woman to make it to the shot put finals in three consecutive Olympics—Zybina made it to three, but not in consecutive Games, and Press had only competed twice. Brown also was the first American woman to break the 50-foot shot put barrier. At one point she ranked number one in the world, the lone American name among a sea of Soviets, Germans, and other Eastern Europeans. Despite all the barriers—lack of funding, lack of training, and lack of family encouragement—Brown competed well among the greatest that the Cold War had to offer.

Bowlarama

Dozens of movies and biographers have told Wilma Rudolph's story. Earlene Brown has yet to be given a full treatment. Biographer Nathan Aeseng, who included the shot putter in his encyclopedia of Black American athletes, called her "the most unheralded U.S. athlete of all time."[40]

If and when they make a movie about Earlene Brown—and surely someone must—the opening scene ought to be in a bowling alley, July 1964.[41] Imagine two huge women, each weighing over 200 pounds and nearly six feet tall, both holding bowling balls in their enormous palms. They toss them from palm to palm as if they are grapefruits. Each flashes a wide, gap-toothed grin. Both are known for their sense of humor, and both are laughing helplessly. Neither speaks the other's language.

A third woman, small, blond, and wiry, tries to translate, but it's confusing. "Here?" she says in Russian-tinged English. "Fingers here?"

The Black woman waves them back to demonstrate. She winds up and whizzes the ball down the lane. It slices through the ten pins, sweeping them up like dust off a broom. The taller one, Tamara Press of the USSR, fits her fingers in the holes, but can't get comfortable with the hold, and it hangs from her thumb and forefinger. She imitates the American, and the spinning ball starts in the lane, but immediately bounces into the gutter and up into the wall. The camera zooms in on a dent.

There was no film crew in 1964 to document when Olympic shot put medalist Brown hosted her Soviet competitors in a detour from their international goodwill tour, a detour to the Bowlarama in Compton. It must have been a sight, a quartet of the world's best shot putters, three immense Russians and one equally strong Black woman playing tour guide. Galina Zybina and Yevgeniya Kuznetsova were with Press when they visited one of Brown's hangouts. No doubt, the quartet were accompanied by a few "security men," i.e., KGB agents, watching anxiously over a tour stop that was "unsanctioned."

After the 1960 Games, Wilma Rudolph stopped competing, wanting to go out on top, uninjured. She toured as goodwill ambassador for the U.S. for a few years, earning widespread praise for her poise, in her own way a model of the exceptionalism that Jesse Owens had experienced. Afterward, she settled down to a quiet family life but died relatively young, aged 54, of brain and throat cancer. By all reports, Rudolph was a long-term smoker.

Earlene Brown had a slightly more colorful post–Olympic career, even aside from her exploits at the bowling alley. Brown became a Roller Derby Queen. This new form of entertainment was rising in popularity in 1966 and paid well on top of the hairdressing. After all, there were no endorsement deals or Wheaties box covers for a female shot putter.

Skating for the New York Bombers, Brown became famous for a signature move called the "bear hug," for which she was particularly well suited. From New York, Brown was traded to the Los Angeles Thunderbirds, enabling her to end her derby career at home in southern California. There was a media splash as the team designed a special jersey for her with a special number: 747. Eventually, Brown was inducted into the Roller Derby Hall of Fame and, posthumously, into the Track and Field Hall of Fame. Like her teammate, Brown died too soon, only age 47, in Compton.

What everyone remembered most about Earlene Brown was her smile, that

Six. The Cold War and the Feminine Mystique (1948-1968)

personality that was both sweet and tough, encapsulating what it was like to be an American rocket launcher: "When I was young, I was ashamed of my size. I never thought something of which I was ashamed—my size and strength—could make me feel proud. But I feel proud now."[42]

The Cold War raged on for another couple of decades, with Soviets continuing to win gymnastic and shot put contests, and Americans dominating the sprints. The rest of the world found other athletic avenues to explore, plenty of them not hemmed in by American prejudices against athletes looking masculine or Soviets obsessed with winning.

Many of them just wanted to play, and play all year round, if they could. There were other ways and places to compete, in the mountains covered with snow or on the lakes covered with ice. If women were going to expand where they competed, they couldn't limit events just to avoid cold weather. They also wanted spots in the Games of Winter.

Seven

The Other Cold War
Winter Games (1924–1956)

Women's participation in winter sports was roughly parallel to their summer experience. Despite competing like the men (sometimes with the men) in games on snow and ice, women were strictly limited when Olympic competitions were first formalized. Countries, and the individuals who ran their country's organizing committees, drew different conclusions about what women could do. If women's encounter with the Summer Games was a series of hurdles, then their entry into winter sports was like a bumpy slalom ski run, full of corkscrews and treacherous moguls.

The launch of the Winter Olympics itself wasn't smooth, either. The IOC had no desire to organize another set of international competitions. Olympics were based on the Greek ideal, and there were no bobsled racers or ski jumpers on the side of the Grecian urns. As others were launching international tournaments, from those Women's World Games and Spartakiads enthusiasm rose for a winter sports competition to join the others. But Coubertin and the committee weren't interested.

So, Scandinavia launched them on their own. Led by Sweden's Colonel Victor Balck, who might be called the "Coubertin of the Winter Olympics," the Nordic Games kicked off in 1901, a mere five years after the Athens Games. This was fitting, given that Sweden had formed that first "Olympic Union" and hosted those precursor summer contests a good sixty years before Coubertin came along.

The Nordic Games included the favorite Scandinavian sports: cross-country skiing, skating, ski jumping, and sledging. Women were welcomed into several events, including cross-country skiing and skating. Balck was for anything that would make Sweden look good, baldly stating: "we should hold our banner high … we should make the Swedish name known and respected."[1]

The IOC criticized the Nordic Games as motivated by a desire for money and to boost tourism, pretending that the Olympics was completely indifferent to spectators. Stockholm's schedule for the Games did include theater, opera, parades, and field trips to a newly created Swedish open-air museum in Skansen. Balck's response to the IOC was *So what? Our Games will attract tourists.*

The success of the Nordic Games in Sweden caught the attention of the hotel and ski industry in the Alps. As the 1924 Paris Olympic organizers began their planning, they added a winter sports festival in Chamonix, a winter companion to the newly crowned Summer Games.[2]

Balck, who was a member of the IOC, voted against the Chamonix idea because it would have directly competed with the Nordic Games. He was mollified when organizers promised not to call their contests "Olympic." Then, Chamonix organizers promptly plastered the "O" word on posters all over town.

In addition, after this new winter sports festival was a success (250 athletes, 16 sports), the IOC retroactively announced that it *had* been the first Winter Olympics. Hence, one purpose for the creation of IOC-sanctioned Winter Olympics was to crush a competing tournament. The IOC didn't want to hold winter Games, but they didn't want anyone else to hold them either.

The Nordic Games ended, partly due to this rivalry, and partly from the loss of its promoter when Victor Balck died in 1928. It didn't help that political disputes between Sweden and Norway had led to boycotts, and some years without snow had caused havoc with the schedule. The last non–Olympic winter festival was held in 1926. The dissolution of the Nordic Games left Olympic organizers with a firm hold on the design and execution of any future Games, so that "winter sports were now brought within the IOC's sporting empire."[3]

In the first IOC-approved Winter Olympics, women were allowed in only one sport. As it happens, it was a sport that Balck had presided over for thirty years, as head of an international sports federation that featured women prominently. Balck led the International Skating Union, shaping what would become one of the most popular events of the Nordic and Winter Olympic Games. In Chamonix 1924, ladies' figure skating first made its debut.

Strenuous and Delightful

Mass interest in Olympic figure skating did not start with the Harding-Kerrigan brouhaha, which will be covered further in Chapter Thirteen. The sport has a long history, even predating an Olympic pedigree that dated back to 1908, predating classic Olympic events like weightlifting and the modern pentathlon.

Twenty-first-century skating has been described as the "quintessential 'girls' sport,"[4] but the practice started out as the exclusive province of gentlemen athletes. In the 1860s, the sport was a way for men to demonstrate their civilized prowess on the ice. Tracing complex figures and striking poses on skates required precision, strength, and flexibility.

Scandinavians Axel Paulsen and Ulrich Salchow invented jumps, while American Jackson Heines added music and dance, ratcheting up the sport's popularity in Europe. When men performed, they were described as skating like a "whirlwind," leaping "like a cat," or "immensely powerful."[5] Originally, competitive figure skating was for men.

But Madge Syers, as noted earlier, caused a stir by coming in second in the men's skate competition in 1902, when no rule prevented her from entering. The figure skating federation (ISU) hastily created separate competitions and events for Men, Ladies, and Pairs, which were added to the 1908 Olympics. For a few years after, the British let Syers compete against men in their national championships, and she continued to win. Thus, skating could be seen as one of the first disciplines where mixed genders could compete.

Skating was also the first "winter" sport to appear in the Olympics, among sports that required unfrozen weather. While Coubertin was not a fan of winter sports overall, he welcomed skating's introduction in London 1908 by praising its intrinsic virtues, calling it "amateur in nature and possessed of a sporting dignity so frank and pure that its exclusion from the Olympic programme robs it of strength and value."[6] Figure skating appealed to the poet in him.

The 1908 London *Olympic Report* had described a "rink [that] was filled to overflowing with an enthusiastic crowd of onlookers, who witnessed perhaps the most strenuous, delightful and varied display of figure skating that has ever taken place."[7]

From this initial viewing in the public sphere, figure skating continued to gain enthusiastic followers throughout the mid–1920s. Not to contest against men, of course, because of the problems with judging the long skirts and so forth. But once the genders had properly been sorted out into categories, ladies' figure skating was welcomed, often lumped with swimming and gymnastics as the acceptable kind of sport that allowed women to look beautiful, as opposed to the running and jumping that caused grimaces and contortions. Paul Gallico explained that figure skating allowed "the female figure in the dance, but freed by the steel blades from the ordinary pull of gravity and lethargy of friction. An entire arena is her dance floor, and there is no costume lovelier or more graceful than the figure-skating dress with its short, flared skirt, and the jaunty caps to match."[8]

Cute costumes or not, figure skaters were considered athletes, and there was respect for the physicality and strength required to leap or for men to lift a partner. Those within the sport knew that skaters worked hard at training, even though they were "schooled to make the difficult look easy,"[9] to the point where their strength was taken for granted.

Despite such support, skating was removed from the 1912 Stockholm Olympics on the grounds that it was not a summer sport. It may also have been because the Swedes were still featuring skating in their own Nordic Games. As it happens, boxing was also removed in 1912, simply because the Swedes didn't care for it. In those early days, sports were still in a revolving door. Tug of war—in! Croquet—out! For the next Olympics in Antwerp, figure skating was back on the menu.[10]

Figure skating in the Winter Games was not just a sideshow, but the marquee event. Skating figured prominently on the schedule for the first Chamonix winter not-officially Olympic/Olympic festival of 1924. Large audiences were expected, even before the rise of the incomparable Sonja Henie.

When the first gold medal in ladies figure skating went to Austrian Herma Szabo, the skater in last place was destined to become the most famous. Norway's Sonja Henie was just 11 years old in 1924, in only her second major skating competition, after winning the Norwegian championships at age ten. During the Olympics, she skated over to the rink side several times to get help from her coach—during her free skate performance.

By 1927, Henie was no longer consulting the coach during the skate. She won the first of ten consecutive world championships, a feat never since duplicated. Still, that first international contest was a close call and a harbinger of some of the judging favoritism that would forever loom over skating.[11]

The 1927 world championships were held in Oslo, Henie's hometown. Three of the judges were Norwegian, while the other two were from Austria and Germany. Henie, 14 years old, faced the veteran Szabo, whose maturity would have had the edge in those high-scoring but nebulous characteristics like grace and carriage. But the three hometown judges voted for Henie over Szabo. Afterward, the ISU changed the rule to allow only one judge per country in future meets.

Yet Henie's talents were not overrated. By the time she skated in the 1928 St. Mortiz Olympics, she received six of the seven first place votes from judges in multiple countries.[12] In the 1932 Lake Placid Games, Henie earned a second gold medal. Austrian Fritzi Burger settled for a repeat silver as Henie swept the judging with seven first places.

Henie was an innovator in several ways. Skaters had been using musical accompaniment since 1908, but she expanded the use of choreography, borrowing heavily from her ballet training. She pioneered the much shorter, fur-lined skirt that Paul Gallico admired so much. She was the first to wear white skate boots, which she claimed were to remind her of the snow in her homeland.

She had several nicknames by then, including "the White Swan" and "the Ice Queen of Norway."[13] She was a teeny-bopper phenom, so popular that when she toured large cities, from Prague to Manhattan, police had to be brought in to handle crowd control.

Her popularity—and the popularity for women skaters in general—created a circular problem of sorts. The more a woman skated with flexibility and speed, then the more popular she became, and the larger the crowds. This led to more coverage emphasizing her looks and feminine attributes rather than her power or training. Popularity led to marketing tie-ins with dolls, makeup, and costume items, which led to even larger crowds and so on. This cycle would repeat itself for multiple skaters, once Henie showed that skating could reap benefits. Financial benefits, to be specific.

It was widely known that Henie's father/manager demanded large sums for her "amateur" appearances. This "expense money" was the way athletes could receive money and still meet amateur rules. Other athletes, like Paavo Nurmi, had been investigated for lesser offenses, but Henie seemed to successfully skirt the rules. This led to the less flattering nickname of "Little Miss Moneybags." Still, the Germans, Swiss, and Austrians were nuts about figure skating, and by the time Henie showed up to skate in the 1936 Olympics in Garmisch-Partenkirchen, she was a superstar.

She had performed in Berlin a year earlier, enthusiastically giving Hitler the Nazi salute, so the German crowd was already in her camp. Between the partisan audience and her two previous wins, she was heavily favored to three-peat and was planning to retire soon after, so she could start earning some real money.

At the same time, there were two youngsters from Great Britain giving Henie serious competition. Fifteen-year-old Megan Taylor and 15-year-old Cecilia Colledge, born within a few months of each other, had already competed against Henie at Lake Placid. Both had been climbing the ladder at the world championships, steadily gaining on the Ice Queen of Norway. Taylor had even placed second behind Henie at worlds in 1934 and 1936, although an unfortunate accident prevented her from competing at the British Trials, which put her out of the Olympics.

Colledge, however, was still breathing down Henie's neck. The older superstar had been Colledge's idol, the reason she decided to take up skating after learning about Henie's first gold medal in St. Moritz. On the way to vying against her in the 1936 Winter Games, Colledge had added a double jump to her repertoire—the first woman to land one. The British teenager was herself an innovator and invented both the camel and layback spins, two key weapons in the arsenal of every skater today.

The Olympic competitions of 1936 included two segments: compulsory figures and the free skate. The compulsories required the athlete to trace out complex patterns on the ice. The free skate allowed creativity but jumps, spins, twirls, and footwork were now embedded in the choreography, thanks to both Henie and Colledge's contributions. After the compulsory figures, Henie was in first place, but by fewer than ten points out of 250. When she read the scores, Henie reportedly ripped the sheet off the results board and tore it up in irritation.[14]

In the free skate, Colledge was scheduled early in the group, an unlucky disadvantage. She came onto the ice and gave the mandatory Nazi salute, which helped to put the crowd in a festive mood. But as she began to skate, the wrong music began, and the delay to search for the proper recording rekindled the opening butterflies. When Colledge began again, she stumbled within the first minute. She recovered to skate well for the rest of her program, but the door was left open. Henie took advantage and received all first place marks, with a conservative but error-free program. Her three-peat Olympic gold was followed by her tenth straight world championship win.

After retiring, Henie starred in movies, then helped launch a new form of entertainment—the touring ice skating show. These quickly became a hit, and she was eventually able to earn millions as a performer. Her celebrity status and three marriages kept her in the tabloids for decades, until she passed away from lymphoma in the 1960s.

While opinions about Henie were mixed, her impact on skating was undeniably huge. She was the first teenager to popularize figure skating, the first female to incorporate ballet and dance into the skate, the first to adopt short skirts and plunging necklines, and the first to demand huge sums as a skating performer.

At the same time, many considered her a traitor for cozying up to Hitler and the Nazis when she skated in Germany. It was widely reported that she had an autographed photo of Hitler prominently displayed in her house during the Nazi occupation of Norway. Later, when she gained American citizenship, she tried to bury the past with charitable appearances and goodwill tours, but many Norwegians still consider her wartime behavior more significant than her multiple trophies.

Colledge and Taylor, the two young British athletes, were expected to wage a terrific skate-off in the Winter Olympics of 1940. War canceled those plans and derailed their careers, as it had many others.

However, the pipeline of young, vivacious, and increasingly physical skaters had been established. Canada's Barbara Ann Scott followed in the Henie model, becoming the first singles skater to land a double lutz. Scott quickly rose to popularity as another fresh face, winning the 1947 world championship and looking toward the Games of 1948.

However, Scott caught the unfortunate attention of Olympic organizers when her hometown of Ottawa gave her a Buick convertible as a "good luck" gift. This was too blatant a violation of amateurism for IOC president Brundage. In tears, she had to return the car, or it would disqualify her for the next Olympics. She did win Olympic gold in 1948, returned home in triumph to Ottawa, and received another car.

What Barbara Ann Scott did for Canada, Tenley Albright did for the U.S., earning a silver medal in 1952 and a gold in 1956, America's first ladies figure skating Olympic win. Albright had survived childhood polio and recovered from a serious skating fall only two weeks before the Olympics. After Albright would come 16-year-old Carol Heiss, future medalist in 1960, then Peggy Fleming, and others.

Fig.19. Sonja Henie appeared in 15 films, not entirely involving skating but all involving showbiz. The "lovely" Olympic female skating costume became even shorter in Hollywood (National Portrait Gallery).

Skating continued to advance in difficulty. In 1956, Dick Button became the first person to execute a triple jump in competition. A Canadian couple, Frances Defoe and Norris Bowman, developed twists and overhead lifts. The Protopopovs from the Soviet Union elevated the level of choreography and technique further, until they ruled pairs competitions throughout the 1960s. Skaters flew, spun, were thrown, and even did backflips. While some saw skating as dance and spectacle, the sport advanced in athleticism.

Despite all the innovations, Scott and her peers were often still reduced to their "doll-like" qualities, the parts that made them so tantalizing to marketers. Some historians argue that this opened athletic doors which track and field did not. "Like Sonja Henie before her, and Peggy Fleming and Dorothy Hamill after her, [Scott] was an 'athlete in disguise' who skated, with unimpaired femininity, into hearts closed to the likes of Blankers-Koen and Ostermeyer."

Like gymnastics, then, figure skating offered opportunity for women. Because of its popularity as entertainment, skating was a way for women to express their athletic talents without being criticized for their lack of femininity. In addition, skating helped pave the way for other sports. The 1908 *Olympic Report* hinted as much: "The successful appearance of ladies in these competitions suggests ... [that it is] illogical ... to provide so few opportunities for the[ir] participation.... More events, in fact, might be open to women, whether they are permitted to compete with men or not.... In rifle-shooting, and possibly in other sports, they may also have a fair chance of success in open competitions."[15]

Basking in the glow of figure skating and Sonja Henie, the ISU confidently added speed skating to the program for the Third Winter Olympiad of 1932. Women athletes looked forward to competing in other winter disciplines, too. Surely slalom skiing and cross-country ski relays, sports that had female champions in several countries, would follow quickly.

But this was women and the Olympics. There was nothing sure about it.

Stalling in the Nordic Events

> "Women's speed-skating, with sanction now given it by the [International Skating Union] will become one of the most popular winter-sports competition[s] ... [with] races [that are] much like the men's."—*Official Report, Lake Placid*.[16]

With the popularity of women's figure skating drawing crowds, the organizers of the Lake Placid Games included three women's speed skating events: the 500, 1000, and 1,500 m. The IOC insisted that they remain demonstration sports only, which meant there were no podium ceremonies and no official records.

Still, the races were considered well contested and the nine medalists were well received. Eighteen-year-old Minnesotan Dot Franey was thrilled to capture a bronze medal, and she looked forward to the ISU launching international championships the following year. There promised to be a full slate of events for the 1936 Games.

However, when the next Winter Olympiad rolled around, women's speed skating was nowhere to be found in Garmisch-Partenkirchen. Promises of turning the demonstration sport into an IOC-approved event went unfulfilled. As it turns out, Olympics speed skating for women didn't reappear for 28 years, until 1960.

Other winter sports also turned women away. Olympic bobsleigh, introduced in 1924 for men, was off-limits for women until 2002. For a while, the U.S. national championships allowed mixed genders until a woman, Katharin Dewey, won the 1940 national championship, along with men on the bobsleigh team.[17] After that, women were banned from U.S. bobsleigh because the sport was suddenly deemed too dangerous.

Men's cross-country skiing events kicked off in 1936, but none for women until 1950. Men's biathlon, which kicked off in 1960, wasn't available for women until 1992. Ski jumping took ninety years. Despite the rosy outlook in 1932, women's winter sports fell vastly short of men's for decades, just as they had in summer competitions.

There have been few exceptions. Luge, where a single-person sled flies down a track feet first, debuted in 1964 for both women and men, simultaneously. Skeleton, where the athlete flies head first, debuted in 2002 for both women and men. The modern "X-Games" winter sports, like snowboarding and ski aerials, were added for women and men simultaneously. Yet most of these were recent in Olympics history. Prior to 1960, only one discipline launched with gender parity: Alpine Skiing.

In 1936, the Alpine Combined ski event was put on the Winter Olympics schedule, with one event each for men and women. In the very next Games, the post-war Olympics of 1948, the Alpine Slalom and Downhill events were added separately, again for both genders. When Giant Slalom and Super G were further tacked on in the 1990s, both women and men had competitions. It raises an interesting question. Why alpine skiing but not speed skating or cross-country skiing?

Danger might have been a valid argument for some winter events, like the bobsleigh. Swimming and sprinting don't send athletes hurtling down a track 90 mph. Although some arguments against women ski jumping were silly (see Chapter Eleven), ski jumping is still dangerous. Crashes do happen frequently in speed skating.

But not all events are so perilous. Cross-country racers might become exhausted, but they don't face the kind of injuries that downhill skiers do. The reasons for acceptance of some sports and disapproval of others can't simply be traced to health-based arguments. Some still tried, as German Alpine skiing champion Christl Cranz claimed: "Cross-country skiing and ski jumping are athletic performances ... for which a lot of strength and endurance is necessary, more than women can give without harming themselves.... Certainly no reasonably sporting girl would think about participating in a marathon or boxing, and that is how it is with us women skiers; there is no interest in running or jumping competitions."[18]

Yet this was from a woman who regularly flew down vertical drops of 2,700 feet at 50 mph.

Safety has always been a matter of perspective, an argument used to justify an already existing bias. After all, figure skaters are injured constantly, in a sport that involves serrated metal toe-picks, sharpened blades, and mistimed jumps that land on concrete-like ice. No one argues that figure skating is inherently dangerous, even though injuries are constant.

The reason for the choice of some sports over others had more to do with the intersection of regional politics, chauvinism, and unfortunate luck, a combination that emerged on a sport-by-sport basis. With speed skating, for instance, ISU president Victor Balck had been one of the strongest advocates for women athletes. But he died in 1927, just after the first Winter Olympics took place, and before he could apply pressure to include women. Women skaters lost one of their biggest supporters, and the ISU, under new leadership, didn't even hold women's speed skating championships until after the Games.

Meanwhile, Norwegians dominated men's speed skating, and they did not share Balck's notions of equality. While Norwegians supported women's rights in general, they could be positively Neanderthal in their athletic clubs, which banned women early in the 20th century. They disdained women's participation in their speed skating events until the 1980s. One historian points out that a Norwegian book, *Stars of the Skating Sport,* published in 1971, didn't cover a single woman in its 200 pages.[19]

Moreover, the skating events in Lake Placid involved major controversies in the men's events that clouded the picture. For the first and only time, the men's races used a mass start at the Americans' request, and the Europeans didn't like it. The Scandinavians preferred to race in timed pairs, highlighting pure speed over tactics.

Seven-time Finnish medalist Clas Thunberg had even reached out to the Norwegians a year earlier to form an alliance, but they spurned his offer. He refused to come to Lake Placid. Not surprisingly, the American and Canadian men took ten of the twelve medals, including all four golds.

The mass start issue was bad enough, but the races were then full of accusations of cheating. In some heats, the judges stopped the race to rerun it, claiming the racers were "loafing." In others, skaters obstructed each other and violated the rules to the point where four countries lodged protests. When the races concluded, the Norwegians, Finns, Swedes, and Japanese lobbied for changes including elimination of the mass start, and they got their wish.[20]

When all of the demonstration medals on the women's side also went to Americans or Canadians, it added to the bad feelings from the competitions as a whole. North Americans may have supported their women speed skaters, but they didn't have the votes from Scandinavia and Germany to lobby when the Games next moved to the Alps and then Norway.

After the war, when the ISU might have come back to the table on the women's behalf, the USSR entered the mix. For the next seventeen years, starting in 1948, female Soviet speed skaters swept every medal in the world championships except for one year. The ISU[21] of the 1950s, whose leadership was from Western Europe, was little interested in lobbying for women's events which might add to the Soviet Union's tally.

Thus, three decades of international politicking passed before women speed skaters were able to get back on the 1960 Olympic schedule. Dot Franey, the demonstration medalist in Lake Placid, couldn't wait that long. She went professional, although there were no money-making opportunities for a speed skater at the time. She joined the only other place open to her—the figure skating shows.[22]

Complex dynamics also affected cross-country skiing, the national pastime of Norway. Norwegians are said to be born with skis on their feet, but although women have feet, too, they weren't always accepted in competitions. Norwegian sociology professor Gerd von der Lippe chronicled the pressures facing a multi-talented Norwegian female athlete, Laila Schou Nilsen, who was pushed out of the men's sports—speed skating, cross-country skiing, and ski jumping. "I quit speed skating and slalom when they did not send me to international competitions any more."[23]

Nilsen had been winning mixed-gender cross-country ski races since age 13. However, when she won a 6 km race by a margin of 6 minutes, an Oslo newspaper suggested she must have cheated, because she was too fast for a girl. Luckily for Norway, Nilsen kept skiing in Alpine events and ended up winning a bronze medal in the Combined Downhill/Slalom at Garmisch-Partenkirchen in 1936.

Like the Canadian Rosenfeld, Nilsen seemed to excel at everything, and even won tennis championships while waiting for the snow to return. Of all sports, though, Nilsen ended up most famous for playing handball and even took a turn as president of the Norwegian Handball Federation. For reasons explained in Chapter Nine, Norwegians considered handball to be a women's sport and certainly a more acceptable place for women athletes to shine.

Another historian describes how Norwegian newspaper *Dagbladet* feigned outrage at a 1950s women's ski race when participants ended "breathless, sweaty, with clumps of ice in their hair, [and] fell exhausted to the ground."[24] It was the Norwegian version of the 800 m races all over again. For men, exhaustion after a 10 k was considered normal, but for women, it spelled F-R-A-G-I-L-I-T-Y.

Overall, the Norwegians did not press for women's events to be included in their beloved sport of cross-country ski racing and even voted against it when the Games came to Oslo. It would take until 2002, when Marit Bjørgen won the first of her 15 Olympic medals (8 gold), for the Norwegians to warm up to women cross-country skiers. Bjørgen is now considered the most successful cross-country skier—male or female—of all time.

Fig.20. Laila Schou Nilsen (NOR, 2nd from left), being congratulated by teammate Per Fossum (far left) and coaches (names unknown) after earning bronze in the 1936 Olympic Downhill/Slalom Combined (Photograph by Albert Cusian, German Federal Archive).

All Downhill from Here

As for why Alpine skiing was welcomed for women when the other sports were not, the easy answer again is regional politics. The 1936 Winter Games were held in Garmisch-Partenkirchen, in the German Alps. Germany had talented skiers, women who took the gold and silver in the Alpine Combined. The winner was Christl Cranz, that athlete who had argued so strongly against other winter women's events. (The bronze went to Norway's multi-talented Laila Schou Nielsen, before she took up handball.)

Thus, Alpine nations saw the benefit of lobbying for women's events when they had women who could win. It was why Americans had pressed for women's speed skating in Lake Placid.

When the Games resumed after the war, another Alpine city—St. Moritz, Switzerland—hosted the next Winter Olympics. Austrian Alpine women took five medals, and Swiss Alpine women took two. After that, Alpine "bloc" countries would continue to support Alpine skiing for women, as their German, Austrian, Italian, and Swiss female athletes continued to win.

The other two 1948 medals in Alpine skiing went to American Gretchen Fraser, gold in the Slalom and silver in the Combined. She was the first American to win any Alpine skiing event. A native of Tacoma, she had won a ski championship a decade earlier and was training for the 1940 Games when war broke out. Fraser didn't even return to competitive skiing until 1947, after she was married and living a quiet domestic life. The USOC had pinned their hopes on someone else, a teenager from Vermont, Andrea Mead.

However, Fraser out-skied the world's best in St. Moritz—including Mead—and returned home to a ticker tape parade. She then spent much of her life back in Idaho, running a club for amputee skiers.

Meanwhile, Andrea Mead Lawrence had unfinished business. She returned to the Oslo Games and fulfilled her potential, winning two of the three available Alpine medals. Together, Fraser and Lawrence proved that Americans could take on the Europeans.

But the Alpine skiers continued to rule their own event. As of 2020, the all-time women's Olympic medalist was Croatian Alpine specialist Janica Kostelić. Kostelić racked up six medals before knee surgery required her retirement at only 25 years old.

One of the most recognized names on the U.S. circuit, Lindsey Vonn, managed three medals and eleven major injuries before retiring at age 34. All in all, factoring in the risk of injury clearly doesn't explain why Alpine skiing was widely accepted for women early on, when speed skating and cross-country skiing were not. National prejudices had a much bigger influence on the arrangements.

Lindsey Vonn, with her World Cup titles and Olympics medals, formally asked the international ski federation (FIS) to allow women to ski against men. It was an interesting request, since conventional wisdom predicts that men would always win. However, one comparison[25] of average speeds suggested the results might be more nuanced.

An analysis from 2018 showed that, based only on skiing speeds, the average downhill male skier would beat the average downhill female skier. On the other hand, the average woman might beat the average man in the slalom. Women's races are typically shorter and less rigorous, which makes comparisons problematic. Yet, when speed isn't the only factor, women might have a fighting chance, at least to get on the podium.

Vonn herself suggested that winning wasn't the only outcome of interest: "I train with the men all the time and I really enjoy it…. They push me to be a better skier. I always find myself skiing my best when I'm skiing against them … so I would like the opportunity to race against them and see where I stand…. I know I'm not going to win, but I would like to at least have the opportunity to try."[26] The "opportunity to try" is a phrase that certainly sounds Coubertin-esque, reminiscent of "the triumph rather than the struggle."

A few winter sports have considered the possibility of mixed-gender events. Pairs Figure Skating isn't exactly mixed gender, but women and men do compete together, and a team event was added in 2014, though differing disciplines compete for placements rather than pure score. More intriguing is the team event in skiing. Team genders are equalized (two women, two men, etc.) and similar genders compete head-to-head, but the tie-breaker is total time. There might be a future possibility of directly comparing male and female skiers. Perhaps Vonn's offer might one day come to fruition.

Women athletes might not all have been as keen as Vonn to compete against men, but if it was a choice of a mixed-gender event or none at all, they would take what was offered. They wanted more chances to compete, but trying to gain more of their own events ran into another problem. The Olympics, as a whole, were just getting too darned big.

Eight

Olympic Gigantism and the Zero-Sum Game (1924–1976)

The Olympic organizers had always wanted to have their cake and eat it, too, to fulfill that after-dinner dream of an international Olympiad populated by exceptional sportsmen *and* to keep the competition limited to individual gentlemen athletes performing the sacred sports from ancient Olympia. It was an argument lost long ago. The public loved contests. Individual countries had lobbied to add their own beloved sports to the schedule, while international sports federations clamored for their athletes to compete on the biggest stage. The IOC was continuously faced with the problem of "gigantism," fearing that the Games had become a colossus out of control.

Grumpy John Tunis had complained back in *Harper's* 1928: "Polo and hockey, football [soccer] and curling, bicycling and lacrosse, these sports are in no broad sense international and have no place in any international sporting gathering like the Olympic Games." He continued with his offhand bombshell that suggested women be excluded as well.

Of course, "in no broad sense international" depends on which nation is doing the sensing. Tunis might have wanted to talk to the Canadians, Russians, and Swedes about hockey and curling, the Hungarians and Serbians about water polo, the French and Italians about bicycling, and everybody in the world about soccer. They might have explained to him that international doesn't mean American. Meanwhile, would discus throwing really be considered international? Do they swim a lot in Norway?

As the Olympics continued, the IOC tried to limit adding sports while being continually peppered with requests to add sports. This would never change. However, it was a pattern that could be put to good use for those who wanted to limit women's participation. While the earliest arguments against more women's events rested on them being unfeminine or unhealthy, later arguments were that there was no more room at the inn. More women couldn't be added because that would make the Games too big.

For example, in the 1955 IOC meeting that was the prelude to the Melbourne Games, board member Gaston Mullegg, the delegate from the Rowing federation, mentioned that there had been proposals from other IOC members to add women's rowing, basketball, and speed skating. Mullegg admonished such proposals: "the members of the I.O.C. have no right to make these proposals, particularly now that the I.O.C. has asked for the last two years the reducing of the programme at the Games, as well as that of the number of athletes ... the proposition which involves an increase in the number of participants is incompatible with the demanded reduction."[1]

IOC president Brundage promised to mention this to the delegates at their later at-large meeting, so that all should know not to make such absurd suggestions. The agenda item of adding women's sports was the final one to dispatch, after which came thank-yous and apologies for the inadequate size of the conference table. In light of the growing size of the Executive Board, they would get a bigger table. But no bigger table for women's sports.

Gigantism has always been one of the happy problems of the Games, a difficulty born out of its popularity. Spectators pay for a big chunk of the contests, so when demand for a new sport rises, so does funding, through sponsorship and ticket sales. But expenses increase as well.

In order to combat spiraling costs, the IOC routinely challenged each international federation to prove that their sport was performed by as many countries and practitioners as possible. Although the IOC argued that adding women increased expense, sports federations in the 1950s began to point out that adding women's events to existing venues would make them more cost-effective. The gigantism argument could be offset if both women and men could compete in the same place using the same staff.

Even if a federation was mainly interested in creating an event for men and just giving lip service to women, it might still benefit from including both genders. Hence, part of the expansion of sports for women between the 1930s and 1970s, aside from the Cold War rivalry, came from federations who saw that their sport could become more entrenched in the Olympics by adding women's events.

Many of those arguments were on behalf of the audience rather than the athlete. Add the event, discipline, venue, or entire wing of contests because people would enjoy watching. Few besides Alice Milliat argued that women deserved any kind of equity or balance in numbers prior to the 1970s.

Between 1936 and 1968, four new sports were opened to women. Two disciplines opened up for mixed genders, where women and men could compete directly against each other. The results helped women gain new respect and new footholds, though there were also headwinds. Those two sports, curiously enough, both came out of the military.

Carried into History

> "Here Come the Girls!"—2020 *Fédération Équestre Internationale*
> (FEI) Website

The Greeks invented dressage. What could be more Olympic than that?
To be clear, the Greeks didn't include equestrian dressage competitions in their

Olympiads. They did use horses, building an entire stadium—the Hippodrome—solely for the chariot races. The Greeks loved horses the way modern culture worships cars.

Further, while Tunis and Coubertin were probably correct that were no Greek Olympic events for women and no women athletes, women were listed among the victors. The official winner of a Greek chariot race was the owner, not the horse or the charioteer, and sometimes the owner was a woman.

A Greek soldier, Xenophon, wrote the original book on dressage, clearly a different kind of competition from a race. Also affectionately (or derisively) referred to as "horse ballet," dressage requires riders to put their horse through a series of patterned moves without using verbal commands. Riders use only their knees and minimal hand gestures to cue the horse to stop, start, turn in circles, and move through multiple changes in gait, direction, and speed. Non-fans complain this is tedious because of its apparent inactivity, but it's comparable to watching someone walk across a tightrope while balancing a martini on their nose. The skill comes *from* the lack of movement.

A veteran of the Spartan-Persian campaigns, Xenophon was awarded for service with a country estate,[2] and he settled down to write books on his military exploits and on riding. His classic, *On Horsemanship*, was a training manual for cavalry in previous eras, and still is recommended to dressage riders. His tips were practical, such as approaching horses from the side with a quiet hand. He wrote that the best horses have "supple loins" with which to display the "noblest feats." Of those feats, he wrote: "A horse so prancing is a thing of beauty, a wonder and a marvel; riveting the gaze of all who see him, young alike and graybeards. They will never turn their backs, I venture to predict, or weary of their gazing so long as he continues to display his splendid action."[3]

Controlling a horse with subtle shifts of the legs and feet while holding a sword was considered a critical skill for cavalry. The displays that Xenophon described demonstrated that skill, much as jousting did for knights. Hence, dressage was designed by and for soldiers, whatever may be thought today when watching a horse performing a *piaffe*[4] to "Ice, Ice, Baby."[5]

Olympic equestrian competitions began in 1912, although entry to all events was originally restricted to military officers riding military-trained horses. By 1924, civilian riders were allowed in the jumping and the endurance contests, although dressage remained the strict province of the military.

Women, whose horse-riding pedigrees were long acknowledged (think of either Queen Elizabeth), could compete in *Fédération Équestre Internationale* (FEI) competitions beginning in the 1930s. But not in the Olympics. In 1938, Rule 214 specified that Amazons (women riders) could qualify for non–Olympic competitions only. Moreover, to help their countries' Olympic teams, women were encouraged to lend their horses.[6]

However, big changes came after a dressage scandal of 1948. In that post-war London Olympics, a Swedish dressage rider named Gehnäll Persson was a non-commissioned officer. Sweden temporarily promoted him to lieutenant solely to meet dressage competition rules. They demoted him a few weeks after Sweden won the gold medal, since they knew he wasn't really an officer. The IOC promptly disqualified Sweden and rescinded the medal.

Whether the disgrace was in allowing the "impostor" or in having ridiculously rigid rules, the FEI wanted to avoid future scandals. In 1952, they opened the barn doors completely. Civilians were allowed—even in dressage—as well as non-commissioned officers. Further, as long as they were throwing caution to the wind, they let women in as well.

The possibility of allowing women in *all* the equestrian events, including show jumping and the endurance race, had even briefly crossed the minds of the FEI committee when they planned for Helsinki. Allowing women into show jumping (called *Prix de Nations*) was discussed but voted down, even though women were show jumping in many national competitions. That decision meant that the lone woman who had earned a spot on the U.S. team had to stay home. Letting women into the endurance cross-country race didn't even make it to the formal agenda. Dressage remained the only equestrian event for women. In 1952, women were acceptable riders, but only for horse ballet.

Yet, for all the cold shoulder given to women in the 1951 meeting, the FEI quickly relented and admitted female riders to show jumping for the very next Olympics. Further, by 1964, women were admitted to the entire competition, including the "endurance" race. Something in the 1952 dressage competitions convinced them that the "weaker" sex had the strength and courage to handle horses. That something was probably Lis Hartel.

Hartel was the Danish dressage champion of 1943, an up-and-coming 23-year-old rider, honing her craft during the war and awaiting the opportunity for post-war competitions. One morning in 1944, however, she woke with a frightening headache. When the symptoms persisted, doctors confirmed the worst: she had contracted polio. Hartel was pregnant when polio hit but, luckily, delivered a healthy baby. However, she was rendered completely paralyzed and told she would not likely walk, let alone ride again.

Sometimes the victim of a disease gets lucky, and sometimes they just need the right motivation. Hartel began physical therapy and slowly muscled her way out of bed and back onto a horse. After years of therapeutic work, she regained some muscular use in her arms and upper legs, though she was limited from the knees down.

Oddly enough, dressage might be the one sport where having such limited use is not necessarily a dream-killer. Had she remained immobile from the waist down, she could not have managed to control her mount, but as long as she had her knees and enough determination, she could compete successfully. The biggest issue was now getting on the horse.

That problem turned out to be the easiest to solve. Plenty of aides were there in the Helsinki Olympics to lift Hartel onto her beloved horse, Jubilee. There were also three other women competing, but Hartel's was the story of the competition.

The best rider in the world, Sweden's Henri St. Cyr, won the event easily, competing in his third Olympics. His Swedish team (including the now-qualifying non-commissioned officer, Gehnäll Persson) also took the gold. But the battle for second and third was between Denmark's Hartel and France's André Jousseaume.

Hartel squeaked out a win by a half point, with a 541.5 score, a mere .09 percent ahead. The drama continued at the medal ceremony. In a gesture of goodwill, gold medalist St. Cyr carried Hartel from her horse to the second place spot on the podium. There probably wasn't a dry eye in the stadium.

Four years later, for the 1956 Olympics, Hartel proved she was no fluke by winning her second silver medal, again placing below the legendary Henri St. Cyr.[7] Germany's Liselott Linselhof took third, becoming the second woman to win a medal in a mixed sport.

Hartel's achievements became a part of history, both for women and for disabled advocates. She further championed efforts for decades to help polio victims and to advance therapeutic riding, eventually regaining some mobility in her legs. She also demonstrated that women could achieve marks equal to or better than men, even under exacting standards.

Linselhof would continue competing for several more Games, setting her own record in her fifth Olympics. By winning the gold medal in 1972 Individual Dressage, Liselott Linselhof became the first woman to win an open mixed-gender competition.

Decades later, Anky van Grunsven of the Netherlands showed further that women could dominate the event, winning nine medals (three gold, five with a team) during the 1990s and 2000s. Isabell Werth currently holds the all-time dressage

Fig.21. The 1952 Equestrian Dressage competition was one of the first mixed-gender events. Lis Hartel (DEN) overcame polio to earn a silver in Helsinki and Melbourne, which helped open all equestrian events to women (LA84 Digital Libraries Collection).

record with twelve medals (four gold, six for Team Germany). Werth competed in her fifties at Tokyo, still winning medals. Dressage riders have been known to compete into their seventies, so unbreakable records may yet be set.

With Hartel and Linselhof impressing the stodgier elements of the FEI, women were quietly granted an advance in Rome 1960 by being allowed to enter the jumping competition. After that, in 1964, they were allowed into eventing, which included the cross-country race. The race was timed with riders in sequence, not run together like a steeplechase—not exactly *National Velvet*. Yet even with riders going one at a time, courses could be difficult and mishaps frequent. Britain's Princess Anne competed in the Montreal Olympics, only later revealing that she had been recovering from a fractured vertebrae and a concussion. Respect for women's capability improved.

A major milestone was finally reached in Tokyo 2020, when Germany's Julia Krajewski became the first woman to win the Individual Eventing gold. Krajewski's feat was notable, in part, because women had dominated dressage ever since the days of Hartel and Linselhof. But they had not yet proven themselves the best across all disciplines—until 2021.

Meanwhile, as they had in several prior Games, women swept the Individual Dressage medals in Tokyo. Across the last nine Olympics, 25 of the 27 medals awarded in dressage went to women. It's a curious result for a sport that started firmly wedded to military officers who, at the time, were decidedly not women.

As it happens, dressage is also one of the few sports that has openly embraced gay male athletes. The first openly gay man to compete in any Olympics was Robert Dover, an American dressage rider, who won four bronze team medals, starting in 1988. A sociologist who analyzed the British team from 2007 to 2009 further found not only a relatively high percentage of openly gay men competing, but a high degree of tolerance from the straight men on the team, who said it was "a positive aspect of equestrianism."[8]

In contrast, many gay men in other disciplines have endured rampant homophobia. For example, diver Mark Tewksbury of Canada was told after his 1992 gold medal that being publicly gay would eliminate his chance for endorsements. Kerron Clement, three-time U.S. medalist in the 400 m hurdles, only came out after 18 years of competing in secret. (Lesbian women's experiences have been similar, as Chapter Fifteen will examine.) Gay men have not been welcomed in sports until very recently. Yet they don't seem to cause an uproar in dressage.

At the same time, dressage is routinely mocked by sportswriters as a "sissy" sport, sometimes by the same writers who worship gymnastics and figure skating. Journalists routinely call it the "equestrian version of ballroom dancing" or liken it to "poodle scuba diving."[9] Either that, or the media ignores dressage completely. For example, the *New York Times* in 1948 didn't even list the American Team Dressage bronze medal on its highlight of medal winners for the day, in its "comprehensive recap." Three days later, when the American team won the entire Eventing competition, the article praised the "hard-riding U.S. Army team,"[10] even though the dressage and eventing medalists were the same people.

Is ignoring or lampooning the sport a byproduct of the sport's acceptance of women? Does it reflect a streak of homophobia? It's not because Americans don't win. U.S. riders have won eight bronze and one silver Team Dressage medals. It's hard to ignore the combination: the strong performance in dressage by women once the sport permitted them to compete, the sport's acceptance of openly gay men, and continual scorn heaped on the event by the media. Whatever the prevailing public opinion about this sport, one of the oldest of the Olympic events, women and men continue to compete together without further hand-wringing.

Another classic Olympic discipline that experimented with men and women competing together beginning in the early 1970s was target shooting. Women had been petitioning to be included in the shooting events for a long time. There were plenty of Annie Oakleys out there, just waiting for their moment to shine. What happened when one finally did shine was strange. When two did, it was even stranger.

The Unthinkable Happens in Small-Bore Air Rifle

Sport-shooting contests have changed over the years, even though the Olympic discipline debuted all the way back in 1896. Like dressage, shooting for sport has close ties to the military, although competitions have attracted plenty of gentlemen non-officers. Coubertin himself was an avid pistol shooter, pleased that the first Olympics included both pistol and rifle events. Early competitions involved both dueling pistols and shotgun contests that used live pigeons. Fortunately, both of those were quickly discontinued.

The oldest Olympian on record was 72-year-old Oscar Swahn from Sweden, who competed in the Running Deer Shoot in 1920. There's also the story of Karoly Takacs, who lost his shooting hand in World War II. He won the pistol event in 1948 after teaching himself to shoot with his other hand. Plenty of drama has taken place in the shooting events.

One curious incident involving women happened early on, in that other most military of multi-events, the modern pentathlon. Coubertin's manufactured event in 1912 included shooting, riding, swimming, *and more*! This was the first year of added equestrian events, and women were specifically barred from riding in those. But they were not explicitly blocked from the modern pentathlon.

An enterprising British gentleman, Ambrose Preece, and his daughter heard of the competition, and 15-year-old Helen wanted to give it a go, after winning a couple of horse shows. It may have been a publicity stunt for Dad's business, but soon local newspapers started showing photos of Preece avidly training for the new event. She applied and was not immediately turned down.

Coubertin, who didn't want women doing anything, passive-aggressively said that since women were swimming and playing tennis against his wishes, he had no grounds to deny them into his pentathlon. He punted the decision to the Modern Pentathlon Committee, which swiftly voted 10 to 2 that Helen was persona non grata. The ballots were secret, so it's not known who those open-minded two voters might have been. Women would have to wait until the 21st century to be admitted into the Modern Pentathlon. They were admitted to other shooting events before then.

Eight. Olympic Gigantism and the Zero-Sum Game (1924–1976)

As women clamored to have more events, the International Shooting Sport Federation (ISSF) took note of the positive press gained from the open equestrian events in the 1950s. They opened the men's shooting events in 1968, and all three of the sub-categories—Rifle, Pistol, and Shotgun—let women compete next to the men.

The motivation might have been partly in response to criticisms of the sport's growth. Olympic shooting had started with only 5 events but increased to 21 by 1920. The IOC pushed them back to 2 contests for 1948, but the numbers had crept up again to 8 by the early 1970s. Each time events were opened, the number of participants per event was also expanded. Appeasing women might have been a way to allow more increases.

Women would still have to qualify, however, through a pipeline that hadn't existed before. Only a few apparently did that in their first two opportunities to join. The ISSF may have counted on that, too, knowing that women had little presence across the national federations. Pistol shooting doesn't require upper-body strength, and longer guns are routinely handled by experienced women. Yet shooting has traditionally been viewed as a men's sport. Some emphasize that prehistoric men were hunters. Sons are far more likely to be taught by their fathers than daughters, although more from tradition than physical ability. Aiming and keeping the body still is gender-neutral.

However, just two cycles after the competitions were opened to both genders, in the 1976 Small-Bore Air Rifle Competition in Montreal, the unthinkable seemed to be happening. A woman—a seven-time world champion, multi-gold medalist from the Pan-American Games, but still *a woman*—was at the top of the leader scoreboard when the last round was completed. Her name was Margaret Murdock.

Murdock was a shooting instructor in the U.S. Army who had enlisted to join the shooting team after a standout performance on the Kansas State University rifle squad. She had trained men, had competed against men, and had beaten men on plenty of occasions. She had set world records. It would not be unthinkable for her to beat this group. It just might not be what the ISSF had in mind.

Murdock's teammate, Lanny Bassham, had entered as the odds-on favorite. He was the returning silver medalist from the previous Games and the most recent world champion. He knew his U.S. teammate well and respected Murdock's skill.

The Individual Air-Rifle competition required shooters to hit a target ten times repeated over four rounds, from three different positions—prone, standing, and kneeling—120 shots in all. Bassham had fallen behind after the second round, and the scores for the final round, the kneeling position, were very slow to come up. When the leader board showed Murdock at the top, he was first to congratulate her. Next came cheers from her parents, family, and five-year-old son.

However, the judges were still conferring in a lengthy discussion that dragged on. Murdock's final score of 1162 had gone up quickly. But Bassham's score of 1161 took a long time and was still in dispute. As Murdock recalls it: "I thought I had won and Lanny said he thought he had one more point. They were going to check our targets and we waited about three hours and finally one of the guys came out and I asked if they had done the targets and he said, 'Oh, yeah, you won.' About a half-hour later they came out and changed it and gave Lanny the other point."[11]

The final ruling was that an official had made an error in writing down a score. They had needed to check the targets more than once. Bassham might have been keeping track of his own shots, all 30 of them in that key final round. Perhaps he and his coaches expected one more 10 instead of the 9 that came up, if he knew those details.

Still, was there extra scrutiny because of whose name sat at the top? Did that require everyone to go through and triple-check their sheets? Did they review all the targets, one more time, with an extra-sharp magnifying glass to see if they had perhaps missed a shot that was one millimeter more into the 10-side rather than the 9-side, for Bassham? Did they do exactly the same with Murdock's targets?

Murdock had, in fact, earned her spot in Montreal with similar drama during the U.S. Trials. She had beaten the gold medalist from 1972 with a tie-breaker based on *her* last set of ten kneeling shots, with one more 10. Here, it seems, she was one short. She was a little concerned. Strange things had happened before, when a woman was atop the leader board: "I had been screwed on a couple of other occasions big-time, so it doesn't surprise you. They said we were both from the same team so they thought it would be OK. We said why don't we have two gold medals and no silver like in boxing, but they said no."[12]

Underdogs have seen this happen plenty of times. Evelyn Hall watched Babe Didrikson given the benefit of the doubt in close calls. Bobbie Rosenfeld had seen smiling Betty Robinson chosen when the photos couldn't tell who had won. The nod to the expected winner isn't always gender-based. Beating the front-runner always requires the one with lower expectations to go beyond proof.

As with hurdler Hall, the American team officials would not have cared which athlete won, as long USA was attached to their name. Many would assume that Murdock would be thrilled just to be there competing or even to get on the podium.

Yet, if she had been a man, would there have been more of an opportunity to protest, or at least for her to question the outcome? On the other hand, more than one coach said later that they were using telescopes and that something had been missed for Bassham. If a score had been missed, then it was right to correct it.

Murdock and Bassham ended in a tie, and the tie-breaker rule, the one Murdock knew well, gave Bassham the edge. He was awarded the gold and Murdock the silver. He said he felt the injustice of it, wanted them both to get the gold, and "gallantly"[13] pulled Murdock up to stand with him on the podium. They listened to "The Star Spangled Banner" together.

Contemporary shooting competitions now have tie-breaker shoot-offs to avoid this kind of incident. But the ISSF made another, even bigger change. By the time the next Olympiad returned to North America in 1984, the open rifle and pistol events were split into men's and women's events. Women gained three events, men kept their six, and two events remained open to both genders in the shotgun groups.

The ISSF hailed it as a step forward. It was also a way to ensure that this awkward situation didn't repeat itself. If it seems far-fetched that the ISSF simply didn't want men to lose to women, consider what happened when history did repeat itself—in skeet shooting.

Skeet shooters use shotguns to aim at clay pigeons, reminiscent of the days of

Eight. Olympic Gigantism and the Zero-Sum Game (1924–1976)   129

aristocratic hunting parties, when dogs (e.g., foxhounds) and horses were specially bred for the purpose and servants were brought in to flush the game. Skeet requires shooters to aim at two separate targets from multiple positions around a half circle. Trap, another shotgun event, involves aiming at targets (Single or Double Trap) in rapid succession.

In 1992, in the still-open division of Olympic skeet, a woman won the gold medal. China's Zhang Shan shot perfect rounds in the qualifying and semifinal heats. She set a record on her way to the first Olympic win for a woman in an open division.

After Zhang's historic achievement, women were barred from skeet shooting in the very next Games. Or, as the ISSF would have characterized it, women were (finally) granted their own competitions in recognition of their demonstrated abilities. Instead of continuing with open events, both Men's and Women's Double Trap events were added, again separating women while appearing to grant them their long-requested additional events. Seventeen-year-old American Kim Rhode won the event in front of a hometown 1996 Atlanta crowd.

Fig. 22. Was it chivalry for Lanny Bassham (USA, center) to let Margaret Murdock (USA, left) "share" the national anthem for his 1976 Air Rifle win? Or was it awareness of something odd in the scoring? Also pictured is bronze medalist Werner Siebhold (FRG) (Associated Press).

The segregation of events continued and so did the criticism. Recently, when a 2014 study of college athletes showed no difference between male and female rifle shooters, USA Shooting explained to the researchers that separating the events was better for women. They said it allowed more growth in the participation of women across these newly added events.[14]

The ISSF also pointed out that because of difference in the number of shots and distance of the targets, Olympic men and women's shooting events are different. This makes results hard to compare. Of course, it is within the ISSF's purview to make them comparable. At least in Tokyo, the plan was for women to shoot the same number of times as men, which was comparable. Also added was a mixed team competition, a compromise of sorts, and a way to move toward balancing the number of athletes by gender. But opening the shooting events to both genders for individual competitions is not under discussion.

Gold-medalist Zhang competed in Women's Skeet in the 2000 Sydney Games but only managed eighth place and bowed out to younger teammates afterward. Rhode came in seventh in Skeet but took a second medal, a bronze in Double Trap. In the next Games, Rhode proceeded to another gold in Double Trap. After that, the Double Trap event was eliminated.

No matter for Rhode, who by then had become one of the world's best Olympic shooters.[15] She took three more medals in Skeet, one in each color. Her bronze medal in Rio 2016 was a record-breaker. She became the first Olympian *ever* to medal across six consecutive Olympics, a feat that neither Michael Phelps nor Isabelle Werth were able to achieve. She is also the only person to medal on five separate continents, a feat that will be difficult to duplicate, since it requires an athlete to have skill, longevity, and the luck to maintain both as the Olympics hop around the world.[16]

This is the full circle, then, from Murdock making history. She beat men to earn her spot and gained the recognition that women could hold their own. This opened the door for other women, even if it closed the door to open-gender events. One of those successors created the ultimate record, one that no one may ever beat—man or woman.

The Zero-Sum Game

Women shooters proved capable of being the best in the world—twice, in open competitions. Proving themselves equal to men was one way for organizers to "find" room for separate extra events. Other sports continued with a more traditional path, simply pushing directly for more. Alpine skiers did it successfully, even though their cross-country skiing and speed skating friends would have to wait decades longer. Sometimes it worked, and sometimes it didn't.

From the IOC's point of view, as the *Olympic Report* from Helsinki noted, the problem was the stubbornness of the international federations, who simply refused to cut back. In 1948, however, one federation set the tone with a compromise that would be the forerunner of future discussions. The event was in canoeing, where adding women became a bargaining chip.

Europeans love canoe racing, almost as much as they like rowing, a discipline where the Finns and Venetians debate who came first. Germans are particularly partial to canoeing. In Berlin 1936, Germany added 9 different kinds of canoe sprints. The paddlers used the same venues as the rowers, arguing that this kept costs down, though that wasn't a prime concern for the Nazis. It seems almost an afterthought to mention that Germany took 7 of the 21 medals, and Austria another 7, so that two-thirds of the medals came from the same region.

As London began planning for the more austere 1948 games, the International Canoeing Federation (ICF) lobbied for more events, naturally. They suggested relays

Eight. Olympic Gigantism and the Zero-Sum Game (1924–1976)

and events for women. The IOC clearly had to rein this in. The London organizers fixed the limit of canoeing events at the number from the prior Olympics. Women or relays could be added, but not both, and only if men gave up an event.

This precedent would echo down through other sports and other countries for years to come. In order to combat gigantism, adding women's events would become a zero-sum game. Adding—whether that meant enlarging the sport as a whole or correcting the massive imbalance between women and men's events—would mean subtracting for the men.

Since the nine canoeing events had only been contested once, it didn't seem too difficult to allocate one to female canoers. Thus, the inaugural women's contest in the canoe spring kayaks, the K-1,500 m, was won by Karen Hoff of Denmark, in front of Alida Geertruida van der Anker-Doedens of the Netherlands and Fritzi Schwingl of Austria.

The battle to add whitewater slalom events started the gigantism complaints all over again. Any host country would now have to build courses unsuitable for other purposes. Munich happily added the slalom events in 1972, but every Games since then has debated whether it's worth the expense to include an entire venue for slalom. Many of those whitewater venues became the poster children for Olympic excess, shown turning to mold and weeds only a few years after the Games concluded. Yet lobbying for the slalom events never stops.

By the time the Games were awarded to Rio 2016, there were 16 separate canoeing events for men and women. The division by gender was still 11 and 5, nowhere near parity. The zero-sum plan for Tokyo in 2020 was thus summarized: "C2 men loses its status as an official Olympic event and is to be replaced by C1 women."[17] Translated: "Men will have to give up their contests for doubles slalom in order for women to have an event at all. Then, both genders will have a Canoe Single Slalom event. They both keep a Kayak Single Slalom event."

It is a simple pattern. Expand, expand, expand, and when parity or fairness is required, complain that the men must "give up" something in order to make room for women, even though the sport as a whole has continuously added. As gigantism continues to be a perennial problem, criticized by every journalist from 1928 onward, it's well remembered that complaining didn't stop the addition of canoeing, slalom, Alpine skiing, synchronized diving, short-track speed skating, and so on.

All in all, after decades of lobbying and debunking the notion of "appropriate" sports for women, after launching into track and field and skiing, bolstered by the popularity of gymnastics and figure skating, women had made decided inroads into Olympic sports, far beyond tapping a few croquet balls. Women were happy by 1960 to be permitted in eight of the eighteen core disciplines. Nearly halfway there, after only 64 years! A giant slice of what remained in the other ten sports were competitions that involved far more athletes. Those were the teams.

The Greek ideal, according to Coubertin was "the individual adult male."[18] The 1896 list of options had excluded both women *and* teams. But it only took one Olympics before soccer, rugby, and the tug of war were pulling groups of athletes into the competition schedule. After teams entered the Paris 1900 Games, they remained a staple of the Olympics schedule ever since. However, the prejudice against women playing in teams stayed firm through the years. Women were barred from Olympic team sports, despite playing them widely in international championships for decades.

This changed in 1964, driven by several forces. The rising ride of feminism merged with nationalism to clamor for more team sports. The zero-sum dynamic was offset by every country's desire to up their own medal count. When women's teams were finally allowed, their stories showed how nations and genders intersect.

One of the first and biggest successes was for a team to rebuild the confidence of a country. It involved another sport that had been popular with the military. That sport was volleyball.

Part III

Fighting for Access

Nine

Nationalism and the Rise of the Teams (1964–1976)

When Japan bid to host the 1964 Olympics in early 1959, they might not have thought the fate of their national psyche would rest on the resilience of six volleyball players gathered from textile factories scattered around the Osaka countryside. They surely didn't know (or care) that it would pave the way for the Norwegian women's handball or Australian basketball teams.

Volleyball wasn't even part of the Olympic program when Japan first bid for the Games. American women didn't play much basketball in college yet. Handball was still a young sport in Scandinavia. The "women's team" question was routinely booted off the Olympic Executive Committee agenda.

Change comes slow to the IOC. Advancement isn't step-by-step but lurches in a drunken walk down blind alleys and through short-cuts that end in dead ends. Progress is haphazard.

The first Olympic organizers didn't want any teams. They quickly softened, and the 1900 Paris Olympics included both teams and women—but no women's teams. As Chart Two in the Appendix shows, rowing, soccer, and water polo were played, but by men only. The oldest team sports were the slowest to allow women, with several taking more than 70 years to relinquish their exclusivity. Water polo took the whole century.

Coubertin's vision was that women should not participate in team sports, unless "absolutely necessary."[1] The organizers strictly adhered to that rule. After all, what exactly did "necessary" mean in the context of a voluntary sports-entertainment undertaking? Evidently nothing.

The ongoing source of the specific resistance to women's team sports was never clear, beyond Coubertin's early pronouncements. IOC presidents did argue that they had to keep the numbers down, and teams added numbers. Women played organized soccer, baseball, basketball, and cricket worldwide throughout the 20th century, but their leagues went unrecognized in the sporting federations, so their opportunities for Olympic play stayed off the table for 68 years.

The door finally opened a crack in 1964 when the first women's team sport was approved. This change came about for two primary reasons.

The first was unabashed nationalism. Countries have their own favorite sports. They want more opportunities to win in them. Americans always think of basketball

Nine. Nationalism and the Rise of the Teams (1964–1976)

or baseball, but the long-standing Olympic countries all have their own cherished pastimes, and most don't start with a "b." The same kind of fevered passion for March Madness or the World Series can be found with water polo in Yugoslavia, field hockey in India, and ice hockey in Canada.

Such fervor for national pride sometimes cloaks itself. Consider the following excerpt from a speech to the IOC:

> Women should have equal rights for participation in the Olympic Games ... it is high time that women should be given equal rights to participate ... in those events at the Olympic Games in which they compete at the official international championships. ...basketball, cycling, shooting, handball, and rowing.[2]

While this may sound like Susan B. Anthony addressing the United Nations, it was, in fact, a speech by the Soviet IOC delegate, Konstantin Andrianov, in 1971. Aside from marching rhetorically with the suffragettes, the USSR also happened to have the world's best teams in the sports on Andrianov's list: women's basketball, cycling, and rowing, as well as a few not on his list, like handball and volleyball. Team USSR had a strong and continuous desire to add as many team events as possible to prop up their medal count. *Votes for women!*

The second reason the door opened a crack in 1964 was legislation aimed to improve education in the United States, although Title IX took decades before it improved the status of women in team sports.

Even if it all started with a whimper, rather than a bang, or even if progress was meandering and erratic, rather than quick and definitive, team play eventually blossomed. From the translation of rules at a kitchen table in Norway, to the back room deal-making in Washington, D.C., to the Nichibo corporate committee aiming to "conquer" other textile firms, the reasons for team play were often unrelated to the goals of the Olympic Executive Committee.

Still, change came, and once the Japanese women worked their magic, assumptions that women's teams wouldn't be compelling to watch went by the wayside.

Enter the "Oriental Witches."

Murderous Exercise

> "The Japanese, who looked like schoolgirls, had been trained by a coach who subjected them to an almost sadistic regime of Zen-like intensity and rigor."—Allen Guttmann[3]

Kasai Masae, captain of the Japanese women's national volleyball team, was no schoolgirl. Kasai was actually 31 years old on the night of the 1964 Olympic final. Moreover, while the brutal techniques of her infamous "ogre" coach, Daimatsu Hirobumi, included long hours and physically punishing drills, the howling disappointment of 97 million Japanese would have been far worse for Kasai if they had lost. The honor of the entire country was put in her hands.

The life of Kasai and her teammates up until then might have sounded familiar to anyone who follows American football. She was recruited to join the Nichibo volleyball team while she was a standout player in secondary school. She was taller than average, with quick reflexes, and the recruiter thought she showed potential. Kasai's parents were thrilled at the offer.

What might not sound as familiar was that Nichibo was a textile company, and the recruiter was hiring Kasai to work at a nearby factory. This was more like Colonel McCombs hiring Babe Didrikson for Employers Casualty than the University of Alabama recruiting a new tight end. Fifteen-year-old Kasai was soon shifted to a bigger factory with a stronger team, then to their Kaizuka branch in Osaka. At the time, Nichibo also consolidated its factory teams into one at Kaizuka, with an explicit plan to "conquer volleyball."[4]

Luckily, they found a Kaizuka factory supervisor, Daimatsu Hirobumi, to coach the women. He had played volleyball. He had also been a platoon commander in the war, so he knew how to get a group in shape. For him, failure was not an option.

But, volleyball? Why was volleyball the women's first team sport, and why in Japan?

Volleyball, as a women's team sport, came late to the party but ended up first to lead the Olympic dance. The game was designed as "mintonette"—badminton with a ball—under rules first devised at the YMCA in 1895, only four years after they invented basketball. Players didn't need to be tall, at least not as tall as in basketball. A game with only a net and a ball, rather than a specially placed basket, was also easier than basketball to play. One scholar also suggests that, because volleyball does not involve physical contact due to the separation of teams by the net, it might have made it more acceptable for women to play.[5]

Exported overseas by the army and the YMCA, volleyball still remained a poor cousin to other team sports in the U.S. and Europe. For years, it was a mere sub-division of the International Handball Federation. The game proved more popular in Asia, though, where Filipinos even pioneered a few key rule changes like the three-hit limit as well as the set and spike, which they called the "bomba."

The Japanese, whose height was not conducive to the YMCA-imported basketball, preferred volleyball. Volleyball required speed, agility, and superior teamwork, and while tall spikers were useful, their advantage could be countered.

After World War II, when Japan's huge textile industry began rebuilding, companies reached into the countryside for inexpensive labor, especially seeking young women who had traditionally only managed the home or worked in cottage industries. As a way of fostering teamwork, companies added intramural games. They chose volleyball as an acceptable female sport. Initially, then, Nichibo's corporate teams were created to make workers more productive.

Meanwhile in Europe, the game also eventually gained a foothold. Frenchman Paul Libaud launched the *Fédération Internationale de Volleyball* (FIVB) in 1947. While shepherding the organization over the next four decades, he made persuasive inroads as a delegate to the IOC. In 1957, "volley-ball" was added to the Games.

A side note in the meeting minutes commended Libaud's patience, noting that the sport had "applied for recognition for a long time."[6] Ten years was long enough, apparently, if the sport was proposed by a Frenchman. In the same meeting, women's speed skating, which had applied for 28 years, was delayed for more information gathering.

On May 26, 1959, Tokyo's bid for the 1964 Olympics was also approved. Japan was itching to show the world their economic miracle, the triumph of hard work and innovation that had allowed the country to rise from the ashes. While it was odd that volleyball was chosen over other sports to inaugurate women's team sports, the host country was all for it. Japan would host the tournament, and, as it happens, they had a women's volleyball team, a good one. Thus, in 1962, the IOC tacked on women's volleyball to the schedule partly because it already had Japanese men's volleyball. As it turns out, the women were better.

Kasai Masae might not have remembered the day her team's 257-win streak started. Once the streak caught attention, nicknames followed. Coach Daimatsu was called "ogre" or "demon" in the Japanese press because his practices were merciless. The athletes would work a full day in the factory, then practice from 4 p.m. until midnight, with only one break. The workouts were nicknamed *satsujin taiso*: murderous exercise.[7]

When Kasai and team finally found themselves invited to the 1960 international volleyball championships, they shocked everyone by winning all but one of their matches. They lost only to the Soviet Union, the winner of the prior two tournaments. The Japanese second place finish was sudden. Soviet journalists deemed it other-worldly and nicknamed the team "Oriental witches."

In the next championship, two years later, the Japanese women continued their magic, thrashing through the pool play and obliterating Poland, Brazil, Bulgaria, and Romania. They dropped the first game in the finals to the Soviets, then never lost a game. They were newly crowned FIVB champions and became favorites for the next tournament, which would be the Olympics.

To beat team USSR, Coach Daimatsu the drill sergeant devised a strategy to counteract taller opponents. His drills worked players low to the ground, requiring hundreds of "burpies" and squats to build strong and flexible knees. Players would frog-hop back and forth across the court and in figure-eights around balls.

Then, they would perform an innovative exercise that was punishing and brilliant in design. It was called *kaiten reeshibu*, rotate and receive. Daimatsu would fire balls hard and low at individual players, just past their reach. The athlete had to run sideways, dive to hit the ball, and somersault through a shoulder roll back onto their feet. They must dive to the floor; there was no way to cheat gravity. Once back on their feet, a ball was already being hurled to their opposite side.

The team would drill for hours, with players sobbing from bruises and nearly dislocated shoulders. If a player was overly distraught, Daimatsu would bark that they should quit and go home to their mothers, or, worse, play for South Korea.

Nichibo allowed the press to cover the practices, and journalists were horrified at the harsh treatment. Labor unions criticized Nichibo, and sportswriters portrayed Daimatsu as a kind of Svengali. An infamous *Sports Illustrated* article described the team as "Driven Beyond Dignity," as the American writer sniffed: "Ah, but then, I said to myself, it's only volleyball, played by girls."[8]

As another journalist observed,[9] no one would have written *it's only high school football, played by boys.* Daimatsu noted: "They do it because they choose to. The preparation for winning is a personal, individual challenge."[10]

For the women, surviving the drill made them battle ready to represent their country. They had the option of quitting, but playing for Japan brought personal honor. The majority stayed. Kasai explained, "Whenever our team won, we were convinced that his hard training was the right way to go, and so we would practice and train hard again, and then we would win again."[11]

Anthropologist and historian Christan Tagsold further put rotate and receive in the context of Japan's economic miracle:

> Daimatsu did for volleyball and Japanese sports, in general, what Morita Akio did as a leader of Sony and what Ohno Taiichi achieved at Toyota by introducing the Toyota Production System. The rolling dive recovered lost time and reduced the burden on Japanese bodies caused by their inferiority compared to Western athletes … the kaiten reeshibu could be read very naively as the story of post-war Japan. The Japanese fell, but they got back on their feet again quickly.[12]

Volleyball was no longer "just a sport" for the Japanese.

Japan had also pinned their Olympics hopes on judo, their true national sport. The country had pinned their hopes on their open-weight champion, Akio Kaminaga, against massive Dutchman Anton Geesink. Unfortunately, Kaminaga took a humiliating beating from Geesink. After that, the Nichibo team, Daimatsu, and Kasai had their work cut out for them. One player quipped that if they did not win, "they would have to leave."[13]

Team captain Kasai had wanted to retire much earlier. After fifteen years of working and playing, she wanted to start a family. She had ended at least one budding romance in order to play. As the tournament began, she saw a friend in the stands with her daughter, and it reminded Kasai of what she had missed. But she had been compelled to stay; "the public did not allow me to retire. The only way to respond to the public expectation was to win the gold medal."[14]

On October 23, 1964, the day after the disastrous open-weight judo final, the women from Nichibo Kaizuka took the weight of the country onto their shoulders,[15] shoulders banged and bruised for ten hours a day, seven days a week, for nearly a decade. They faced a crackerjack, sophisticated Soviet squad nearly six inches taller on average. Up to that point in the round robin tournament, Team USSR hadn't lost a game.

Between the hubbub of the press, the entry of visiting dignitaries like Princess Michiko, and pre-game ceremonies, the start was delayed for an agonizing half hour. The gymnasium was stuffed to the rafters with 4,000 hopeful fans. An estimated 90 percent of Japan tuned in to watch on TV, still the highest-rated program ever in Japanese television history. Streets were emptied as people rushed home to watch in their living rooms. The country paused and held its breath.

When the game finally began, the women briskly got down to business, steaming through their first two sets, 15–11 and 15–8. Japan pushed forth in the third set, quickly jamming in points until the score was 11–3.

As successful service points mounted, it was as if they could see the end on the horizon, after all the hard work, all the demonic workouts. The princess was clapping and smiling, the crowd on its feet. Yet each one-more-point began to feel like pushing a boulder uphill.

That boulder got heavier. The towering Soviets didn't give up easily. At 13–6, they battled back, using their own counter-strategies. For example, instead of spiking the ball downward while facing the net, they would smash it sideways. It was hard to predict and even harder to defend.

The score reached 14–8, but Team USSR was not going away without a dogfight. Not as much has been written about the Soviet workouts compared with Daimatsu's murderous exercises, but volleyball teams today routinely perform "Russian drills." The Soviet players had their own techniques, incentives, and burdens.

Team USSR pushed a little harder to take momentum away, and, suddenly, the score was 14–13. Daimatsu called a much needed time-out: "What are you doing? Calm down. All you need is one point to win, right? Take it easy."[16]

Captain Kasai took the serve back. Both sides had dug their trenches deep. Volleyball rules at the time still only allowed scoring for the serving team, and the service switched back and forth, five times in a row. The tension corkscrewed further.

The ending, when it came, was abrupt. Japan served, and a Soviet player prepared for one of their signature sideways smashes. This time, as her arm extended to push the ball over, her hand flopped on the net. The whistle blew. Cameras of the world caught the error and showed it—still show it—highlighted and magnified. Point to Japan. Game over, because of the Soviet foul.

The Japanese players screamed with relief and exhaustion. Daimatsu, true to his stoic nature, stayed frozen in his seat as his team celebrated. The years of work had ended for him as well.[17] Later, after the dignified medal ceremony, the team would toss him, smiling, in the air.

The win for the women's volleyball team was Japan's proof that they had risen from the ashes. The press might call the volleyball players schoolgirls, robots, or witches, but Japan recognized them for the athletic warriors they had become.

Kasai finally got a boost in her marital search. She was introduced to her future husband by the prime minister himself. When Daimatsu retired in 1965, Kasai retired shortly after, and married Nakamura, a career military officer.

The matchmaking press followed the romances of all the players as if they were part of one big Japanese family. One by one, the athlete's courtships and nuptials made the papers, until the last of the team was married off, and the public could close the book on them.

In later years, the Japanese women's team won two more golds and a silver at the Games. The men's team itself eventually earned a silver, although years after the 1964 spotlight. Over time, the textile industry declined, too, as automation and cheaper overseas labor forced Nichibo and others to diversify or merge with other companies.

Volleyball is still popular in Japan, and corporate team volleyball still exists, but now under Toyota and NEC. Japanese teams have ceded their national pride to others from Brazil and Cuba.

Lost in all the hoopla was the original resistance against women's Olympic teams. The IOC had long wondered whether women's teams possibly could be worth

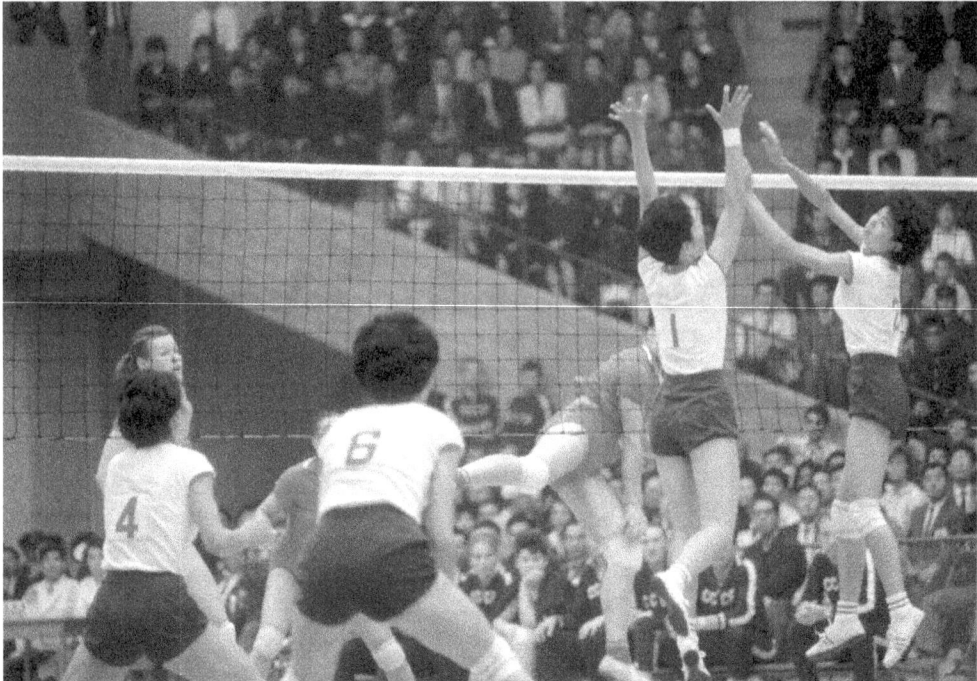

Fig.23. Japan's 1964 Women's Volleyball team became national heroes after beating the taller Soviets. Kasai Masae (#1, right) and Miyamoto Emiko (#2, right) jump to the net, as Tatyana Roschina (USR, left, opposite), Yuriko Handa (#4) and Sata Issobe (#6) watch (courtesy of the International Olympic Committee).

watching. Ninety percent of the Japanese public answered with a resounding yes. Women could take on all the hopes of a country, even when the strongest man in their national combat sport could not. The innate aversion to women's teams had been worn down, a little.

Handball: Pink in Norway, Blue in Germany

Konstantin Andrianov got his wish for more women's Olympic teams, although it took another dozen years. The IOC continued at its snail's pace. Yet, if the Soviet Union's ulterior motive in advocacy was cultural world domination, the Soviet delegate's persistent advocacy on behalf of women's sports benefited everyone when the logjam was broken.

Three women's disciplines were finally added in 1976: handball, basketball, and rowing. Handball's journey is a particularly illuminating example of how sports can be gendered, even unintentionally. As Professor Gerd von der Lippe explains,[18] handball developed remarkably different approaches by gender and by country.

Today in Norway, women play handball. In Germany, men form most of the handball teams. For example, in 1990, 66 percent of the registered handball players in Norway were female, while in Germany, 70 percent were male. The reason for the difference has to do with historical origins.

For the unfamiliar, handball is a goal-based game, similar to soccer but with an indoor field about one-third the size. The goal and teams are also smaller, with seven on a side. Hands are allowed while feet are not. Offensive players can pass, dribble, or throw the ball at the goal, but they must stay behind a marked "safety zone" near the goal, until the ball leaves their hand. Scoring is frequent and fast.

Handball is a sport virtually unknown to Americans, whose version of a similarly named game against a wall bears little resemblance to the wildly popular European pastime. On the other hand, the Danish, who are passionate handball players, feel about basketball much the way Americans feel about handball. *Huh? What's basketball?*[19]

The Danes and Germans collectively invented handball, although Denmark can trace its origination of rules back to 1906, while Germany can claim it was first to organize national handball competitions in 1920. The sport was so popular in Northern Europe that when the International Handball Federation was created, basketball and volleyball were originally included as sub-categories.

German handball may even have been originally designed for women, whose turn-of-the-century restrictive clothing and presumed-inferior athletic capabilities were thought to better fit a game where the ball was thrown from a standing position rather than while running.[20] In fact, in the initial 1919 German version, "all body contact and aggression were forbidden."

The problem in Germany for handball aficionados of the 1920s was that the sport wasn't catching on. Karl Schelenz, a teacher at a German school for physical education wanted to boost handball's popularity. He proposed hockey-like combat rules to the men's version, turning it into a *Kampfspiel,* where players could hit or punch the ball out of an opponent's hand.

Within a decade, twice as many men as women were playing German handball. Today's rules—which are now the same for men and women—no longer allow this type of grappling, although incidental contact is allowed. The game is still popular (for men). Modern German men's league play has been known to fill 40,000-seat stadiums.

In Norway, however, the game has long been viewed as a "women's game." The current Norwegian women's team is considered one of the best in the world, having appeared in 22 of the last championship finals. Meanwhile, the men's team in Norway often falls short of Olympic qualification.[21]

Von der Lippe traces this gender division back to 1937, when the Norwegian Handball Federation was first formed. The just-elected president sat at a kitchen table to choose rules. He adopted from the Swedish version, not the German version, choosing rules which didn't allow "combat." The Swedish version allowed some physical contact, but with emphasis on "speed [which] suited [women's] techniques and tactics ... [and] tended to avoid aggressive body contact."[22] Within three years, women made up 69 percent of the total Norwegian players, and the rest is "herstory."

Von der Lippe also noted that Norwegian female athletes, skilled in the sports that men dominated, like speed skating or cross-country skiing, were routinely pushed toward handball as a more acceptable sport. For instance, Laila Schou Nilsen, who won that first Alpine skiing medal for Norway described in Chapter

Seven, ended up better known as a star handball player. Nilsen even served as the first female president of the Norwegian Handball Association in the 1960s.

Overall, even though handball today is essentially the same sport for men and women worldwide, it is perceived to "belong" to different genders, depending on the country.

A recent controversy in the 2020 Youth Olympics brought the European sport into the world-wide spotlight. Beach handball was added as a brand-new sport to the Youth Games, with rules mandating swimsuit-like uniforms. Its better-known cousin, beach volleyball, no longer required bikinis, but beach handball pulled out a much older rulebook. Female players had to wear bikinis, of the super-skimpy kind. This created problems, especially when many of the players were under legal age. American Samoa, a country known for religious conservatism, nearly forfeited their spot in the world qualifiers because of the optics of young girls playing in such little cloth.

Meanwhile, the Norwegian teenagers took matters into their own hands and wore swim shorts similar to the men's uniform. They were fined. The backlash in public opinion surprised the rule-makers, who hearkened back to days when they could command any uniform they wished, those days when long skirts prevented women from swimming. The discussion launched a cascade of tut-tutting over beach handball, and many in the U.S. confused the sport with its volleyball cousin. The controversy may even have a side benefit, by piquing the interest of outraged American feminists enough to bring them to the sport.

On the other hand, the highest average temperature in a Norway summer is a balmy 71 F (22 C), which is just barely warm enough for a bikini. The handball players may end up wearing long woolen underwear beneath those swimsuits anyway.[23]

All the World Loves Women's Basketball

Like handball, basketball rules have also ebbed and flowed, by gender and by country. Unlike handball, though, basketball has been popular worldwide, for both men and women, since the game's invention at the end of the 19th century.

The first U.S. women's college basketball game (1896) happened only a year after the first U.S. men's college game (1895). Many Olympic athletes started in basketball, especially those who gravitated to track, from Babe Didrikson to Wilma Rudolph to Jackie Joyner-Kersee.

But women's basketball is also big in other countries. In Australia, women's basketball is one of the most popular sports, even though it came in through something of a back door. When basketball spread to Europe in the 1900s—exported by the YMCA like volleyball—gym teachers in London altered the rules to appeal to women who still wore restrictive clothing. The teachers created a variation called "netball," where the ball could only be passed or shot at the basket. Netball has no dribbling, no running with the ball, and no excessive physical contact. Perfect, if playing in a corset and a long skirt.

From London, the game spread through the British Commonwealth, eventually to Australia. The Australians took to it with a passion, until netball became the most popular women's team sport in the country. It still ranks in the top ten. Over time, as skirts shortened and women sought more challenge, some netball players shifted to basketball.

As a result, the women's Australian basketball team developed into a top-tier team. After five Olympic medals, the women outranked their country's men's team, which has had numerous individual stand-out players, but no team medals as yet. Of course, men have long had other team sports to choose from, including soccer, rugby, water polo, and their own favorite contact sport, "Aussie rules football."

In the early half of the 1900s, Russia and other Eastern European countries flocked to basketball as well. In fact, the first international women's basketball match was played in St. Petersburg in 1909. By the mid–1970s, the USSR had built a strong talent pool on their women's team and was vying for basketball world domination, right along with their petite gymnasts and muscular track stars. After the women's game was admitted to the Olympics, helped by the strong urging from the Soviet delegation, Team USSR's women quickly equaled the number of golds as their men (two), even though the men had a two-decade head start.

The U.S./USSR women's basketball rivalry in its heyday was as strong as the men's. The first 1976 team final between the U.S. and USSR featured multiple legends. Nancy Lieberman and Ann Meyer were two of the pioneers on the American women's side. Meyer was the first woman offered an athletic scholarship (to UCLA) and the first to sign a contract with an NBA team. Lieberman played on professional women's teams, coached briefly in the NBA, and became an announcer for an NBA team. On the opposing side, the Soviet Union featured the best player in the world at the time, seven-foot tall Uljana Semjonova.[24] All

Fig.24. Seven-foot Uljana Semjonova (URS) won gold medals in 1976 and 1980 and never lost a game in international competition. Semjonova shoots over Japan's Keiko Namai, as USSR's Tamāra Daunene, left, waits for the rebound. The Soviets won the qualifier over Japan 98–75 (courtesy of the International Olympic Committee).

three women were inducted into the first class of the Women's Basketball Hall of Fame.

The Soviets took the 1976 gold medal. After the boycotts, American women got their revenge in the 1988 Seoul Olympics, beating Team USSR in the semifinals. A solid Unified team took the gold back in 1992. As the American and Soviet teams continued their slugfest, other teams burned to knock both of them off the podium. Australia has been recently climbing the ladder, along with Spain, France, and Serbia. Overall, women's basketball today thrives around the globe.

Still, American women's basketball waxed and waned against international competition. Strong in the heyday of Employers Casualty, the pipeline was depleted by the 1950s. Other countries had sports schools, robust club networks, and textile corporations to build out their talent pool. U.S. men's players came from colleges, but, in 1976, American colleges hosted only a handful of women's basketball programs. To transform into the powerhouse Olympic teams that compete under the American flag today, women athletes in college needed more support.

That support came from Title IX.

Ten

Not So Fast

The Tortuous Journey of Title IX (1972–2000)

> "They learned the hard way that even groundbreaking civil rights laws are not self-executing."[1]—Kelly Belanger

Nationalism may have driven the Japanese to volleyball and the Australians to basketball, but many countries expected America to lead the way in sports, especially in those invented in America. Instead, U.S. women lagged behind in the sports until a second significant change raised worldwide competition for the better.

When the U.S. Congress passed Title IX in 1972, some thought that American women would immediately gain all the freedom to play the sports that had eluded them. The USOC, of course, was staunchly behind Title IX, knowing that it would likely improve America's Olympic positioning for international medals. *The Future Is Feminist!*

It wasn't like flipping a switch, though. The 1972 amendment to the Civil Rights Act was a handful of words that said simply that women had an equal right to education. Next came years of stonewalling by educational institutions, uneven regulatory enforcement by political bureaucracies, and infinite patience while women took freezing showers and used playing fields at midnight.

Eventually, Title IX helped elevate U.S. women's teams into a better competitive position on the world stage. Where the U.S. went, other nations followed, as stronger-funded teams improved competition for everybody. Soccer, water polo, rowing—with America finally fueling a pipeline of talented athletes through college, international rivalries developed in full.

But it did seem to take forever.

Just a Few Simple Words

> "No person in the United States shall, on the basis of sex, be excluded from participation in, be denied the benefits of, or be subjected to discrimination under any education program or activity receiving federal financial assistance."[2]—Title IX, Section 1681, part (a)

At 17, American swimmer Donna De Varona had no place to go. She had set 18 world record titles and earned two Olympic gold medals. But in 1964, there were no women's swimming programs in colleges, no scholarships, and no organized competitions. In comparison, 18-year-old Mark Spitz performed poorly at the 1968 Olympics, despite holding several national records. He went on to Indiana University to train with the Hoosier swim team, improving his technique enough to return to Munich in 1972, where he won a record-setting seven gold medals. De Varona retired and became a sports broadcaster.[3]

These days, potential female athlete superstars, like Katie Ledecky (swimming), Breanna Stewart (basketball), or Megan Rapinoe (soccer), are bombarded with college recruiting offers. They now hone their skills in universities, as the men do. Unlike De Varona, swimmer Dara Torres won a 1984 Olympic medal while in high school. Then Torres swam for the University of Florida on a scholarship, earned a sackful of Olympic medals while she was still a Florida Gator, and parlayed her success into four more Olympic appearances, medaling until she turned 41. This was the impact that Title IX could have. But why was it necessary for college sports?

Colleges are critical to the American sporting infrastructure. In Europe and elsewhere, the club/league model successfully supports basketball, volleyball, and water polo. However, in the U.S., the club/league model only works for certain sports.[4] When leagues are fed athletes from colleges, as with football and basketball, the leagues are powerful. U.S. leagues that are stand-alone, like judo or fencing, only develop the occasional standout athlete.

In the late 1960s, U.S. women's college sports were few and underfunded. Increasing numbers of women were motivated by watching celebrity athletes, like Wilma Rudolph and Billie Jean King but struggled to find programs. They struggled to find other educational opportunities, too, as women then still made up only tiny percentages of graduate students and professors. The 1964 American Civil Rights Act, which ended discrimination in public accommodations, voting, and employment, had overlooked education.

American women pressured their legislators to close that gap. Congresswomen Patsy Mink and Edith Green worked with Bernice Sandler, a women's rights activist, to gather data and hold hearings in order to draft legislation. Women's sports were included but never the main objective.

Girls' sports were still primarily handled by physical education teachers, who maintained the stance they had held for nearly a century that competition was not a good path for athletics. The gym teachers stayed firm that schools should promote health for all females rather than developing athletes who also happened to be students. The old slogan "a sport for every girl and a girl for every sport" still held sway.

In 1967, the national group of physical education teachers created a separate Commission on Intercollegiate Athletics for Women, partly to create guidelines for national championships. Core to their beliefs was that such championships should promote broad participation because sports brings everyone a "sense of enjoyment, self-confidence, and physical well-being derived from demanding one's best performance."[5] Sports should bring out the best in *all*, not just in the *best*. A new organization, the Association for Intercollegiate Athletics for Women (AIAW) would oversee the task.

The AIAW then built out this cognitive-dissonant program. They set up national championships with an implicit goal of avoiding too much competition. At the time, they still barred colleges from recruiting and banned athletic scholarships.[6]

Their other immediate concern was to avoid conflict with the powerful National Collegiate Athletic Association (NCAA), the behemoth that ran men's events and had a stranglehold on media arrangements. In the late 1960s, the NCAA didn't take women's sports seriously and was happy to ban female athletes outright to prove their lack of interest.

Although the AIAW rules did limit the development of elite athletes, they were still strong advocates for women's sports and lobbied hard for Title IX. Their efforts on behalf of girls in elementary and middle school were especially needed. They didn't want girls to compete, but they did want them to play. In 1972, only one in 27 girls played sports at all, and only 2 percent of athletic budgets were allocated to women.[7]

When Title IX did pass on June 23, 1972, American schools took a deep breath to see what would happen next. The answer was nothing. Schools would need a lot more nudging before offering sports or shifting their budgets. The infamous experience of the women's Yale Crew team provides a classic example.

Women's rowing was added in 1972 at Yale, a school that had long boasted the "oldest college boat club in America." However, women didn't feel much like part of the grand tradition, as they were treated as second-class citizens when allotted inconvenient practice time, worn-out equipment, and spartan facilities. In particular, the existing boathouse had only one set of changing rooms and showers, designated for men only. All the women had was one tiny multi-use toilet.

After a sweaty, exhausting practice, the Yale women rowers would have to sit wet on the bus—often in freezing temperatures—for the long ride back to campus, often after waiting for the men to shower and change. Illness was common, and some even contracted pneumonia.

The women petitioned Yale to add facilities and, since Title IX had already passed, assumed their request would be honored. Instead, the Athletic Department installed a few extra porta-potties. The women pressed further, and plans to expand the boathouse were developed, then shelved due to budget constraints. This went on for four years.

Fed up in March of 1976, the women marched into the assistant athletic director's office to "take a shower." They pulled off their clothes, revealing the letters T-I-T-L-E-I-X inked on their backs. As it happened, they had invited the press and photographers. The photo of scantily clad women, as a "protest story," made its way into national news, including the *New York Times*. Yale expanded the boathouse.

However, Yale's administrative embarrassment did not start a trend. For several years after the act's passage, school districts and colleges dragged their feet, complaining that the words "no discrimination" were too vague. How was discrimination even defined? How were they supposed to achieve equality? Did the act even apply to sports?

The 1976 equal-rights-friendly U.S. Department of Health, Education, and Welfare (HEW) spent three years building out clarifying regulations. Meanwhile, less friendly congressmen passed amendments that sequestered funds for their beloved football. By the time the rules were in place in the 1980s, the government had switched political leanings, and enforcement by the Office of Civil Rights (OCR) was lax. Often, universities preferred to wait for a lawsuit, then spend money on defense lawyers rather than just building out their women's programs.

One key U.S. court case, *Grove City College vs. Terrell H. Bell,* proved a major setback for Title IX proponents. The 1984 Supreme Court ruled that Title IX didn't apply to the entire school, but only the part that received federal funding, which was rarely the athletic department. Growth of many women's programs screeched to a halt. In 1988, Congress amended the act to cover that loophole, but progress had slowed.

The back-and-forth continued. The Clinton administration in the 1990s strengthened enforcement in its Office of Civil Rights; the Bush administration in the 2000s relaxed control. A new batch of "reverse discrimination" court cases were filed. Men's sports that didn't end with "ball" complained that they were getting cut.

Wrestling programs, in particular, cried that they were being gutted because of Title IX. However, details in court (*National Wrestling Coaches vs. Department of Education,* 2004) showed that more wrestling programs had been cut before Title IX enforcement than after. Because wrestling programs couldn't show that weakening women's sports would restore their programs, their case was dismissed.

The less popular men's sports were correct that added women's programs were shrinking resources. Re-allocating budgets, by definition, is that zero-sum game again. For women to get anything, the money had to come from the 100 percent allocated to the men's side. Because huge budgets for football and basketball were treated as untouchable, all the other poorly funded sports would have to make the up the difference. Olympic sports were hit especially hard.

Of all things to benefit disproportionately, women's rowing actually got a boost, even if for the wrong reasons. Because rowing encompassed several events, with multi-person boats, rowing allowed schools to add bodies by the handful. In many cases, a program might end up with 60 women, which didn't exactly create "opportunity" for all of them. Rowing wasn't a panacea either. Boat shells and facilities were expensive, not to mention that plenty of schools weren't near water, especially in the cities.

Another sport that benefited was women's soccer. Shortly after the passage of Title IX, in 1975, only 80 schools carried soccer programs. By the year 2020, that number had jumped to 1,500.[8] (There are also 1,400 men's programs.) Colleges found soccer an easy sport to add because it only required a field and a ball. Teams were large, again bringing in lots of female bodies to help offset those football programs.

The impact on women's soccer was quicker than in other sports. Within ten years after Title IX, All-Americans from Stanford, the University of North Carolina, and UC Santa Barbara were stars for the U.S. National Women's Soccer Team. It was good timing. Women's soccer was rising in popularity worldwide just as U.S. women were getting more opportunities to play the sport. The Federation of Association Football (FIFA) had already been planning to add a Women's World Cup.

That first American group cobbled together from various colleges to play internationally was still woefully underfunded. Author Karen Blumenthal, whose book *Let Me Play* details the early experiences of female athletes under Title IX, says that her 1985 team headed to their first international tournament with no uniforms. "The day before the team was supposed to leave, they got all these boxes of shorts and shirts and sweats, and they were in men's sizes. So the team members stayed up into the night, sewing, taking in these clothes, so they would have something to wear."[9]

In their very first tournament, the Americans tied a much more experienced squad from Denmark. By the time of the first Women's World Cup in 1991, the ragtag band of U.S. women upset Norway. A loss in 1995 (to the Norwegians) was followed by a dramatic win over China in a penalty shoot-out in 1999, which led to an exultant Brandi Chastain ripping off her shirt. The image of Chastain became a recruiting poster. Some argue today that soccer has become the most ubiquitous extracurricular sport in the country.

Much was made over the U.S. women's "lesser" results in the past two Games after winning several Olympic and World Cup tournaments. In Rio, the Americans didn't advance out of the quarterfinals, and, in Tokyo, they eked out a bronze after lackluster games against Sweden and Canada. But, if anything, the media obsession over whether the women lived up to their potential was a different kind of signal. The women were finally being taken as seriously as the men, if they were now being subjected to the same nasty invective lobbed at men's teams that don't win. The P.E. teachers were not entirely wrong.

By 2010, Title IX's passage had finally reaped broad-based benefits. High school girls' sports participation had increased from 7 percent to 41 percent of all athletes, while women increased their college athletic pursuits sixfold. Women's college athletic budgets blossomed from 2 percent to 40 percent of total budgets in that 1972–2010 time period, and women students by then comprised 53 percent of the student population.[10]

There were two significant casualties, aside from the perceived loss to men's sports.[11] With opportunities for TV revenues from growing women's sports, the NCAA became interested in running things again. They maneuvered their way back into a coordinating role and, by 1983, had effectively swallowed up the AIAW.

The second major casualty was women in positions of power as coaches and administrators. When Title IX was first implemented, women made up 90 percent of the coaches of the tiny programs. As significant money was allocated to sports, male coaches were hired until that number had been cut in half by 2006.[12] New opportunities, new challenges.

Title IX, now past its fiftieth birthday, helped American women's teams compete. Still, for a truly great rivalry to be established, it takes two or more to tango. The newly strengthened U.S. women's teams were ready but needed to find other countries with the same passion for play. Romania and Australia, to name just two examples, were waiting in the wings.

The Carousel of Rowing Dominance

Rowing was the third new women's sport added in 1976 and provides a useful illustration of how national dynamics intersect with Title IX's impact. One of the oldest sports in the world, rowing is second nature to a dozen cultures—the Finns, Dutch, Italians, and even Pacific Islanders. Rivalries are fierce, whether between schools like Harvard and Yale, Oxford and Cambridge, or towns like Pisa and Venice.

Alice Milliat herself was an avid rower in the early 1920s, but women were considered too frail for Olympic rowing. The international rowing federation, *Fédération Internationale des Sociétés d'Aviron* (FISA), long supported the opinion that for women the sport was just too strenuous. Even when women were allowed, like into the hallowed 1927 Oxford/Cambridge Boat Race, the female crews rowed on the river separately and were judged on rhythm and style, rather than speed.[13]

It took years of persistent solicitation from rowers like Nelly Gambon-de-Vos of the Netherlands to persuade FISA president Thomas Keller. Keller finally admitted women to rowing events in the mid–1960s, although with distances half what the men rowed. Naturally, once FISA accepted women, they wanted more Olympic events, so Keller himself lobbied the IOC for inclusion.

He chose a tactic as old as the hills. The "typical" female rower he chose for the IOC presentation was single-sculler Ingrid Dieterle, who just happened to have "fantastic legs and a beautiful figure and long fair hair."[14] As the IOC debated which three events they should include, Monique Berlioux, a French Olympic swimmer and rowing enthusiast, insisted on "all six" FISA-sanctioned events. Men rowed in eight FISA events (and still do). Berlioux got her wish.

Adding rowing in 1976 affected women's Olympic sports for an entirely different reason. The first U.S. team was captained by a Philadelphia law student who led the team to a bronze medal. Despite taking up rowing only recently at tiny Connecticut College, Anita DeFrantz became the first Black American athlete to compete in U.S. Olympic rowing. When the 1980 boycott ended her brief rowing career, she sued to be allowed to compete. She lost the suit but impressed the IOC, who awarded her special recognition. Rowing was just the start of DeFrantz's Olympic experience, though. Bitten by the Olympic bug, DeFrantz embarked on a lifelong career promoting women athletes, and was ultimately elected to the IOC board, only the fifth woman to serve.

Additionally in 1976, that inaugural year of women's Olympic rowing, East Germany flexed their Cold War muscles and won four of the six races, while medaling in the other two. Germany had long invested heavily in the rowing and canoeing programs that they loved, including for their women.

East Germany had been especially progressive toward women participating in sports, both as a reflection of their Marxist, egalitarian philosophy and of their interest in "winning" the Cold War. Women made up 40 percent of the East German 1976 Olympic team, compared with only 25 percent on the American team.

However, East Germany's wins had benefited not only from their world-class sports scientists, but also from their large-scale doping system.[15] Ironically, by insisting upon shorter 1000 m distances for the "delicate" women, FISA had encouraged boats to crew with weightlifters, which East Germany happily supplied. This prompted FISA to make a major change in 1988, lengthening the distances to 2,000 m, the same distance as the men. Later races would favor endurance and technique rather than pure strength.

With the fall of the Berlin Wall went the East German teams and their doping programs. After 1991, a unified Germany won a few medals, but no longer all of them. Meanwhile, building on a single bronze in 1976 and broad success in Los Angeles 1984, the Romanian women rowers had risen to become the best in the world. Instead of steroids, they focused on technique, talent, and innovative coaching methods—much like those of Japanese volleyball.[16]

Their coach, Nicolae Gioga, was known for his lengthy and difficult workouts. Gioga also designed a "deadly effective" style in rowing mechanics. "At its most simple—they moved their hands very fast away from the finish of the stroke and followed with a really fast body swing forward. Then the slide was taken very—very slowly (in proportion to the hands and body movement). They crept up the slide as slowly and delicately as possible."[17]

Like volleyball's rotate and receive, the Romanian technique was innovative and led them to back-to-back-to-back medals in the women's eight.

Gioga lucked out with talent, too. The extraordinary Elisabeta Lipă won eight rowing medals for Romania, in four different disciplines, including both sculls and sweep. After a successful single, double, and quad sculling career, Lipă moved over to the women's eight and helped them win all three golds. The cox of the eight, Elena Georgescu, was another superb athlete who spanned five Olympics. With talent, longevity, and a great strategy, the Romanian rowing squad became one of the most dominant rowing teams—one of the most dominant teams in any sport—that most people have never heard of.

Whether because of Title IX or because timing brought the right combination of coach and athletes, U.S. women's rowing rose to answer the challenge. Often finishing last in the 1980s and 1990s, USA Rowing brought in a new coach, Tom Terhaar

Fig.25. Romania (ahead, left) is beating Great Britain (foreground) and the Netherlands (background). The Romanian women rowers dominated the sport, winning three straight gold medals in the Eights and going unbeaten for nine years (Wikimedia Commons).

from Columbia University. Terhaar instituted a multi-year "Beijing Plan" which changed recruiting, techniques, and motivational attitudes. He lengthened workouts and rotated rowers across disciplines to give them a better feel for the boat. He mixed and matched athletes to get the best team combination.

In addition, the American cox at the time, Mary Whipple, matched Terhaar's scientific training with a fierce hatred of losing. She was an elf with a truck driver's vocabulary, who also knew how to time the change in the boat's stroke rate with devious perfection. In 2004, she coxed a boat that lost to the Romanians by barely a whisper.

The U.S. women's eight took the gold not only in Beijing, but also in London and Rio, echoing the three-peat from the vaunted Romanian team. But the athletes know how competition works: "complacency can't be [present]. Just when you think you're fast enough, someone else is up there, going faster. You're constantly pushing yourself, day in and day out while still maintaining your health and being uninjured and taking care of your body."[18]

As it turns out, the bronze medal in 2016 behind Team USA went to their new/old friend, Team Romania. Then, in the first rowing championships after the Olympics, the new winner was Romania, ahead of the U.S. eight, which was then edged out of the medals by a surprising young squad from New Zealand. New Zealand was the team to beat in 2020, but the rematch was won by another tired-of-losing squad. The Canadian women's eight hadn't won gold since 1996, watching Romania, the U.S., and others year after year. Their game plan in Tokyo was to lead wire to wire, a difficult plan to execute, but one which sometimes works. It did for Secretariat. It also did for the Canadians, who were queens of the river at the Tokyo 2020 Games. For the moment.

All these countries helped sustain a great, ongoing rivalry. But America was still slow-walking many of its women's teams in the 1990s. Other countries could continue to take the lead. To bring water polo—the oldest Olympic team sport—into contention for women, another country would take up the challenge. This time, it wouldn't be coaches in the spotlight, but athletes and their passion for winning.

"Female Involvement Not Allowed"

Water polo, one of the oldest Olympic sports and one of the most popular team sports in Eastern Europe, took the longest journey of all the Olympic women's team sports. Neither the Europeans nor the Americans—who both developed top-ranked squads—played the key role in bringing women into the water polo arena at the Games after a century. That challenge was taken up by the women from Australia.

Invented in Great Britain as "water rugby" in the late 1800s, the game is rough-and-tumble. It's a sport which leads to fistfights among fans and requires players to have their nails checked before the starting whistle. Americans added moves like the "toe jiu-jitsu" in the early days, while the Hungarians perfected passing. When the sport emigrated to the Land Down Under, a country that thrives in the water, the Australians embraced it long before playing internationally. As Australian historian Annabel Sides described, women had been playing the game in Australia as long as the men, just not in formally recognized leagues.[19]

Team Australia's women faced the same challenges as elsewhere: no funding, no media, no social approval. Nevertheless, they played with ferocity and developed rivalries between state teams like Victoria and Tasmania. By 1992, Australian sportswomen were itching to play internationally. Star player Leanne Barnes began lobbying the *Federation Internationale de Natation Amateur* (FINA) to permit women to play in the Olympics awarded to Sydney for the year 2000. The IOC had finally made noises about addressing gender equity by the 1990s, while privately it was still putting up barriers. They claimed any new sport had to be played in 40 countries on 3 continents, a tall order for those just adding women's teams.

The Australian women were also caught up in a "bureaucracy loop-de-loop" among the IOC, sports federations, and organizing committees. It was like Alice Milliat being shuttled between the IOC and IAAF all over again. Each group would shrug and point at the other two when asked which was the decision maker. In the case of women's water polo, the IOC would only vote after a formal application was made by FINA. But any sport included at a specific Olympics also needed approval from that country's organizing committee.

FINA told women's water polo that they were "a priority" in 1993. In October 1995, a commission on women's water polo met with FINA in Sydney and agreed to support a proposal to the Sydney Organizing Committee (SOCOG). An enthusiastic group, including Leanne Barnes and another water polo pioneer, Pat Jones, made their pitch to SOCOG, including a video: "Sydney 2000 Women's Water Polo.... It's Time!!!"

Barnes was skeptical about the platitudes coming from FINA. "We've hit barrier after barrier since 1983—we'd start to talk, and they'd tell us to go away and do something different to what they told us in the last meeting. We just keeping getting sent back to square one."[20] Everyone expressed approval in the fall of 1995, but when the IOC met the following year to finalize the sports for Sydney, women's water polo wasn't even on the agenda.

The Australian women had had enough. When FINA board members came to Sydney for an April 1997 meeting, they were met at the airport by protesters in swimsuits and water polo caps. The women carried signs: *FINA = Female Involvement Not Allowed*. As their Yale rowing counterparts had learned, women protesting in swimsuits tended to bring the media. They received major press, most of it positive.

Yet in the next 1997 FINA meeting, the last for finalizing the aquatics program, water polo was still left off the discussion. Even worse, synchronized swimming, a recently invented sport with relatively few participants, was added. Water polo lobbyists had been told repeatedly that there was no room for more athletes.

The Australian women dug in their heels. They pushed to have FINA reduce the number of players on the men's teams from 13 to 11—only 7 players are in the water at a time—in order to free up enough spots for women's water polo. They also lobbied the IOC, who kicked it back to FINA. In their July 1997 meeting, FINA members pushed back and took "strong exception" to SOCOG's criticism. They claimed "the

Olympic swimming quota has always been flexible as it allows for swimmers from as many countries as possible to compete."[21]

This was the argument, then. It was more important for all, i.e., "mediocre swimmers,"[22] to compete than for outstanding athletes from water polo to get a chance. Finally, the women threatened FINA with legal action. FINA caved. The men's team rosters were reduced from 13 to 11. In the men's gold medal match in Sydney, Hungary beat Russia, 13–6, in a less-than-riveting final.

The women also got to play in Sydney and their match was far more interesting. The Australian women and their 4–1 record were at the top of the small, plucky group of six entering squads. They ended up meeting a young American team for the gold. The young Americans had a mixed record, having only recently been pulled together from fledgling women's college programs in California, at Santa Barbara and UCLA.

The home crowd in Sydney Stadium was packed and roaring with excitement. The inexperienced but spunky Americans put up a valiant struggle and were down by only a goal to Team Australia with 13 seconds left. Brenda Villa, a stand-out player from Stanford, managed to tie the game at 3–3, quieting the rowdy crowd.

With only 1.3 seconds left, though, a controversial foul was called. Australia's Yvette Higgins was allowed a shot on goal. Higgins threw hard, and it was tipped by an American defender high up to the left, just out of the outstretched arms of the American goalie but snugly into the left corner of the goal. The Sydney auditorium of 18,000 burst into "Aussie! Aussie! Aussie! Oi! Oi! Oi!" It was the storybook ending, a fitting reward for the women who had protested in their Speedos.

Fig.26. Goalie Kelsey Wakefield blocks a shot at the 2013 World Championships. The Australian women maintained their passion for water polo, winning additional medals in 2008 and 2012, though they have yet to repeat gold as of 2021 (photograph by Maxisports © Dreamstime.com).

It lit a fire under the crestfallen U.S. squad. By the end of the decade, the American college pipeline had vastly improved. The highly regarded coach of UCLA, Adam Kirkorian, was brought in to manage the women's Olympic team, which had followed the silver in Sydney with a bronze and another silver.

Kirkorian planned bigger. Like Gioga, Terhaar, Daimatsu (and legendary women's coaches like Tara Van Derveer, Pat Summitt, and Pia Sundhage), Kirkorian assembled a talented crew, honed their technique, and stoked their competitive urges. It was a good sign when he noted that they played cutthroat dominoes.

Kirkorian's squads took golds in London, Rio, and Tokyo. At one point in 2020, they had won 69 straight victories. But who did Kirkorian's team lose to in January 2020? The Australians, of course.

While women's water polo in Australia had fallen on hard times in the past few years, they have been climbing the rankings. Brisbane is scheduled for 2032, so perhaps the Aussies are biding the time to peak again at home. They'll keep their swimsuits at the ready, to play or protest, whatever it takes.

All or Best?

Olympic women's teams are here to stay. It's even hard to remember what it was like before Australia vs. the U.S. in water polo, the U.S. vs. Norway in soccer, or Norway vs. Denmark in handball. The struggle over water polo merely resurfaced the old AIAW debate. Should we have more "mediocre swimmers" or an outstanding water polo team? Should there be a sport for every girl, or should girl's sports be the best that they can be?

Title IX was a watershed for the U.S. It did bring to women's sports all the things that the AIAW had warned against: recruiting scandals, doping, and sports injuries. But the activity level has increased for girls at all ages. It's true: girls don't get injured when they are never allowed to play.

Critics sometimes complain about the new pressures on athletic teenage girls, saying that Title IX puts adolescents in "a game that forces high-schoolers to make one of the most important decisions of their lives, where they go to college, based on how well they can kick a soccer ball."[23]

Such a paternalistic complaint—*these poor girls shouldn't be forced into such a choice*—ignores the obvious. The same teenager could still choose a college for another reason, for all the reasons they chose before soccer became a choice. Potential scholarships simply offer an option that wasn't there before. The alternative—no scholarships, no competition, no challenge—is no choice at all.

Is sport about developing the best athlete in every person? Or developing the best athletes? For the Olympics, it has to be the latter. If there is no standard of excellence, if all are winners, then those who are the best have little to strive for. It's an argument that would be unimaginable on the men's side.

By focusing on the best, everyone is pulled upward. As Coubertin himself said, there will be stress in that challenge: "Peace could be the product only of a better world; a better world could be brought about only by better individuals; and better individuals could be developed only by the give and take, the buffering and battering, the stress and strain of free competition."[24]

Title IX helped accelerate the advance of Olympic women in teams. But even after its passage, that illusive concept of gender equity was still decades away. Even though it had become more acceptable for women to compete without losing their femininity, there were still open questions about whether individuals had the stamina and endurance, especially for any sport involving distance. Those medical arguments still reared their ugly head, as they had for a long time.

Eleven

See How She Runs

Gender Politics and Racing (1948–1984)

"People felt like if you were going to coach women, you had to be gentler with them. The periods in the international game were shorter, just like there was a period where women were not allowed to run marathons because it was feared that their uterus would descend and fall out. The evolution of women's sports is the evolution of understanding how strong they are."—Anson Dorrance, UNC women's soccer[1]

Just as the women's team competitions were gearing up for the Moscow Games, the U.S. boycott brought Olympic momentum to a crashing halt. The decision by the American government to ban athletes from going to the Soviet Union for reasons unrelated to sports ended the career of rower Anita DeFrantz, basketball player Carol Blazejowski, and many others.

However, the interruption may have had a side benefit. When the next Games premiered in Los Angeles, shunned in turn by the Soviets and their allies, Americans predictably dominated the wins. More American women than ever were seen winning. More importantly, they were seen successfully competing in ways that they hadn't been seen before.

Many of the athletes who would be helped by Title IX were still waiting in the wings in 1978. Another legislative Act in the U.S. may have had a more immediate impact. When Los Angeles was awarded the bid for the 1984 Olympics, Congress decided to formalize the American Olympic sports structure. The 1978 U.S. Amateur Athletics Act put the USOC in charge of all American Olympic sports, with sport-specific divisions such as USA Gymnastics, USA Track and Field, etc.

This change wrested control away from the AAU, which had kept some long-held restrictions for athletes, ostensibly for medical reasons, since the days of its creator, James L. Sullivan, Mr. Anthropology Days. The limitation on women running middle- and long-distance races had remained since 1928. The USOC, however, was becoming more interested in medals than tradition, and the organizational change helped chip away at the limits imposed on women runners.

For women cyclists, another kind of distance athlete, restrictions were also loosening. Women cyclists had been attempting to launch female versions of the Tour de France, championed especially by the British grande dames of racing. The downstream impact helped bring the first women's road race to the 1984 Olympics.

Women who had been slipping into marathons and organizing multi-stage cycling races butted up against years of medical objections. Those "doctor's orders" had railed against athletic pursuits, claiming risks to mothers and potential mothers. Those risks began to evaporate from lack of scientific evidence. Even when the roads opened up, though, there still remained resistance to lengthening the distances. Racing had its own poisonous stew of politics. Part of the antidote was visibility.

Doctor's Orders and the Flying Housewife

Medical arguments against female athletes had their own ludicrous history. Ever since the Industrial Revolution put science on a revered pedestal, radical ideas like hand-washing helped doctors improve their success rates. But other unproven ideas followed, treated with the same level of reverence. For example, Victorian doctors spread ideas that women were too fragile and nervous to exercise, punctuating their explanations with inaccurate diagrams of the female anatomy.

By the end of the 19th century, women were proving that good health came *from* physical activity rather than from its avoidance. However, male physicians still clashed with athletes over whether exercise put women's most "sacred function"—reproduction—at risk. The stages of female reproduction, from menstruation to childbirth to menopause, were commonly described using the language of illness. The medical community "privileged reproduction over other functions, portraying fertility as the litmus test of female health and the first casualty of exercise."[2]

A popular medical concept from the 1920s was called "vital force." This notion held that human energy was limited and should not be squandered, especially by women: "Every girl, it seems, has a large store of vital and nervous energy, upon which to draw in the great crisis of motherhood. If the foolish virgin uses up this deposit in daily expenditures on the hockey field or tennis court, then she is left bankrupt in her great crisis and her children have to pay the bill."[3]

Medical analogies like these were used to justify excluding unmarried women from the playing field. Once married, while doctors admitted that physical activity could be beneficial, they urged exercise to be limited to sweeping, dusting, and washing dishes: "use your monotonous routine as a means of physical culture."[4]

Even when the vital force theory finally fell out of favor, other theories about the potential negative impact of sports on reproductive capability persisted. As early as 1912, *Harper's Bazaar* wondered, "Are Athletics a Menace to Motherhood?" As late as 1987, the same magazine headlined an article with nearly identical wording: "Can Sports Make You Sterile?"[5]

This was perhaps the biggest concern from the results of the 800 m in Amsterdam. Women collapsing was a pitiful sight, but the real horror was that they "would be 'desexed' and their reproductive capability impaired by such 'terrible exhaustion.'"[6]

For over a century, doctors had been warning about the risk of uterine prolapse, the specific medical term for when the uterus shifts out of position. Exercise was long theorized to be the cause. A doctor warned in *The German Journal of Physical*

Education that "violent movements of the body can cause a shift in position and a loosening of the uterus ... with resulting sterility, thus defeating a woman's true purpose in life."[7]

Such extreme advice was so commonplace that the rules for women's basketball were initially designed to avoid the jumping that was thought to cause prolapse, another reason for the tamer rules of netball. The concept of the Falling Uterus was also behind the rationale that banned women from Olympic ski jumping, which lasted all the way to 2010. It was also given routinely as the reason that runners should limit their distances. Even in the 1960s, women were being told that running would "make their uterus fall out."[8]

Once a woman had given birth, physical activity was thought to impair breastfeeding or to risk future pregnancies. But medical restrictions depended on the sport, as women in so-called aesthetic sports, like diving or gymnastics, weren't criticized. American diver Pat McCormick completed back-to-back double golds in 1952 and 1956 with barely a mention that she gave birth only a few months before the Melbourne Games. However, running mothers were another thing entirely, rare and discouraged.

Dutch track star Fanny Blankers-Koen, a 30-year-old mother of two, was one of the first to break the mold. When she entered the 1948 Olympics, she was greeted with disapproval, even inside her country. As she described it: "I got very many bad letters, people writing that I must stay at home with my children and that I should not be allowed to run on a track with my—how do you say it?—short trousers."[9]

The criticism against running mothers came from two fronts. Doctors said sports put mothers at risk of being able to have more children. Added to that was the belief that competing would distract women from raising families.

Blankers-Koen planned to correct both notions. She had been a star-struck 18-year-old on the Dutch track team in 1936, with her Olympic highlight being obtaining Jesse Owens's autograph. After the Berlin Olympics, Fanny married and gave birth to a son. War came, and families nearly starved, surviving on potatoes and "very thin milk" from the undernourished cows. During the war, she and husband, Jan, had a second child, a bright spot in a bleak time. Even with food shortages—horse meat was common as a protein supply—her body was resilient.

She returned to training, consulting with her doctor about running while breastfeeding. He suggested exercise in moderation, and she found she "had more and more food for the girl than before."[10] She pedaled to training with her two children in the basket of her bicycle. As she began to win races, the sportswriters dubbed her "The Flying Housewife."

When London 1948 approached, she was practically ancient compared to the world-class sprinters of the time. That's when the nasty letters started landing in Blankers-Koen's mailbox. Yet a woman who had lived through the war with young children had a long stubborn streak. A few 1948 "trolls" were nothing after four years under the Nazis.

She entered four events: the 100 m, 200 m, 80 m hurdles, and the relay. She won all four, equaling Jesse Owens's accomplishment of four track gold medals. Blankers-Koen remains the only woman to win four track events in a single Games.[11]

Afterward, she paraded in a carriage through the streets of Amsterdam, and a candy bar was named for her. Sportswriters included her among the Greatest Female Athletes of the 20th century. When a category of Greatest Mother Athletes is created, she will surely top that list as well.[12]

Ultimately, the scientific community relented on their uterine prolapse fixation, but they remained adamant that women could not run distances safely. Remember all those women collapsing in the "pitiful spectacle" of the 800 m?

For decades after 1928, doctors continued to claim that women didn't have the stamina for long distances. Those who protested the lack of evidence were provided circular logic as explanation. For example, as late as 1971, Dr. Nell Jackson of the AAU ruled: "I wouldn't give permission [for the marathon].... Only two medical studies have been done, and they're still in progress."[13] With so few women able to run distances, there were never enough athletes to populate research studies. Studies weren't funded without the athletes, and without the studies, the women weren't allowed to be athletes.

Research on women's training finally began trickling in during the 1970s, showing what women had felt all along. Women runners had no more cardiac or

Fig.27. In the 1948 Olympic 80 m hurdles final, Fanny Blankers-Koen (far right, NED) just edged Maureen Gardner (GBR) in the next lane. Also pictured, left to right: Shirley Strickland (AUS), Yvette Monginou (FRA) and Libuše Lomská (TCH) (National Media Museum).

lung risk than men did. At last, in 1979, the American College of Sports Medicine (ACSM) issued a critical opinion: there was no evidence to show that women would be harmed by long-distance running.[14] As far as the doctors were concerned, women were free to run. And run they did.

Erasing the Pitiful Spectacle: The Marathon

Early on the morning of August 5, 1984, a small crowd gathered in Santa Monica Community College Stadium, flag bearers leading a procession of fifty women dressed as sparingly as modesty would allow. The breeze was drifting in from the southern California coast, slowly dissolving the fog. The women enjoyed a brief time in the cool air, knowing they would shortly head inland, where the smog would thicken.

Although other marathons had been including women now for more than a decade, it was still an historic occasion. Ever since Stamata Revithi had been turned away at the starting line in Greece, women had been formally barred from long-distance running until only recently. This race would mark the first time any woman had run longer than four laps around the track in an Olympic stadium.

Two of the race favorites were from Norway. Grete Waitz, 30 years old, had won nearly all the recent marathons—28 races in a row at one point—and was ranked #1 in the world. Her teammate, Ingrid Kristiansen, was also a world record holder, ready to become equally famous.

Others also sought notoriety. Rosa Mota of Portugal, half a foot shorter than Waitz, was new to distance running, but had recently won the first Greek women's marathon in Athens. She liked the heat more than the Norwegians. Representing the host country, the Americans paraded in last. First, there was Julie Brown, an American record holder, and then the other J. B.: Joan Benoit.

Benoit, like Mota, was short for a distance runner but made up for it by channeling her hardy Maine stamina. She held the best record for a women's Boston Marathon, set a year earlier.[15] On the other hand, she had been significantly challenged by recent injuries. Seventeen days before the U.S. Trials in May, she had arthroscopic surgery to remove a plica rubbing against her tendon. Somehow, she won the Trials, but the knee was still a work-in-progress.

She was well aware that Waitz had beaten her ten of the eleven times they had run together. The slim Norwegian towered over her by six inches, all of it leg. Despite the challenges, Benoit knew, as every runner does, that each race depended on a hundred little factors—weather, knees, stomach, placement of the water stations, training—the "conditions." It was, realistically, anyone's race.

A few friends and family watched the runners bunch up on the small track behind the starting line. They were outnumbered by the full complement of TV cameras with wide-angle lenses and tripod mounts. There was also a motorcade of mini-cars and motorcycles, waiting to surround the runners. The men would go through this later in the week, when their marathon would close the Games, by tradition. But they would start at 5 p.m., after the day's heat started fading. At the moment, the sun was still rising.

Shortly after 8 o'clock, the gun sounded, and the women took off together.

Nearly 90 years had passed since Spiridon Louis followed a man on horseback shouting *A Greek! A Greek!* Fifty-six years had passed since the 800 m had been misreported. Even with film evidence available to prove otherwise, people still repeated the false stories of women collapsing in Amsterdam.[16] When the IOC reconsidered adding back the 800 m in 1957, the American delegate, J. J. Garland, still blanched at how he was "shocked by this women's race that featured in the Programme." Words in print, magnified and multiplied a thousandfold, became stone tablets. The committee eventually voted 26 to 22 to allow the 800 m back into the Games.

The women's 800 m had finally returned in 1960, and Soviet Lyudmila Lysenko had edged out Australian Brenda Jones in an exorcism of the "pitiful spectacle" from Amsterdam. A few years later, in 1972, the women's Olympic 1,500 was added, followed by the 3,000 in 1980. It was very slow progress.

Other distance race organizers moved at a similarly glacial pace. The AAU grudgingly added a few laps to the track races—the 800 m in 1958, the 1,500 in 1965, and the 3,000 in 1970. At a rate of 1,000 m added every five years, it would take a century for the marathon to be approved.

The women-oriented AIAW had been persuaded to go slightly longer, adding a 3-mile (5k) race to college events in 1969. In similar circumstances, men might run 5, 6, or 8 miles. The guideline for women was set, for no particular reason, at half the distance: "Men ran 10 kilometers, so women's distances were standardized at five."[17]

Moreover, the maximums varied by organization, which created weird discrepancies. For example, the IAAF and AAU (amateur track federations) bumped up their distances, but the AIAW and NCAA did not. Suddenly, 18-year-olds were running farther than their older sisters in college. The older sisters pressed for more.

Here in Santa Monica, barely nine minutes into the Los Angeles women's marathon, the runners passed the longest distance ever run by female Olympians. The pack making its way down Ocean Avenue was arrow-shaped, with the favorites in front, running shoulder to shoulder. This vanguard of runners heading toward Los Angeles had been in the vanguard of cross country for years, running into spaces where women had never been visible before.

Even though the medical concerns about running had begun to fade, familiar criticism remained. First, women who ran were still labeled unfeminine—same old, same old—but the nasty comments lobbed at marathoners still stung. Many runners, like cross-country runner Julia Chase-Brand, always dressed up a little, "curled my hair and put on goddamn lipstick," wanting to give no excuse.[18]

Another word frequently used was "embarrassment." Marathoners were made to feel ashamed, as if running was doing something wrong. For instance, when Chase-Brand finished a 1961 AAU men's race without registering, the AAU threatened her with expulsion because she had "embarrass[ed] them by going on the road in a men's race."[19] The AAU agreed to open up a women's only cross-country event the following year, but only if the women would stop trying to run with the men.

Even Benoit, who trained alone most of the time along back-country roads of rural Maine, had felt the disapproval: "When I first started running, I was so embarrassed I'd walk when cars passed me. I'd pretend I was looking at the flowers."[20]

Among this clump of runners in Los Angeles, Benoit was getting antsy barely twenty minutes in. She couldn't find the right rhythm within the pack and intuitively felt that she was not running efficiently.[21] She was accustomed to running without a pack, and as they passed the first water station, she moved out ahead. She turned her white painter's cap back to front, to shelter her fringe of dark hair from the coming heat.

Waitz watched her shift into the lead. She thought it too early. While runners in a pack can't draft off each other as bicyclists do, they benefit from pacing together. Running out alone too early had been a bad idea since the very first marathon, when Albin Lermusiaux tried it and collapsed mid-race.

Waitz was famous for her strong late-race kick. She would lope along for the first 20 miles, then flash out on those long legs for the final 6 miles. As long as she could stay close, she believed she could pass Benoit, who might by then be wilting in this heat.

Benoit's splay-footed gate didn't seem especially efficient to those watching on TV. She ran without apparent fear or looking at a watch. She later said she "never worrie[d] about splits"[22] or who else might be running. At six miles in, she had built an eleven-second lead; by nine miles in, it was up to a minute.

Flopping along mile after mile of gray concrete, by herself, Benoit started to zone out. When they had first begun near the beach, spectators lined the streets. By mid-race, the path pushed her up and onto the Marina Freeway, where traffic had been halted. She ran alone, although in the footsteps of the hundreds who had pushed their way onto the track.

By the 1960s, women had gotten over feeling embarrassed, and they had pushed into more races. The pushback had been even stronger. The core concern was no longer injuries or appearance. The resistance was more fundamental: You Don't Belong. That is, women didn't belong on the road, which was men's space, a men's-only club.

It was one thing for women to earn the right to compete against each other on their own. But the marathons in Boston and London were for men, many of whom didn't want to compete with women, at all. The women didn't think of it as competing against men. Completing a marathon was like climbing Everest—a human challenge. But the men didn't like it, and, for a long time, the AAU wouldn't allow it.

In response, a group of open-minded men and women had formed their own sanctioning body, the Road Runners Club of America. Other women ran without registering, such as in the Western Hemisphere Marathon of 1963, when Merry Lepper and Lyn Carman hid in the foliage near the starting line. Lepper recalls someone saying mid-race—"A girl, why doesn't she give up?"—but she finished without harassment. Carman, unfortunately, was accosted by race officials who tried to grab her. She punched one of them, knocking him to the pavement, then kept going. But she burned too much adrenaline and, later, failed to finish.[23]

Roberta Gibb decided to use the bushes trick in the 1966 Boston Marathon. She had attempted to register legally the previous year but was turned away, told that it wasn't medically safe, and refused because organizers couldn't "take the medical liability." Gibb persevered, thinking that if anyone saw her run, even at the back or coming in last, it would prove she could do it. She hid in a hollow, covering her long hair with a hoodie and her body with men's Bermuda shorts. She also wore nurse's shoes because there were no running shoes for women. Others who had worn flat sneakers had lost toenails. Gibb finished without incident, though the head of the Boston Athletic Association (BAA) later refused to acknowledge it. He claimed she merely "covered the same route as the official race" and continued to maintain that "no girl has ever run in the Boston Marathon."[24]

The reception of Kathrine Switzer the following year was less positive, though perhaps more useful to women in the long run. Switzer registered to run under her initials and, thus, received a race number, #261. She ran with her coach as well as her boyfriend, an ex–All-American football player. It didn't seem to bother nearby runners, but when the media noticed, the word got out, and organizers were outraged. The co-race director, Jock Semple, ran up behind her and tried to rip off her official number: "Get the hell out of my race and give me those numbers!"

Switzer's boyfriend, the ex-football player, took Semple out, while her coach told her to "run like hell!" After the race, Switzer was officially thrown out of the AAU and all its sanctioned races. The formal reason was "running without a chaperone."[25] Ironic, since she had two chaperones.

A woman being "man-handled" on the race course didn't sit well with the public. Gibb and Switzer received a flood of positive publicity. Gibb had been right. Being seen to run and finish did energize others. More women starting running unofficially. There was nothing the organizers could do when the venues were public. Women could run on the streets alongside others without registering.

Activist runners took other approaches. First, they spread the word. *If you start, you must finish.* They didn't want the discussion to center around whether women

Fig.28. Kathrine Switzer, center, registered for the 1967 Boston Marathon under her initials. Race organizer Jock Semple, behind, was trying to remove the number but was thwarted by Switzer's coach Arnie Briggs, left, and boyfriend Tom Miller, right (Recuerdos de Pandora).

were too weak to complete the race. Women "didn't want to give them an inch."[26] They also met extensively with event sponsors, engaging them as allies to lobby for inclusion. Nike saw the handwriting on the wall; more women running would sell more shoes, opening a huge new market for them. They were all for it.

Finally, pressuring the marathon organizers paid off. The AAU agreed to add women, but with conditions. For the 1972 Boston Marathon, they insisted women start separately, a half hour earlier. This turned into a logistical nightmare as men and women were all mingling early, so the organizers merely ended up lengthening the starting line and making the women start on the sidewalk.

New York tried the same tactic. They allowed women in for the 1972 New York Marathon but wanted them to start ten minutes ahead of the men. The organizers called the six women to the starting line to begin the race, but when the gun went off, all the women sat down. For ten minutes. Then, the men lined up with women, and they all started together. After that, there was no more talk of starting separately.

Not all the media coverage was positive. A *New York Times* write-up of the New York Marathon from 1973[27] focused on the now-famous Switzer and another marathoner, Nina Kucsik. But the story didn't cover the race. Instead, it detailed how both women were getting divorced from their running husbands, attributing the break-up of the marriages to the women's athletic activities.

Switzer, meanwhile, had become energized by the negative attention and turned into a marathon evangelist. She started working to persuade the IOC to bring the women's marathon to the 1984 Games in Los Angeles.

Curiously enough, Peter Ueberroth, head of the Los Angeles Olympic Organizing Committee (LAOOC), later claimed that it was his group that concocted the plan to persuade the Olympic Committee. "We wanted to break through the glass ceiling of the marathon," Ueberroth said in 2004. He said it was known that the Soviets didn't support long-distance running. His solution was to take the Soviet ambassador to Disneyland.[28]

However, according to another marathon historian, the real lobbier—literally—was Switzer.[29] When the IOC Executive Board Meeting met in Los Angeles in February 1981, the decision about the women's marathon was on the agenda. There were nine votes on the board: four were thought to be supportive, while the Soviets and four others were not. The Belgian delegate was undecided. Switzer approached him in the hotel lobby the night before and made her pitch. He took notes. The vote ended up being 8–1, with the Soviets still vetoing the idea. Switzer's impassioned plea turned out to be more pivotal than Disneyland.

All in all, it had taken a marathon of persistence and persuasion to bring the women to Los Angeles. Here, the race was on, at long last.

After an hour, it had become clear that the weather forecasters were on the nose. The smog was taking over. Eighty-five degrees might not seem that hot, but it was windless and runners were surrounded by nothing but gray road and glassy buildings, which magnified the sun's glare. Julie Brown, the other American, had grown increasingly uncomfortable. By mid-race, she dropped off the pace of the front group.

At 19 miles, Mota pushed forward briefly, probing the dwindling pack. Waitz seemed to take it as a signal to start her attack. She had watched Benoit recede but there might be room to close the gap. She had done it before. She made her move, gradually beginning her 7-mile kick. Kristiansen and Mota, the remainder of the original vanguard, would battle for the bronze.

Later, Waitz would note that she had runner's stomach and had been feeling cramps for a while. But that was normal for her and not a race killer. Later, she would say, "I was prepared for warm, but I thought it would be warmer."[30] Later, she would also say, "I could perhaps have run faster, but because of the heat, I was afraid of dying."[31]

All of it was true. Waitz closed the gap, but even seven miles of acceleration is not long enough if the front-runner never slows down.

As the runners approached the final leg to the stadium, spectators reappeared along the boulevards, pushing against the restraining rope and sitting on tree branches. They waved signs and applauded as Benoit went by, her gray suit darkened with sweat. She seemed oblivious to them when she entered the final tunnel.

She enjoyed the dark and cool, soaking up the solitude for a last brief minute. She wondered who in the heck would get up early to watch this race, on a hot Sunday morning? Surely, the stadium would be empty? Still, she told herself, "Once you leave this tunnel, your life will be changed forever."[32]

She popped out of the tunnel into the glare of the sun, her first sight a group of men in orange polyester—race assistants—pointing the way. The cameras had multiplied. The crowd roared so loudly that she almost stopped running. Her knees were wobbly. This was not the back highway of Maine after all. She couldn't simply stop and pretend she was looking at flowers.

Waitz, outside the stadium, heard the cheer. She had been steadily accelerating, but emerging from the tunnel, she saw Benoit all the way around the track, nearly a minute ahead. The marathon's last lap into the stadium is cruelly designed; after 25 miles, the one in second place must still watch the one ahead, knowing they can't catch them. Occasionally, races are close but not here and not today. The woman from Maine put on a clinic in pacing.

Benoit's finish in Los Angeles was the third fastest in women's marathon history. Her time of 2:24:52 would have won 13 of the 20 Olympic men's races to date. She ripped off her cap coming off the last straightaway and waved to the crowd, putting both arms up across the finish line. "I was so charged that when I broke the tape, I could have turned around and run another twenty-six miles."[33]

Waitz crossed less than two minutes later, just a little disappointed with a silver. Rosa Mota came around the track as well, and she loped into third. The first Portuguese woman ever to win a medal was emotional, covering her mouth, then clasping her hands against her chest.

Only a few seconds later, Norway's Kristiansen came in fourth, grimacing. Fourth place always earns a grimace. Cameras clicked away.

More women poured in. Britain's Priscilla Welsh, in sixth place, clapped for her teammate, Joyce Smith. Smith, at 46 years old, had been running since the early 1970s. Finishing eleventh, Smith went over to congratulate Benoit, and both hugged with warmth. Benoit later called it a thrill to be embraced by this racing "matriarch."³⁴ There was a group hug among all those making history.

Nearly an hour later, Leda Diaz de Cano of Honduras was told to stop. Although her time of three-hours plus was not unusual in a marathon, the Los Angeles officials wanted to open the freeway. Not all women will be allowed to run wherever and whenever they want.

The battle to be seen running would continue. Even as late as 2015, when the CEO of the U.S. Track & Field and Cross-Country Association was asked why women still run shorter distances than men, he continued to urge caution. He patiently explained that "when you increase the distance, it shrinks the depth of competitive runners."³⁵ This is correct. Making an athletic task more challenging will reduce the number of people who can accomplish it. At first.

Fig.29. Joan Benoit-Samuelson crossing the finish line in 1984, the culmination of years of work by long-distance runners to bring the women's marathon into the Olympics (photograph by Jerry Coli © Dreamstime.com).

Eventually, the women will get there. Because they belong there.

Disaster, Inspiration, Disaster, Regret

While Joan Benoit's successful finish erased the memory of the 800 m in Amsterdam, two other 1984 Olympic incidents courted potential disaster for women runners. The first, also in the marathon, nearly brought the whole effort down. The second turned an over-hyped distance-running showdown into an international incident that ruined reputations.

In the marathon, about the time Benoit was crossing the finish line, one runner forgot to grab water at the last water station. Gabriela Andersen-Schiess was an avid Alpine skier and experienced cross-country runner. To her, missing the water station was simply an oversight. However, because of the oppressive heat, her body started to become uncooperative within minutes. As her legs cramped, Andersen-Schiess considered stopping, but the Coliseum was already in sight. The tunnel felt blissfully cool, and there were just those last few hundred meters around the track. She had come this far.

The world watched as Andersen-Schiess lurched into the stadium, wandering across lanes of the track and hobbling for six agonizing minutes to the finish line. Because of her awkward gait and limp left arm, she was immediately approached by medical personnel. She told them she was hurting but wanted to complete the race. She was perspiring and lucid, both signs that she was not in danger. To touch her would lead to disqualification, and she adamantly did not want that. They let her go.

The spectators in the stand gasped and cheered, alternately inspired and horrified. TV anchor Al Michaels, more familiar with baseball than track, found her courageous. But his partner, Marty Liquori, an experienced runner, decided it was shocking. Her mind was "gone," he claimed. The medical assistants were derelict in their duty: "I can't stand to watch it."[36] He mentioned brain damage.

Next day, when journalists interviewed those involved, they highlighted the opinions of Joan Benoit's (male) coach, her husband, and Andersen-Schiess's husband, Dick Andersen. After trailing her all race on a motorbike, Andersen had been prevented from following her into the tunnel and "would have liked to take her off the track." Benoit's coach echoed the sentiment: "If it was Joan, I don't care how mad she was, I would have taken it down."[37] What the athlete knew—and what the field doctors knew—about her own situation seemed irrelevant. Clearly, other men would have known better how to handle the problem.

Except that Andersen-Schiess was correctly diagnosed by the field doctors. She was not delirious. She was not experiencing brain damage. Instead, she was suffering from dehydration, which is uncomfortable but not life-threatening like heat stroke. The track-side medics acted appropriately, even though others speculated that she might have been near collapsing, as in another race long ago.

After replacing some fluids and getting a good night's sleep, Andersen-Schiess was almost back to normal, to the surprise of many spectators. Her biggest feelings were of embarrassment, of being a spectacle, and of making others worry.

Today, Andersen-Schiess's story is no longer used as a cautionary tale about the risks of letting women run, but instead called "inspiring." Most summaries now explain medically why she was safe. What would have happened if an official had been flexible enough—as the sportswriters thought should have happened—to let a man drag his wife off the track after 26 miles and 250 yards?

Forty-four of the 50 women (88 percent) who entered also finished the race, including the dehydrated Andersen-Schiess. It would have been 90 percent had they allowed Diaz de Cano to cross the freeway. In the men's marathon, 78 out of 107 (73 percent) finished, despite starting when it was cooler. Some of them suffered from dehydration, too, but it didn't make international news.

Ultimately, the women's marathon was a great success, the longest distance run by women in the Olympics. In 1984, the second longest race was the 3,000 m. But here there was a second disaster, in a race that became famous for less inspiring reasons.

Mary Decker, or "Little Mary Decker" as she had been dubbed as a teenager, had dominated middle-distance running in America for over a decade. She had missed Montreal due to corrective surgery and Moscow due to the boycott. But missing out had redoubled her desire to capture a medal. By 1982, Decker had set world records across distances from the 1,500 m to the 10,000 m. Luckily, the next women's Olympic 3,000 m would be held in her backyard, only a few miles from her southern California home. She would be able to get her Olympic medal at last![38]

Another teenager, however, threatened to spoil those plans. Seventeen-year-old Zola Budd had broken the world record in the 5,000 m just that spring. But Budd was from South Africa, barred from the Games because of its apartheid policy. Great Britain allowed her to speed-apply for dual citizenship, which thrilled Britain and angered everyone else, particularly the Americans. Budd, of course, just wanted to run. However, as Helene Mayer had discovered in Berlin, no Olympic athlete represents only themselves.

American Decker was the heavy favorite, and the American pre-race hype was massive. Everyone was on edge, more than usual. Medals were at stake after years of waiting. The setting courted disaster.

The real problem in the race was that Budd and Decker had both always been so much faster than their peers that neither was accustomed to running in a pack. At the beginning, the pace was leisurely and cautious. The pack was especially dense, with Budd in the lead mid-race and Decker on her heels. Literally.

Decker, following too closely, stepped on Budd's back foot. Budd jumped as if electrified, and, as her back foot kicked out, she tripped Decker, who fell to the infield. The American landed awkwardly, injuring her hip. Her Olympics was suddenly over.

Stunned and distraught, Budd fell off the pace. Romania's Marcica Puica took advantage and out-kicked Britain's Wendy Sly to an unexpected gold. Budd finished seventh. Decker's boyfriend and future husband, discus thrower Richard Slaney, carried his sobbing fiancée chivalrously from the track.

Budd reportedly tried to apologize as they exited through the tunnel, but Decker was having none of it. Pressed by a crowd of reporters to make a public statement, the American runner held an impromptu press conference. She railed at the unfairness of it all and angrily suggested that the tripping might have been intentional.

The press had egged Decker on. Now, it feigned surprise at her emotional "outburst." Decker was criticized for being unsportsmanlike, after being goaded into it. U.S. team officials briefly sought Budd's disqualification, arguing that she had cut in front of Decker, but the officials saw something else on the tape. Decker should have given more room and could herself have been disqualified.

Over the years, Decker's comments became increasingly sincere and conciliatory: "some people think she tripped me deliberately … [but] the reason I fell is because I am and was very inexperienced in running in a pack."[39] Yet because of her frustration on camera right after the race, Decker has been required to repeat the explanation and relive the incident on every "anniversary."

On the world's biggest stage, there is no room for tears, especially from women who want to remain serious athletes. The marathoners—even the dehydrated one— had all behaved with grace. It was as if the press were looking for embarrassing behavior and found it. One woman had the audacity to switch countries in her lust for glory. The other was subject to emotional outbursts. Few interviewed or even mentioned Romania's Puica, the actual winner.

Both the women's marathon and the 3,000 m captured the world's attention, for better or worse. Still, in these same Games, a much quieter revolution had also taken place. In a distance event of a different kind, for the first time ever in the Olympics, women's cycling had also come to town.

Let the Women Vote with Their Bikes

The 90-year delay for cycling was particularly ironic, since 1896 happened to be the year when Susan B. Anthony enthusiastically endorsed the bicycle. Anthony called it the ultimate "freedom machine" for women, which had "done more to emancipate women than any one thing in the world."[40] Women had been riding and racing bicycles for as long as men had, yet with virtually no recognition or accolades.

For example, Britain's Beryl Burton had ruled as the British time-trial champion, the best among men and women for 25 years (1959 to 1983). She set a record in a 12-hour race by riding past 99 men, including Mike McNamara who was setting the "men's" record. Yet Burton was simply known "as a Yorkshire wife and mother, a part-time cycling star with no sponsorship and no coach."[41]

Another grande dame of British cycling, Eileen Gray, founded the Women's Cycle Racing Association in 1955 in order to pull women's racing out of the shadows of the men's tournaments, especially the Tour de France. The famous Tour had launched only a few years after the Athens Games, languished during the wars, then bounced back more popular than ever in the 1950s. The women's version, the Tour de France Feminine, which launched in 1955, didn't attract enough interest or attention—even from the riders. One reason? The stages were too short.

While men were riding stages of 50 to 150 miles, women might ride only 30 or 40 miles, barely two hours a day. Resistance to lengthening the routes came from the governing federation, the *Union Cycliste Internationale* (UCI). Although women created the circuits, they had to stay within UCI guidelines, which limited the distances. The Tour de Feminine courses weren't challenging or long enough to capture attention, and the women's tour didn't last. Subsequent attempts for other multi-stage tours would start up and fold in similar fashion every decade or so.

But Gray, Burton, and other pioneers kept racing, and Gray kept nibbling at the organizers. First, she persuaded the UCI to recognize women's records.[42] As Alice Milliat had learned with the IAAF, when the records count, the athletes are legitimized within the sport.

Secondly, Gray kept after Lord Killanin, the long-time British delegate to the IOC. The IOC argued that women's cycling did not have enough participants to be an international sport. However, Gray kept pointing out to Killanin that international participation was supposed to be evaluated at the sport level—cycling as a whole.

The choice of events within a sport was up to the UCI, as federations well know. For instance, a women's canoeing event was added when one of the men's events was eliminated, once canoeing was already a recognized Olympic sport. It was up to the canoeing federation.

Cycling already hosted seven men's events, which often changed. Over just two decades, for example, the UCI had added Men's Individual Pursuit in 1964, dropped Men's Tandem in 1980, and added a Men's Point Race for 1984. Sporting federations changed their events all the time.

It was still a long hard road of persuasion, as it had been for advocates of the marathon. The IOC wasn't the only problem. Up and down the cycling world, women encountered barriers. The UCI limited the women's cycling distances, just as the AAU had arbitrarily limited women's running distances. Meanwhile, velodrome track owners would sometimes ban women. National federations wouldn't provide enough funds for women to transport their gear, so they would have to pass the hat. During one British women's competition, a male staff member left early, deliberately taking away all the women's spare tubes and tires that they had bought with their own money. For years afterward, Gray said, it made her "blood boil."[43]

Still, Gray's pestering paid off. She finally convinced Killanin to support her push to the IOC and UCI. The cycling federation finally agreed to support an Olympic women's road race event, approved for Los Angeles. Only 45 women were allowed to enter, compared with 135 men. The distance would be only 50 miles (79 k), compared with 118 miles (190k) for the men. It was practically a two-hour "sprint." However, any race was better than none.

In the inaugural race, two Americans were favored, along with a handful of powerful Europeans. Connie Carpenter was another in the parade of multi-talented female athletes, an Olympic veteran from another sport. As a 14-year-old speed skater in the Sapporo 1972 Games, she had finished seventh. For years, Carpenter held the distinction of being the youngest female Winter Olympian. Later, while attending the University of California, Berkeley, she rowed in the national championship in the coxed boat of four.

Carpenter was known in the cycling world because she was also dating (and would later marry) Davis Phinney, another cyclist on the U.S. Olympic team. Phinney himself would compete in the men's road race scheduled later the same day. He ultimately finished fifth but then rode in the men's team time trial and earned a medal. Luckily, men had the seven events to choose from. Women only had the road race.

Rebecca Twigg, Carpenter's teammate, would help on the road. Cyclists worked together in packs or in small breakaway groups, taking turns drafting off each other. If they each did their job, they would be near the finish line together and then could separate and sprint like the dickens to be first over the line. Twigg was far less experienced, but with fresher legs. She had a strong chance of winning, too.

Rounding out the favorites were distinguished riders from West Germany and France. Sandra Schumacher and Ute Enzenauer were contenders, as was Jeannie Longo. Longo was in the first of what would become seven Olympic appearances. After 1984, Longo would go on to win cycling medals by the sackful, although involvement in a doping scandal near the end of her career would threaten her legacy. In this, her fate would be similar to those of better-known male medalists, proving that men had no monopoly on scandal. During the final sprint in 1984, though, Longo was near the front, but collided with another cyclist, lost her chain, and won neither Olympic glory nor disfavor in 1984.

In that final breakaway sprint, Twigg and Carpenter were in front as predicted. Twigg started her sprint a little too early and drifted sideways, losing several feet. Carpenter timed and aimed her final sprint more carefully and clipped Twigg by a few centimeters.

One cycling recap notes that Carter-Phinney threw her bike forward at the end with a "racing move taught her by her husband."[44] This innocuously named "racing move" refers to when a rider extends their elbows right at the finish, pushing their front wheel forward like a runner leaning for the tape. Twigg and every other woman behind her made the identical move at the exact same time, although no one mentions which men taught it to them.

Even with shorter distances and fewer cyclists than the men, the 1984 Olympic women's road race still helped persuade the UCI to add more women's races. The eight international women's road races in 1982 rose to 42 by 1983 and 50 in 1984. Women continued to push for longer distances. It remained still slow going. In the 1990 multi-day Women's Challenge race in Spokane, the six stages only totaled 180 miles. The UCI limits frustrated riders: "I do 80–90 miles all the time. To do this breaks my heart. It's embarrassing."[45]

At last, here was embarrassment as empowerment. Women were embarrassed to compete because they knew they could do more, not because they felt they didn't belong. Another organizer planned a race with 17 stages that totaled 663 miles overall. The UCI complained that those race organizers had used "excessive" distances. The organizing staff got creative, selling T-shirts that said: *Let's Get Excessive!* They also told the UCI: "Let the women vote with their bikes…. If they don't like the race, they won't show up."[46] The women showed up.

Thirty years later, though, Olympic road race stages haven't changed much. In Rio 2016, the men's road race invited 144 cyclists to race over 150 miles (240 k). In comparison, only 67 slots were given to women, who raced 88 miles (141 k). At least in Rio there were the same number of cycling events for men and women: nine.

In late 2020, the longest women's road race held was 170 k. It was hailed as a breakthrough past the UCI's artificial constraint of 160 k. In the multi-stage Gira Rosa race, 85 women finished all 603 miles. Plenty of women voted with their bikes, and they were all in favor.

It Runs in the Family

The resistance to athlete mothers and to women competing over longer distances finally seemed to crumble by the 2010s. It's still a work in progress. It took until the 2020 Games for the 1,500 freestyle swim to be staged for women,[47] even though the first women's world record was set in 1922. In the decades since the Los Angeles Games, attitudes took time to evolve.

Only two days after Joan Benoit won the 1984 marathon, the headline in the

New York Times headline was "Life's Other Joys." The story emphasized how Benoit was planning her wedding, presumably ready to move on from racing.[48]

Benoit did get married. She also kept running.

Years later, she was still running. Benoit qualified to run in every U.S. Olympic Trials up through age 50. She missed qualifying at age 54 by less than two minutes. At 62, she ran the Boston Marathon with her adult daughter Abby, less than 40 minutes off her original time from 1979.

Greta Waitz became a great friend, even though they still raced against each other. Waitz passed away from cancer at only 57, and Benoit mourned the loss of their friendship.

Kathrine Switzer found that having her number torn off in Boston gave her a voice, and she dedicated her life to inspiring women and to lobbying for changes in racing. She ran in the Boston Marathon at aged 70 on the 50th anniversary of her first attempt. This time, no one tried to stop her.

Over time, the narratives shifted further away from medical concerns and conflicts with husbands. Before, when women ran, they had to stop to focus on family. By the 21st century, they were competing while also having families. Sometimes they compete *with* their families. In middle- and long-distance running, everyone came to know about the Dibabas.

When Tirunesh Dibaba won her first world championship at age 17, they called her "little girl." Later, they nicknamed her "baby-faced destroyer."[49] As of 2016, she had amassed three Olympic golds and three bronzes in the 5,000 and 10,000. Her sister Genzebe shattered the 22-year-old record in the 1,500 m and also won silver in Rio. Older sister Ejageyehu has a 10,000 silver. Their aunt Derartu Tulu has two golds, and a bronze in the 10,000. Perhaps all along, women should have been running with their families.

Women now run not only the 10,000 and marathons, but also ultra-marathons— races more than 100 miles. Often, they beat men in those longest of races. In fact, medical studies have shown for decades that women may be more suited than men to long endurance races. Men have bigger hearts, more lean muscle mass, and better VO2Max, but women move more efficiently. Research now shows that efficiency can outperform VO2Max if the distance is long enough.[50] The days of the "weaker sex" are over, at least when it comes to long open-water swims or punishing trails.

Studies have also shown that runners may perform better after giving birth. Norwegian Ingrid Kristiansen, the fourth place finisher in Los Angeles, won more races after having children. Women are even running triathlons and ultra-marathons while pregnant or soon after having children. It's not always easy. Thirty-five-year-old Jasmin Paris, in the middle of a 268-mile face over a mountain ridge, had to stop to express breast milk for her baby daughter.

In addition, they sometimes get surprised by age-old prejudices. Emelie Forsberg, a successful ultra-racer, had just entered the 12-hour Courmayeur-Champex-Chamonix race. She also had recently had a baby. An Instagram poster wondered, "If you run for 12 hours, who takes care of your baby?"[51] The answer, of course, was "somebody else," the same answer that a new father might give to such a question.

Still, there has been progress. As late as 2019, Nike was still pulling sponsorship money from pregnant athletes. Sprinter Allyson Felix, winner of 11 Olympic medals, helped pressure them to stop when she opted to take a break to have a child. She then requalified to return to Tokyo and ended up with two more medals. Runners with children have now not only become commonplace, but fashionable. Overall, attitudes about mothers as athletes have evolved leaps and bounds since the days of Fanny Blankers-Koen.

Some who classified the Los Angeles Games as the most "feminine games yet"[52] pointed to the IOC's addition of "women-only" events, rhythmic gymnastics and synchronized swimming, as proof of positive progress. Not everyone understood the irony. After decades of skirmishing to add in a few long-sought distance competitions and to stop harassing mothers who wanted to compete, the IOC leaped to add new events which emphasized feminine form over pure athleticism. The numbers of international participants for those competitions didn't come near the numbers of runners or cyclists, but the IOC makes exceptions for the right kind of sport.

Yet giving women their own "feminine" sports was still missing the boat. Women wanted to do what the men were doing. Some of the biggest fights over women's sports were yet to come.

Twelve

Them's Fighting Words (1988–2012)

Combat sports were the last bastion of resistance by the conservatives sprinkled throughout the Olympic bureaucracy and in the sports community at large. It was a big bastion, too. A comparison of Charts Three and Four in the Appendix shows that one of the bigger obstacles to women achieving gender parity in Olympic events was all the combat events.

However, the very notion of women fighting each other or, worse, men fighting women, was considered so extreme that objections persisted into the 21st century. Boxing, they said, was unfeminine, made women masculine, and was practiced mostly by prostitutes through "ritual[s] of degradation."[1] Co-ed wrestling was the devil's playground. Traditional judo sparring was sacred and, therefore, forbidden to women. As the Olympic movement closed in on the end of its first century, many of the oldest sports remained off-limits to female athletes.

Women had actually been boxing and wrestling since the ancient times. Sometimes they fought to demonstrate strength, sometimes for spectacle, and sometimes just for exercise. Women also learned fighting sports for an entirely practical reason—self-defense. The suffragettes, for example, were infamous for hiring skilled women bodyguards to fend off angry crowds as well as the law. Both the bodyguards and the women on the picket lines learned jiu-jitsu, an ancient Japanese fighting method designed to fend off stronger or armed opponents. The appeal of such techniques was immediate and the term "suffrajitsu" soon came into common use.[2]

Jiu-jitsu did not become an Olympic sport, but its cousin judo did, in no small part because its founder was an honorary member of the IOC. Judo seemed tailor-made for a Coubertin enterprise, though it took until 1992 to include women. Taekwondo, a more recently invented sport, quickly followed. Wrestling took even longer to be approved, and boxing longest of all.

The self-defense argument became a double-edged sword. Self-defense classes helped women act assertively to take charge of their own lives. Learning to say "No" or hit an attacker back was empowering. Yet women who wanted to fight as athletes felt pigeonholed by the focus on self-defense. After all, it's not self-defense to pin an opponent for 30 seconds or to use a rope-a-dope strategy in the ring, when a simple heel kick to the instep would do.

The feminist argument that women needed self-defense because the female "body is often construed as the object of patriarchal violence" also inherently limited fighting athletes. The ability to freely display aggression needed to be part of the solution for combat athletes, not lumped with patriarchal violence. As historian/MMA fighter L. A. Jennings asked, "If men are inherently violent, does that not make women inherently passive? ... Why is it more acceptable for me to train for self-defense than competition in a fighting sport"?[3]

Fighting athletes had to move beyond training only for self-defense. They also had to move beyond badgering their aristocratic friends or protesting in swimsuits. In order to be taken seriously for these sports, they needed the lawyers. Female practitioners of judo, wrestling, and boxing learned to use the legal system on their behalf, enlisting the ACLU and other groups to file anti-discrimination cases.

Thus, although the growing feminist movement hailed 1984 as the Year of the Woman, plenty of athletes were kept from competing even after the Los Angeles Games. These women had to fight to earn the right to fight. Being aggressive by nature helped, once they could get the right lawyers and the public on their side.

Or, as Rusty Kanokogi, "the Mother of Women's Judo," said, a person could be the hammer or the nail. Better to be the hammer.[4]

Judo, the Gentler Way and the Not-Always-Gentler Sex

Judo, a fighting system designed to help the weak overcome the strong, might have seemed a no-brainer for women to learn. However, when judo paraded proudly into the Olympic Nippon Budokan arena in 1964, it was reserved for men only. While the Japanese supported the triumph of their world champion women's volleyball team, they did not allow women in their national combat sport.

Since judo's invention prior to the end of the 19th century, women had had to battle their way into the dojos, the competitions, and, ultimately, the Olympics. Though only 28 years ultimately passed between the entry of men and women into Olympic judo, it took nearly a century for women's judo to gain acceptance in Japan—100 years, and a succession of stubborn women, many from outside the country.

Japanese educator Kanō Jigorō created judo as a fighting system wedded to a moral philosophy. Standing only 5'2" and weighing 90 pounds, Kanō had learned jiu-jitsu to overcome the bullies of his youth. He had even traveled to America to demonstrate jiu-jitsu for President Grant. While overseas, Kanō studied the American teaching methods of John Dewey and returned home with ideas to modernize education. Kanō and Coubertin had a lot in common. Both were born in the 1860s and both were fervent in the belief that sports improved moral and physical health.

The exercise approach Kanō developed was called the "gentle way" (*jū* and *dō* mean "pliancy" and "way"). He combined different parts of jiu-jitsu to deliver "maximum efficiency through minimum effort." Judo similarly used principles of leverage and balance to help the weak resist the strong. Kanō further attached the idea of *shushin-ho*, the cultivation of wisdom and virtue. Overall, judo was meant to be a way of life rather than just a sport.

While such a system might seem ideal for women, the Kodokan School founded by Kanō did not see it that way. Judo consisted of three parts: *kata* (study of forms), *shiai* (combat sparring), and *randori* (free practice). From the outset, women were only permitted to learn kata.

Kanō himself was not a strict traditionalist. He was both modern and scientific in his approach. Rather, he was concerned about women becoming injured and consulted the best medical experts at the time—Western doctors of the 1880s—who told him that women's essential fragility prevented strenuous activity. Strenuous, at the time, applied to almost any kind of exercise.

Yet Kanō believed judo could improve anyone's physical condition, and he watched with approval when a sickly female student become "sturdy and healthy" with judo. When it appeared that learning forms was safe for women, he modified the kata and "adjusted exercise routines"[5] for women's practice. He taught forms to his family. His daughter, Noriko, would later run the women's division. Kanō respected their efforts enough to tell male students, "If you really want to know true judo, take a look at the methods they use at the Kodokan *joshi bu* (women's section)."[6]

One of his greatest students was Fukuda Keiko, who became legendary for her perfect execution of kata and its connection to spiritual philosophy. She received the 5th *dan* in Japan, the highest black belt ranking allowed for women, and taught judo well into her late nineties. Yet, even the perfect disciple believed women should stick to kata, echoing the old guard that women were creatures of gentility and fragility. She discouraged the participation of women in men's tournaments, saying, "Does a bent ear or a broken nose look beautiful on a woman? I don't think so."[7]

Meanwhile, Fukuda herself remained hemmed in, unable to advance higher than 5th rank because the leaders of the Kodokan believed women need go no higher, even though 10th rank was the highest available.[8] Moreover, the black belt for women carried a white stripe. The stripe was supposed to represent purity in the kata forms, but it actually signified different, lesser, not a true black belt.

Foreigners came to Japan to study. Kanō didn't mind. He wanted others to take judo back to their countries. Even women came to Japan to study. Sarah Mayer, a married British actress, became the first non–Japanese woman to earn a black belt. As a woman of independent means and spirit, she traveled to Japan and talked her way into the men's classes.

At first, they laughed Mayer out of the dojos, but the men let her stay when she persisted, and she improved. Eventually, they were slapping her on the back and cuffing her on the head like one of the boys. Her being non–Japanese likely made a difference. Promoted to black belt in 1935, she posed for a photograph: cross-legged, with short hair, and wearing a belt with no stripe. She had learned in the men's schools; she was awarded the men's belt.

Like Mayer, others outside Japan would see a judo demonstration and immediately want to learn. One New Yorker was destined to play a big role in expanding judo, all the way to the Olympics. Rusty Kanokogi, born Rena Glickman, grew up on the streets of Coney Island, ran with the girl gangs, and learned how to chase away the rats. But she was Jewish and female, which in her world meant being treated as weak. Wanting to lift weights like her brother, Kanokogi went to the weight room at the YMCA only to be turned away—no women allowed. She went back, talked her way into the Y, saw a judo demonstration, and was hooked. There were local classes that let her learn, and she took them to "calm down,"[9] she said. However, they would not let her compete with men.

Kanokogi cut her hair and bound her chest before slipping into a 1959 men's YMCA tournament. Women were not technically barred, but her team kept quiet, especially when she won her match. Standing in line to receive her trophy, she was told to see the tournament director and knew the jig was up. She expected mainly to be told to leave, but he chewed her out and told her women could never learn judo. Those were the magic words. She would never quit now.

By 1962, she had traveled to Japan and earned admittance to the Kodokan school. She was quickly moved over to train with men because she was "pulverizing" the women practicing kata.[10] There, she met her future husband, Ryohei Kanokogi.[11] They returned to New York, and Kanokogi dedicated the next two decades to teaching women and organizing tournaments, ultimately being named the U.S. National Judo coach.

She learned to spar in conference rooms the way she sparred in judo, aggressively and well prepared. Kanokogi would storm into meetings with tournament officials armed with a tape recorder, minutes from previous meetings, and *Robert's Rules of Order*. If women participants were to be excluded, she would bark out objections—then mention lawyers. In the 1977 Maccabiah Games, a sports tournament in Israel, she threatened a court injunction if women were prevented from competing. Women were admitted.

Kanokogi aimed next for the Olympics. She tried to brazen women's judo into the 1980 Moscow Games, but, even before the boycott, the IOC sent her packing. She was told to establish a women's international tournament first. Fine, she thought. She could put one on at home in New York.

The AAU, still in charge of such tournaments at the time, demanded a $50,000 guarantee from sponsors. Kanokogi claimed she had it, though the truth might have been stretched, she later admitted. She ended up maxing out her personal American Express card. Fortunately, the event was a resounding success. Like the Women's Games of the 1920s, there was pent-up demand, and 140 women from 27 countries competed in front of a thousand spectators.

Impressed, the IOC said in 1983 that they would consider adding women's judo. But in their next executive meeting, they didn't even put the subject on the agenda. When Kanokogi got a sneak peek at the July 1984 meeting minutes, she realized this meant no women's judo for another four years, at least. She was livid. She started dialing the ACLU—in the middle of the night.

A janitor finally answered, and she told him it was an emergency. Ramona Ripston of the Southern California ACLU eventually called her back (in the daytime) and helped her file a discrimination lawsuit against the IOC.

The IOC tried to drum up public support for their refusal. Their director of sports, Walter Tröger, told the press that women's judo was still considered "a new sport," and that the "Olympic Games are not a playground for new sports."[12]

The comments were both insulting and inaccurate. Judo was not, in fact, a new Olympic sport, not since 1964. Women's judo was considered a new event, and adding events was the purview of the International Judo Federation (IJF). When men wanted new cycling or canoe events, they could petition their federation to shift existing events around. The ACLU successfully argued, and the IOC folded. Women's judo came in as a demonstration sport in 1988 and, ultimately, as a full sport for the 1992 Barcelona Games.

Kanokogi passed away in 2009. She is now widely considered the "Mother of Women's Judo." Not everyone loved her "mama grizzly" approach. When asked about her, Frank Fullerton, president of U.S. Judo, Inc., said, "I'd rather not discuss her." It was reminiscent of how Avery Brundage had characterized Alice Milliat, that she was always "making a nuisance of herself." No doubt Kanokogi thought being called a "pain in the ass"[13] by Fullerton was the ultimate complement.

It may be a surprise to some that in the first Olympic tournament, the most successful women's team came from France. Since the 1960s, France had quietly become judo-crazy, second only to Japan. Physical therapy engineer Moshe Feldenkrais[14] studied judo under Kanō in Paris and was so enthusiastic about it that he created the first judo club in France. By 1992, French judokas were world class, and the French women took four of those first medals, including two gold. Team France even beat Team Japan in the 2020 inaugural Mixed-Team competition.

One of the great recent women's battles showed how far the sport had progressed. France's world champion Audrey Tcheuméo was popular enough in France to be recognized on the street and hailed with sobriquets like "Tchoum," "The Tank," and "Le Bouef."[15] But, in the 78 kg final in 2016, Tcheuméo faced long-time rival American Kayla Harrison. After a defensive stalemate that lasted nearly the entire six-minute match, Harrison ended the bout dramatically, with a grappling technique called an armbar (*Ude Hishigi Juji Gatame*). It was a fitting end to the old

Fig.30. Rena "Rusty" Kanokogi, the "mother of women's judo," who helped open up the Olympic sport for women. She would charge into judo organizing meetings armed with her Coney Island take-no-prisoner's attitude, Robert's Rules of Order, and a tape recorder (courtesy of the Kanokogi family).

school attitudes of the Kodokan, who had not only frowned on women sparring, but expressly forbid grappling. Crawling around on an opponent to twist an elbow into submission was not especially aesthetic, but it would earn a gold medal.

Over time, Japan became concerned that "the women's section of the sport was being stolen by foreigners"[16] (those French, Cubans, and Americans). They brought women into advanced training and, in doing so, uncovered a star who would rise to become the greatest Olympian judoka of all time, male or female.

Standing only 4'9", extra-lightweight Tani Ryoko *nee* Tamura ultimately loomed large, winning nine world championships and five Olympic medals, two gold. Her mastery was not immediate. In her first Olympic final, Tamura lost a close battle to Cecile Nowak of France. She was then upset in the 1996 finals, after winning 84 matches in a row. She lost to an unheralded North Korean, then didn't lose again for 12 years, winning back-to-back golds in 2000 and 2004. By then, she had turned a dramatic foot sweep and hip throw into bruising perfection.

In between Olympics, her life became more complicated. Tamura Ryoko fell in love with Tani Yoshitomo, a baseball player for the Orix Buffaloes. As it had with the Japanese volleyball players, the press obsessed over their courtship. The media loved to transition female athletes into the traditional Japanese role of "good wife, wise mother" (*ryosai kenbo*). The nation followed the Tamura/Tani nuptials, and their wedding was carried on live television. The birth of Tani's child even caused reporters to camp out at the hospital.

Tani came back to compete in a fifth Games in Beijing. A little older and a little slower, she again fought, conservatively, although well enough to earn a bronze. It was a fifth medal, a record no female or male judoka has matched to date. As with the runners and cyclists, it helped shift Japanese attitudes that Tani became a mother while she was competing—and kept competing. Perhaps women in Japan may someday be routinely known as "good wife, wise mother, strong athlete, and beloved champion."

The Wide World of Women's Wrestling

Judo did not pave the way for other combat sports, unfortunately. Female wrestlers had to make their own push and hold their ground, all over again, even though international women's wrestling had an even longer and more varied history than judo.

Women's grappling in the ancient world could be traced back to Greek mythology, when the speedster Atalanta defeated Achilles's father Peleus in a wrestling match, long before she ran for golden apples. Spartan women and girls were known to wrestle for fitness.

Non-European countries had long-held wrestling traditions as well. Brazilian women folk wrestlers practiced a style called *huka-huka*, while Bolivian "cholitas" wrestled as theater, not unlike the more storied "lucha libres" in Mexico. Ritual female wrestling was also common in African countries, from Gambia to Nigeria. In some tribes, the winner in the women's tournament would marry the winner in the men's tournament.[17]

Throughout America, women wrestlers were part of the vaudeville acts of the 19th and 20th century, wearing bathing suits or pin-up style outfits replete with sequins and capes. But for serious contests, American female athletes were barred from athletic wrestling bouts. In the 1950s, amateur wrestler Jerry Hunter was prosecuted in Oregon for being of the "feminine sex" and "participating in wrestling competition."[18]

Hunter appealed her conviction to the Oregon Supreme Court, but the court denied her request, declaring that the state had a legitimate interest in protecting public safety and morals. They ruled that sports like wrestling and boxing were not constitutional rights. Moreover, since it was 1955, the court further took the opportunity to rail against women's advances in society, suggesting that their decision would stop "the ever-increasing feminine encroachment upon what for ages had been considered strictly as manly arts and privileges."[19] This attitude signaled decades more of American resistance to come.

Other countries were more progressive. France, once again, led the way in combat sports. French gym teachers taught wrestling in school just as they had taught judo, even to the girls. One of the first all-woman clubs, the French Tourcoing Wrestler's Union, was launched in 1974. French wrestler Denise Picavet and her husband then helped get the national tournaments off the ground, persuading Belgium and Norway to enter the first international women's tournament.

Norway had developed a burgeoning women's wrestling community, too. The general secretary of the Norwegian Wrestling Foundation, Ove Gundersen, had built a thriving women's practice. In 1979, he was approached by 14-year-old Marit Foss, who wanted a wrestling coach. He told her he would do it—if she brought five friends. She did.

Curiously enough, the preferred Norwegian style of wrestling was Greco-Roman rather than freestyle. Invented in the classical revival of the 19th century, the Greco-Roman rules were created based on interpretation of the painted urns. No one knew whether the ancient Greeks actually wrestled with only the upper body, without using their legs or allowing holds below the waist. However, the Scandinavians were partial to that form and earned several Greco-Roman Olympic medals, even the women, in national matches. While some have argued that women are incapable of proper Greco-Roman wrestling because of their limited upper body strength, that's originally how women wrestled in Norway and Sweden.

However, when the United World Wrestling Federation (FILA, the *Fédération Internationale des Luttes Associées*) drew up the women's rules in 1987, they opted to use the French/Belgian approach. There was even brief debate over whether women should primarily be judged based on aesthetics, such as the performance of different holds in terms of grace and femininity. Fortunately for the athletes, those suggestions were voted down.

By 1987, women's wrestling was deemed a full international sport. But with only 19 nations, supporters knew that they needed twice that many to be taken seriously. They kept recruiting until, by the year 2000, the world championships had over 40 participating women's teams. By the time the IOC executives voted in 2001, women had put together what they needed to propel wrestling into Athens in 2004.

USA Wrestling, meanwhile, had lagged far behind the rest of the world. Because American athletes attracted American television and its revenue stream, everybody wanted the Americans on the mat, but the country routinely snubbed women wrestlers. Title IX, which was intended to broaden women's athletic participation, expressly exempted contact sports: "boxing, wrestling, rugby, ice hockey, football, basketball, and other sports...."[20]

At the same time, men's wrestling had sued over Title IX, for "reverse discrimination," as universities cut wrestling programs. Chapter Ten pointed out that the situation was complicated. Wrestling programs *were* being forced to close as universities looked for ways to cut costs and wouldn't touch the huge budgets for football and basketball. When college wrestling programs couldn't show that their reduction was caused by expanding women's sports, as opposed to other reasons, they lost their court cases. This meant men's wrestling programs were loath to support women wrestlers, whom they blamed for dwindling resources.

Furthermore, many girls who wanted to wrestle in U.S. middle and high schools were blocked from doing so, which kept the pipeline into colleges small anyway. Often, when a teenager wanted to join a team, there was no program for girls. If schools allowed girls to join the boys' team, the girls would have to wrestle and beat boys. For the historically puritanical U.S., this was a huge can of worms. Many parents believed that their son would be ashamed to beat a girl, sexually aroused, or—worst of all—humiliated by losing.

Lawsuits were filed in multiple states by girls trying to gain access, but it was a poor solution. For instance, the ACLU successfully argued on behalf of Texas high schooler Courtney Barnett that being prevented from wrestling was a violation of the Equal Protection clause of the Fourteenth Amendment. She won damages, but, by the time her case had finished its appeal, she had graduated. The strategy of stonewalling by school districts meant that girls who eventually won cases or appeals would be far past the age where training as a youngster was useful. Cases were not necessarily treated as class-action suits, so the next girl would have to start through the courts from scratch.

Boys also often forfeited matches. One researcher describes how this method let those who refused to wrestle girls cloak their discrimination in a combination of chivalry and pseudo-feminism—"I didn't want to hurt her." This turned them into media heroes and turned the girls into the villains.[21] It was another way to deny young women the opportunity to wrestle.

The experience of Olympian Helen Maroulis is a case in point. Maroulis was allowed into the ring as a child in the early 2000s, during one of her brother's tournaments. With no other girls available, she wrestled boys. When she lost, it was fine. But when she won, she began to hear catcalls from the bleachers: *kick that girl's ass* or *get that dyke off the mat.*

At one point, boys forfeited ten matches in a row rather than wrestle her, which made it impossible for her to learn or improve. Her high school coach finally told the other schools that he would forfeit every match or, next time, show up with 14 girls and win everything. Maroulis finally got partners. After climbing in the state rankings, she got a call from the Olympic training center to train with other teenage girls. Finally, she even earned a scholarship to Simon Fraser University, which had a strong women's wrestling program—in Canada.

Overall, when the U.S. might have promoted wrestling for boys and girls, local organizations chose instead to put money into lawsuits. The sport stagnated, and the U.S. went from being the best in the world in 1984 to barely winning any medals by 2000. By then, wrestling in America was in disarray and even scandal.[22] With few recognizable American names to cheer, the Olympic audience dwindled.

Olympic arena tickets went unsold, and potential revenue for the IOC dropped. The IOC decided to pull the plug in 2013, booting wrestling out of the Games entirely to make room for more popular and more lucrative sports, like skateboarding and golf. Women wrestlers had barely begun to grow their sport when it looked like the whole thing would fold.

Part of the IOC's concern was, in fact, wrestling's persistent hostility toward women. Decades earlier, the IOC had itself put up some of the biggest obstacles for women athletes, but, by the new millennium, attitudes had shifted. The Olympics no longer wanted to support organizations that overtly discriminated.

FILA, heeding the warning, brought in a new president willing "to modernize and democratize the sport"[23] and add women to decision-making committees. Olympic wrestling was reinstated within a year, back on the schedule at least through 2024, as long as the sport maintained a more progressive outlook.

The fortunes of three countries in the 2016 Olympics—Japan, the U.S., and India—suggest a promising future for women in the sport. Japan, for example, built upon its knowledge of judo by developing a best-in-class wrestling team under a coach who designed an approach specifically for women. Women have less upper-body strength than men but more flexibility, so Coach Sakae Kazuhito created techniques that keep women low to the ground, using angles that give the wrestlers a stronger defensive footing. Japanese matches are low-scoring, but their athletes excel at holding off attacks and converting them into scores. In Rio and in Tokyo, Japan won four of the six weight classes outright. Icho Kaori even won a record fourth gold wrestling medal in 2016, the first woman to do so in any sport. Three of her teammates won their first gold medals, suggesting that Japan's reign as a team will likely continue.

But most eyes in Japan were on the country's favorite, Yoshida Saori. Yoshida, another legend seeking her fourth Olympic gold in 2016, had been wrestling since age three, trained by her coach and father. Coach Yoshida Eikatsu passed away in 2014, which led Japanese media to create a script where daughter Saori would win the 2016 gold in her father's memory.

American Helen Maroulis rewrote the ending. Thirty-three-year-old Yoshida fought too cautiously, as if there was too much to lose. Even though she had beaten Maroulis before, multiple times, she lost a hard-fought 4–1 decision. Yoshida was devastated, and the media squeezed apologies out of her for months. But time may soften the blow. Yoshida was popular enough to be chosen as one of only three women athletes to carry the Olympic flame in the Tokyo opening ceremony.[24]

In the U.S., the Maroulis win, a triumph of the underdog, was seen as a big boost to the national program. In USA Wrestling, their recent six-year-plan put high priority on bringing more girls into the sport, and their glossy brochure prominently featured wrestler Maroulis as the shining example for achievement and recruitment. The payoff in Tokyo was nine medals for the U.S. team, sprinkled among both men and women. Maroulis even won a bronze medal, though this time she lost her semifinal to Japan's Kawai Risako, who took the gold.[25]

India's recent foray into women's wrestling also bodes well for growth in the sport. The country had no women on the team when Olympic women's wrestling first premiered in 2004. Dirt wrestling in India had its own long tradition (*pehlwani*), though for men only. Pride in the sport prompted former male champions to look for talent in the other genders. National champion Mahavir Phogat didn't look far; he brought in his family.

According to Phogat's biography and Disney's loosely true biopic, *Dangal*,[26] Phogat wanted to train a son. Unfortunately, his careful plans were thwarted when his wife gave birth to four girls. He trained the girls anyway. Rural India was not known for its progressive attitudes, but they approved of winners. When Phogat's eldest daughter, Geeta, beat teenage boys in local contests, "the hecklers were replaced with applause."[27]

Geeta and sister Babita were wildly successful. Both won medals in the Commonwealth Games, and Geeta Phogat became the first Indian woman to wrestle for India in the 2012 Olympics. Wrestler Sakshi Malik likewise trained under her grandfather and won the first bronze medal for India in 2016.

The future looks better for women's wrestling, and Olympic wrestling as a whole. As Kent Bailo, creator of a U.S. national high school girl's tournament, said, "the answer to the survival for men's wrestling is women's wrestling ... interest follows opportunity, not the other way around."[28]

Fig.31. Geeta Phogat defeating Emily Benstead (AUS) at the 2010 Commonwealth Games. Wrestling in India is ancient, but competition only recently opened to women like Phogat and Babita Kumari, sisters who competed in London and Rio (Indian Ministry of Youth Affairs, ID 30854 and CNR 33878).

Interest in American women's wrestling has been steadily rising. Where only 3,800 women wrestled in high school in 2004,[29] that number hit 21,000 by 2019. Larger programs will improve competition, which in turn will boost international programs as well, ensuring the continuation of this ancient sport in the Games. Rather than having small groups fight over small funding, recruiting more people—as Ove Gundersen said to Marit Foss, *bring five of your friends*—will raise the profile of the sport. Either bring five of your friends or find a former wrestler who has four daughters.

Boxing in Skirts

> "When the bell sounded and the girls charged to the center of the ring to begin pummeling each other, I couldn't quite decide if I was witnessing a great step forward for the female gender or the end of civilization as we know it."—Bill Thompson[30]

Boxing, more than almost any other Olympic sport, seems to bring out negative opinions. Women's boxing, in particular, creates a hurricane of invective from chauvinists and feminists. Is it degrading? Racist? Salacious? Anti-feminist? Throw in unscrupulous promoters, talking heads on the sports networks, and old-guard protectionists, and it's a wonder any woman has even been allowed to box, ever.

Centuries ago, British women boxed for the same reasons as British men, to entertain and to prove their prowess. British boxing legends like Elizabeth Wilkinson Stokes and "Bruising Peg" Malloy were renowned in the 1720s and would issue public challenges in the newspapers with an Ali-like braggadocio. Stokes boasted in print to "ass driver" Ann Field: "doubt not that the blows which I shall present her with will be more difficult for her to digest than any she ever gave her asses."[31]

Historian Christopher Thrasher argues that Stokes's reputation was equal to that of Jim Figg, the best known male boxer of the time. The journals of 1870 were full of her exploits. However, a few decades later, she was no longer mentioned, while Figg was dubbed the "father of modern boxing."[32]

The reason for the shift in attitudes for British men, according to Thrasher, was fear of loss of empire and of the encroachment on their terrain by suffragettes. Likewise, American men were concerned about becoming soft as their labor was replaced by machines and as they moved more into offices. Such social forces may have provided the rationale to build a masculine moat around boxing, "defend[ing] the sport as a curative to the 'mere womanish' of modern civilization."[33]

Curiously enough, Coubertin thought girls and young women should be taught the "sweet science" of boxing as part of physical education, provided it was "under the orders of a prudent master."[34] Coubertin just didn't want anyone watching them in the ring.

Thus, female boxers would now have to pass two different hurdles. As before, they would have to prove themselves as athletes against those who thought they were physically incapable. Secondly, they would have to contend with resistant spectators.

Discussions over women's boxing were preoccupied with who would want to see it, and, if so, how it should look.

Boxing was part of P.E. class in Britain and continental Europe for decades, although not in the U.S. The largest coordinated American program for young people was the Golden Gloves, organized through private gyms. The official national policy of the Golden Gloves for decades was No Girls. However, the Golden Gloves were locally operated, and a few trainers were more open-minded.

For instance, Dallas coach Doyle Weaver believed that girls should not be treated "like breakable pieces of glass."[35] Weaver created a Missy Junior Gloves Program in 1966. Despite many venues barring his club from competing, he pressed forward anyway. He believed that "if the sport was right for boys, that it was also right for girls."[36] The program eventually attracted more than 300 participants.

By the late 1970s, professional female boxers were also nibbling around the edges of restrictions. Jackie Tonawanda, billed as the "female Ali," had found enough places to build an impressive amateur record (31–0), but she was prevented from going professional. The chairman of the New York boxing commission did not want to license female boxers and erode the sport.

Tonawanda sued, lost, and appealed, claiming that the state's ban prevented her from earning a livelihood. New York ultimately relented and issued her a license, rather than continue to pay for lawyers. But years had passed, and her career was shortened. Tonawanda managed only one successful win before retiring.

While Black fighters like Tonawanda and Marion "Tyger" Trimiar had pressured the New York Athletic Commission for years, the organization gave its first licenses to them and to a white fighter, 25-year-old Cat Davis. It was Davis, though, who first appeared on the cover of *Ring* magazine in 1978. She was paid $20,000 to fight in North Carolina, an astounding sum at the time.

The focus on Davis, a white woman, contrasted with the lack of attention paid to the other Black women athletes, adding racism to the already-charged discussion. *People* magazine in 1978 suggested, for instance, that Davis didn't fit the "stereotype," while other articles called her the "Great White Hope." Also not subtle was the attempt to suggest Davis was a different kind of boxer, an aesthetic one, who "look[ed] more like a ballet dancer."[37]

While Sweden and other countries lifted their bans on boxing in the late 1980s, most of the world was waiting for the Americans. U.S. courts finally began intervening. One court ruled that teenager Dallas Molloy should be allowed to box under the Equal Protection clause of the Fourteenth Amendment. After Molloy won the right to box, USA Boxing finally dropped its nationwide restriction in 1993. In 1995, the New York Golden Glove Association began sponsoring amateur women's fights, and, in 1997, Golden Gloves went national.

As a result, some call the 1990s the Golden Age of women's professional boxing in the U.S. Fighter Christy Martin's bout with Deirdre Gogarty in 1996 was the first recognized by the World Boxing Council for a world championship. Martin fought in pay-per-view events as well and on the same card as Tyson and Holyfield, helping "legitimize" the sport for women. Landing a *Sports Illustrated* cover in 1996 was a high-water mark for Martin. She, too, had to contend with negative press. Headlines questioned whether she was "Admirable or Abominable," while magazine photo spreads might show her vacuuming as often as sparring.

Still, other female boxers multiplied, notably daughters of former boxing stars, like Jackie Frazier, Freeda Foreman, and Laila Ali. Ali's famous father did not want her to box, but she quickly amassed 24 victories. She then was able to turn her competitive successes into a TV career, which helped boost the positive image for women's boxing as a whole.

Women's international organizations began to coalesce and expand. Women's boxing petitioned to be added to the Beijing Games but was rejected. However, the rhetoric was friendly, and they were encouraged to return when they had more countries on board. By 2009, the IOC formally approved women's boxing for the London 2012 Olympics.

However, there were two problems. First, there would only be three weight classes for women, compared with ten for men. Women's flyweight maxed out at 51 kg and lightweight at 60 kg. Men's weight classes across the same range included divisions of 49, 52, 56, and 60 kg—twice as many groups. Compressing the weight classes reduced opportunity for the athletes as well as interest by spectators who would have to watch the same women fight repeatedly against each other. Boxers couldn't build much of a career just fighting the same opponent.

The second problem involved the uniform—a decade before the beach handball controversy. When International Boxing Association (AIBA) president Dr. Ching-Kuo Wu enthusiastically announced women's boxing had been admitted to the 2012 Games, he explained that the AIBA wanted female boxers to wear skirts in the ring. Many people, Wu said, "can't tell the difference between the men and the women."[38]

The women were dumbfounded. Three-time Irish world-lightweight champion, Katie Taylor, rejected the idea out of hand: "I don't even wear miniskirts on a night out, so I definitely won't be wearing miniskirts in the ring."[39] Sportswriter Katrina Onstead complained, "Being asked to wear miniskirts is a little like saying, 'Come to the party, but use the back entrance—and dress like it's Slutoween.'"[40] This was the penalty for getting the sport intended for manly men to accept women: female athletes must become sex objects, downplaying their capabilities and offsetting their displays of physical aggression with suggestive dress.

The AIBA had already required skirts at the 2010 world championships, so the organizers didn't understand what blew up into a huge controversy. But a change.org petition quickly gathered 50,000 signatures in favor of ditching the skirts. Boxer Queen Underwood told the press that the potential uniform included not only a skirt but also a padded bra, impractical for sports.

The media tried to strike a "both sides of the issue" tone. Many articles cited women boxers who claimed it was fine. Some said they didn't mind, in the same tone once used by those who "didn't mind" being limited to three track events or "didn't mind" starting on the sidewalk to run the Boston Marathon. "Didn't mind" might mean "whatever it takes, if that's how I can finally get in the ring."

The coach of the Polish team endorsed the idea of giving a "womanly impression." The coach of the Australian team countered that "people shouldn't be there to watch their arse ... [but] their gloves."[41] Boxing Canada came out against the rule. Ultimately, the tone-deaf AIBA backed off from the requirement, grumbling that it was only a suggestion.

When women's boxing debuted in London at last, the first three wins went to women whose subsequent careers justified their Olympic success. Britain's Nicola Adams, a hometown heroine in 2012, followed up with a second flyweight medal in 2016 and was awarded an OBE after retiring.

Katie Taylor brought thrills to Ireland and parlayed her London medal into a professional career. She was still ranked in 2021 as the best pound-for-pound women's fighter in the world. Claressa Shields, also a double gold medalist in London and Rio, followed up with a 10–0 professional career.

Shields has been especially assertive outside the ring as well. She used her celebrity status to advocate on behalf of her neighborhood in Flint, Michigan, the town where the water was poisoned by overly budget-conscious state officials. She highlighted the lack of sponsorship she received compared with male gold medal winners. She said she had been told to tone down her aggression, normally a boxer's best asset.

Even after winning a second gold medal, Shields found few opportunities to fight. By 2021, she was frustrated enough to arrange for her own pay-per-view

Fig. 32. London 2012, the first Games to allow women boxers, was the perfect place for British flyweight Nicola Adams (left) to shine. Adams fought brilliantly against China's Cancan Ren (right), eventually winning back-to-back golds (photograph by Kent Capture, Wikimedia Commons).

evening with an all-women card. Sales passed expectations, and she punctuated the night of boxing with a decisive win over her opponent, Marie Dicaire.

While Shields tried to use the event to push for more pay, others tried to turn the clock back. During the publicity run-up to Shields's all-women event, ESPN's Stephen A. Smith complained that he didn't want to see women punching each other or engaging in any "pugilistic sports." Not only was it twenty years out of sync, it wasn't even pertinent to what he was asked, which was about women filling leadership positions in sports.

This was another way of using women's boxing as a dog whistle. Turn a question about the business end of sports—why women don't get paid or have access to equitable jobs—into an ancient gripe about how women look. His comments drew as much negative publicity as the boxing match. At least he didn't claim that civilization was at an end.

Meanwhile, in 2020, the zero-sum game was put into effect in Tokyo, but with surprisingly little hue and cry. Women's boxing weight classes were expanded from three to five and men's dropped from ten to eight. Most of the criticism of Olympic boxing, however, centered on judging controversies and fighters who didn't handle losing well,[42] rather than the idea of shrinking opportunities. One of boxing's key organizing groups, the AIBA, had encountered so many other problems that they were stripped of the right to run the Olympic tournament. Boxing as a sport faces multiple challenges, but no longer from women participating—sixteen different countries took medals in Tokyo 2020, suggesting that women's boxing may continue to grow.

Taekwondo Signals a Sea Change

The acceptance of combat sports may have signaled the end of an era of resistance to women athletes. Taekwondo is a case in point. While women's wrestling and boxing had to push for recognition for decades, taekwondo was admitted in 1992, when women's judo made its debut.

The sport of taekwondo was itself only a few decades old, a mere baby compared to Greek wrestling or African boxing. Still, taekwondo burst forth in the Games with both men's and women's divisions, only a few decades after establishing a world championship. Why were women accepted so quickly at the Games? The answer was not about taekwondo but more about what had finally changed at the IOC.

The committee had finally admitted women to its ranks.

In 1981, two women—Venezuela's Flor Isava-Fonseca and Finland's Pirjo Häggman—were elected to the IOC board. They were the pebbles that started an avalanche. Anita DeFrantz was added in 1986, then asked to chair the 1992 IOC Women in Sport Commission. Soon after, the IOC launched a Women and Sport Working Group, a World Conference on Women and Sport, and an ongoing working group to promote women in sports. Isava-Fonseca was bumped up to the IOC executive board in 1990, and a few years later DeFrantz elected IOC vice-president.

Amid this growing expansion of women's voices at the leadership level, the IOC passed and implemented a critical change in 1991. Any new sport pushing for inclusion in the Games had to include both women's and men's events. Full stop.

The 1991 change didn't make sporting headlines. Other changes drew more attention at the IOC, like its finally admitting South African, the fall of the Soviet Union, and the end of amateurism. With its attention elsewhere, the IOC no longer wanted to maintain its wall against female participation.

The rule change regarding gender equity hardly made news, but it was a huge milestone. For the first time, women would be treated equally with men. Debates might continue over differing rules, uniforms, compensation, or number of participants, but the basic rule of thumb was now gender parity. Any sport added—from BMX to rugby to surfing—must include an equal number of events for men and women.

This move toward parity, so long in coming, reflected the persistent and patient advocacy of women at the IOC: DeFrantz, Isava-Fonseca, Häggman, and others. Outside groups like the Women's Sports Foundation and National Organization of Women also helped with advice, persuasive statistics, and legal support. But there was another crucial change at the IOC, and it came from the top.

Just as the personal opinions of Coubertin and Brundage had locked the door against women's entry, the more recent IOC presidents would give women the key. Juan Antonio Samaranch, a Spanish businessman, started taking a more global and financial approach to the Games, seeking growth, financial stability, and broader participation. Some of his decisions would lead to scandal and others clashed with long-held traditions. It was under his tenure that the amateur prohibition was dropped.

But, to his credit, Samaranch was unabashedly supportive of women's competitors. While he may not have joined the feminists protesting in swimsuits at the airport or put the ACLU on speed dial, his rhetoric and actions were as supportive of women athletes as anyone in his era. Said DeFrantz of him: "He couldn't live without having women be a significant part of the world of sport … [Samaranch] said: 'We need more ideas, we need more women. We have to use that vast, untapped resource.' He understood that there shouldn't be a boundary for women."[43] Samaranch's support helped female athletes and leaders establish themselves firmly among the IOC patrons. He walked the walk.

There were still obstacles. The 1991 provision had a grandfather clause. Any men's events already in the Games could continue to bar women as they pleased. The trials and tribulations of water polo, wrestling, and boxing continued as a result.

There were other stubborn hold-outs. Pole vaulters were told by coaches and tournament organizers that women simply didn't have the upper-body strength to compete. Women weightlifters also had to press for inclusion against the existing bias against muscled women lifting giant barbells. Five-foot-tall Morghan King reminded organizers that weightlifting also had size classes.

Ski jumping was also infamous for resisting, up until the 2010 Olympics. Old-fashioned attitudes led Gian Franco Casper, president of the International Ski Federation (FIS), to comment as late as 2005 that it "seems not appropriate for ladies from a medical point of view."[44] There were mumbling references to uterine prolapse and "technical reasons" why women didn't qualify, even though international competitions for women's ski jumping had taken place for decades. The IOC finally admitted ski jumping in 2014, and Germany's Carina Vogt made women's sports history with the first gold.

The IOC leaders after Samaranch—Jacques Rogge and Thomas Bach—continued a welcoming attitude toward women. By the time Rogge was elected in 2001, women had become 38.5 percent of the athletes at the Games. Bach was proud to proclaim for Tokyo 2020 that gender equity had been achieved—at 48.8 percent.

Nevertheless, it had been a long road to gaining entry, sport by sport, and athlete by athlete. Women had moved mountains to get the IOC to open venues, reduce ridiculous rules, and close the gap toward gender parity. However, just being allowed in didn't end all bias. Even while female athletes increased participation, they faced new tests.

Boxing had hinted that visibility was problematic, which meant there might be a new kind of barrier. Between the decades of the 1950s and the 1990s, television coverage had grown exponentially. What audiences could see, "up close and personal," were athletes digitized and multiplied on giant screens and instant replays. People became cartoons—some heroes and some villains—and competitions turned into legends.

In theory, the Olympics arrived in people's living rooms live and unscripted. In reality, many events were edited into stories crafted for public consumption. The choices of the television directors would heavily influence how and whether an athlete was viewed. Women had yet another challenge to overcome.

They had to learn how to take charge of their own visibility, and they had to take back control over the camera.

Part IV

Being Seen

Thirteen

The Camera Changes the Narrative
Gymnasts, Skaters, Racers, Villains (1972–2000)

On the opening night of the 1972 Gymnastics Team competition, a diminutive Russian in pigtails stood on the top of the uneven bars and jumped off—backwards. It was a playground dare, a "watch-this-mom!" moment for the world. Today, there are dozens of videos of it in slow motion, taken from multiple camera angles. This was Olga Korbut's introduction to the world, and not only did it herald a change to gymnastics-as-we-knew-it, but the image of it would start a temblor that would ripple across the entire sport.

Three days later, in the Gymnastics Individual All-Around, Korbut made several errors in the same bar routine. Team USSR was not surprised. Seventeen-year-old Korbut had been an afterthought for the team, a last-minute addition. Her coach, Renold Koysh, was "something of a renegade"[1] who thought it innovative to have his gymnasts show skills from one apparatus on another, like tumbling on a balance beam or the bars.

But the Soviet coaches knew Korbut lacked international experience and expected this to be her breaking-in Games, perhaps the first of many. Latynina had been 19 in her first world championships and had only won a team medal. She aged into gymnastic prominence like fine wine. Others were expected to do the same.

However, by 1972, worldwide television audience had climbed to 28 million viewers.[2] The dynamics of TV fans were different; they looked for stories as much as good competition. When Korbut, looking more like age six rather than the seventeen that she was, dissolved into tears and cried in the arms of her coach, the camera stayed on her. Suddenly, Korbut's emotions became the story. The main story.

Roone Arledge, director of ABC's Olympics coverage, simply wanted to play to his audience, as any TV director would want to do. Arledge's *Wide World of Sports* had broken the mold in televised sports by concentrating on highlights rather than presenting competitions in a straightforward manner. *Wide World* worked by promising to show "the thrill of victory and the agony of defeat." Arledge's choice of how to present Korbut was a watershed moment in Olympic history.

Women had come so far, pressuring intransigent Olympic committees and arguing with sports federations to let them play. They had helped pass legislation, filed lawsuits, and even talked their way onto committees to promote women in sports. But this was a new kind of barrier.

The media had always been an extra force to contend with, especially when they misreported results like the 800 m race or crowned victors before races had been run. But as TV audiences geometrically multiplied, those who presented sports had a bigger opportunity to put their thumbprints on the competition. TV directors could control the story, especially when 80 percent of the televised events had a time delay that allowed for editing.[3] Women athletes would now have their images manufactured for spectators.

After Korbut, Olympic gymnasts would shift younger, which would upend the sport. Because of Korbut, gymnasts—all women athletes—would become increasingly aware of how they looked on camera. They would be prompted to smile regardless of how they felt. They would be plastered in makeup under the bright lights of the cameras, no matter how strange it might seem on a pre-pubescent face.

Because a television director decided where to aim the cameras, and later how to edit the feed to tell the desired "story," lives would be changed. It was no longer enough just to excel at a sport, but now athletes must be seen doing it with the proper smile, a positive attitude, and the necessary charisma to attract the eye of the director and the eye of the camera.

Perfection and Power in the New Pixies

> "We're here to crown the new Nadia, the new Mary Lou."
> —Dick Enberg, NBC Gymnastics commentator at the 1988 Games[4]

Ludmilla Tourischeva was the 1972 Women's Gymnastics All-Around champion at the tender age of 20. She earned her second team gold, since she herself, age 16, had helped Team USSR in Mexico City fend off Czechoslovakia. Doubtless Tourischeva had been waiting years for her chance to shine, once Latynina and Čáslavská had gone. Somehow both lithe and curvy, Tourischeva had the grace and refinement of the balletic champions of yesteryear.

By the time she had finished her third Olympics in Montreal, Tourischeva would amass four golds, three silvers, and two bronze medals. For a nine-time medalist, though, she ended up the answer to a trivia question: Who actually won the All-Around in the year that Olga Korbut debuted?

Like Korbut, Tourischeva also wore pigtails, although they didn't have the same effect, at least not on the American TV crew and audience. "She was a woman of regal poise and stunning beauty … but her physical maturity and pronounced muscularity proved less exciting to the media and the public than Olga Korbut's 'pixie' charm."[5]

Korbut came in seventh in the All-Around after her uneven bar disaster, although she bounded back to take gold in the floor and balance beam and a silver in the bars. Still, it was the tears that had made her a star: "Before anyone had heard anything of her background or even knew what her voice sounded like, she was adored by millions."[6]

Despite the seventh place, Korbut was named Sportswoman of the Year by the BBC. She became the headliner for a new set of tours, international goodwill tours which had been popular ever since the Press sisters went west to Compton and Wilma Rudolph took Europe by storm. When the Soviet gymnast came to Chicago, the mayor proclaimed it "Olga Korbut Day." This was the golden era of sports *glasnost*, the decade of the ping-pong diplomacy that helped the Nixon administration establish a relationship with China. Korbut toured and toured, until Lord Killanin started complaining that the Soviet gymnastics team was violating the amateur rule.

Gymnastics in America rode the popularity wave as well. This was slightly ironic, since American gymnasts had won no Olympic medals since the Soviets had entered the Games in 1952. But the most talented U.S. gymnast to date was Cathy Rigby,[7] who also debuted in 1972 to help a plucky young American squad earn a highly respectable fourth place.[8]

Tourischeva, Korbut, and Rigby's fortunes played out in front of the cameras. But there had been changes to the apparatus behind the scenes, too, in the decade prior to Munich. The women's uneven bars had started as men's parallel bars with one side set higher. Women performed the men's routines with variations. Only in the late 1960s were the uneven bars redesigned to be a separate structure. More space was placed between the bars, which were also more firmly anchored to the ground. All of a sudden, women could swing on the bars as men did on their single high bar. The back-flip that Korbut performed happened after the alterations.

Likewise, the floor surface changed as well. Gymnasium floors had been hardwood, typically covered by only a single thin mat. In Munich, the floor had "heavy-duty carpeting." Despite the carpet burns, more padding at least allowed more tumbling. Even 5'4" Joan Moore on the U.S. team could fly through aerial somersaults and cartwheels speedier than Vera Čáslavská did in Mexico City, leaving one announcer to gasp, "Isn't that unbelievable, that a girl that looks as feminine as this can tumble as Joanie tumbles?"[9]

Lastly, the vault had gained a springboard, longer runway, and padded landing mat. Latynina had trotted slowly enough down the vault path to roll into a cartwheel that moved up and over the horse and let her land lightly on her feet. Only by the 1970s could gymnasts sprint down the runway and launch into multiple somersaults onto a surface that wouldn't tear a knee ligament.

Scoring had evolved, too. New skills now gained more points, where once the goal would have been perfecting the simpler skills. Television made Korbut a household name, but scoring and apparatus changes had only recently made what she did possible.

Korbut's celebrity on the international tours might also have put the cart before the horse. When she returned to the 1976 Olympics, Korbut had not blossomed into the team star, though she did add a team gold and a silver medal to her stash. The American analysts decided her lack of repeat stardom was because she was too old, but it's possible she had never reached the standards of excellence expected by the Soviet team.

Korbut also claimed that scores were negotiated in advance by the judges and coaches. She reportedly clashed with her coaches and suggested they chose someone else to earn the high marks. TV audiences certainly couldn't always match scores to the performances. It's possible it wasn't age at all, but Korbut's confrontational nature that let her down: "Korbut, in particular, was more beloved in the West than she had ever been in her homeland."[10]

Korbut's teammate Nellie Kim was the anointed 1976 star for Team USSR. At 18, Kim's long hair was pinned back in an adult-like bun or tied in a demure ponytail, both of which suggested schoolmarm rather than cherub. Kim had the combination of grace and precision favored by the newly crowned Soviet coach, Larysa Latynina. Gymnastics, despite scoring and apparatus changes, might have returned to favoring Soviet women with experience.

But in 1976, there was a new country, a new coach, and a new athlete in town. Romania had stumbled upon a dynamic trainer named Bela Karolyi, and he had discovered a talented youngster to offer the world. At 14 years of age—three years younger than Korbut at her debut—Nadia Comaneci would make the revolution in gymnastics complete.

Comaneci also wore a ponytail, but her yarn ribbons looked playful rather than simply ornamental. The beehive hair styles of Čáslavská's day had dissolved into simpler styles, which accentuated the downward shift in age. Since 1964, the average age of female gymnasts had dropped eight years. The average age of male gymnasts had only dropped a year, traceable to the apparatus improvements.

The Romanian teenager was slender as a willow, with none of the curves of Tourischeva or even of the petite Rigby. Some have noted that Twiggy-like androgyny was the fashion. If so, Comaneci was fashionable. The Romanians also had vertical stripes on the sides of their uniforms, which seemed designed to show the judges exactly how straight Comaneci's arms and legs were. They were—perfectly straight.

Worldwide audiences didn't know diddly squat about judging mechanics, apparatus changes, or acrobatic maneuvers. They just knew that 1.00—the first Olympic Perfect Ten—was something special. Comaneci's first ten on the compulsory routine for the uneven bars flashed on a scoreboard that had been designed for only three digits. The gymnastics federation (FIG) had insisted to the Montreal planning committee that gymnastic scores stopped at 9.95.[11]

Scores had been drifting upwards with the increasing difficulty on the newly designed apparatuses. The athletes were pushing up against what the scoring could accommodate. As gymnast Dvora Meyers explained in *The End of the Perfect Ten*, Comaneci's score was both evolutionary and revolutionary. The ten was an artificial barrier, like the four-minute mile, with no intrinsic meaning. There was an unwritten rule about not awarding tens, but when one compulsory routine was performed noticeably better than those awarded 9.95, the barrier had been breached. Perhaps each of Comaneci's judges thought theirs would be the high score thrown out. They clearly judged the routine consistently, since all awarded tens.

Once the wall came crashing down, eight more tens were awarded in Montreal, two to Kim and six more to Comaneci. By the time the Olympics were over, the Romanian had won the all-around and three more medals. Kim's superior tumbling brought her in a close second, but Comaneci's extra four inches and longer-pointed toes were more impressive on the bars and beam.

Coach Karolyi reportedly was a rough taskmaster to the Romanian team, either beating or at least browbeating his young charges. Teenagers living in state-sponsored camps run in communist dictatorships would have little opportunity to complain. Karolyi also believed overall fitness helped. He had the girls run laps, do push-ups, and lift weights as Russian ballerinas would never have done. Comaneci claimed that some of the coach's harsh methods helped give her the toughness required for international competition.

On her own, Comaneci might have been a Mozart of the sport, a freak of nature to be so good, so young. But she followed Korbut, who had looked like a child. Together, their apparent stature as teeny-boppers reordered the old school judging that had preferred grace and experience. Going forward, gymnasts must be younger, more flexible, more impressionable, and more acrobatic.

As before, American audiences ate up the 1976 results. Comaneci's miraculous ten on the bars and the beam drew so much attention that ABC re-aired the routines several more times. They even added music, a soap opera theme already borrowed from an obscure movie. The rechristened "Nadia's Theme" went platinum. Comaneci had effectively been commodified for American consumption.

Fig.33. Nadia Comaneci's (ROM) ponytail and adolescent body belied her maturity on the bars and balance beam. Once she broke the barrier of receiving a perfect 10.0 at the 1976 Olympic Games, more tens would follow for her and others (Comitetul Olimpic si Sportiv Roman).

Not everyone welcomed the shift toward teenagers. Olympic historian Guttmann grumbled that Korbut "won hearts unmoved by exhibitions of athletic skill" and lamented that "pixies" had "displaced women and ... transformed [gymnastics] into children's acrobatics."[12] Others dismissed Korbut and her "intensely televisual elfin charm."[13]

Just as journalists declared that Korbut was past her prime in 1976, the same was said of Comaneci herself when she competed in Moscow in 1980. She was taller and sported a much more feminine silhouette. *Sports Illustrated* emphasized that "as a result of that much publicized puberty, Nadia now has breasts."[14]

Puberty was used to justify why Comaneci was no longer always perfect. When she fell off the bars in the team competition, the breasts were to blame. Yet she still competed with power and precision, and Coach Karolyi loudly griped that the scores were predetermined. Bias was highly probable, with the Soviets winning most of the medals in Moscow, but difficult to prove.

Comaneci, in fact, barely missed the gold medal in the all-around. The growth spurt clearly had not ruined her career. At the World University Games a year later, against many of the same athletes, she took individual firsts in everything except the floor exercise.

Then, Comaneci retired, in part because she lost her coach. Whether due to Comaneci's waning stardom, the restrictions of the Romanian regime, or his own confrontational personality, Karolyi decided to defect from Romania in 1981.[15]

Karoly timed his move to surf the rising tide of gymnastics interest sweeping America. The U.S. had been slow to the party, but gymnastics in America was now jumping on the teenager bandwagon. They needed to import the coaching philosophy. Who better than the man who said that "a female gymnast's best training and competing years were from eight to twenty," years when "there is no fear ... no problems."[16] Karolyi set up shop in Texas and quickly attracted scads of young women who wanted their own theme songs.

However, he was no longer looking for sylphs like Comaneci. He had shifted his preference to more compact forms, women with sturdy shoulders and thighs. One of his first stars, Dianne Durham, would become the first Black female gymnast to win the U.S. national championship. Karolyi's other discovery would go even further.

Mary Lou Retton was a pint-sized dynamo, 4'9" but constructed "like a cast-iron toy truck." She was small like Korbut and perfect in execution like Comaneci. Her curves were muscular rather than womanly. She didn't have the elegant lines that seven more inches would have given her on the bars or beam,[17] but her explosiveness led to jaw-dropping vaults.

Meanwhile, the exercise surface had acquired even thicker foam padding, called a "springboard floor." It allowed Retton to fly into punch-backs and double somersaults that would have ripped ankles in 1956. She was the complete package: the "wow" factor in athleticism coupled with a million-dollar smile. Retton was a walking Wheaties box cover.

Like Korbut, Retton was actually 17 but appeared to be years younger because of her size, high-pitched voice, and bubbly manner. As she vied for the All-Around title with Romanian Ecaterina Szabo (born two days earlier than Retton), the cameras again picked up another story.

Karolyi, always larger than life, had clashed with the USA Gymnastics establishment from Day One. U.S. head coach Don Peters, in particular, didn't appreciate his antics, and the two were engaged in an alpha male standoff over control of the team. Rules had been created which prevented personal coaches from leaving the stands, which might have been dubbed the *No Karolyi Rule*, a rule which he seemed ready to break.

The cameras, trained relentlessly on Retton once she became a serious contender for the all-around title, noted her going over to Karolyi, nestled among the press photographers at the railing, for "unofficial" coaching. It had the feel of a little girl listening to daddy.

In the final rotation, when Retton hit her vault, she squealed and leapt into Karolyi's arms as he crossed the barrier. There was a brief moment of concern that she might be assessed a penalty point for hugging her coach. Was the concern real or a manufactured part of the story, this intrigue between coaches and judges? It certainly seemed disconnected from the competition, from how many somersaults were executed, or from her score. She earned a perfect ten and won the gold medal.

That vault launched Mary Lou Retton into becoming the most popular women's athlete in America, if only for a moment. Olga Korbut had started a tide of interest in gymnastics, but under Retton, it became a tsunami.

A similar wave had already begun in another sport that also appealed to ballerinas—figure skating. That sport also had its share of young idols. In 1976, another teenager danced and giggled her way into a gold medal and TV stardom. They named an athletic maneuver after her, but what really made her famous was her hairstyle. Even Nadia Comaneci wore a Dorothy Hamill cut when she competed in Moscow.

Once Olympic TV cameras magnified the images of athletes, the two most feminine of sports were attracting huge audiences to watch every move, both in and out of the sporting arena. Gymnastics coverage dominated American

Fig.34. Mary Lou Retton (USA), winner of the 1984 Women's All-Around, dialed the popularity of gymnastics up a notch with her perky personality and dazzling smile. Her broad shoulders and muscular thighs also opened the door to a new type of gymnast (photograph by Jerry Coli © Dreamstime.com).

television in the summer, but figure skating commanded the winter. The same set of countries were still pirouetting and tumbling for medals. The women involved encountered similar problems. Like tsunamis, popularity would leave wreckage in its path, regardless of where you came from or how you competed.

Socialism, Sequins, and a Whack in the Knee

Korbut, Comaneci, and Retton all had something else in common. They were all teenage Cold Warriors. Despite the eye shadow and the crowd-pleasing booty-shaking that accompanied the handsprings, these young women were still soldiers in the battle for cultural hearts and minds that had begun in 1952.

In the 1980s, the Cold War was stronger than ever. When the U.S. hockey team upset the Soviets in the Lake Placid "Miracle on Ice," Americans treated it like V-E Day. Though Team USSR had boycotted the Los Angeles Games, Retton beat women from autocratic Romania and China. As far as Retton was concerned, the jingoistic "We're #1" chants for her gold medal mustered the same enthusiasm that Bob Mathias had worded decades earlier: "You just loved to beat 'em. You just had to beat 'em."

The Cold War was also in full swing in figure skating. Athletes from Eastern Europe and the USSR were as strong on the ice as on the uneven bars. However, in figure skating, the Westerners were also darned good. Combat had been ongoing since the 1950s, with Soviet pairs like the Protopopovs and Rodnina/Zaitsev setting the standard in pairs skating, while John Curry, Robin Cousins, and Dorothy Hamill had defeated East German and Soviet men and women in the singles.

When the U.S. installed Pershing missiles in Western Europe in 1983, tensions between East and West skyrocketed. East German women gained a kind of revenge by defeating American skaters, three Olympics in a row. Two of those golds were won by "the most beautiful face of socialism,"[18] Katarina Witt.

Witt was attractive and athletic. She was a mere 19 in 1984, although she didn't skate like an ingénue. Famous for wearing provocative feathered costumes with plunging necklines, Witt skated for East Germany with a steely-eyed gaze that never seemed to crumble under pressure. In the Sarajevo Olympics, she defeated America's "best bet," Rosalyn Sumners, with two extra triple jumps.

Four years later, she faced another American, Debi Thomas, a better jumper. Thomas was the first Black woman to win a U.S. national and world championship. She also happened to be a Stanford pre-med student and had impressed audiences with her intelligence and poise. She skated with enormous expectations.

For better or worse, both Thomas and Witt chose similar theme music for the 1988 showdown in Calgary. The media labeled their final performances "Battle of the Carmens." On the men's side, as Canadian Brian Orser faced American Brian Boitano, the announcers called it the "Battle of the Brians"—some of the hype was simply repetitive.

Thomas planned a more ambitious program in Calgary than Witt's, opening with a triple-triple jump combination, a maneuver that the East German would not attempt. However, Thomas missed the combination and soon found herself unable to recover the remainder of her program. After more errors, she fell to bronze. Despite the disappointment, Thomas remains the only Black figure skater with an Olympic medal.

Witt's "Carmen" was another thing entirely. Witt was a solid jumper, but her programs were getting simpler as she got older. Lower risk led to fewer errors, and she received the benefit of the doubt in high artistry scores.

Her outfits were also much shorter, and her routines made the most of them. Witt's 1988 Calgary costume displayed so much skin that afterward the ISU added a costume rule which forbade bare buttocks and G-strings. The East German skater was unapologetic about what showed whenever she jumped: "I rather think every man prefers looking at a well-built woman [rather] than someone in the shape of a ball."[19]

Many criticized Witt's blatant appeal for higher scores through "lipsticked lips drawn up in an exaggerated pout."[20] Some described her as a Mata Hari, a femme fatale seducing judges for communism. Other male scholars argued that "we"—presumably the male gazing audience—could "have it all" by appreciating her fine figure "as a competitor" while "simultaneously be[ing] stirred by the erotic appeal of her gliding, whirling, spinning, leaping figure."[21] Especially in a G-string.[22]

Meanwhile, Witt had her own concerns off the rink. Like Comaneci, she was watched incessantly by the East German Stasi, who had kept a file on her since she had attracted national attention at age eight. The government had plied her with luxury items, like cars, televisions, and apartments, to keep her from defecting. Many outside East Germany called her a collaborator, and Witt understood that she was on a velvet leash. "It was a class war, undeniably," she once said. "For the Americans as much as for us. It was a face-off between two opposing political systems."[23] When she won a gold medal, communist North Korea celebrated with a special postage stamp.

After the Berlin Wall came down, the Cold War battle among sequined femme fatales and pixie warriors ended, even though the same cast of characters vied for the top spot. The other underlying battle in ladies' figure skating—between athleticism and appearance—became more pronounced. This tension surfaced, in part, because it was becoming more acceptable for women to be more athletic and more muscular. As women became stronger jumpers, it sharpened the contrast between skating as a sport and a display.

Paul Gallico's words still hovered over the judges' table: "the female figure in the dance, but freed by the steel blades from the ordinary pull of gravity and lethargy of friction." Just as importantly, there was "no costume lovelier or more graceful than the figure-skating dress with its short, flared skirt, and the jaunty caps to match."[24] The jumpers ventured higher, but the costumes became shorter and jauntier.

The 1992 Olympic gold in Albertville went to American Kristy Yamaguchi, a competent all-around skater. Like Witt, Yamaguchi was not the strongest jumper but performed with flair and without error. Two women competing against her had planned more difficult programs. Both wanted to be first to land the jump that, up until then, only the men could do: the triple axel.

Midori Ito of Japan had wowed audiences both in Sarajevo and again in Calgary with seven triple jumps, the first woman to do so. With Witt out of the picture, Japanese fans expected Ito to leap her way to victory. In the 1992 final, though, she fell on her first triple axel, and her subsequent scores pushed her into silver.

Nevertheless, she attempted and landed another triple axel near the end of her program, leading the announcer to gasp that "every skater in the building knows how difficult that is."[25] Ito apologized for disappointing Japan, but being the first woman to land a triple axel in the Games cemented her legacy as one of the greatest athletes in skating history.

Yet Ito was not done in just by missing one jump. For Ito and contemporaries like Surya Bonaly of France, the problem was what happened between the jumps. A skater who only jumped would spend most of the rest of the time simply marching up and down on the ice. Witt, Yamaguchi, Hamill, Fleming, and even Sonja Henie knew that what came between the jumping—sparkling footwork, elegant hand positions, and sustained flexibility—was as important. After all, ballerinas don't just jump.

Fig. 35. "The most beautiful face of socialism," Katarina Witt (DDR) spun and jumped to two figure skating golds in 1984 and 1988. She skated with grace and fluidity, but also wore such racy outfits that the skating federation rewrote the costume rules (photograph by Wolfgang Thierne, German Federal Archive).

Some skaters bristled at the perceived lack of appreciation for their athleticism. Bonaly and her fans complained that she was kept out of the medals because of racism. She could perform multiple jumps and even a backflip, yet received poor artistry scores. The problem was again the between-jumping-part, where Bonaly would lumber up and down the ice, arms mostly at her side.

Classism was the complaint from the other skater with a triple axel—Tonya Harding.

Harding would bring skating a much-bigger audience, but not because of her jumping. She was the first American woman to land a triple axel, in a 1991 competition. She couldn't quite manage it in Albertville and was edged out of the medals by Yamaguchi, Ito, and another American, Nancy Kerrigan.

When Kerrigan, a polished but lackluster skater, appeared to be crowned as the heir apparent for the 1994 Games in Lillehammer, it irked Harding to no end. Kerrigan was even less athletic than Yamaguchi, but slim and graceful, oozing refinement from her fingertips. Judges loved her style.

In comparison, Harding had the jumper's thighs of Midori Ito. However, like Ito and Bonaly, Harding didn't seem to know what to do between jumps. She would gesture with bent elbows like a waitress carrying plates or a lumberjack with an armful of wood, both tasks familiar to her in blue-collar Portland.

Judges told Harding that she should lose weight because of those thick legs that gave her such lift. In skating, judgment was based on appearance, an unfair but acknowledged part of the sport. After a hundred years of Olympic competitions, both men[26] and women were still routinely criticized for their "hairdos and costumes and earrings and eye makeup and teeth (and … failing to change such details might well result in lowered scores)."[27] Harding was told she was too fat and that her costumes, which she could only afford to sew by hand, were too gaudy.

There was a clear double standard. Men got high scores for triples—Brian Boitano won a gold medal with a huge triple axel in 1988—but women needed dance moves and expensive outfits rather than eye-popping jumps. The front-runners used top fashion designers like Christian Lacroix (Surya Bonaly) or Vera Wang (Nancy Kerrigan). Harding had a sewing machine.

Ironically, despite Harding's complaint about "wealthy" opponents, Kerrigan's family was also barely head and shoulders above working class. Her father, a welder, had worked three jobs to pay for Kerrigan's coaching, practice sessions, and costumes. Vera Wang fashions only emerged after Kerrigan's talent had attracted international attention. But Harding saw the fancy white lace outfits and dangling earrings and felt that the judges and media perceived her rival as elegant while she was treated like "trailer trash."

What Harding wanted most of all was the glamor and the magazine covers that came so easily to Kerrigan. *Newsweek*'s "Guide to the Winter Olympics" for the 1994 Lillehammer Games even featured the heir apparent in a dancer's pose. Harding had beaten both Yamaguchi and Kerrigan with that triple axel at the 1991 U.S. Nationals. But that was three years earlier. Harding had not landed the jump in competition since then.

She had also gone through several coaches and been married, separated, gotten a restraining order, and reconciled with her husband, Jeff Gilooly. The struggles on the ice and in her personal life were punctuated by the constant media attention paid to the-winner-in-waiting. Somehow, if Harding could clear the path in front of her, she believed the triple axel could make her famous.

At home, with Gilooly and their friend and bodyguard, Shawn Eckhardt, Harding seethed at the unfairness of it all. They joked around. Someone made a comment, *If only Kerrigan could be taken out....* Harding remembers responding forcefully, *Hey, I can skate! I don't need that.* Eckhardt, who apparently imagined himself playing a cameo in *Goodfellas*, took it as a signal. He knew a guy. Gilooly and Eckhardt met privately. The details are murky, but it seems that Harding wasn't involved in any advance planning, though she may have chosen to ignore what she inadvertently observed.

Thirteen. The Camera Changes the Narrative

The day before the finals of the U.S. Nationals, as Kerrigan left the practice ice in her white spandex, she was approached in the hallway. The hired acquaintance of the bodyguard/friend of the estranged-then-reconciled husband of the disrespected jumper hit the front runner of the Ladies' Figure Skating competition in the knee with a police baton.

Harding got more fame than she bargained for. The media surrounded her house for months, pressing for the interviews that she wanted, but also going through her trash, puncturing her tires, and bugging her phone. To add insult to injury for Kerrigan, she received similar treatment.

While the authorities in law enforcement and the skating federations debated over what to do about Harding, she won the U.S. Nationals, with Kerrigan off recovering. The IOC and ISU further dithered for months over whether to let Harding skate in the Olympics. Ultimately, they allowed her in.

The media feeding frenzy in Lillehammer was even bigger than it had been in America, nearly overshadowing the rest of the Games. Every private comment the two women made was caught on mic. Every time they took the practice ice, the cameras clicked as journalists tried to capture them close enough to be photographed "together." It paid off for CBS, which enjoyed its highest-rated week ever.

When Harding finally competed, she broke a skate lace and had to beg for time to fix the problem. The cameras followed her backstage as she sniffled her way to the skate repair. It was a mini-drama to add to the big drama, which further left the actual competition behind. Harding did not complete her famed triple axel, and her predictably shaky skate dropped her to eighth place.

Meanwhile, Kerrigan had worked her tail off just to get back on the ice. She later said her two Lillehammer performances were the two best skates of her life, which was remarkable given the public scrutiny. While most of the press had treated her with sympathy, some late-night comics and tabloid photos mocked her sobs after the attack: "Why? Why?" Others complained that Harding's triple axels had been unfairly under-scored, without noting that Harding had not landed those jumps when given the opportunity to do so.

Enter a skinny teenager from the Ukraine named Oksana Baiul. Baiul had started as a ballet dancer but, of all things, was told she was not thin enough. She had gravitated toward skating instead. Her ultra-classical style was conservative but had the energy that Kerrigan lacked and the leaping that Harding had missed. It was chock full of judge-pleasing ballerina moves. In a pink feathery tutu, she tippy-toed across the ice to "Swan Lake" and became the judges' solution to the ugly mess.

The 1994 Ladies' Figure Skating event earned a 40 share, one of the highest TV audiences ever. The collateral damage on the skaters was bigger.

Baiul, for starters, parlayed her gold medal into an international skating tour. Among the older Americans and Russians on the tour bus, the alcohol flowed freely. The under-aged Baiul developed a severe drinking problem. She was further told to ignore injuries which developed during the grueling performance schedule. By the time she went into a substance abuse program and treated her knee issues, her competitive and professional skating career was over.

In the months that followed, Harding pled guilty to knowing about the attack after the fact, but not reporting it. While she did not serve time, she was banned for life from competing. Desperate to gain respect, Harding had created conditions which guaranteed she would never be respected.

Kerrigan herself found the glare of the cameras off the ice to be oppressive as well. She was caught on mic criticizing Baiul while waiting for the podium ceremony, after mistakenly being told that the ceremony was delayed for the Ukrainian to reapply her makeup after crying. Kerrigan's comment, "Why? She's just going to cry again" was portrayed as another example of an American bully.

Later, Kerrigan's comments were picked up by another hot mic complaining during a Disneyworld parade that it was "corny." Now, she was being mean to Mickey Mouse! She explained it was because Disney required her to wear her Olympic bronze medal, which she found embarrassing. By the end of her Olympic journey, Nancy Kerrigan was just happy to be forgotten by the press.

Overall, women figure skaters before and after Lillehammer seemed to pay a very heavy price for the magazine covers. The list of medalists "opening up" about mental health issues—bipolar disorder, depression, suicide attempts, panic attacks—became long: Hamill, Sumners, Thomas, and, more recently, U.S. national champion and 2014 bronze medalist Gracie Gold. Eating disorders (Kerrigan, Adam Rippon) and substance abuse issues (Tai Babilonia) also became common.

A sport which Coubertin once praised because of its "sporting dignity so frank and pure" had turned on lights from television so glaring that few seemed to escape unharmed. In front of the camera, the women were "darlings on the ice." Behind the camera, they were a mess.

And the cameras kept coming. Even avoiding the cameras could turn a star athlete into a recluse—the ultimate sin. When the cameras were deployed to create heroes and villains, it could be hard to play either role. It was especially hard when a whole country was gunning for you.

The Camera Anoints, the Camera Condemns

> "The 400 m in Sydney was not a race against Cathy Freeman, it was a race against an entire nation which had its problems.... I was only prepared for a 400 m."[28]—Marie-José Pérec, two-time 400 m gold medalist

The city of Sydney decided to do something special to celebrate the centennial of women's Olympic participation in the year 2000. The opening ceremony for their Olympics paid reverent homage to women athletes. Australia was determined to show throughout their Games that they had purged their history of racism and sexism. They were also going to make sure they eliminated any obstacles that might block that plan, even if they had to be racist and sexist to do it.

During the 2000 opening ceremony, a little girl flew across the sky in wonder, watching the rise of aboriginal culture across the outback and the arrival of settlers who had made it to Australia's faraway shores. Several segments highlighted

Australia's multiculturalism, showing migrants from Africa, Europe, and Asia mingling happily with the natives, who danced in colorful costumes.

At the finale, as pictures of past torch relays flashed on giant screens above the stadium, the athletes on the field parted to create a path. Torch bearers entered through the crowd, unknown to the spectators (and TV audience) until a close-up camera revealed them. All were women, some of the greatest athletes from Australia's Olympic history. There were Betty Cuthbert and Shirley Strickland, the speedsters who between them had gathered five gold medals in Melbourne 1956. There was Dawn Fraser, who won the Olympic 100 m freestyle, three times in a row.

Then, in the most iconic moment from those millennial Games, a figure covered in silver took the torch and briskly climbed the steps to cross a pool of water. As she held aloft the torch, the water rose, echoing the fire and water symbols that had flared and flowed throughout the entire ceremony. She knelt down to light the water around her, and a circle of flame rose, floating upward to light the cauldron above the stadium. There was a brief moment where the mechanism stalls, but it corrected itself, and the circle of light, water, and athlete emerged as perfect. Certainly, perfect enough for photographs that still astound, years later.

Sydney manufactured this perfect image, when their beloved native daughter, Cathy Freeman, lit the Olympic cauldron. Never mind that many in the audience were descendants of the colonizers who arrived from Europe, Asia, and elsewhere to oppress Freeman's ancestors. Never mind that when Freeman, an indigenous Australian, had waved the aboriginal flag after winning a race a few years earlier, a Commonwealth Games official pressed for her expulsion.[29] Or, that when Freeman had won races as a youngster, the white girls had been given trophies for coming in second and third, while she received nothing.

Freeman's lighting of the torch was Australia's demonstration that they had eliminated the prejudice of yesteryear:

> She is not only the heroine of the Olympics, of Australia's rare track golds, but also, for many Australians, the symbol of reconciliation between black and white. Her image promotes airline companies, mobile phones, the assets of the jet Australian consumer. She is depicted as a happy-go-lucky lover of freedom, a "good sport," the highest praise Australians can give. At the same time, her aboriginality is a strong part of her public identity.

For a long time the opening ceremony had been just a sideshow, important to classics scholars and Coubertinistas but actually dull to observe. Prior to 1980, the launch of the Games consisted of speeches, classical music snippets, the long parade of athletes, and more of the same. In 1980, organizers for the Moscow Games added several feel-good history pieces from the birth of the USSR, presumably leaving out the gulags and the KGB.

Los Angeles, of course, had to top the Soviets with 85 grand pianos and a man flying in on a jet pack. When television packaged the ceremonies for a much larger audience than those in the stands, a country could use the opportunity to whitewash its past. Muhammad Ali lit the torch in the 1996 Games in Atlanta, as if the U.S. had forgotten he was once sentenced to prison for evading the draft.

Australia in 2000 also set out to prove its past was over, in full view of the world. It was thrilled to use Freeman and other female medalists as a backdrop. There was no acknowledgment, for example, that the women's water polo team had had to protest in swimsuits for their sport to be included in those same Games. There was no memory of the New South Wales Ladies Amateur Swimming Association forbidding their swimmers to race in public.

What Australia also needed was for Cathy Freeman to win the 400 m. She had taken the silver four years earlier, but, in 2000, she was now the front-runner, certainly as far as the country was concerned. Winning the gold medal would close the loop on the perfect image. Freeman needed to win the gold so that Australia could prove it was no longer racist.

Only one problem—the other runners.

Marie-José Pérec, Freeman's main competition, was tucked away in a hotel room in Sydney. She was skipping the opening ceremony because, from the moment she had arrived, she had been surrounded by the Australian press. She refused to live among the athletes in the Olympic village. She refused interviews. She refused to cooperate.

Pérec was the two-time defending Olympic medalist in the 400 m. She had also taken gold in the 200 m in 1996, which had surprised her coach, who had told her that running the 200 was not such a hot idea. But Pérec was legendary for going her own path and doing things her way. It ticked off her team, her own country's media, and now the Australians.

Ironically enough, Pérec herself was a native of Guadeloupe, a Caribbean island, which the French characterized as an "overseas 'département,'" i.e., a French colony. Pérec, in other words, was an indigenous person like Freeman, exported to France at age 16 when she was discovered to be really fast. Her indigenous status is rarely mentioned in her bios.

By her early twenties, Pérec had set records across multiple sprint distances, breaking 11 seconds in the 100 m and 50 seconds in the 400 m, both near-record times. Once she became an expert in the 400, with her two golds in 1992 and 1996, the French press had nicknamed her *La Gazelle*, a nod to Wilma Rudolph. Both had those long legs to help them whiz around the track.

But Rudolph had been coached to be patient with the press. Pérec was not patient. She didn't care for either the press or the French authorities. At the peak of her career, she had developed a reputation even at home as hostile, reclusive, and eccentric. One coach said she had a "difficult temper." She went through several coaches.

Still, Pérec had every intention of defending her 400 m Olympic title in Sydney against Freeman. The Frenchwoman said she was not afraid of running against Freeman and boasted that she might even be able to run under 49 seconds, as both had done in Atlanta. It was a long shot, however, even though she was the reigning champion.

At age 32, her body was finally catching up with her, and she was still recovering from a string of injuries, including a long bout with Epstein-Barr virus. She was not in her best form. Yet she had come to Sydney, hoping to keep the race close and perhaps use her experience to eke out a win against the younger Freeman.

Even this level of competition seemed too much for some Australians. While

Pérec was criticized for separating herself from other athletes, every time she went out in public, she was harassed "at her hotel, in supermarkets, and everywhere else. 'There wasn't a day that I wasn't tracked, like an animal, truly,' she said."[30] There were scads of emails, "threatening gestures." Tabloids carried unflattering photos of her and stressed repeatedly how badly she had been running recently.

A few nights before the preliminary heats, there was a knock on her hotel door. When she answered, a man threatened her and tried to force his way in. According to Pérec's agent, the man "told her he would find her wherever she went and there was no point calling the police because there was little they could do to protect her."[31] Pérec had had enough. Suddenly, "nothing else mattered, not even the gold medal I came for."

The hotel manager, in later interviews, scoffed at her claim. He said there was 24-hour security, as if a guard in the lobby would stop random strangers from knocking on doors and making threats. He stressed that she never complained.

Nevertheless, Pérec headed straight to the airport with her boyfriend. They flew first to Singapore, but while waiting for their connecting flight back to Paris, a TV cameraman pestered them so much that Pérec's companion got into "an altercation." The police were called, and Pérec plus boyfriend were detained at the airport for several hours to answer questions. The Singapore airport police could somehow not understand what might have sparked such a confrontation, why someone who had been harassed while trying to buy lettuce and been chased after constantly by paparazzi would be upset. Even the *New York Times* asked, "*Why did French runner run away?*"[32]

And the word used was "run," clearly to contrast with how Pérec did not run in the Games. Every article in the aftermath used similar phrases: *run away, flee, done a runner*. The *Sydney Morning Herald*, with a front-page photo of Pérec turning away from huge flashbulbs, chronicled the list of her transgressions: "August 4: fails to race…. August 5: pulls out…. August 16: Announces she will not run because of her injury…. September 8: brushes way past waiting media…. September 19: Fails to appear at a press conference."[33] The last two seemed to underline the biggest sin, which was refusing to talk to the media.

The Daily Telegraph, an Australian tabloid, was even blunter with their front page: "MADEMOISELLE LA CHICKEN!" The French sprinter was showered with a host of adjectives often applied to women athletes who displayed (à la Mary Decker) "emotional outbursts." Pérec was "temperamental" and had an "emotional breakdown."[34] One Australian columnist made a list of the words used by his colleagues: "'Petulant.' 'Temperamental.' 'French missy.' 'Precious mademoiselle.' 'Scared.' 'Seriously disturbed.' 'Fantasist.' 'Sadly deluded.' 'Brittle.' 'Disgraced.'"

Because Pérec had not reported any of this harassment to the police or the hotel manager—the Australian police, the Australian hotel manager—there was the strong implication that it was all in her deluded mind. Except that the photos of her being chased by cameramen proved that she was harassed right out of the country.

As Australians high-fived each other for pushing their main rival out of the race, Freeman herself was gracious and not thrilled with the media. "I hope that you guys are treating her nicely and giving her all the respect she deserves."[35]

The country celebrated with abandon when Freeman did win the actual 400 m final. Her time was nowhere near a record or below the previous Olympic results, nor was any other runner close to her. At the end of the fated race, as she passed the finish line, there was no smile and none of the grateful tears common to winners. Her immediate facial expression was grim, with exhaustion and gloom running across her face. *Thank heaven this nightmare is over.*

After the race, Freeman sank to her knees and covered her face, ready to let the weight of the country lift off her shoulders. A smiling Donna Fraser from Great Britain—who had herself just missed out on the medals—ran up to embrace her in joy, but Freeman remained on the ground, still panting, almost afraid to acknowledge that she had done what was demanded of her.

She smiled at last when she got up to move toward the photographers, who surrounded her in a pack.

Fig.36. Cathy Freeman (AUS), stalked by photographers after winning the 400 m in Sydney 2000 (photograph by Ian © ThePaperboy.com, Wikimedia Commons).

Fourteen

Showing the World (1988–2016)

The rise of the cameras in the 1970s and 1980s showed women just how carefully they would have to manage their public image in order to compete successfully. The whole world was watching, at least what was captured by those cameras. Those who learned the lessons of their predecessors could use it to their advantage. They couldn't compete if they were hounded by paparazzi. They also faced headwinds if they were trivialized, treated as children, or didn't fit the "proper" image.

Those who were marginalized—young women and women of color—might find the glare harshest. They would have to be the strongest, the most daring, and the most thick-skinned if they wanted to compete and earn respect.

Plenty answered the call. One of the smallest was one of the most courageous of all.

The Greatest Vault in History

It makes every American list of Top Ten Olympic moments.

A little girl with a worried expression walks down the gymnastics vault runway, glancing at the sidelines and shaking her leg. Her coach in the stands, a tall man with bushy eyebrows, barks at her repeatedly, "You can do it! Way to go! You can do it…" as he points and urges her back to the starting spot. She's mouthing something: "Do we need this?"

The crowd is shrieking. A few seconds earlier, as a replay shows, she under-rotated slightly on her vault and slipped backward, landing on her posterior. She appears to have injured something, an ankle or knee. She continues to shake out her leg as she looks at the sidelines. Her parents in the stands both simultaneously clasp their hands above their head. Her teammates look anxious, so clearly there is a team at stake here, too.

She looks to be about nine years old, chewing at her lip. In reality, she is 18½, old enough to vote. She raises her arms above her head and stares at something. Then, she blows air out of her cheeks and takes off, elbows pumping to accelerate quickly.

This most famous vault in Olympic history—one of the most famous *moments* in Olympic history—has stirred controversy ever since.

Kerri Strug, the final vaulter on the U.S. women's gymnastics team at the 1996 Olympics, was competing in the last rotation for the team medal. The American squad had never reached higher than silver, and that was only when the USSR boycotted the Games. But, in Atlanta, the Americans had been brilliant, and they had a realistic chance at winning. However, one of Strug's teammates, Dominic Moceanu, had fallen twice on her earlier vaults, and the scores were agonizingly close. Russian Rosa Galieva was about to start her floor exercise, her final event, so it was not known what vault score the U.S. would need to win.

When Strug sat down on the mat after her first vault, she had heard a pop and felt something twist in her ankle. She knew she was hurt. Her coach, Bela Karolyi, probably knew it. She vaulted again anyway, risking the medal, her leg, her pride, and her gymnastics career.

The questions have surfaced repeatedly: *Did Team USA need the vault to win? Why did the coaches urge her on, without checking on her more thoroughly or reviewing the score? Did she know she was injured? Why did she do it?*

Gymnastic team scoring was complicated. In the 1948 team final between Czechoslovakia and Hungary, the teams were tied at 316.7 going into the last rotation. They hadn't known how close it was at the time because scoring with paper and pencil took hours. Even a half century later and with computers available, team totals which depended on a routine that hadn't yet started were hard to evaluate.

Strug's first vault score was 9.162. It was high because, although she had landed poorly, the vault was difficult and otherwise well-executed. Since the Russian Galieva had not finished, the U.S. team thought they *might* need Strug's second vault—a better vault—in order to improve on Moceanu's lower scores.[1]

No one on the team had apparently calculated that they did not need Strug's second vault. Decades later, it's still not clear who did know it. Some now claim it was obvious: "Producers in the TV trucks, parents in the stands, officials at the scorer's table all knew the answer.... Only the coaches and the athletes didn't know."[2] But the complexities of throwing out the lowest scores for multiple teams required computations *not* available to the TV producers and parents. Moreover, Strug and her coaches thought they only had thirty seconds to decide. No one knew in those thirty seconds whether the vault was necessary, certainly not everyone watching without access to all the judges' totals.

For nearly a century, women had been considered too frail to be athletic—too delicate to run the 800 m and too fragile to attempt the ski jump. Lots of women were tired of being told they couldn't do it. In particular, Strug and her college-aged gymnastics teammates were treated like 12-year-olds in public, with announcers routinely commenting on how adorable they were. *You just wanna pick 'em up and hug 'em!* Women athletes, despite their popularity, were still not taken seriously. This was especially irritating for gymnasts, given the contrast with their brutal training in private.

Only a year earlier, sportswriter Joan Ryan had published an exposé of women's gymnastics and figure skating titled *Little Girls in Pretty Boxes*.[3] Ryan had detailed, for example, how young women were exposed to extremely limited diets. Many of Karolyi's former students said that he and his wife were manic in insisting their gymnasts subsist on inadequate calories, shaming them anytime they ate a French fry or "pizza with cheese."[4] Coaches would check the incoming teens' luggage for food, and additional food sent by parents would be confiscated. Recently, records from Romania even surfaced which described similar or even harsher practices by the Karolyis in the 1970s. Some of Nadia Comaneci's teammates had taken to eating toothpaste just to have something in their stomach.

The AMA had coined a new medical condition—the Female Triad.[5] Women were showing up at doctor's offices with eating disorders, menstrual dysfunction, and low bone mineral density. It wasn't from being an athlete; it was from the combination of intense training and insufficient calories typical to those who were shamed for appearing too fat.

Additionally, gymnasts were practicing when severely injured. One of Ryan's chapters was titled "If It's Not Bleeding, Don't Worry About It." Gymnast Betty Okino, from the bronze-medal-winning 1992 team, described training with Karolyi on a knee that desperately needed rest and recuperation. Another Olympic alumnus from 2000, Jamie Dantzscher, talked about training with "plantar fasciitis so painful that I couldn't stand on carpet; with my hips going out of alignment on a daily basis; with sprained ankles, broken toes, fractures in my back, and torn cartilage in my wrist and ankle."[6]

This was not a uniquely American gymnastic complaint nor was it limited to the Karolyis. Russian and Soviet female gymnasts had been increasingly coached by men who emphasized difficult complex techniques over the choreography. The apparatus and scoring changes had led to higher degrees of difficulty but also to moves which were more dangerous. Promising Soviet gymnasts had ended up as quadriplegics.[7]

Strug herself had already been seriously injured, more than once. She had torn a stomach muscle in 1993. A fall from the uneven bars led to her being carried out in a stretcher with a serious lower back sprain. "That really scared my dad," said Strug. She had also felt for years like "second fiddle. If they took two girls to the finals, I was third. If they took three, I was fourth."[8]

Thus, in private, many of the pixies were starving or walking wounded. In public, they were viewed as cute and cuddly, rather than strong. Strug, perhaps, had just had enough of the contrast. "Everyone always said I was the baby. This was my time and I said, I'm going to prove it. People have the wrong impression, that [gymnasts] are robots and don't think. I was upset with people blaming Bela [for my decision to vault again]."[9]

As Strug walked back to the starting position, mulling over whether to repeat the vault, her decade of struggle made the choice an easy one. She flew down the runway, fists clenched, then shoved downward, palms spread wide. Her hands pushed off the board and on to the vault as she sailed into a straight-legged, twisting flip.

Both feet landed straight downward and both hands went up, as if Strug hoped raising her arms would lessen the pain that was coming. Gravity intervened. As the weight settled on her injured ankle, it rebounded as if touching hot coals. She hopped on one foot in two directions, arms in the air, in the mechanical salute to audience and judges that all gymnasts have been taught. Then, she crumbled to her knees, her face contorted in pain.

As if surprised, the TV announcer gasped, "Kerri Strug is hurt!"

Kerri Strug was hurt on the first vault. Her coach knew it. Strug had shredded tendons in her ankle. While she would vault again, she would never compete again.

Many athletes have done remarkable things while competing injured. Los Angeles Dodger Kirk Gibson limped to the plate before hitting the winning home run in the bottom of the ninth of a 1988 World Series game. Emmitt Smith led the Dallas Cowboys to victory with a dislocated shoulder. Greg Louganis hit his head on the diving board, then won gold in the finals with his head bandaged. Most of the famous injured athletes to date had been men.

Strug saw herself joining this hardy breed:

> I knew I needed to land the second vault well in order to feel good about myself and my Olympic performance, secure the team gold medal and also qualify for the all-around finals.... I was the one that decided that I would and could do the vault again. I wanted to show the world how hard I had worked, that I could do the vault well, and to make sure we would win the team gold.[10]

When the gymnasts mounted the podium, Strug was carried in Coach Karolyi's arms. The image was again one of a little girl in daddy's arms rather than a heroic athlete who had braved pain to deliver a patriotic victory for Team USA. A wheelchair might have made more sense, but someone—the TV director? the team? Karolyi himself?—seemed to prefer the optics.

For the gymnastic exhibition, Strug was also carried in by the all-around men's medalist, Russian gymnast Alexei Nemov. In later years, Strug allowed herself to be carried in by Barry Switzer, Shaquille O'Neal, and several ESPN anchormen. She has never minded jokes about being portrayed as a helpless female. Everyone in the world knows that when the camera was on her at the moment of truth, she wasn't helpless.

Those first gold-medal-winning American women gymnasts were dubbed "The Magnificent Seven" by the media. The use of nicknames, too, would become an important part of controlling what people thought. It wasn't a nickname the women chose. Over time, they would need to grab the reins back from the cameramen, the media, and the coaches, in order to drive their own safe athletic destiny.

Strug upended conventional notions of what gymnasts were capable of doing. Others would also find ways to change the paradigm, sometimes finding controversy, but ultimately trying to govern their own public image.

From Unaffected Grace to Refreshing Boldness: Jackie & Flo-Jo

> "From her clothing choices to her fingernail colors, Flo-Jo's appearance fostered more public awe and scrutiny than did her athletic accomplishments."—Lindsay Pieper[11]

While gymnasts were often infantilized, women of color had also long been slighted. When women's participation in sports widened at the end of the 20th century, opportunities increased for competitions that required power and strength. For Black American women, their increasingly spectacular feats of derring-do resurfaced long-held biases. Some athletes blunted criticisms with grace and elegance, while others used fashion to wrap their muscularity in femininity.

Despite the treatment of Marie-José Pérec in Australia, very few Black track stars were chased after by photographers. Bias was more subtle. Back in the 1930s, when Black female American track athletes first appeared, they were often ignored entirely. Tidye Pickett and Louise Stokes had experienced this when lesser-qualified white substitutes were given their racing spots in the 1932 Games.

Nevertheless, Black athletes continued to perform and excel, especially in track and field. As noted in Chapter Six, white women were pressured to abandon track after the 1940s for cultural reasons that did not necessarily affect Black women. The Black community supported athletes, as Susan Cahn explains in *Coming on Strong,* who could "affirm the dignity and capabilities of African American womanhood."[12] On the other hand, those outside the community might use the track stars to "confirm derogatory images of both black and athletic women." The media sometimes dismissed the success of Black female track athletes entirely by claiming they were the "inevitable result of 'natural,' 'masculine' prowess."

Moreover, Black women were often characterized in racist terms, e.g., as animals. Black athletes were compared with gorillas if they were strong and gazelles if they were fast. Worse, they were characterized in highly sexualized terms as "lascivious and apelike," in contrast with the delicate, "asexual purity among highly 'civilized' white women."[13] A Black athlete trying to navigate these prejudices must tread carefully.

This was why Tigerbelle Coach Ed Temple had taken the charm school approach. Forty years later, the perfect example of charm school medalist, who exhibited that contrast between deeds and temperament could be found in the other Greatest Woman Athlete of the 20th Century, Jackie Joyner-Kersee.[14]

Joyner-Kersee rose to national attention in 1984 with a silver medal in the heptathlon, followed by back-to-back golds in 1988 and 1992. She added three medals in the long jump, just for good measure. Yet she smashed records, as *Sports Illustrated* termed it, with "unaffected grace."[15]

One way the media resolved the contrasting image, the image of the "good Baptist" who obliterated her competition, was to frame stories of the "modest" Joyner-Kersee with her coach and husband, Bob Kersee. Kersee was a big part of helping Jackie attain her extraordinary results, but the two were always treated as a duo in interviews. They were pictured together, even if it was a cover piece on the "world beater," and Kersee was quoted nearly as much as his accomplished wife.

Some stories even focused on how "Jackie has to be horse-whipped to run any distance"[16] or how Bob ordered her around like a "marine drill sergeant."[17] Showing Joyner-Kersee controlled by a male authority was another way of blunting her power. It was a unique take for someone considered the World's Greatest. How often was Babe Didrikson photographed with Colonel McCombs? Does anyone know the name of the coaches for decathletes Ashton Eaton or Daley Thompson?[18]

Joyner-Kersee seemed unbothered by the focus on her husband and primarily let her competing do the talking. Six medals in the heptathlon and long jump, spanning four Olympics, said quite a lot. Other Black athletes, however, might take a different path, draping their muscularity within a mantle of femininity.

First and foremost of these was Joyner-Kersee's sister-in-law, Florence Griffith-Joyner. "Flo-Jo"—for she was flamboyant enough to garner her own celebrity athlete nickname—was a legend in her own time. She was a sassy, brassy sprinter who punctuated her unprecedented performances with elaborately designed fingernails and eye-catching track suits. She silenced critics of her one-legged outfits and extravagant hairstyles by running races with times that were extraordinary.

Like her heptathlete in-law, Florence Griffith made a relatively modest debut in 1984 in Los Angeles, taking a silver medal in the 200 m. The family connection was especially tight. Griffith was dating triple jumper Al Joyner, Jackie's brother. That future husband won a gold in Los Angeles while his sister was jumping and his fiancée-to-be was sprinting. When silver didn't meet Griffith's dreams, she left running to work full-time at a bank and part-time at a hair and nail salon. Yet she was still dating Joyner, and the track beckoned her back.

By 1987, she had changed her mind and was impatient to get back in shape. Joyner proposed and starting coaching her in tandem with Kersee. She became a fanatic about weight training, first to shed pounds and secondly to find an edge against the competition. "If you think of running like a man, you have to train like a man, and weights are the main factor."[19]

Unafraid of the "mannish" label, Griffith-Joyner did lats and squats for hours every evening. With huge, new quadriceps, she started exploding off the blocks, and her times rapidly improved. It led to accusations of steroid use, but Flo-Jo passed all the drug tests. The accusations came anyway. She did more squats. She added more glitter.

Even in Los Angeles, her four-inch-long curved fingernails had made news. For her comeback at the 1987 World Championships in Rome, she arrived in a hooded speed skating outfit, and wrists festooned with bracelets. She came in second in the elite field.[20]

For the following spring, Griffith-Joyner showed off an entirely new set of designs—the one-legged track suits. Some were purple or aquamarine, while others sported lace or leopard print. She said she sometimes brought a dozen outfits to each meet.

People didn't know which to criticize: the peek-a-boo lace or the muscles? The "dragon lady" fingernails or the lightning-fast starts? The massive quads or the bling? Some argued that Griffith-Joyner's fashion choices were "supporting the sexual exploitation and subjugation of black women ... promot[ing] a racialized binary of sexual difference."[21] Others wanted to know where they were sold.

Many griped about her quick rise to popularity, and how endorsements started rolling in for her before she had won any medals. They claimed she was "a 'shameless' self-promoter who presented herself as an 'exotic alien' in order to 'seduce' and 'titillate' the public."[22] The bare leg, which "appeared more naked than any other bare limb in the race" certainly shifted the conversation off her muscles.

Plenty also applauded her embrace of "sports and eros."[23] Olympic historian Guttmann called her the "brightest star" of 1988 with "her flamboyant, intensely colorful space-age"[24] suits. Cultural historian Cahn pointed out that Griffith-Joyner's "refreshing boldness ... demanded recognition of ... femininity and strength."[25] The one-legged suits made her a "fashion pioneer," according to *Vogue*. As a true pioneer, she then went out and smashed the record books.

In an early heat for the 1988 U.S. Olympic Trials, as Griffith-Joyner lined up in an electric plum one-legged suit, the announcers noted that the wind was too strong for new records. Earlier heat times had already been fast, but the wind was over the legal limit. At the start, Griffith-Joyner erupted from the blocks and left the others several steps behind her long, flowing hair. Her time of 10.49 was an astonishing 0.27 seconds below the existing record. The AAU certified the record because the wind gauge showed zero, although later analysis showed the timing instrument was probably faulty. The time may have been incorrect, but the distance between her and everybody else was not.

Babe Didrikson had likewise come out of nowhere, going in just two years from picking up a javelin to smashing half the records in her events. Like Didrikson, Griffith-Joyner had been obsessed with training, reportedly staying at the track until one or two in the morning. But in the early days of steroids, any rapid improvement might be suspect. Plus there was the wind. One of the TV announcers scoffed, "No one can run that fast."[26] Clearly, someone could. In the semis and the finals, Griffith-Joyner did it again, with times of 10.70 and 10.61.

At the Games in Seoul, Griffith-Joyner had to wear the plain red-and-white Team USA uniform. She did, however, paint her nails different colors—red, white, blue, and optimistic gold. In both the heats and finals, for both the 100 and 200 m, she breezed to the finish, knocking the 100 m Olympic record down to 10.62 and the 200 m world record down to 21.34.

Complaints about substance-abuse got louder, especially after drug testing in those Games caught Canadian sprinter Ben Johnson. Yet Griffith-Joyner failed no tests, despite being tested—according to the chair of the IOC's medical commission at the time—with all "possible and imaginable analyses."[27] Her mother said she kept copies of all the clean tests because she was so angry at the continued, unproven accusations.

Fig. 37. Sporting peek-a-boo lace and eye-popping muscle definition, Florence Griffith-Joyner (USA) set records at the 1988 U.S. Olympic Trials that still held firm in 2021 (photograph by Jerry Coli © Dreamstime.com).

After her amazing, blazing runs in the U.S. Trials and in Seoul, Griffith-Joyner parlayed her success into endorsements, exercise videos, books, and a seat on the Presidential Commission on Fitness. There were suggestions that she left the sport suddenly and suspiciously before random testing was introduced, but she was 29, ready to have a child, and wanted to earn money from endorsements, still banned for "amateurs." No one had speculated so hard about why track legends Rudolph and Didrikson had retired after only one Olympics.

Griffith-Joyner did attempt a comeback in 1996, after giving birth in 1990. Injury and age intervened. Then, in 1998, she died suddenly in her sleep. Rumors surfaced again, and the medical examiner was brought in. The only drugs found in her system were Tylenol and Benadryl. She had died from a seizure. Her family revealed that it had not been the first.

The total for the glamorous sprinter was three gold medals from Seoul. One more gold than Babe Didrikson and one fewer than Fanny Blankers-Koen. Florence Griffith-Joyner had earned them with unparalleled flair.

The flair was catching and even swept up her sister-in-law. In 1996, as Joyner-Kersee competed in her fourth and final Olympics, she appeared in a remarkable ad. In a soothing voice over black-and-white views of her running in slow motion, she said, "I can throw a nine-pound shot put fifty-one feet. I bench press 155 pounds. I jump further than all but 128 men in the world. And I have red toenails."[28]

It was an ad for Avon makeup. While a few criticized the trivialization of Joyner-Kersee's athletic accomplishments by comparing them to her makeup use, most saw the ad as a strong positive image—for both the athlete and the makeup. After all, the toenails came last.

The commercial wasn't about how ornamentation superseded her muscularity, or about how Joyner-Kersee was abandoning her athletics for makeup. Unlike Paul Gallico's 1930s article "Babe Is a Lady Now...," this ad showed how Jackie Joyner-Kersee had always *been* a lady, *and* how she still jumped further than all but 128 men in the world. Strength *and* femininity, with neither needing to compromise.

Fashioning Their Own

Griffith-Joyner and Joyner-Kersee would not be the last to celebrate their muscular femininity. Two other Black Olympic athletes took a similar approach to winning with strength and style. The first one picked up the baton the same year as the Seoul Games. In 1988, Serena and Venus Williams burst into the country club world. Afterward, tennis would never be the same.

They were a talented pair, raised to play tennis almost before they could walk. Sixteen-year-old Serena and 17-year-old Venus made it several games into the 1988 Australian Open. Venus beat Serena to make it to the quarterfinals, the first of many meetings between the sisters high in the brackets. Venus won the Mixed Doubles (with Justin Gimelstob), also the first of many.

In Australia, the sisters also claimed they could beat any man ranked over #200. Both were quickly beaten by the #203 ranked player, but it did get them attention, and they did start climbing the rankings. By 2000, both were winning Grand Slam finals, a few years after tennis had finally made it back to the Olympics. In the Williams sisters' Women's Doubles Tennis Olympic inaugural appearance in Sydney, they took the gold at ages 19 and 20.

They seemed made for the Games. Venus in 2020 sat at the top of the all-time Olympic tennis list with five medals: a Singles gold in Sydney, Doubles golds in Sydney, Beijing, and London, and a Mixed Double silver in Rio (with Rajeev Ram). Serena earned a Singles gold in London, and the three Doubles golds with her sister.

Twenty years after Sydney, though, Serena had eclipsed her sister as a singles player. She is widely regarded as the greatest women's tennis player of all time, after amassing 23 singles Grand Slam titles plus 14 doubles titles with Venus. Her monster serve and muscular ground game shifted the way women's tennis is played. While she never did defeat highly ranked men's players, videos have surfaced of her being challenged by ordinary male players, who were then bounced off the court with her 128-mph rockets.

She has also been called every name in the book. Thick-legged. Gorilla. Breasts that are "registered to vote." Covered with "thick, muscled blubber."[29] She has said that she learned early on not to read everything written about her. She simply let her tennis do the talking. As it had with Joyner-Kersee and Griffith-Joyner, her winning had a lot to say. However, when Williams grabbed the reins of tennis, taking over the #1 ranking in 2002 and hardly letting go for fifteen years, she also chose to make fashion statements.

They were loud statements. There was the short-legged leather cat-suit for the U.S. Open in 2002. She followed with denim-and-leather "rebel" outfits in 2004. Both Puma and Nike signed her to wear their creations, and she designed some of her own. Many caused raised eyebrows, like the white trench coat at Wimbledon worn on a cloudless day in 2008. But as the designs extended into jewelry, handbags, nails, and hair, their exaggerated femininity offset the constant hand-wringing over her grunting, muscles, and hard-hitting play.

Fig.39. Muscular femininity was on display when Serena Williams fired a rocket return at the 2015 U.S. Open. The front pattern of her dress was as intricate as the ripples in her powerful thighs (photograph by Zhukovsky © Dreamstime.com).

A full-length cat-suit meant to help prevent blood clotting took special criticism in the 2018 French Open and was banned. (Perhaps too much fabric?) Her outfit at the very next tournament was an off-the-shoulder top with an exaggerated tutu.

In 2021, trying a comeback after maternity leave, injuries, and the COVID hiatus, Williams made it to the semifinals of the Australian Open sporting a pink-and-black one-legged cat-suit. She flatly declared it an homage to Flo-Jo. Both athletes smashed records—one in a brief blaze of glory and the other by "out-muscling" one teenager after another for decades. Both athletes achieved their extraordinary results with deliberate, calculatingly beautiful style.

At the Rio Olympics, on August 9, 2016, the Williams sisters ended their bid for a third consecutive doubles Olympic gold medal. Serena was unable to advance to another Singles medal as well. Their Olympic journey may or may not continue, but their reputation was assured.

Two days later at the same Rio Games, the women's shot put competition highlighted a third powerful Black athlete who put on a show of muscles and haute couture. Thirty-one-year-old Michelle Carter had also hunted for Olympic glory before, although unsuccessfully. This time, she came with better throwing technique and a full complement of lip gloss.

Carter is the daughter of the silver medalist from the 1984 shot put, Michael Carter. She had shied away from her dad's sport, trying other pastimes, until a high school teacher suggested it, unaware of her dad's history. She was a natural and made the U.S. National Team at age 15. An athletic scholarship soon put her through the University of Texas, and she kept throwing and improving after college—for nine more years.

What makes Carter unique, aside from her strength and technique, is that she is also a certified makeup artist. A sharp dresser off the field, she brings as much style as possible on the field—especially on the field. This might mean diamond-studded earrings, sculpted gold nails, intricate headbands, and/or thick, extra-long fake eyelashes. She explained that she chooses carefully how she will appear: "I'll lay out the makeup I want to put on: a brow filler, a lipstick—there's a NYX red one that looks great with those Team USA uniforms—and my lashes. I have to have my lashes."[30]

IOC President Brundage once said that women should avoid track and field and stick to swimming, fencing, and gymnastics, in particular, because "the shot put does nothing for them."[31] Brundage might have changed his mind had he seen Carter. Or the entire field of powerful women who lined up for the 2016 competition.

While Carter, who calls herself the Shot Diva, was an elegant stand-out, what was notable was the variety in shapes, sizes, and styles among these strongest women of the track and field events. Some were tall, like New Zealander Val Adams, two-time gold medalist, who is 6'4", with whip-like forearms. Adams would fold in half almost gently, like a Greek statue, before launching the shot into the dark. Other were short and squat, with most of the power in their legs, and wore simple shorts with their country's uniform top.

Many, like Carter, were in full makeup, and many were not. Canada's best thrower, Brittany Crew, wore ruby red earrings below her maple leaf baseball cap. Iran's Leyali Rajabi wore a bright blue hijab. Trinidad and Tobago's Cleopatra Borel, a three-time Olympian, sported cherry red lipstick that matched her bright red uniform.

Carter has spoken out for years, since she started winning the first of her seven national championships, on the importance of confidence and body image. "We're girls and we can throw heavy balls and be in the dirt and we look good while we're doing it."[32]

As a woman who often weighed more than 200 pounds, Carter struggled with body-shaming, magnified every year by the Internet and social media trolls. She doubled down by creating a confidence-building sports camp for girls to counteract such messages. She particularly emphasized that different looks support different sports: "I tell people all the time if I was built like (gymnast) Gabby Douglas, I could not throw the shot put the way I throw the shot put. And if Gabby Douglas was built like me, she could not flip in the air the way that she flips in the air. And so you have to understand, everybody's body is built to do something different."[33]

In 2016, during a Brazilian night at Joao Havelange Olympic Stadium, after an introduction by samba drums and dancers, an array of strong and glamorous women tossed balls into the dark sky. Carter saved her best for last, launching one for a new national record and an Olympic medal on her final throw. Adams followed with the second best throw of the day, earning a silver to set next to her two golds. This time, it was Team USA's turn to win its first gold medal in the women's shot put and its first medal since the incomparable Earlene Brown took a bronze back in Rome.

When she watched the New Zealander's throw land a trifle short, Carter seemed stunned briefly, then teary-eyed. Practicality overruled the emotions. Before going back in front of the cameras, she carefully dabbed below the corner of her extra-extra-long lashes, then reached into her bag, fishing out what she needed most: fresh lipstick.

The Final Five

Twenty years after "Magnificent Seven" Kerri Strug's vault in Atlanta, and a week before Michelle Carter flung an eight-pound cannonball half the length of a football field, the five women of the 2016 U.S. Women's Gymnastics team did

Fig.38. Michelle Carter (USA) combined strength with beauty on her way to a 2016 gold. Bigger than the 1950s rocket launchers, Carter wore well-manicured hairstyles, makeup, and jewelry, down to the charm bracelet above the hand cradling the 8.8 lb shot put (photograph by jenaragon94, Wikimedia Commons).

something else remarkable. After winning their second Olympic gold medal in a row in the team competition, the quintet hopped up on the floor exercise dais to take a bow. They huddled inward like a football team, touching hands, calling the break, then turning to crowd and cameras and shouting in unison: "We are the Final Five!"

Choosing a nickname may not seem revolutionary. Maybe it's even a little corny. But it was an interesting way to turn the tables on all the camera's scrutiny. The team had coyly refused to share their choice with the media until after the competition was over. The announcers had played along, even commenting that the audience would "have to wait to find out" what the team would be called.

In years past, the media had chosen the names. At the previous Games, a sportswriter had used "Fab Five," until a basketball team later huffily "claimed" the name. The team had offered up "Fierce Five," which hadn't stuck. The women had learned a lesson about how names had power. And how it might be more powerful to choose one's own.

The "Final Five" signified it was the last year where five could compete for a team. Future teams would only allow four members, at least until the gymnastics federation changed the rules again, as happens often.[34] The squad was also the last five under the dominance of the Karolyis. It was the first where the women started making choices for themselves.

There was a noticeably different vibe on the sidelines among the 2016 American team. For two decades, the camera had caught them walking past each other with grim stares, as if giving themselves reminders that they were all in a competition. Intimidation is always a weapon in the athlete's arsenal. But the gymnasts would stare daggers at each other even when they competed *as* a team. This competitive game-face started during the run-up to the Games, at the Olympic Trials. These, too, had evolved to being televised on Saturday night at prime-time.

All nations and federations have some approach to determine who becomes an Olympian. A giant team like the U.S. typically has many athletes to choose from, and the trials are highly competitive. Coaches have always used judgment and instinct, factoring in previous Games' experience, injury history, and an athlete's "momentum." In USA Gymnastics, Márta Karolyi had the responsibility for choosing the finalists. She was known for making non-standard choices. In 2016, for example, she decided to skip over the fourth-, fifth-, and sixth-place Trial finishers, instead choosing Gabby Douglas, previous All-Around winner and Madison Kocian, who was a specialist on the uneven bars.[35] Such selections were commonplace but also made the Trials interesting.

Since 2001, the team choices had been Marta's choice. Then, beginning in 2004, NBC had opted to film the Olympic Trials like episodes of *The Bachelor*, as Dvora Myers describes it, with announcers breathlessly wondering, "'Who will be on Martha [sic] Karolyi's Olympic team?' … NBC's cameras panned the row of girls for their reactions. The network seemed to relish the opportunity to show young women getting their dreams dashed in real time."[36]

The cameras created additional drama to entertain the public. It was good for TV ratings, but not for athletes who needed to go into their next tournament confident, rather than fearful that someone else could take their spot if they falter. Only women's gymnastics seemed to have unnecessarily turned the experience into the *Hunger Games*.

Cruelty had become something of a standard in American gymnastics as it raised the bar for quality. Strug had tried to exorcise the demons of fragility, to prove that even a 4'8" gymnast could contain the heart of champion. By impressing the world, she had poured gasoline on the fire of dreams for other future stars. Starting in 2004, Americans were thrilled when Carly Patterson, Nastia Liukin, Shawn Johnson, Gabby Douglas, Aly Raisman, Simone Biles, and Suni Lee each took a medal in the All-Around in their respective Games. Every four years, the media would try to pick the "next Mary Lou," rather than looking at the team as a whole.

When the team competed in the Games in Athens, Beijing, and London, the cameras would show them practically stalking around each other like caged leopards. That was an intriguing part of the story for the audience. There was, after all, only one All-Around winner, so that medal took precedence for some. What more could a nation want than an unending stream of small but fierce warriors?

It might have wanted them safe.

The atmosphere among the team along the sidelines in 2016 was in stark contrast to prior years. When American gymnasts Biles and Raisman each performed their routines in the All-Around, for instance, they would close with a warm embrace of one other, as if they weren't even competing. They held hands, smiled, and engaged in a lengthy conversation. These women had been brought up to vie against each other for the few precious spots in the limelight. As of 2016, they just weren't having it.

What became known later—and was certainly known to those athletes at the time—was that a sewer of evil had been running below the surface of all that joy. Less than a year after the 2016 team's success, the cover was pulled off, exposing a flood of horror to the world. His name was Larry Nassar.

Nassar was the team doctor for USA Gymnastics for 18 years. Old footage from Atlanta even shows him leaning in, looking concerned as Strug is scrutinized after her vault injury. Nassar had been sexually assaulting the gymnasts all those years.

Multiple women had complained and been brushed aside by USA Gymnastics. Only the organization knows exactly how many were ignored. Maggie Nichols, who would be a member of the 2016 national team, was one of the first to go to the police and identify herself publicly, but several others followed suit. The list quickly grew into the hundreds. When the case came to trial in late 2015, over 265 women had been identified as victims. Some examples dated back to the late 1980s. Four out of the Final Five had been abused by Nassar.

Nassar also wasn't alone. Coach Don Peters, who had gotten into the coaching tussle with Bela Karolyi all the way back in 1984, was ousted after multiple women accused him of inappropriate sexual relations. John Geddert, who had a close partnership with Nassar in Michigan, was also investigated for physical assault.

Furthermore, Nassar's crimes had been covered up by another half dozen administrators. Steve Penny, the USA Gymnastics CEO, had tampered with evidence, while Michigan State University president Lou Anna Simon had lied to the police. Court documents showed that USA Gymnastics had received sexual abuse complaints against 54 coaches, but barely followed up and had allowed even those who were convicted sex offenders to continue their membership. The Indiana Field Office of the FBI had compounded the problem by ignoring the complaints for months, then lying about their lack of investigation, potentially leading to hundreds more incidents of assault.

Even after Nassar's conviction, the one Final Five gymnast who hadn't been assaulted by Nassar—Laurie Hernandez—went public about abuse from her own coach, Maggie Haney. Haney had harassed Hernandez mercilessly about her weight. She had also pulled her hair, threatened to commit suicide, and forced Hernandez and others to compete with serious injuries.

It was *Pretty Pink Boxes* times 100, with allegations that were more serious, widespread, and covered up by the U.S. gymnastics infrastructure at the highest level. It also wasn't only Americans. As if on cue, Olga Korbut went public in 2018 with accusations of sexual abuse from her coach at the time. While some in Russia scoffed, four other Belarussian gymnasts provided similar stories of the same coach from the same time period. Gymnasts over the past four decades had been going through private hell. They weren't going to take it anymore.

Biles, the All-Around winner, had especially emerged from her shell. As an athlete capable of extraordinary feats far beyond her peers, she had moves named for her even before competing in Rio. Prior to 2016, though, she had taken a page out of the Ed Temple book and stayed poised and cheerful during interviews.

However, after the Games, she pushed hard not just for Nassar to receive justice but for more actions by USA Gymnastics. Her social media commentary became increasingly pointed, asking in November 2019: "What's it going to take for a complete and independent investigation of both USOPC and USAG???"[37] In 2020, before the Tokyo Games were postponed, she wasn't even sure if she wanted to compete: "they haven't taken accountability for their actions and what they've done. And they haven't ensured us that it's never going to happen again."[38]

Biles's hesitancy flared up again in the 2020 Olympic Trials when her characteristic cheerfulness accompanied a few stumbles. By the time she arrived in Tokyo, her image was magnified and multiplied across every network, magazine, newspaper, and website. All those expectations that others put on her didn't sit well, particularly when no one seemed willing to address her open questions.

During her first vault in the team event, she felt disoriented and failed to complete what she had planned. She knew something was wrong and chose the opposite path from Kerri Strug—for the same brave reasons—to show the world how women athletes can conduct themselves. She chose to step aside, anxious of ruining the team's chances and risking a career-ending injury. The team took the silver. With her, they might have won gold or won nothing, if her continued experience of the "twisties" had hurt their scores. By pulling out early and staying on to cheer and advise, she helped the team continue to contend, and contend they did.

Those who considered Biles to be the "face of the Olympics" were disappointed. One announcer, hearing the news live, expressed sadness for her millions of fans who had been waiting and watching. Lengthy discussions ensued about the need for mind and body to be in synch, and the many athletes who had struggled with anxiety said a silent thank-you. The Face of the Olympics reminded everyone that athletes are not automatons. Some called her a quitter, but most applauded her choice. No one called her frail.

Biles was finally able to compete on the balance beam and squeaked out a bronze medal. But by choosing not to compete in the team event and the all-around, despite the pressure to do so, Biles may have sealed the deal on a new era for gymnasts to choose their own destiny.

Because the gymnasts also used their social platform to push for social change, this may be the beginning of an end, at least of the worst abuses by the coaches. It's too early to see whether changes will be permanent, but it's difficult to imagine a return to the days when teenagers had to eat toothpaste or were set on each other like something out of a dystopian novel. The 2016 medalists may indeed have been the Final Five. They may have been the final five to be treated as cuddly and cute in public and vulnerable in private, commodities for the world and prey for others.

For these women, using the camera's fascination with their "stories" to control their own public image before *they* were controlled was vital. To do so, athletes had to be visible and vocal. Talented women of color might always be in the potential

Fig.40. The "Final Five" chose their name, heralding a new focus on gymnasts controlling their path. It would foreshadow Simone Biles' choices in Tokyo 2020. Pictured left to right: Aly Raisman, Madison Kocian, Laurie Hernandez, Gabby Douglas, and Simone Biles (photograph by Zhukovsky © Dreamstime.com).

spotlight whether they liked it or not. Elite female gymnasts would have a billion pairs of eyes watching as long as their sport remains popular, which seems likely to be a while.

But another group has struggled with visibility for entirely different reasons. For lesbians and bisexual women, for all LGBTQ athletes, just getting into the public eye has always been an uphill climb.

Fifteen

Erasing the Specter of Lesbianism (1896–2016)

Coming in a respectable fifth place in her first Olympics, U.S. shot putter Raven Saunders would not be considered particularly fashion-forward. Unlike Michelle Carter, her gold-medal-winning teammate who doubled as a makeup artist, Saunders's style choices at the 2016 Games consisted of a magenta-tinted, close-cropped Afro, oversized men's basketball shorts, and polka dot socks. It was a look, though not one which would make *Vogue*.

Saunders, who grew up deep in the American South, was nicknamed the "Hulk" because she was friendly off the field but strong and ferocious inside the throwing circle. The friendliness was natural but also a helpful part of her public image. For her, crafting a comfortable public persona could mean the difference between invitations and ostracism, between safety and harassment. Because, as much progress has been made toward LGBTQ+ rights, Charleston, South Carolina, is still the front lines for a Black lesbian Olympian.

Women had very slowly made their way into Olympic competition, finally reaching 4,305 athletes (41 percent) by 2004. But lesbian and bisexual athletes had been glacially slow to emerge into the open. Civil rights groups could still count on one hand the number of publicly declared LGBTQ competitors as late as the Athens Games.

Of course, there had been lesbian athletes since the first women had picked up golf clubs and tennis rackets in Paris 1900. But cultural and legal reasons had prevented them from openly embracing their sexuality, even as other women became comfortable with their athleticism. Sometimes, things even seemed to go backward.

First treated as invisible, then as Public Enemy Number Two, athletes in same-sex relationships had to navigate especially treacherous waters. Some were outed before they were ready. Others were non-controversial in their home country but found themselves making international headlines, once the tabloid press smelled a potential scandal. Eventually acceptance of LGBTQ Olympic competitors allowed them to come out in the open without hysteria. Like advancement for women as a whole, acceptance has taken its own sweet time.

Miss, Mrs., Mr., or It

Lesbian athletes probably didn't mind being invisible at the outset. Queen Victoria allegedly left women out of the British statute which reaffirmed criminalization of sex between two men because "women do not do such things." That's an urban myth, historians say, because the queen technically cannot personally influence legislation. It was, in fact, the British Parliament that decided lesbians didn't exist.

At the end of the 19th century, as both men and women began playing more sports, public lesbian relationships were rare. When those early athletic women—like Suzanne Lenglen and Gertrude Ederle—were criticized for their "mannish" behavior, they weren't being called lesbians. Not at first.

Initially, as previously mentioned, there were two primary concerns over women's growing participation in the rapidly expanding sporting world. One was medical obsession with damage to the reproductive system from too much exertion or jumping. The other was the over-development of muscles, which might turn women into "muscle molls." But, as historian Susan Cahn points out, "there was one note of agreement.... All sides presumed heterosexuality."[1]

The biggest worry was that women who participated in sports would become highly sexualized and lose control of their passions and dignity. The word "moll" meant a promiscuous, lower-class woman, the kind that hung on the arms of gangsters or prowled the back alleys. Experts prior to the 1920s warned against excessive exercise out of fears that women would have moral and physical breakdowns. To become "mannish" originally meant that a woman athlete might become as sexually aggressive as a man.[2]

Some doctors also specialized in diagnosing the disease of lesbianism, calling it a "symptom and effect of an inverted gender identity."[3] When women had an "inverted" male soul trapped in their body, they might enjoy sports and exhibit same-sex desire. But these early analyses were obscurely scientific and highly speculative. There was far more focus on whether the majority of women might lose their Victorian virtue if they developed a particularly strong serve or golf swing.

There were varying solutions offered to offset the concern about the "amazon" athletes. Turn-of-the-century physical educators considered competition to be the culprit, so they embarked on their campaign of play days and mottoes that recommended "a sport for every girl." Taking a different tack, the fledgling AAU supported competition, especially if they could dictate which events were considered sufficiently feminine. Hence, swimming might be allowed, though perhaps not in public, and some running, though not as far as 800 m.

As more women competed in more sports, making their way into the Olympics and holding their own Games in the 1920s, they also pressed for freedom in other ways. The flappers of the Jazz Age pushed the boundaries of acceptable behavior by embracing shorter hemlines, smoking, and wearing cosmetics. The flapper was free to dance—and compete—as long as the end goal was marriage.

Thus, Cahn points out, the line of "deviant sexuality" shifted. Where before sexualized activities might lead to a loss of virtue, by the 1920s, sex appeal could be pursued in its own right because marriage was the end state. Sexy heterosexuals

Fifteen. Erasing the Specter of Lesbianism (1896–2016)

were now fine. Not fine were those on the other side, either the newly designated "Victorian prude" or the "mannish lesbian."[4]

Hence, while "muscle moll" might have started out referring to women of the streets, by the time Paul Gallico wrote a 1931 diatribe against muscle molls in *Vanity Fair,* he meant something else. His criticisms of the "strenuous and hippy ladies"[5] who invaded the golf course and swimming pool was not out of a concern that they were oversexed, but rather that sports made them unattractive. Even worse, they might no longer be interested in attracting men.

The label "mannish" multiplied in parallel with the rising number of athletes, but now it represented a different underlying anxiety. If women were increasingly moving into men's sphere, as with athletics, that would upset the natural order of things. The more muscular the woman, the more likely the world would be turned upside down. Hence, "manly women" began to be described as "nature's greatest failures."[6]

As Chapter Four detailed, "muscle moll" Babe Didrikson gave the sportswriters of her day fits. Gallico obsessed repeatedly about her boyish appearance, even though the main difference in photos between Didrikson and her contemporaries seemed mostly to be the length of her hair. Gallico was so bothered by Didrikson's appearance and singular focus on athletics that he speculated whether she belonged to a "third sex," and whether she (and any like her) "should be addressed as 'Miss,' 'Mrs.,' 'Mr.,' or 'It.'"[7]

Didrikson found the obsession annoying, "They seem to think I'm a strange unnatural being summed up in the words Muscle Moll, and the idea seems to be that Muscle Molls are not people."[8] A muscle moll, by 1936, meant a short-haired athlete spending too much time on sports and not enough time "man-snatching."[9] Annoyed or not, though, when Didrikson took up golf, she found the opportunity to end the constant attacks by marrying someone she met on the golf course—George Zaharias.

Biographers have pointed out that during her marriage, Didrikson Zaharias developed an intimate relationship with fellow golfer Betty Dodd. They roomed together on tour, then stayed together after Didrikson separated from Zaharias. Dodd was by her bedside through the majority of Didrikson's cancer treatment. However, the athlete never said a word about anything but friendship. She remained so silent, in fact, that Olympic historian Guttmann claimed that the couple's marriage broke up because Dodd had an affair with George rather than with his wife. Dodd and Didrikson's biographers have since confirmed otherwise, but Babe remained close-mouthed about it to her death. The closet was very deep.

A few notable contemporaries of Didrikson were also lesbians, although it could be mentioned only many years after they competed. The list included Canadian Bobbi Rosenfeld, who ran wearing men's hockey socks, as well as sprinter Helen Stephens, who had been falsely accused of being a man after her 1936 win in the 100 m. The list was short. Few women competed, and even fewer had biographers dig into their personal lives enough to uncover relationships they were hiding. Gertrude Ederle's bio simply says she remained single and lived to age ninety-eight with only female companions. They kept their intimacies private. Cahn called it "Play It, Don't Say It."[10]

During the war, more women played team sports like baseball or basketball as substitute entertainment while the men were away. More women on the field meant that more lesbians might find kindred spirits in group venues, enjoying the camaraderie of teamwork and sometimes creating deeper relationships. They continued to play even after the war was over, although the semi-pro leagues disbanded. Many women continued on casual teams anyway. As lesbian writer and publisher Barbara Grier pointed out, in the 1950s and 1960s the softball diamond would be the "place to go where you knew there would be dykes."[11]

But if more lesbian athletes were finding each other, they were even more reticent to make it public. When the 1947 House Un-American Committee (HUAC) investigations went into high gear, homosexuals suddenly became the second biggest threat to the U.S. after Communist spies. While daily televised interrogators attempted to root them out of the government and the Army, no athlete would voluntarily identify themselves as LGBTQ.

The physical educators changed tactics as well. The teachers who had tirelessly promoted participation in sports found themselves accused of lesbianism in their often all-women ranks. Partly to offset the allegations and partly to follow the cultural drift toward overt heterosexuality, their curriculum shifted from the rules of sports and health to techniques for improving personal appearance. In posture contests, college classmates clandestinely rated their peers on how they stood, sat, or walked, believing that better posture led to more marriage proposals. Co-ed non-physical contact sports like bowling, volleyball, or shuffleboard began to be encouraged instead of basketball.

At the same time, there was a new concern over "conversions," especially in education. While McCarthy and friends were trying to root the "homosexual menace" out the State Department, educators were trying to eliminate predatory lesbians in the school system. The bogey-man (or bogey-woman) was now the gym teacher, and the specter of lesbianism loomed anywhere there was a community of women, from all-women's colleges to softball fields. Teachers were routinely fired; lesbian bars were raided; divorcing women lost custody of their children.

Thus, by the late 1950s, no matter how much at home they might be on a track, tennis court, or baseball diamond, lesbians rarely discussed being lesbians openly. The penalties for discovery were now far worse than being called a muscle moll.

Yanking Out, Stuffing Back in the Closet

The passage of Title IX and the first gay pride parade took place only two years apart. With pressure for recognition of women's and LGBTQ rights happening together in the early 1970s, the time might have seemed ripe for recognizing lesbian athletes as well. Nothing could have been further from the truth. LGBTQ athletes were kept quiet, for several reasons.

First, a rift had opened in the feminist community between progressives and moderates. In 1969, the lesbian president of the National Organization of Woman (NOW) was pushing for improved LGBTQ rights. Others even further left called for women to separate from the patriarchal culture entirely. Mainstream feminists—notably Betty Friedan—feared that the extremists and the "lavender menace" would derail feminism and cause others to dismiss women's demands as mere sour grapes from "man-hating" lesbians. While NOW and other feminist organizations thrashed out their philosophical struggles by purging lesbians from the ranks, those who wanted more opportunity to compete in the male-run Olympics found little support from either side.

In addition, women were just beginning to make their case to expand competitive opportunities, through Title IX and other means. These new ventures did not want distractions. After women's Olympic basketball made its debut in 1976, the Women's Basketball League (WBL) launched in the U.S. with Olympian Ann Meyer and rising star Nancy Lieberman promoting the league.

Following the 1973 Battle of the Sexes, when Billie Jean King beat Bobby Riggs, King used the momentum to create a women's union for tennis, the Women's Tennis Association. The WTA lobbied for increased prize money, more tournaments, and return to the Olympics. King also launched the Women's Sports Foundation, with swimmer Donna de Varona, skier Suzy Chaffee, and (later) skater Peggy Fleming. The WSF would eventually grow into one of the most important advocacy groups for women athletes in the world, but while fledgling women's athletic ventures were still starting up, they preferred to avoid controversy. Heterosexual athletes bent over backwards to resist being called "lesbians." LGBTQ athletes went deep into hiding in order to have more chances to compete.

The American political climate was also growing less hospitable as well. Conservative politicians, bolstered by religious fundamentalists, were elected on anti-gay "family values" platforms. Even the U.S. Supreme Court got in the act. In 1986, the court decision of *Bowers vs. Hardwicke* reaffirmed the rights of American states to criminalize sodomy. President Reagan was personally indifferent to LGBTQ causes (despite having a gay son), but several of his advisers were notoriously homophobic. Cabinet discussions routinely referred to Title IX as the "lesbian's bill of rights."[12] When Reagan's Secretary of Education Terrel Bell argued against further postponing Title IX's implementation, Attorney General Ed Meese asked him whether the pattern on his tie was a hammer and sickle.[13] Hence, thirty years after the HUAC hearings, homosexuality and Communism were still being treated as the biggest threats to the American way of life.

Outside the U.S., there was also hostility and indifference. Some countries were less homophobic than America, but others, even Olympic host countries like South Korea, formally considered homosexuality "harmful" or "obscene." European countries which *had* adopted more progressive stances were considered outliers, while America's allies didn't seem interested in getting too far ahead of the U.S. The IOC, the least progressive entity on the planet, would definitely not lead on this issue. They had barely just added a couple of women to their ranks after 90 years of competition.

AIDS was also just becoming an issue. When men in cities with large LGBTQ populations began dying of strange cases of pneumonia, doctors named the disease Acquired Immune Deficiency Syndrome. The less charitable called it a "gay plague," and one prominent CEO wondered with a smirk if G-A-Y stood for "Got AIDS Yet."[14]

The disease had little or nothing to do with lesbian athletes, but LGBTQ activism quickly focused on seeking increased AIDS funding and more humane treatment. Lesbian issues took a back seat on the bus, and lesbian athletes were told they could get off the bus entirely and wait for the next one.

Against this backdrop—freezing cold public sentiment, hostile legislators, mainstream feminists conducting witch hunts, and progressives focused on other causes—Billie Jean King found herself thrust into the headlines. For once, it was not for promoting women's sports. In 1981, King was named in a palimony lawsuit by her female secretary, with whom she had been having a long-term intimate relationship. King and her husband, Larry, had also been letting Marilyn Barnett live in their house rent-free as well as paying her other expenses. Barnett, as a thank-you, kept copies of receipts and threatened to go to the press if she didn't receive more money. The Kings brushed off her extortion demands. She went public and took them to court.

Whether the public was ready for lesbian rights or not, they were not ready for ugly public details of an extramarital affair. King first denied the relationship, then called it a mistake and reaffirmed her strong "attachment" to her husband. Even so, the tennis legend lost all her endorsements within 24 hours of being outed. Additionally, while LGBTQ athletes might have taken heart from King's same-sex announcement, they would not have felt supported by her denials. Besides, the table had been set. If anyone else planned to go public, they would walk into a hurricane of tabloid-style press.

In 1981, partly because of King's efforts to increase worldwide popularity of women's tennis, the IOC voted to bring tennis back to the Olympics in 1988. King would have been the last person to want an interruption in momentum. The big stars of the day were eager for the news: Chris Evert, Steffi Graf, and the newly naturalized American citizen Martina Navratilova. Navratilova had defected from Czechoslovakia six years earlier and had just

Fig.41. Billie Jean King in the Wimbledon semifinals at age 38, 1982. The tennis world loved when King beat Bobbie Riggs and applauded her 23 Grand Slam titles. The tide turned quickly, though, when she reportedly "confessed" to a lesbian affair (photograph by Jerry Coli © Dreamstime.com).

gained her citizenship in 1981. She had won a couple of Grand Slam titles but had also lost badly to Evert and was taking her approach to tennis to another level.

Working with rising basketball star Nancy Lieberman, Navratilova stripped her game apart and put it back together. She adopted a more aggressive game, full of volleys to offset Evert's grinding baseline strokes. Navratilova further added muscles in new places, increased her stamina, and used innovative cross-training methods, just as Griffith-Joyner had used weight training to create more explosive starts. As a result of the changes, the revised tennis style helped Navratilova go 86–1 in one stretch during 1983.

Between 1982 and 1986, she built up a winning record so massive that it was considered the "most dominant unbroken spell in the professional era."[15] Because she used cutting-edge training approaches—as a man might—some called her a "bionic sci-fi creation." The tennis media started griping that she was simply "too good."[16]

Navratilova had also been in a romantic relationship with lesbian writer Rita Mae Brown. A reporter threatened to go public. Although the media at least waited until after she had earned her citizenship, Navratilova was pressured into an interview with the *New York Daily News* where she discussed her sexual orientation. She begged them to delay publication, but they did not. In July 1981, the story went out into the world, only a handful of months after King had been thrown to the tabloids.

Navratilova told the interviewer that she was bisexual. She was reported to be in a relationship with Lieberman, though the young basketball star denied it at the time (and still does today, though biographers suggest otherwise). Labels didn't matter. After the interview, no one would endorse Navratilova. She reportedly had to design her own tennis dresses because no sponsors would put their name on one.

By 1984, as the bionic creation continued setting winning records, she began dating Texas housewife Judy Nelson. When she later broke up with Nelson after several years, another lesbian palimony lawsuit kept the media busy. Two lesbians in fifty years had publicized relationships. Both resulted in messy palimony lawsuits—Navratilova's was even televised. Both women had been thrown out of the closet against their will.

It wasn't only a few messy relationships that impaired the climate for lesbian athletes. As Title IX began to fund women's sports, those who had fought hard for more resources found themselves pushed out of those newly funded coaching jobs. The first ones let go were lesbians. Some straight female coaches, who had also lobbied hard to get their own positions, had no intention of letting fear of lesbians derail their work. Some acted out of fear; others were simply homophobic. Coaches and athletes were subject to purges.

Coach Rene Portland of Penn State[17] was especially notorious. From 1980 to 2007, she systematically tried to ensure no lesbians played on her basketball team and went out of her way to tell visiting parents that she would eliminate all such activity. She bragged to the *Chicago Sun-Times* in 1986: "I will not have it in my program."[18] Even though Penn State had passed an anti-discrimination policy covering sexual orientation in 1981, they didn't enforce it, despite complaints about Coach Portland. Nearly half (46 percent) of her athletes left the team after a couple years, twice as many as under other coaches.

Such attitudes chilled other programs, too. Helen Carroll, the openly lesbian coach of the University of North Carolina–Asheville, explained, "Straight coaches used being gay as a recruiting tactic to persuade families against letting their daughter play.... They'd say 'That's the gay team.' It creates a wall of fear for female coaches, who don't have a tremendous amount of job security to begin with."[19] Whether LGBTQ or not, many players and coaches found the atmosphere damaging to athletics.

Title IX seemed to be having the opposite effect as intended, at least for LGBTQ players: "As more and more straight women claimed their right to play sports, homophobia has become more and more prevalent on the courts, tracks, and in the locker rooms. Women's sports promoters [were] working very hard to clean the dyke image off the face of women's athletics."[20]

Even when lesbian athletes appeared in a quasi-sympathetic way in popular culture, it wasn't really positive. The first (and still only) movie about lesbian Olympic track athletes, *Personal Best*, was given high marks for its emotional content and "sensitivity."[21] The story follows the budding relationship between two women, both competing in the pentathlon for a spot on the U.S. Olympic team, and includes one of the first on-screen same-sex kisses.

However, lesbians had little to celebrate in the plot. In the movie, the "more experienced" athlete, played by Patrice Donnelly, gives training advice to young Mariel Hemingway after they fall in love. The coach (Scott Glenn) rants that the relationship is interfering with their training: "Do you actually think that Chuck Knoll has to worry that Franco Harris is gonna cry 'cause Terry Bradshaw won't talk to him? ...that Lynn Swann is pregnant, that Rocky Bleier forgot his Tampax."[22]

Through an unlucky accident involving sticky tape, Hemingway is injured, and Donnelly is incorrectly blamed. However, rather than the lovers being reconciled, as might happen in a lesbian romance, the plot shifts to a heterosexual romance. Hemingway ends up in the coach's bed—somehow not deemed inappropriate given their working relationship and age differences—and then falls in love with a male swimmer. Safely ensconced back in the heterosexual fold, Hemingway thrives in her competition. At the end, even Donnelly remarks that Hemingway's new boyfriend is "cute." All is right with the world, as both would-be lesbians have returned to that more normal female sport of "man-snatching."

Overall, by 1986, the tally made things clear. Two same-sex tennis players with failed messy relationships. LGBTQ activities made illegal in several states and several countries. Colleges purging the lavender menace from their teams and coaching staffs. Popular culture showing LGBTQ athletes the error of their ways. Anyone else want to come out now? Closet doors were not only slamming shut in the late 1980s, but there was an increased sound of locks being turned, up and down the sports world.

The Girlfriend in the Stands (and on the Field)

Nowadays, when lesbian marriage and birth announcements are commonplace, it's hard to fathom the culture of fear that existed only a few decades ago.

Between 1981 and 1998, the athletes who announced their LGBTQ orientation could be counted on one hand. Many athletes came out after—years after, decades after—their competition days were over. The list of athletes known *after* the fact is getting long.

The list of those who went public *at the time* is tiny and subject to debate[23] over degrees of openness. For example, Brazilian volleyball player Jacki Silva, who won gold in beach volleyball in 1996, may have been out in Brazil, but American recaps of the tournament never mentioned it. Tennis player Jana Novotná won a silver in the inaugural Olympic Tennis Doubles in 1988. Did the Czechoslovakian press note that she was a lesbian? The international press didn't highlight it when she was competing, perhaps because there was no palimony suit involved, and she wasn't a #1 player.

When there were no affairs, where athletes were from smaller countries, or where the sport was lesser known, the press might pay a lot less attention. Robert Dover, the Olympic equestrian bronze medalist mentioned in Chapter Eight, told the team and the media in 1988, "I'm the token Jewish gay boy on the U.S. Olympic team."[24] He says reporters followed him around, but his sexual orientation didn't make national headlines.

The first lesbian athlete whose orientation made headlines and who did compete in the Olympics was probably French tennis player Amelie Mauresmo. It was big sporting news when she upset American Lindsay Davenport in the 1999 Australian Open as an unseeded unknown. Only 19 years old, the French player then mentioned her girlfriend, almost casually, to the media in the follow-up conference.

The press jumped on the story, especially after Davenport commented that Mauresmo "played like a man." Davenport quickly backtracked, stating that she simply meant her opponent had powerful ground strokes. Martina Hingis, who beat Mauresmo in the finals, was happy to be more explicitly negative, saying that the French teenager was "half a man" and had the gall to bring her girlfriend to the match.

The girlfriend in the stands was becoming a familiar trope, even with only a couple of examples. The cameras in the 1980s constantly showed reactions shots from Judy Nelson when Navratilova was winning all those Grand Slam titles, before Nelson sued and wrote tell-all books. Whether the TV directors initially intended the views to be titillating, the repeated shots had the opposite effect. When Nelson, as well as Mauresemo's friend Silvie Boudon, appeared as ordinary as the family members of other players, viewers found it hard to see them as ogres. Instead, the cameras played up the love story angle.

Mauresmo had second thoughts about having her love life featured in the tabloids. It became a huge distraction. "I have never regretted the fact that I came out, but I do regret how I said it. It was too brutal. I could have done it in a much easier way. [Being gay] was no big deal for me. But I didn't realize what a huge story it was going to be."[25]

Eventually, Mauresmo focused enough to reach a #1 ranking and earn a silver medal in the 2004 Athens Games, making her one of the first openly declared lesbians to win an Olympic medal.[26]

It was a Scandinavian couple that really opened the floodgates. The sport was handball, so naturally the teams involved were the handball-loving Norwegians and their perennial powerhouse rival, Denmark. Camella Andersen and Mia Hundvin were Scandinavian stars. They were on opposing teams. And they were married.

In 1989, Denmark had quietly legalized same-sex registered partnerships, de facto marriages, while other countries were still trying to decide whether LGBTQ citizens should be executed, jailed, or merely publicly shunned. Andersen and Hundvin met while playing against each other in pre–Games matches, a year before the 2000 Olympics. They weren't the first lesbian couple ever viewed in a stadium, but they were the first where both were athletes, competing against each other. It was tailor-made for giant headlines. After all, it was Sydney, in 2000, and the press was just warming up their pressure campaign toward sprinter Marie-José Pérec. The tabloids needed practice.

The two women were not necessarily prepared for the level of curiosity displayed by the international news services. At home, they had been a curiosity, but most Scandinavian sportswriters were too interested in the actual matches to obsess about the personal lives of the players. Australia was different.

Writers showed up in droves to the handball post-game conferences to pester the women about their relationship, displaying little knowledge of or interest in handball. The IOC tried to dampen the salacious interest by omitting the partnership info in the women's athlete bios. The omission was leaked to the media, which only made them ask about it, every single time.

In a random fluke of scheduling, the two top-seeded teams played each other in the very first game. Both women found it hard to concentrate, and neither played their best. Norway won, 19–17.

The two teams advanced to the round of eight in separate tracks, and their paths diverged. Denmark muscled their way to the gold medal, with Anderson ending as the team's top scorer of the tournament. Norway lost in their semifinal, but scrapped their way to the bronze. Hundvin scored the game-winner. It was a breakthrough, not just in positive LGBTQ press, but also showing that athletes could compete despite being treated as media oddities.

Sports Illustrated picked up the love story angle, and, while the reticent Andersen and Hundvin found it a little exaggerated, they *were* the first Olympian LGBTQ couple. They fretted about journalists "blaring about their private life,"[27] but they did talk to the media. Non-LGBTQ observers might still squirm at the idea of "mannish" athletes, but it was getting harder to conjure up demons with two pleasant-looking women (as so many athletes are) simply holding hands. It likely helped that their sport was completely foreign to American tabloids. Journalists understood fundamentals. Love and sports. And family.

In years past, lesbian athletes had been kicked off teams because, they were told, basketball games were "family" events.[28] Playing the "family" card, especially in conservative American regions like the Bible Belt, meant that homophobia could be legitimized. But once lesbian couples were on national teams, even if it was those progressive Danes, the media could look at family in a different way.

One of the earliest golfers to come out as a lesbian was Patty Sheehan, back in 1998. When ESPN ran a recent update on her, they headlined it "Life after Golf Has

Been All about Family for Patty Sheehan."[29] Meaning children. Meaning spouse. Meaning parenting. All the same old boring shtick, just with differing pronouns.

A player with a girlfriend, partner, or wife in the stands, arguably just wanted what everyone else had. The general public stopped obsessing over whether "womyn" were attempting to overthrow the patriarchy. The media could circle the wagons when talking about relationships.

The list of LGBTQ athletes who went public after 2000 grew quickly. Many were still brave to be the first in their sport or region, but they were starting to follow a trail. Golfer Rosie Jones in 2004. Canadian hockey player Sarah Vaillancourt in 2006. Softball players Vicky Galindo and Lauren Lapin in 2008.

One of the biggest American names was Sheryl Swopes, Olympic basketball gold medalist. Swopes was in the still-new WNBA, and her announcement generated some backlash from the basketball community. But she explained that she was tired of hiding her relationship with her partner of several years.[30]

Whether there were 2, 4, or 5 LGBTQ athletes in Athens is unclear. But, by Beijing 2008, there were 15. At London 2012, there were 23, and, by the 2016 Rio Games, 68 athletes were open about their LGBTQ sexual orientation while competing. It started to seem silly to count when, in Tokyo, the number went into triple digits.

Some LGBTQ athletes found the new obsession with their relationships annoying. In 2018, Ireen Wüst became the most decorated Dutch speed skater of all time, with eleven Olympic medals in total. She won five in Sochi alone in 2014. But journalists in Sochi kept asking about her girlfriend, who happened to be another skater on the Dutch team, until she griped, "You are not asking [Dutch skater] Sven Kramer about how his relationship is going. So why would you ask me? If I would've had a relationship with a guy, you wouldn't have asked me either."[31]

Handball couples continued to capture the attention of northern Europe. Andersen-Hundvin split up, but 2008 teammates Norwegians Katja Nyberg and Gro Hammerseng became the "it couple." Fans started creating homemade videos[32] showing the couple in clipped newspaper photos surrounded by heart-shaped graphics and set to syrupy music. LGBTQ couples had really arrived, if they were receiving the Justin Bieber treatment.

In Brazil, during the 2016 beach volleyball tournament, married volleyball players Larissa França and Liliane Maestrini were prominently featured by the TV cameras. França had long been among the best players in the world. Partnered with Talita Antunes, she played well enough to earn a bronze medal match against the American powerhouse duo, Kerry Walsh-Jennings and April Ross. Since American audiences apparently loved bikini-clad players, a lot of beach volleyball made it to prime time. Cue multiple shots of Maestrini in the stands.

The lesbian athlete who gained the largest celebrity in 2016 was probably Megan Rapinoe. Rapinoe had been added to the national women's soccer team in 2009, helping them win a World Cup in 2011 and the Olympic gold in 2012. Rapinoe also went public in *Out* magazine in 2012, describing her relationship with an opposing team's star—shades of Andersen-Hundvin!

By 2016, Rapinoe had dyed her hair, made provocative political comments, and was pressing for equal pay for the soccer team, all of which attracted far more attention than her love life. When she struck up a new relationship with Olympic and WNBA basketball star Sue Bird, some described them as the newest power couple in women's sports. If the media had finally gone from frowning to fawning over same-sex couples, then it might be time for the tabloids to return to UFOs and the Kardashians.

Certainly, many LGBTQ athletes aren't married or in relationships. But when the "queer" head counts climbed over a hundred, more athletes could be open about their sexual orientation without having a love story as background. Thus, when Raven "Hulk" Saunders returned to the shot put venue in Tokyo, she had an entire Hulk persona: green and purple hair, facial jewelry, wrap-around sunglasses, and a creepy grinning mask that she wore when she competed. She glowered, she twerked, and she threw a personal best that earned her a silver medal.

On the podium, with visibility fought for and earned, she crossed her arms above her head in a gesture of solidarity. It brought the newspapers and the IOC running. She explained that it represented all the oppressed communities that she embodied—those Black, poor, LGBTQ, or struggling with mental health issues. There were a few op-ed pages grousing about political grandstanding, but most telling was the interview with the local Charleston news media, where they gushed at her braveness and celebrated her win for the hometown. Thus, the finger-pointing at lesbians seems finally to have stopped or at least reached the yawning stage, even when the athletes link their sexual orientation to political statements.

But challenges over women's athletic visibility are not entirely over. There is one more issue that remains unresolved. Remains, in fact, messily, loudly argued from several sides, reflecting ever-changing-rules and standards unresolved. That is the issue of gender identification.

As the world increasingly views gender identity as on a continuum rather than resting on binary opposites, policies left over from earlier times become harder to justify. Recounting the journey of the IOC in developing gender-based verification reveals how deeply ingrained the bias was against any who didn't fit the rigid notions of proper womanhood.

In 1976, Dr. H. Howard of the Federation International Societes d'Aviron (FISA), the IOC's Medical Commission, labeled the tests by their true intent. Howard called it "femininity control."

Sixteen

Femininity Control (1936–...)

> "Competitors who have been registered as females must report to the femininity control head office as soon as possible after arrival."
> —Memo from FISA to all athletes, 1976

Fairness certainly seems like such a simple idea. Like *amateur* or *peace*. The IOC had to abandon their amateur rules when the enforcement became absurd, with some athletes thrown out for wearing the wrong T-shirt and other "amateurs" paid full salaries by their governments. Likewise, peace is great in theory, but the devil is always in the details. So, too, with fairness, which is why gender verification, even though applied under the guise of fairness, was problematic from the beginning.

Yet, fairness appears so straightforward. Have all the competitors start at the same place and run the same distance, using the same equipment and the same training—well, not those last two. Surely, athletes ought to be judged equally, using the same rules and without favoritism, such as not having judges from the same country as the athlete. Strike that. Let's just keep the part about using rules. But also allow judges to factor in unwritten rules about how athletes look. Not so simple, is it?

How about just dividing athletes based on their chromosomes? That male Y-chromosome gives men an advantage over women—although not in equestrian, shooting, archery, or endurance races—but let's assume it always does. Divide athletes based on genetic advantages like extra muscle, height, and oxygenated blood. Actually, people who are tall can keep their advantage, which dominates in swimming and sprinting. Plus, people who have better-oxygenated blood or more fast-twitch muscles can keep those advantages. Just regulate the muscular distinctions between men and women, based on hormones. No need to split the men into large-hormone and small-hormone groups, of course. Also, since some men have hormones low enough to fall into the "average" women's range, don't test anyone who labels themselves a man. Just determine the exact amount of hormones that define the appropriate woman and cut off every female athlete above that. Ignore any other potential advantages—genetics, coaching, funding, family history, sponsorships, equipment....

Plenty of unfair advantages are allowed in competitive sports. The arbitrary gender[1] line is one of the few that the IOC has attempted to regulate. The rhetoric about dividing genders in the Olympics has relied on soothing words about ensuring fair competition. However, the application of gender verification has led to misapplied science, public humiliation, changing standards, and unfair exclusion. Although the current policy of the IOC (and IAAF, USOC, etc.) may be trying to create the fairest possible competition, the approach rests on a legacy of attempting to "police the binary"[2] and to enforce the IOC's image of a proper female gender.

Solutions have frequently been designed to gerrymander competitions around specific individuals. Rule changes put in place to prevent Person A from having an "unfair" advantage will then give Person B an advantage. There may be no solution that makes competition fair—without advantages—for everybody. What is clear is that the frontiers of gender keep shifting, which may just drag the regulating sports federations with them.

The path forward is murky; the path behind has not been so rosy, either.

Apparent Characteristics

> "I do know that the question of the eligibility of various female (?) athletes in several sports has been raised because of apparent characteristics of the opposite sex."—Avery Brundage, 1936[3]

Many sports histories date the start of gender testing to the 1966 European Championships in Budapest. However, gender testing, meaning sexual verification and gender segregation, goes all the way back to the dawn of the Games, when women were entirely excluded in the first place, being considered too frail to participate. Once those tennis players, swimmers, and divers were allowed in, the IOC still kept women out of track and field because it believed that running and throwing would unsex them.

Those early policymakers were not overly concerned with fairness. When the first rule makers—Coubertin, Latour, and Edström—were deciding which competitions to allow, their big concern was to prevent women from looking muscular. Brundage was happy to let in any events where women were "[as] beautiful and adroit as they are ineffective and unpleasing on track."

The primary beef has always been about how women appeared when competing. While the flappers of the late 1920s were allowed some freedom to compete, influencers at the time still criticized "grim-visaged maidens of sinewy build, hard and tough and set as working women in [their] forties; some with brawny throats, square shoulders and stern loins that would do credit to a prize ring."[4] Sports was ruining the natural beauty of women, and less-than-delicate-featured athletes were evidence of that problem, rather than proof that non-women were competing.

Before the 1930s, then, few raised concerns that men might masquerade as women to win Olympic medals. So few women's sports were allowed, and so few female athletic accomplishments taken seriously, that there was little value attached to winning as a female. Ultimately, women had to stage their own popular competitions in order to expand their opportunities. The Games absorbed women for the same reason that they absorbed the winter sports: the IOC doesn't like rivals.

In the mid–1930s, before women had competed in more than a handful of track and field Olympic tournaments, complaints began to surface. Not all track athletes were petite and cute teenagers like Betty Robinson. Even before sprinter Helen Stephens was accused of being a man by a Polish journalist, Brundage received complaints about her, about a tall U.S. runner with a "deep bass voice." (Stephens had been victim of a childhood accident in which a piece of wood pierced her larynx.[5]) However, to Brundage, Stephens was not necessarily a man in disguise, but another example of the female athletes he'd been complaining about, with charms of "less than zero."[6]

It was really two 1936 news reports, one coming just weeks before the American team sailed to Berlin, which caught Brundage's attention. Two former European female athletes transitioned to men when the new science of sex reassignment was barely a few decades old. These examples of athletes who had set women's national track records caused special consternation.

Mark (born Mary) Weston of Great Britain, nicknamed "The Devonshire Wonder," held international shot put and javelin titles and competed for the British team in the 1926 Women's World Games. A decade after retiring from competition, Weston emerged in 1936 after a set of surgeries as Mark Weston. The story was covered in the Western press, where British writers took exceptional care to note that Weston had made "an honest mistake, not a case of fraud."[7] Thus, no fraudulent titles for Britain.

Another athlete, Zdenek (born Zdenka) Koubek, had set Czechoslovakian records in the long jump, high jump, and running events. Koubek had even won the controversial race—the 800 m—at the Women's World Games in 1934. Within a year of those contests, though, Koubek also chose reassignment surgery. After recovering, the Czech left sports and traveled to America as a cabaret performer. He gave interviews to generate publicity for his show, and *Time* magazine wrote two stories on the topic of the "Change of Sex."[8] The August 24, 1936, story, crafted in time for the opening ceremonies in Berlin, provided readers the detailed mechanics of how sex organs were exchanged, stressing the rarity of such occurrences, the confusion of the pre-surgery body, and its resolution by the heroic doctors.

Curiously, the article's last paragraph describes another poor "pseudo-hermaphrodite" soul in jail, a prisoner who had developed venereal disease in both sets of genitalia. Naturally, the "prisoner had indulged" with both sexes; the author is unable to consider that the prisoner might have been assaulted when cell mates discovered unusual body parts. Coming at the end of a sports-themed story, the anecdote acts as the moral of the tale for those who might exhibit sympathy toward Messrs. Weston and Koubek. A reader who then learns that American Olympic president Brundage is worried about these cases will wish Mr. Brundage well in ferreting out such deviants.

Mere weeks after Weston's account was published in the British press in late May, the American team left New Jersey for Berlin on their cross-Atlantic voyage. Somewhere at sea, swimmer Eleanor Holm drank too much and was kicked off the team by team chaperone Brundage. Somewhere, as well, he prepared his report for the IOC session in Berlin, to be delivered in their July pre–Games meeting. In a separate letter to IOC president Latour, Brundage described his rationale:

> I don't know if hermaphrodites are as common today as they evidently were two thousand years ago ... but I do know that the question of the eligibility of various female (?) athletes in several sports has been raised because of apparent characteristics of the opposite sex ... [e.g.] the case of an English athlete who after several years of competition as a girl announced herself (?) to be a boy ... it might be well to insist on a medical examination before participation in the Olympic Games.[9]

Two things happened at the Berlin Games that are often incorrectly cited today as validation for the lurking suspicions. Both are shaded by things that were not known at the time. The primary concerns of Brundage and the IOC before the 1936 Games was clear: athletes who had been girls who then announced they were boys.

The Stella Walsh/Helen Stephens brouhaha is widely reported now in discussions of the history of gender testing even though it didn't factor into the IOC's future gender protocols. If anything, it is evidence that the IOC hadn't thought much beforehand about what those protocols would be.

It was ironic. Walsh was herself intersex—not publicly known for 40 years—but it was something she knew. Yet it was Stephens who was accused and forced to disrobe. Other women had noticed that Walsh did not disrobe in the locker rooms, but she was not included in the inspection. The whole thing seems especially bizarre. Reports that Walsh started the rumors make no sense, unless she wanted to be exposed herself, which seems unlikely.

Some even suggest that Brundage recommended widespread gender verification as retaliation for "his" American runner being accused by a foreigner.[10] But Walsh wasn't really foreign, as Brundage was well aware. She was criticized for being a traitor to the U.S., for running under a Polish flag even though she had grown up in Cleveland. Brundage could have accused Walsh himself of being intersex at the time[11] if retaliation was on his mind.

A second incident involving an athlete with gender dysphoria also occurred in Berlin. The athlete in question did not win a medal, and the situation was only discovered years later. However, because the Nazis interfered in the women's event itself—the high jump—stories have characterized it as a Nazi plot.

As described earlier, Germany persuaded Helene Mayer to compete as their token Jew on the fencing team, but no one else. When Jewish high jumper Gretel Bergmann won the German national trials, the Nazis declined to invite her to Berlin, claiming her performance was inferior, despite her setting a national record. They took two other athletes—Elfriede Kahn and Dora Ratjen. Ratjen, it turned out, was an unusual case.

The 2009 movie *Berlin 36* describes it in tantalizing terms: "Gretel was one of Germany's best gold medal contenders. She was also Jewish. Her skill and ethnicity undermined the Nazi belief that Aryans were the superior race, so the German authorities schemed to replace Gretel with another woman—but 'she' had a secret that, if uncovered, could be even more embarrassing to the Nazis." The problem is that there was no dastardly scheme to replace Bergmann with Ratjen.

Dora Ratjen was born in a rural part of Germany. As with Stella Walsh, a country midwife declared the baby first a boy, then a girl. Since Frau Ratjen certainly changed the baby's diapers, she could have reversed the choice if it was unambiguous, so something about Ratjen, Jr., must have seemed borderline. The child was brought up as a girl.

However, during "Dora's" puberty, a deep voice and facial hair suggested to the teenager that he was not the girl that his parents insisted he was. Still, Ratjen began competing in the high jump on the girl's team. At the 1936 Olympics, 17-year-old Ratjen managed to take fourth place in Berlin, and, in a 1938 competition, set a world record.

Just days after the 1938 championships, though, the high jumper was reported to police at a train station for appearing to be a man in women's clothing. Since it was the start of a time when LGBTQ Germans were being hauled off to concentration camps, the police arrested Ratjen for cross-dressing. After some additional tests, a medical exam, and a stay in a sanitarium, Heinrich Ratjen, Jr., was officially allowed to don men's clothing and change his gender identity on his papers.

The details of this 1938 arrest, though, were only uncovered by a journalist in 1957. Whether teammate Bergmann or anyone else had been suspicious at the Olympics, Ratjen's dysphoria was never discovered while competing. The Nazis did not use Ratjen as a pawn to replace a Jewish high jumper with a man in drag in order to win a German gold medal.

Neither Heinrich Ratjen, Jr., nor Stella Walsh were ever men who posed as

Fig.42. Gender testing in 1936 did not start because of Olympian high jumper Dora Ratjen (GER), though Ratjen's case was curious. Ratjen was raised as a girl but went through male puberty. Ratjen competed as a woman, but an encounter with German police later convinced Ratjen to go by Heinrich (German Federal Archive).

women to cheat. Moreover, neither was the reason for the adoption of the gender verification policy.

Brundage had recommended to the IOC that the sports federations require women to bring medical gender certifications to competitions, following August 1936. The presumption was that even a personal doctor would nip in the bud any attempts by an individual man or "pseudo-hermaphrodite" to don a women's uniform. Cheaters, in this view, were individuals, not part of large-scale conspiracies.

However, that view was short-lived. Certification was in the eye of various beholders, and there were no clear rules about what exactly the doctor needed to certify. Could someone receive the feminine stamp of approval just for wearing the right shoes or hat? Could someone be eliminated simply for having muscles in the wrong places or hair that was too short?

The IOC mandated doctor's certificates for the 1948 London Games, the first Olympics staged after Berlin due to the interruption from World War II. But as the Soviet and Eastern bloc countries began sending athletes to international competitions—athletes who were bigger, stronger, and unafraid to display muscles—the concern over cheaters intensified. An atmosphere of inquisition settled over the women's locker room, and examinations became less private.

The Inquisition, Legs Wide

While the IOC take-over of the business of sex verifications didn't formally begin until 1968, the national committees (NOCs) approved by the IOC did assume authority over the grim inspections shortly after gender certificates began to be required in 1936. As prestige had blossomed for women's athletics, so came increasing concern about cheaters, increasing incentives for others to point fingers, and increasing anxiety by the athletes. According to biographer Max Dohle: "The *Dutch Journal of Medicine* reported in December 1936 that three British athletes refused to undergo a gynecological examination … many women were under suspicion. There were so many tough girls on the track that there was a veritable manhunt for 'impostors.'"[12]

Dohle joined another Dutch biographer, Kees Kooman, in describing this new chilling climate in international women's sports. According to both writers, Dutch track star Fanny Blankers-Koen was known to spy on teammates in the shower. Kooman says that Blankers-Koen herself had been suspected of being a man by at least one rival "until she became a mother,"[13] and that one of her nicknames was the "queen with the man's legs."[14] In Kooman's "warts-and-all" biography of Blankers-Koen in 2003, several witnesses said that husband/coach Jan Blankers advanced rumors and may have prompted his wife to peek around corners.

The subject of Dohle's biography earned far less attention. Her name was Foejke Dillema. Dillema may have been the first documented case of a woman denied the official stamp of femininity required to run. Dillema was a rising star shortly after the London Olympics, in 1949. She beat Blankers-Koen in several races as the multi-gold medalist began training for a repeat for Helsinki.

But, in the following July 1950, when all women going to compete at the European Championships were scheduled to report to the Dutch sports medical committee, Dillema canceled her examination. Although she had clocked some of the best recent performances for the Dutch team, the medical board quickly suspended her. Dillema's coach, Tonnis de Vries, spoke to her after a race, but she again refused to go. The next day, an official yanked her off a train heading to another competition, and she was permanently exiled from sports. Dillema went home and reportedly didn't leave her house for a year. She never discussed the subject again.

After Dillema's death in 2007, her family consented to allow a scientific team to perform a DNA test. The team concluded that Dillema may have had a disorder of sex development (DSD) known as 46,XX/46,XY, also called mosaicism, which led to hyperandrogenism.[15] The condition typically provides higher-than-normal levels of testosterone, which can enhance speed. Dillema may have had characteristics of both sexes that she feared would be discovered in a thorough exam.

Yet Dillema lived her entire life as a woman. Rivals said the Dutch sprinter had facial hair but also breasts, which suggests something other than a man dressed in women's clothing. Standing next to Blankers-Koen after a 1950 race, she simply seems smaller, more slender, and with a more-pronounced Dutch nose and chin.

Fig.43. Foejke Dillema, left, and Fanny Blankers-Koen in 1950, after Dillema broke Blankers-Koen's 200 m record. A month later, Dillema would cancel her nationally-mandated gender verification medical exam (photograph by Ben van Meerendonk, Wikimedia Commons).

In this newly crafted world of gender examinations, it was not enough for an athlete simply to show that they weren't strapping down male genitalia. Female competitors needed to have next to no body hair, large breasts, and all the lower body parts required for procreation. Dillema's Dutch teammate Puck Brower described how "the examination was 'about the bottom and not the top.' She had to sit in the delivery chair with her legs drawn up to be examined. 'Legs wide, like this,' she said jokingly."[16]

For more than 20 years, state-sponsored doctors performed these exams on women athletes in order to prove they were 100 percent female. As Soviet and Eastern bloc countries entered the picture, the suspicious atmosphere intensified. Rooting out Communists and homosexuals at home went hand in hand with eliminating potential cheaters in the war in sports. Despite intrusive examinations being performed on athletes by approved doctors, sometimes multiple times, the IOC and IAAF decided in 1966 that they needed even more proof.

The concern was twofold. First, countries had begun using drug cocktails on athletes ever since anabolic steroids were first synthesized in Eastern Europe in the 1930s. The Soviet Union was believed to be giving steroids to weightlifters, so it was possible all the athletes were partaking. Prior to 1968, such chemical use was frowned upon but not banned. Anabolic steroids could create hair growth, deep voices, and other changes that might have failed a female athlete in a thorough exam. Thus, the sports federations were essentially using sex verification tests as a substitute for drug tests. Instead of putting resources into detecting unnatural and potentially harmful substances, the medical commission reasoned that they could catch women who had been doping with a visual inspection.

The bigger concern was the sheer size and strength of the Soviet women, the shot putters and discus throwers in particular. State-sponsored sports academies had recruited women who were even taller and more muscular than the "muscle molls" that sportswriters had griped about back in the 1920s. IOC official Monique Berliox tried to frame it with the "simple fairness" argument: "nature can play some funny tricks and … a baby can be declared of masculine or feminine sex at birth because its physical structure is such that it is possible to make an error … it is the duty of everyone to make sure that the situation is not abused…. Nothing is more prejudicial to female sport than this charlatanry."[17]

Berliox was essentially suggesting that any tall, muscular woman might be intersex. That was a lot of funny tricks. Yet, because of the cultural biases against women developing muscles, some could not fathom that a woman might spend years training and lifting weights expressly to do so.

The Eastern bloc countries, for their part, didn't understand this policy of "neglect [of female athletes] in … the enlightened nations of the West." An East German spokesman explained that "we beat them overall because they are not tapping the full potential of their women."[18] The West, in contrast, viewed it as "communist-gender pollution."[19]

Rumors continued to fly. In a 1966 *Time* magazine article about the coming changes to gender verification, the writer mentioned a North Korean athlete, Sin Kim Dan, who was a world record holder in the 400 m. Sin was barred from competing in the 1964 Olympics, not because of suspicions over her gender, but due to an international dispute between the IOC and North Korea. The ensuing publicity led to a televised reunion with the father, separated from her in the war.

In the article, though there was no evidence to support the claim, the *Time* reporter claimed that the father had "recognized Sin as the son he had lost."[20] Subsequent biographers note that Sin had passed many gender verification examinations and later married and gave birth. Why *Time* mislabeled her gender is a mystery, other than that, as a North Korean, she could not dispute the story. Yet, because of the comment, Sin is now regularly included in gender variance lists, despite there being no public evidence of her gender dysphoria.

Into this environment, where accusations sufficed and any masculine characteristic would be proof over all other feminine characteristics, the mid–1960s sports federations instituted the "naked parades." The large-scale attempt to root out cheaters began with gynecological exams at the Commonwealth Games in August 1966 in Jamaica. A few weeks later, an IAAF-chosen panel also performed inspections at the European Championships in Budapest, though this may have only required a walk-through *sans* clothing. "They let you walk by ... turn and face them, and that was it."[21]

But the exams varied from panel to panel. For the 1967 Pan-American Games in Winnipeg, U.S. shot putter Maren Seidler described the atmosphere as being more than perfunctory:

> They lined us up outside a room where there were three doctors sitting in a row behind desks. You had to go in and pull up your shirt and push down your pants. Then they just looked while you waited for them to confer and decide if you were OK. While I was in line I remember one of the sprinters, a tiny, skinny girl, came out shaking her head back and forth saying, "Well, I failed, I didn't have enough up top. They say I can't run and I have to go home because I'm not 'big' enough."[22]

If nature was playing tricks, these tricks could include anything: less-than-buxom chests, hairy legs, or fuzzy upper lips.

The 1966 European contests in Budapest were the ones that the Press sisters, who had been called the "Press brothers" for years, decided not to join. As Chapter Six noted, both had been accused of being men practically from the moment they stepped on the field. Tamara Press was 5'11", the same height as Wilma Rudolph. She weighed 225 pounds, roughly 20 pounds less than her shot put rival, American Earlene Brown. Yet, Arthur Daley of the *New York Times* still said Tamara was "big enough to play tackle for the Chicago Bears" and that 5'6" Irina was the size of "a running guard." Poetic license? Perhaps, but neither an intersex condition nor steroids would have made them tall.

Still, the Press sisters' decision to opt out of the 1966 competition and then retire was treated as ironclad proof that both the Soviet track stars were men in disguise. Most descriptions blandly state that they "dropped out of competition when gender tests were introduced."[23] This is not quite true, of course, since there had been mandatory verification tests within each country since 1936.

It is likely that the Press sisters had been given "vitamins" as part of their Soviet sports academy training, probably including steroids. They might have known, or their trainers might have known, that the drugs created noticeable physical changes.

When they abruptly canceled their plans to compete at the 1966 tournament, the sisters indicated plans to visit their mother, who was ailing at the time. Within a year, both of them retired formally from the sport.

They pleaded age, which was a legitimate excuse. The Soviet Union was known to routinely kick older athletes off teams, as they had with shot putter Galina Zybina, to make room for the younger generation. Tamara Press had been competing nonstop for a decade, with a history of injury. When the gold medal shot putter officially announced her retirement the following year, she said she had "devoted more than 10 years of my life to sports … and I would like (cede) my place … to young sportswomen … to help my successors."[24]

The court of public opinion had already found them guilty. Gynecological panels were finding women guilty if they had insufficient bosoms or chin hairs. The "chief sex tester" in the 1968 Games, Ludwig Prokop, said his exams "convinced him that sports made [female athletes] ugly, with hard stringy bodies, and, in some cases, hair on their chests."[25] Even if the sisters were not both intersex, could they both have passed such exams? And, if they had passed in Budapest, would they have passed in Winnipeg, and Kiev, and every single time someone turned on a flashlight and got out a magnifying glass?

Soon-to-be-Doctor Press was an intelligent woman. Sister Irina, in her last Games, had lost out on medals in two successive Olympics. They both may have seen nothing to gain from hobbling in on 30-year-old knees to pull down track shorts so that a panel could determine whether there was too much hair or not enough hair or to measure whether their hips were wide enough for child-bearing. Retiring caused all the accusations to become permanent, but Tamara and Irina kept their medals and their records.

The IAAF initially crowed with satisfaction that their system was eliminating cheaters when athletes like the Press sisters dropped out. But women found that the search for cheaters became increasingly humiliating. Even the men began to get embarrassed at the spectacle. The president of the Polish Olympic Committee, Wlodzimierz Reczek, wrote the IOC that "repeated gynecological examinations of the young girl athletes, even several times in the course of one year, make an unpleasant environment around those athletes and are a form of discrimination … and the light-minded arbitrariness in the interpretation of the results of examinations may harm the examined persons."[26]

Brundage, who had long abandoned his early support of women athletes, brushed aside the criticisms, simply saying the subject should be "approached with great caution … to prevent stigma on innocent persons."[27] In other words, the need to catch the guilty was still strong enough to warrant exams; they just needed less publicity, especially fewer women complaining about being probed to their families or the press.

Yet the indignities of the nude parades led the IOC to alter their plan. Beginning with Mexico City, they would end the practice of asking athletes to climb into the stirrups to prove they were female. The IOC stopped trying to have women prove they were women on the outside. Instead, they wanted women to prove they were women on the inside.

Guilty Unless Proven Women

At the 1968 Games in Mexico City, the IOC stopped the physical exams, thus ending three decades of inconsistent, arbitrary, and intrusive physicals. Thus began five decades of poorly designed, misapplied, and constantly changing scientific standards. Chromosomal testing was a brand-new toy in the hands of scientists, ever since Watson and Crick had described the double-helical structure of DNA in 1953. If genetic science could solve mysteries like Downe's syndrome (the cause of which was finally identified in the late 1950s), then maybe it held the key to resolving the slippery determination of gender.

Jacques Thiebault, head of the IOC's medical testing in Mexico City, reinforced that what they were looking for was "hybrid" athletes, athletes who were insufficiently attached to the feminine binary. He said that these "so-called women" were "collecting records.... Sooner or later, the true representatives of the weak sex will feel cheated."[28] It was another warning: strong women need not apply here.

At first, however, the IAAF experimented with a combination of both external and internal tests. For the tests at the 1967 European championships in Kiev, examinations started first with the stirrups. Polish sprinter Eva Klobukowska, a willowy, attractive 21-year-old, had taken an Olympic bronze medal behind American sprinter Wyomia Tyus in 1964 as well as anchoring the Polish team to a gold in the 4 × 100 relay. Even though Klobukowska had passed multiple previous inspections—locally, nationally, and internationally—this time, the doctors saw something questionable.

The Polish sprinter was given the secondary chromosome test. Klobukowska's sample came back as failed. She had "one chromosome too many."[29] Her chromosomal characteristics were XX/XXY, and that extra Y-chromosome ended her career. She was further stripped of her world records and Klobukowska returned home to marry, have children, and remain baffled about her permanent exile from women's athletics.

The IOC deemed the genetic testing a success, though they found their initial approach cumbersome and expensive. The medical team was using hair samples, which might take several. One athlete complained, "I remember almost having a bald patch once because they kept pulling out so many hairs."[30] They switched to a "buccal smear" test, taking DNA from the inside of the cheek. This test was specifically designed to look for the Barr body, that second or inactive X-chromosome, which distinguishes XX females from XY males. Critics of the test pointed out that Klobukowska's XXY had the requisite Barr body, yet Klobukowska remained exiled, and her case was not revisited.

The plan was for the IOC to sample about one-fifth of the athletes in the 1968 Winter Olympics, then all Olympic women athletes going forward. As they had with physical inspections, national teams began performing their own versions beforehand. The Austrian ski federation turned up another unwitting violator.

Erica Schinegger, a sensational 18-year-old downhill skier, was discovered to have internal male sex organs (surprise!) and an XY chromosome. The doctors gave her a choice. She could have them surgically removed, take hormones, and continue living as a woman. In theory, this would have allowed Schinegger to keep a medal earned in the 1966 World Ski Championships, although she would no longer be able to compete internationally.

Or, she could move forward with gender reassignment surgery and transition to a man. Schinegger chose the latter and became Erik, forfeiting the previous medal and enduring public scandal for a time at home. He married and fathered children, embracing his new gender. In hindsight, teammates claim they knew it all along, although no suspicion had fallen on Schinegger prior to the internal test.

The IOC moved forward in Mexico City with the brand-new tests, applying them to all 781 female athletes. They had learned from the process to use more discretion. For a while, there were no more widely reported cases of gender failures, though it's not known how many women were told by their ski clubs that their competitive career was over because of internal features discovered from a cheek swab.

Almost immediately, other scientists began to criticize way the chromatin tests were being used. A key British researcher, Malcolm Ferguson-Smith, refused to allow his lab to evaluate tests for the 1970 Edinburgh Commonwealth Games. Ferguson-Smith explained that having an XY chromosome did not automatically give someone a male physique.[31] Some women could have androgen insensitivity syndrome (AIS), where an internal portion of their genetic makeup said "male," but their body was insensitive to male hormones. Women with AIS would have, for athletic competition purposes, no special advantage. Furthermore, an athlete who was male and had physical advantages could, through a Barr-body test, qualify with an XX chromosome to compete against women. This was what all the hullabaloo had been designed to prevent.

In the meantime, unnatural substance abuse was growing into a much bigger problem. Advancing drug testing science sooner, instead of obsessing over gender lines, might have been more helpful. Throughout the 1970s, the East German swimmers were walking, breathing steroid experiments who did not fail the new chromatin screenings despite deep voices and other signs of steroid abuse. Later data showed that they had been forced to take drugs that caused great bodily harm.[32] They won medals after passing the gender verification screenings, even though many were later unable to have children or bore children with birth defects. Some developed liver and heart disease, and at least one track athlete felt it necessary to undergo gender reassignment because of irreversible side effects from massive state-mandated illicit steroids.

Still, the IOC and IAAF continued forward with their obsession with sexual verification tests, ignoring objections. More data showed that androgen insensitivity was not uncommon. One in every 421 athletes might have some sort of DSD that would lead to a positive test. Among the 4,000 Olympic women competing, as many as 10 might routinely be excluded, not to mention thousands of women athletes across multiple sports. The number of "nature's funny tricks" continued to climb.

These weren't all just faceless numbers, either. A high-profile case in 1985 seemed to turn the tide, at least against widespread chromatin testing. Spanish hurdler Maria Martínez-Patiño took the required gender verification test as part of the World University Games in Japan. A devout Catholic, she was highly offended when informed she was essentially a man because of an internal XY chromosome. Although she had AIS, which meant she was not benefiting from the configuration as an athlete, she was told to step down. The committee suggested she fake an injury. She was outraged and refused. She competed, won her race, and was subsequently thrown out, with her past records expunged.

When she was disqualified, she also lost her athletic residence and scholarship back in Spain. Martínez-Patiño told the press, "I knew I was a woman in the eyes of medicine, God, and most of all in my own eyes ... if I hadn't been an athlete, my femininity would never have been questioned."[33] She continued to fight to be reinstated. After three years, she prevailed at the Court of Arbitration for Sport (CAS), demonstrating that the test which disqualified her inappropriately ascribed to her an advantage which she did not have.

The IAAF went back to the drawing board. They concluded in 1992 that "gender screening based on finding Y chromosomal material should be abandoned" and that "only masquerading males (individuals reared and living as men) should be excluded."[34] Further, the rising number of athletes opting for gender reassignment surgery—transsexual athletes—led to guidelines that described the conditions under which they could compete as women, based on their hormone levels. International track and field was moving forward.

The Olympic Committee was not as ready. The IOC still dragged its feet, trying to uncover masquerading males with genetic tests. In the 1992 Games, they chose a different screening test, which still had scientific problems. In the Winter Olympics of 1994, the host country of Norway refused to help the IOC with the sex testing protocols because of their inaccuracy. IOC scientists had to be flown in from Albertville, site of the previous Games. Finally, in 2000, the IOC ended their mandatory gender verification protocol. They stopped testing everybody.

From now on, they would only test women who were suspicious. It was back to peeking around shower corners all over again.

Simple Biology

The case of Caster Semenya seems to encapsulate the entire history of femininity control within a single person. That history covered a myriad of changing rules and attitudes about what defines a woman athlete. In the past dozen years after Semenya first zoomed onto the scene at the 2009 World Championships, she was included, excluded, accused, tested, cleared, speculated about, argued over, drugged, held up as a shining example, pilloried as a cheater, and won two gold medals.[35]

While the IOC and IAAF did loudly end chromosome testing of all athletes in 2000, they quietly retained the right to test anyone for other reasons. Submitting a urine sample for illegal substance testing was now routinely observed by medical personal, which ought to eliminate any man donning a woman's uniform in disguise. (No more Dora Ratjens!) But the track federations would also test the chromosomes of anyone if a competitor had "lodge[d] a complaint ... because of an outstanding performance or masculine-looking features."[36] So it was back to finger-pointing again.

By 2006, scientific research had shown that women could exhibit several genetic variations from the textbook XX chromosome arrangement. The two most common are AIS and hyperandrogenism.[37] The first contains that extra Y chromosome which does not necessarily convey physical advantages. The second means that higher-than-average levels of androgen (i.e., testosterone) are being produced, which could lead to competitive advantages. Yet, in 2006, the IOC and IAAF made no distinctions. They weren't testing everybody, but if an athlete was suspected, and subsequent testing revealed they were not strictly XX, their competing days were over.

Indian runner Santhi Soundarajan, also determined to be "male" by this testing, had emerged from the poorest of the poor region of Tamil when she won a few races in 2005 and 2006. The highlight of her career was a silver medal at the Asian Games in 2006. But, in a now familiar refrain, she was asked to visit some doctors because someone thought she had too many muscles. She then heard on the news that she would be stripped of her medal because she was really a man. She was so ashamed by the public announcement that she attempted suicide. After recovering, she tried to get a job in sports, but the news caused Indian organizations to shun her. A ten-year battle finally assisted her in gaining permanent employment as a track coach. All of this, even though Soundarajan had AIS, which meant that her invisible intersex condition would not have benefited her as a runner in the first place.

The rumors circulated again when 18-year-old runner Semenya emerged into the senior circuit to set blazing times in the 800 m at the 2009 World Championships. Her times had improved rapidly in the past year, which raised suspicions. Semenya had only recently begun racing, but rapid time improvements can indicate drug use. Yet the track world had forgotten that teenager Betty Robinson had set a world record only three months after picking up track shoes.

Semenya's drug tests were always clean. So complaints about her included her physical features, like in the old days. She had muscles. She had chin hairs. She wore her hair short. She dressed like a boy and didn't wear makeup.

However, unlike in Soundarajan's case, Semenya's coaches argued that they had performed a thorough physical inspection on the South African sprinter. "'She is a female,' insisted general manager Molatelo Malehopo. 'We are completely sure about that. We would not have entered her into the female competition if we had any doubts.'"[38]

Because Semenya had won by such a distance in her heats and semi-final at the 2009 competition, she was asked to take a gender verification test, and that request was leaked to media. Normally with potential drug violations, nothing is said until A and B samples are confirmed, and only after the competitions are finished. Here, before the final had even been run, a teenager was being thrown to the wolves of the international press. At least for Semenya, South Africa fought energetically on her behalf. They angrily complained about the information leaked to the press, which created rumors based on half facts.

Part of the problem was that the IAAF and IOC were not being specific about what would disqualify women who were determined to be not-average women. They were hoping that athletes told that they had some gender-varying condition would simply agree not to run. Semenya did stop, for a year, waiting for an appointed medical panel to make a decision. They emerged in 2010 and cleared her to compete, allowing her to keep her previous medals. What the agreement entailed, though, was a request for her to take hormone-suppressing drugs. She had been told her condition was hyperandrogenism. Drugs would dampen her body's high level of androgens, and she could run.

For the London Games in 2012, the IAAF also picked a number. Going forward, women who had too much naturally occurring androgens—specifically, above 10 nannomoles/per liter (nmol/L)—would be required to take drugs or be excluded. This would also allow those with other intersex conditions, like AIS, to compete as well. At last, there was clarity.

However, another Indian runner, Dutee Chand, also bumped up against the rules and disagreed with the approach. After winning sprint races in the 2014 Asian Junior Championships, Chand was barred from further competition because she had hyperandrogenism. Again, the publicity was humiliating. "For days, Chand cried inconsolably and refused to eat or drink. 'Some in the news were saying I was a boy, and some said that maybe I was a transsexual.'"[39]

But Chand pushed back. Supported by legal experts Davies, Ward, Philips & Vineberg, Chand took her case to the CAS. Her lawyers argued effectively that

Fig.44. Dutee Chand (IND), left, was another sprinter excluded for failing a chromosome test. Refusing to accept the judgment, she went to the Court of Arbitration for Sport, arguing insufficient evidence to prove that her genes gave her an advantage (Asian Athletics Association and Odisha government).

choosing to eliminate athletes based on a natural condition was discriminatory, and a violation of the Olympic Charter. They also pointed out that the IAAF had never established scientifically that 10 nmol/L—or any other particular number—was the right amount of hormones. Chand was reinstated and allowed to run, including in both the 2016 and 2020 Olympics. She did not move beyond the heats in either Games but proudly became the third woman to represent India in the sprints.

The ruling also cleared other athletes—like Semenya—to compete and to discontinue taking hormones. Semenya ran in the 800 m in Rio and took a gold medal. Semenya also had recently come out as a lesbian and married her partner the previous December. A happy ending seemed likely to ensue.

However, in the 2016 800 m Olympic final, all three medalists were from African nations. All three were muscular and swift. All three were immediately suspected of crossing the gender line. Several others in the finals—white runners from Canada, Poland, and Great Britain—complained loudly. Britain's Lynsey Sharp said it was as if there were "two races." Polish runner Joanna Jozwik, who finished fifth, declared she was the "first European and the second white."[40] The racers accused the three African runners of having an unfair advantage. Bishop, Jozwik, and Sharp wanted them eliminated because they might be intersex, which would, logically, mean that Bishop, Jozwik, and Sharp would win the medals.

In 2016, the IOC allowed the three African runners to keep their medals. Later tests did confirm that all three had hyperandrogenism. The IAAF kept poking around in the science, looking for another approach. After two more years, they found more data they believed would show the way. By this time, there was research that suggested women in middle distance races, specifically between the 400 and 1,500 m, would have an advantage unless they lowered their testosterone levels to below 5 nmol/L. This happened to exactly encompass the races that Semenya (Niyonasaba, Wambui…) were running, but at least there was some data behind it.

Opinion pages around the world kept busy. Several who pressed the need for fairness pushed the "simple biology" argument. One in the *New York Times* declared,

> Understanding the rules and why they make sense is hard. They are based in biology people don't know or don't like to talk about. … Replacing traditional sex classifications with classifications based on gender identity certainly has steep costs in contexts like competitive sport, where the likelihood of success is precisely about sex-specific biology … a simple testosterone test establishes this fact one way or the other.[41]

Such arguments hearkened back to the days that mandated a clear binary, the opposing poles of male and female. Women with excessive muscles according to "simple testosterone tests" would be unfairly advantaged. The word "traditional," given gender testing history, sounded rosy enough. But did traditional mean the 1950s, when national teams would probe tall women with a bit too much hair until they found something untoward? Or could it be the early 1970s, when other tests might reveal something on the inside that was a complete surprise to the runner? The older rules had been based on an incomplete understanding of biology.

Despite the alleged simplicity of the science, after the 2018 decisions were made, other researchers took issue with the *British Journal of Medicine* study that the IOC

Fig.45. The 2016 Women's 800 m. Left-right: Wambui (KEN), Grace (USA), Sharp (GBR), Arzamasava (BLR), Jowzik (POL), Niyonasaba (BUR), and Semenya (RSA). The three Africans took medals but were all later labeled hyperandrogenic, banned unless they took hormones (photograph by Celso Pupo Rodrigues © Dreamstime.com).

had relied on. One review charged that it contained several errors—duplication of data, incorrect calculation, and mismatched athletes and times.[42] Other researchers noted that studies which calculated valid testosterone ranges specifically excluded so-called "outliers," such as when the female athletes had DSD or other conditions. That reflected somewhat circular reasoning, since the whole point was to define a range across an entire population, not merely measure the population already defined.[43]

In addition, there has been disagreement over which research to use, since some studies show actual overlap between the low end of the male range of testosterone and the high end of the female range, rather than a statistically significant distinction. Five nmol/L was the number as of 2021, but, as more data is gathered, that number may shift or eventually disappear altogether.

Dutee Chand was cleared to compete in Tokyo 2020. Others were not. More African runners were excluded based on the current rules: 400 m runners Christine Mboma and Beatrice Masilingi from Namibia and Maximila Imali and Evangeline Makena from Kenya. The list is getting long, which may prompt future changes.

Semenya herself has come full circle. She refused to return to taking hormones to dampen her testosterone levels to the required range, claiming they made her sick. Discouraged but stubbornly refusing to give up, Semenya attempted to qualify for races of different lengths—the 200 m and the 5,000 m. However, there were already many specialists in those races, and she was unable to meet the Olympic standard. At 30 years old, she seemed destined to hang up her track shoes, carefully gerrymandered out of the races that had gained her two medals.

However, there is a subtle lifting of the clouds over gender testing, behind the lengthy diatribes for and against whether Semenya and others ought to be able to participate in the 800 m. As a result of the disputes and rulings, because of the bravery and perseverance of Semenya, Chand, and all their predecessors, the international athletic bodies have agreed to allow women with DSD conditions and transgender women athletes to compete. There is a ceiling of testosterone which they must meet, but only for three races: the 400, 800, and 1,500. In the other nearly three hundred events, there are no more requirements for women to prove that they are women. At least for now, no more parades or stirrup examinations or mass cheek swabs.

O Brave New World

Nearly a century of attempting to regulate gender through sex verification testing ended up causing more harm than good, certainly harm to the IOC's reputation for holding fair and impartial contests. Attempting to police the Eastern bloc countries through naked parades and with microscopes may have eliminated a few athletes, but it left a legacy of shattered dreams.

The true parade was the long list of women who were told they were men, then barred from competition. Many were stripped of records and medals which had to be later reinstated. Some accused would be cleared today. The Press sisters and Stella Walsh would be allowed in 2020's racing environment, assuming they passed illegal substance tests. The rules might yet change again, leading to more reinstatement, more confusion, and more head-scratching about why the arguments about fairness don't seem to be fair.

Twenty-first-century standards on gender have shifted to much blurrier lines, too. The whole issue of gender testing practically started because of transgender (FTM) athletes in the 1930s. Now the policy incorporates rules for transgender athletes. Those choosing to adjust their bodies' hormone levels consistent with their gender identity competed openly in Tokyo for the first time. New Zealand weightlifter Laurel Hubbard heard plenty from the Internet trolls but entered and competed.

Nearly a half dozen athletes who consider themselves non-binary or transgender competed in Tokyo. There is a backlash against these athletes as well. American politicians have been fund-raising on promises to eliminate the horrors of DSD athletes competing in high schools and colleges, just as they once railed against LGBTQ marriage. The hue and cry against non-binary athletes who are not excluded from the 400, 800, or 1,500 may get louder, if and when they win medals. The IOC, for the moment, has moved on.

The idea of mixed competition as a possible solution to the thorny sexual verification question has also resurfaced. Men and women competing together would eliminate concerns about the gender binary. This was an irritant with Coubertin early on and part of his rationale as to why women should not compete. "Let us not forget that the Olympic Games are not parades of physical exercises, but aim to raise, or at least maintain, records ... women cannot claim to outdo men in running, fencing, equestrian events, etc. To bring the principle of the theoretical equality of the sexes into play here would be to indulge in a pointless demonstration bereft of meaning or impact."[44]

Others have obsessed over a similar idea. Historian Guttmann ended his landmark survey *Women in Sport* with a painstaking analysis of why men will remain "superior to women in most sports that require strength and speed."[45] His thirty-year-old argument seems outdated in opining that women could never play in the NFL or lift seriously heavy weights.[46] But he also showed performance gaps that had been steadily narrowing. His stance that exceptional women ought to be allowed to challenge men, "if they feel they must," is simultaneously open-minded and weird. Women competing against men was not what women had been fighting for all this time.

Tokyo added nine mixed events, from judo to table tennis to shooting, both as a way of addressing gender segregation complaints and to move closer to gender parity. Most mixed teams had equal numbers of each gender competing against each other, not qualifying women competing against qualifying men. Still, as far as gender testing goes, the solution was never to mix everyone together for every event. The excitement of sports is in watching different people with different skills compete against those similarly skilled. No one would suggest mixing all the weight classes together, or asking the pole vaulters to compete on the balance beam. As the man said, these are not "merely parades of physical exercises," but contests. Athletes and spectators will probably prefer the fragile compromise of the 5 nmol/L to a giant soup of mixed men-women team competitions.

The gender verification rules have shifted forward, time and time again. In this, they have echoed the experience of women athletes as a whole, the push against one barrier after another. Women fought to get into the Games in the first place, then sport by sport and event by event, making their cases based on persuasion, exemplary performances, and legal means when necessary. So, too, have women slowly but surely eliminated the walls surrounding the pedestal of femininity, of delicate features and slender limbs as the only acceptable type of athlete.

Women have taken control of their own idea of gender and have defined femininity however they choose. That could mean thick eye makeup à la Simone Biles, who likes to plaster on plenty of glitter before executing a Yurchenko double pike vault, a maneuver so challenging that no women had ever done it in competition before 2021. Or, it could be a Raven Saunders Hulk mask, accentuating the sight of an eight-pound cannonball arcing into the sky. Perhaps the perfect examples in female sports might be sprinter moms 36-year-old Allyson Felix and 29-year-old Quanera Hayes at the June 2021 Olympic Trials, introducing their toddlers to each other, once their track shoes stopped smoking from their blistering 400 m. Or, non-binary Canadian soccer player Quinn, helping Canada win their first gold medal in Women's Football. However they appeared on the outside and whatever hormones and genetic combinations they carried on the inside, women had gotten into the stadiums and were running, throwing, wrestling, cycling, swimming, leaping, and tumbling into the record books.

Coubertin had once asserted that the athlete—"the adult male individual"—was an "officiating priest of the muscular religion." He saw Olympism as "consisting at its centre of a moral Altis."[47] But at the site of Olympia, priestesses also officiated. While many Greek historians stress that the *only* woman allowed to view the Games was the high priestess of Demeter, the Altis still contained the Temple of Hera. The Temple of Zeus may have been bigger, but the Temple of Hera was the oldest and most venerated of the religious buildings. In modern times, it is a priestess at the Temple of Hera who lights the modern Olympic flame, borne by torch relays to the Olympic cauldron at the host city.

The baron cited the Olympic motto—*Citius, Altius, Fortius*—in explaining why women ought not to compete. He reasoned that they could not be *Faster, Higher, Stronger* than their male counterparts. But as the passing Olympiads have proven, their deeds can be just as inspiring as those of men. Every greatest Olympian list now includes men and women. Perhaps not in equal numbers, but give them time.

To observe these phenomenal women in Tokyo… Paris… Los Angeles… Brisbane and centuries into the future will remind us not only of their athletic accomplishments but also their personal fortitude in refusing to leave the field just because someone told them that they play like a girl. Moment after moment of their triumph and struggle will remind all of us how far and how fast women have come, how high they can go, and how strong they will remain, no matter what obstacles they encounter.

Citius, Altius, Fortius, indeed.

Afterthoughts: On Visibility

They're just sports, some might say. They're just games. With all the other problems facing women in the world—unequal pay, threats of violence, repression of abortion rights, transphobia—why focus so much on trivialities? Sports are a microcosm of our culture. A society is reflected by its entertainment and its art. Besides, if the highly skilled, heroic deeds of brave women in the arena don't command respect, how can the rest of us hope to do so?

Five thousand women competed in Tokyo, and never were the Olympics needed more. After more than a year of restrictions and lockdowns, the world needed a moment to see the best that humanity has to offer. There were no spectators, and the roar of the crowd was missed. But how much worse to have no Games all? Despite the risks of holding contests in the last stages of a pandemic, despite controversies over gender testing and whether marijuana should be banned as performance-enhancing, the Tokyo Olympics provided welcome relief from a year of hard times. We're not through yet. Neither are the Olympics.

Part of what the isolation from COVID has taught us is the need to see and be seen by other people. If out of sight equals out of mind, then the cure needs to be in sight, and top of mind, as much as possible. It seems especially fitting, since the battle for women to gain access to the Olympics, time and time again, was itself about visibility.

First, women were advised not to make a spectacle of themselves. They were told they were incapable and would look ridiculous. When they proved quite capable, many were criticized for looking strained, red-faced, or, worst of all, muscular. Anyone who didn't appear svelte in a bathing suit was called a mannish lesbian, which caused the lesbians decades of grief. When mere words didn't sting sufficiently enough, the sporting federations resorted to doctors, speculums, and cheek swabs to keep out any deemed unworthy for being too strong or too fast. The result, time and time again, was one brave woman after another refusing to go home, refusing to be told they didn't have an entry ticket, they didn't have the priest's blessing, or that they simply weren't allowed.

When I started this project, I considered myself pretty knowledgeable about the Olympics. I had watched a lot of footage, read countless stories, and still owned home-made grainy videotapes dating back to Barcelona, Seoul, and Los Angeles.

But I had no idea.

I had no idea of the bravery of Stamata Revithi, the pioneering spirit of Alice Milliat, the sheer gall of Rusty Kanokogi, and the skills of multi-talented women from around the world like Bobbie Rosenfeld and Laila Schou Nilsen. To my credit, I had watched Olympic handball, but I had no idea it was the most popular women's sport in Norway or that some of the first competing LGBTQ couples came out of handball. I had never heard of the Press sisters or Lis Hartel.

All I knew about Stella Walsh was that she was discovered to be "a man in disguise." I did not know she was once hailed as Stella Walsh, "All-American Girl," and allowed by the U.S. to run for Poland, before she was pilloried as a traitor for doing it the second time. That she won a beauty contest to try to dampen the criticism. That she married someone in the 1950s just so that she could compete under the American flag, only to fail in the heats at the U.S. Trials—at age 45. She had already won the U.S. long jump title again, a few years earlier, 21 years after she first took that title over Babe Didrikson. Well into her late sixties, she could still run the pants off whippersnapper male journalists. That's not hyperandrogenism or being "Stella the Fella"; that's just sheer obstinacy of spirit. That's an unwillingness to let gender or age define who you are and what you can do.

Just as Caster Semenya seems to embody the entire mini-history of gender verification in a single person, Stella Walsh seems to encapsulate the entire struggle for women in the Games, continuing to strive despite encountering one obstacle after another. Some battles she lost; some she won. She was killed buying ribbons to award children competing in yet more races. No doubt, plenty were for girls. What bothered people most was how Stella looked. She never let it get in the way of competing.

As this is not an encyclopedia, there was not enough room to cover all the competitions. Many sports deserved more attention than this treatment could give. Pole vaulting, weightlifting, and ski jumping all had their own heroes and heroines who pestered IOC officials until women's divisions were added. Resistance to female athletes in those events carried the same familiar refrain. *She doesn't look right. She doesn't have what it takes. It doesn't seem okay from a medical point of view.* Thank goodness that their advocates paid no attention to the barking of the chauvinists. The Baroness of Ski Jumping, Austrian Paula Lamberg, probably deserved an entire chapter. Or another entire book. All these women do.

New sports were added in Tokyo and will be in Paris. One of the men's street skateboarding favorites, 26-year-old Nyjah Houston, got in hot water a few years ago after telling an interviewer, "Some girls can skate but I personally believe that skateboarding is not for girls at all. Not one bit."[1] He backtracked quickly, explaining that skateboarding involves falling, and he didn't like to see girls get hurt. Tucked beneath the words was the mindset that still haunts road cyclists and long-distance runners, that viewpoint still hearkening back to the 1928 800 m "pitiful disaster." He doesn't like to *see them*.

Fortunately, millions got to watch the 13-year-old phenomenons Hiraki Kokona, Rayssa Leal, and Sky Brown win skateboarding medals.[2] When Okamoto Misugu fell on her final run and slipped out of medal contention, the other women—American, Japanese, Australian—lifted her up onto their shoulders in a show of solidarity. The picture became one more shining example of Olympism, of athletes respecting each other in the buffering and battering of competition.

That is what Coubertin objected to and perhaps feared the most. Women could play at sports as long as nobody was watching, but they should not make a spectacle of themselves. Fortunately, hundreds fought to earn their place on the track and in the arena and become that spectacle—become, in fact, truly spectacular.

Even the newest sports can carry outdated attitudes. The more things change, the more women will fight the same battles over again. That's okay. The young 'uns have been emboldened by their mothers. They won't take no for an answer. They will demand to be seen and heard as their grandmothers and great-grandmothers of sports showed them how to do.

They won't stop now.

Further Reading

A more in-depth look at a few of the personalities covered here can be found in my first work, *Outside the Rio Spotlight: American Triumphs You Didn't See at the 2016 Olympics*. The book covers twelve stories of American winners whose competitions were exceptional despite receiving little press or focus on prime-time television. For example, the stories include Helen Maroulis, wrestler par excellence; Kim Rhode, first medalist on five continents; and Claressa Shields, the boxer from Flint.

All told, the dozen stories cover both men and women who won medals in the lesser-known sports, events aside from the marquee sports of gymnastics and volleyball. The narratives provide a detailed bio of the athletes, a history of each event and explanation of the rules, and a full description of the tournament which led them to their medal.

Or, for a lighter take on Olympic subjects, there's *The A to Z Olympics: 26 Torch-Worthy Tales and Tidbits*. These 26 essays are perfect short reads, which run the gamut on all things Olympic. Read about why badminton is popular in Indonesia or the Curious Case of the Unknown Coxswain. It's a handy book to have when the Olympics start to make their quadrennial journey and there's a need to refresh the memory.

More information can be found at my author's website, kajmeister.com, as well as wherever books are sold.

Appendix: Charts

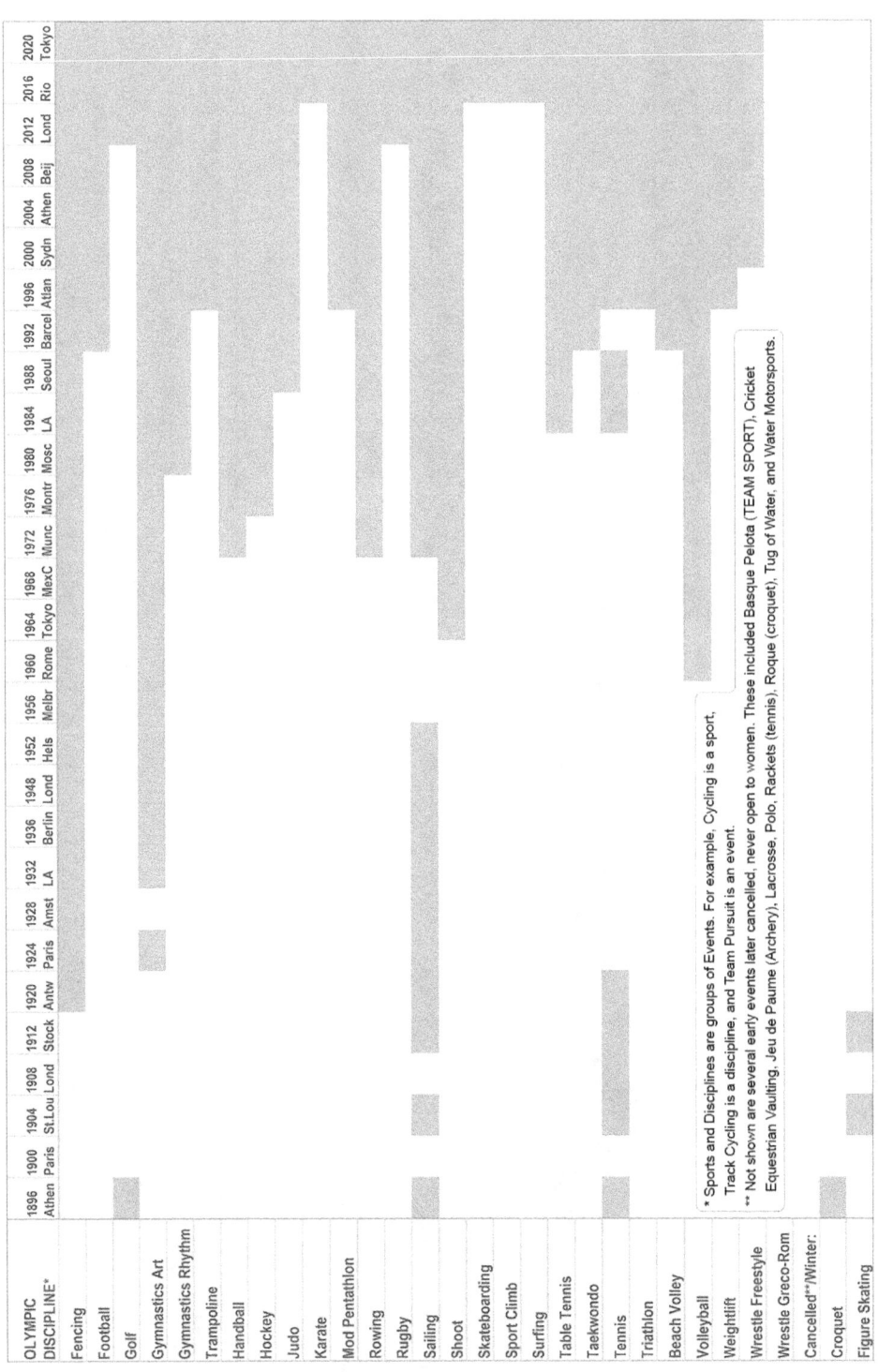

Chart Two. Women's inroads into Olympic disciplines and events were more haphazard than organized, decided by committee members and sports federation organizers. Only after the 1990s was the notion of gender parity even considered (author's chart design based on data compiled from Olympanalyt.com, Olympedia, Wikipedia, and the Official Olympic Reports).

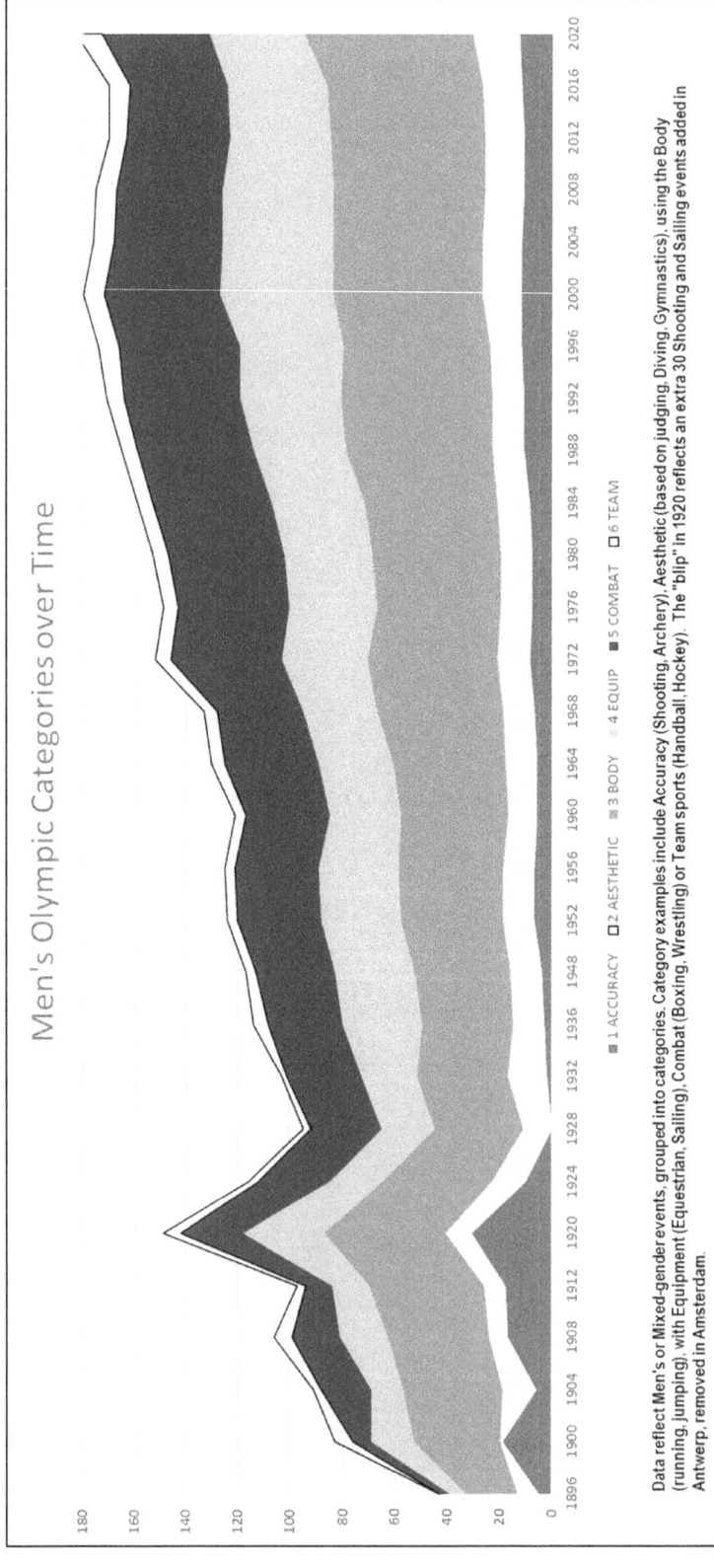

Chart Three. Men's Olympic events steadily increased. Sports using the whole body, with or without equipment (boats, cycles) loomed large, but combat sports also covered a large portion of men's events (author's chart design based on data compiled from Olympanalyt.com, Olympedia, Wikipedia, and the Official Olympic Reports).

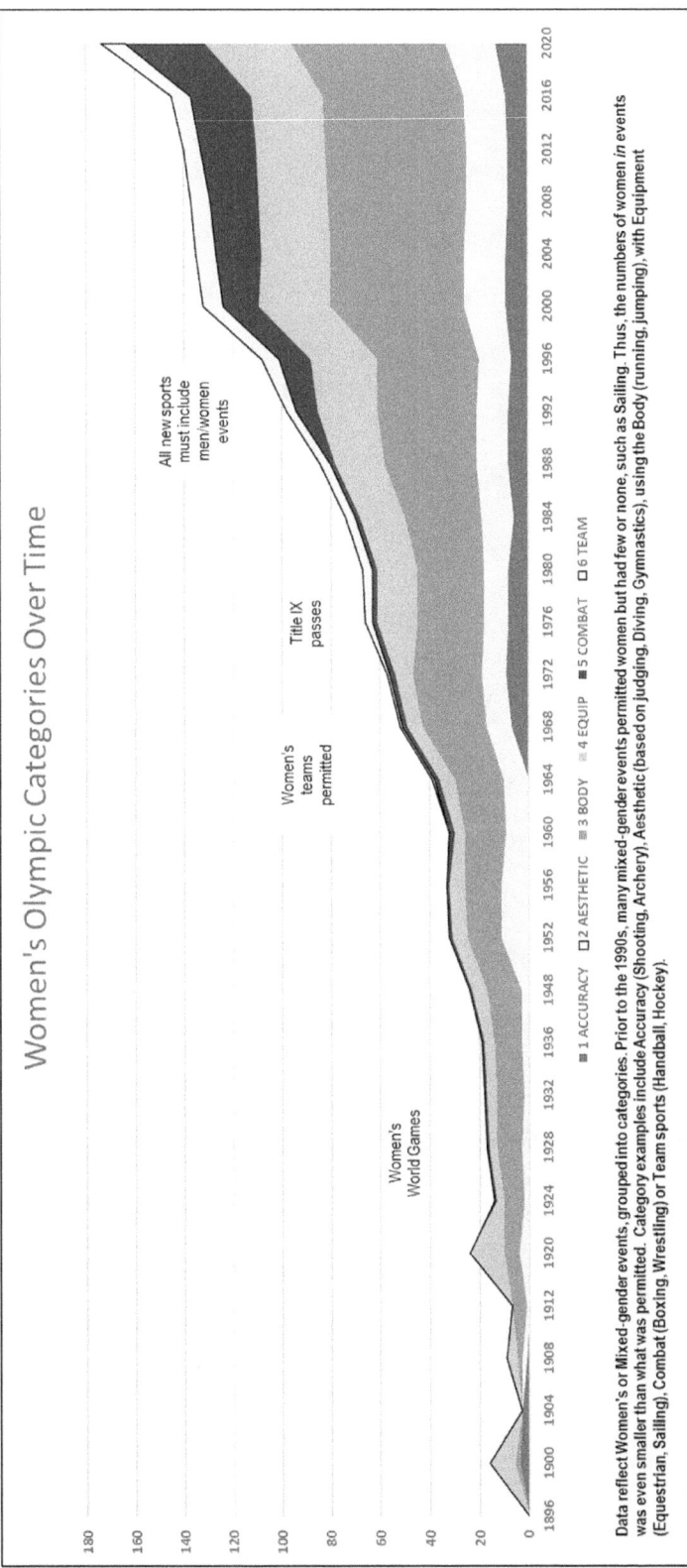

Chart Four. Women's event numbers paled next to men's, with the lack of combat sports accounting for much of the difference. Aesthetic sports (gymnastics, diving) were a high percentage until the 1970s. Gender parity via Title IX etc. didn't take hold until after 2000 (author's chart design based on data compiled from Olympanalyt.com, Olympedia, Wikipedia, and the Official Olympic Reports).

Chapter Notes

Introduction

1. Tunis, John R. "The Olympic Games." *Harper's Magazine,* August 1928, pp. 318, 323. https://harpers.org/archive/1928/08/the-olympic-games/. Accessed August 22, 2020.
2. Historian David Young has noted that women were listed as victors in the chariot races when they owned the horses. While they could not compete, some thought that they could sit in the audience if they were married, though what their husbands thought of that is another thing entirely. Young, David C. *A Brief History of the Olympic Games.* Blackwell Publishing, 2004, pp. 113–120.
3. Goldblatt, David. *The Games: A Global History of the Olympics.* W.W. Norton, 2016, p. 139.
4. Author's chart based on data from Olympanalyt.com, Olympedia, Wikipedia, and the Official Olympic Reports.
5. "IOC Takes Leadership Role in UN Women Sports for Generation Equality Initiative." *IOC News,* March 9, 2020, https://www.olympic.org/news/ioc-takes-leadership-role-in-un-women-sports-for-generation-equality-initiative. Accessed August 15, 2020.
6. Longman, Jere. "Women Move Closer to Olympic Equality," *New York Times*, August 20, 2000, https://www.nytimes.com/1997/08/10/sports/in-footsteps-of-history-it-s-suzuki-in-marathon.html. Accessed August 16, 2020.
7. Goldblatt, *The Games,* p. 422.
8. Goldblatt's *The Games* and Alan Guttmann's *The Olympics: A History of the Modern Games* (University of Illinois Press, 1994) cover such critiques in full detail.

Chapter One

1. The Greeks used the Julian calendar until 1923, so the newspapers noted the date as March 30. It was definitely not summertime, the more common period for the Summer Games.
2. The details in this narrative of Stamata Revithi were provided in a 1997 article by Athanasios Tarasouleas in *Olympic Review.* To build his portrait, Tarasouleas extracted portions of articles from Greek newspapers, namely *Estia* and *Asty* from March and April 1896. He provided his own "free hand drawing" of Revithi and descriptions of conversations, which may reflect some artistic license on Tarasouleas's part but feel faithful to the time. Tarasouleas, Athanasios. "Stamata Revithi, 'Alias Melpomeni,'" *Olympic Review* 26, no. 17, October–November 1997, pp. 53–55. https://library.olympic.org/Default/doc/SYRACUSE/353009/stamata-revithi-alias-melpomeni-by-athanasios-tarasouleas. Accessed August 1, 2020.
3. In current day Marathon, Greece, a stadium has been built which holds an annual "Authentic" marathon each November. There was no special marker in 1896.
4. Goldblatt, *The Games*, p. 8.
5. As of 2021, the contests are still called the Much Wenlock Olympian Games. While the IOC probably bristles at the use of their hallowed trademarked word, Brookes and his progenitors had changed it just slightly from "Olympics." Besides, they could prove prior use. See http://www.wenlock-olympian-society.org.uk/history/first-wenlock-olympian-games/.
6. Although the 134th athletic competition was canceled due to COVID, Much Wenlock did hold the art competitions in 2020.
7. "Ancient Games as Modern Inspiration." *Olympic.Org.*, 2020. The International Olympic Committee, 2020. https://www.olympic.org/pierre-de-coubertin/ancient-games-as-modern-inspiration. Accessed August 23, 2020.
8. The 1870s saw a rise in archaeology, in part, from Heinrich Schliemann's search (and claim of discovery) for the remains of the ancient city of Troy.
9. Coubertin, Pierre de. *The Olympic Idea: Discourses and Essays.* Editions Internationales Olympiques, 1970.
10. An earlier version of the organization was even called the Committee for the General Propagation of Physical Education. Goldblatt, *The Games,* p. 32.
11. Goldblatt, *The Games,* p. 38.
12. "Pierre de Coubertin," Wikipedia, August 13, 2020. https://en.wikipedia.org/wiki/Pierre_de_Coubertin. Accessed August 23, 2020.
13. Hirtler, George. "Coubertin Quote for Jan.

03." https://coubertinspeaks.com/quotes/jan/03/. Accessed August 7, 2021.

14. Guttmann, *The Olympics: A History of the Modern Games,* p. 13. It's ironic that Guttmann used the pronouns "his or her," since those who advocated for amateurs at this point in history also believed women should not be competing in athletics.

15. Goldblatt, *The Games,* p. 37.

16. Boulongne, Yves-Pierre. "Pierre de Coubertin and Women's Sport." *Olympic Review* 27, no. 31, February–March 2000, p. 23. LA84 Foundation, Digital Library Collections, https://digital.la84.org/digital/collection/p17103coll1/id/36808/. Accessed August 20, 2020.

17. *Ibid.,* p. 24.

18. *Ibid.*

19. Shaulis, Daun. "Pedestriennes: Newsworthy but Controversial Women in Sporting Entertainment." *Women of Achievement and Herstory: Spotlight on Pedestriennes,* Spring 1999. http://www.thelizlibrary.org/undelete/woa-spotlight/02-pedestriennes.html. Accessed August 24, 2020.

20. Goldblatt, *The Games,* p. 110.

21. Bandy, Susan J. "The Female Athlete as Protagonist: From Cynisca to Butcher," *Aethlon* 15, no. 1, Fall 1997, p. 84.

22. Lindsay's character was fictional, but based on the real Lord Burghley, who did win at the hurdles—although not the 110 m in 1924 but the 400 m in 1928. It was Burghley, not Harold Abrahams, who did race successfully around the courtyard of Oxford. Burghley later became an MP and went on to preside over the International Amateur Athletic Foundation (IAAF). He was on the IOC from 1948 to 1968 and was the one who presented the medals to the gloved Tommie Smith and John Carlos before their controversial black power salute.

23. Goldblatt, *The Games,* p. 26.

24. Coubertin wrote his "Ode to Sport" in 1912. He submitted the poem to the Olympic literary competition for the Stockholm Games under the rather thinly veiled pseudonym of Hohrod and Eschbach—villages near his wife's birthplace. As it happened, he won first place. Curiously enough, his address was used for all the submissions, so it's possible he may also have been a judge. Coubertin, Pierre de. "Ode to Sport," 1912. Reposted by jmsgale, "Poetry in Surrey Libraries," September 19, 2020, https://npdsurrey.wordpress.com/2020/09/19/ode-to-sport-by-pierre-de-coubertin/. Accessed August 7, 2021.

25. Tarasouleas, "Stamata Revithi, 'Alias Melpomeni,'" p. 54.

26. Sportswriter Jere Longman quotes Frank Shorter, the American Olympic marathoner, who said the route out of Marathon was "bleak, desolate, and hot. The whole point is, you block it out." Longman, Jere. "In Footsteps of History, It's Suzuki in Marathon." *New York Times,* August 10, 1997. https://www.nytimes.com/1997/08/10/sports/in-footsteps-of-history-it-s-suzuki-in-marathon.html. Accessed August 13, 2020.

27. Famed photographer Burton Holmes even captured a trio of Greek runners practicing, puffing along a line of olive trees. "1896 Olympic marathon." June 1, 2018. https://commons.wikimedia.org/wiki/File:1896_Olympic_marathon.jpg. Accessed August 23, 2020.

28. Dispensing watches and other prizes didn't last long. Once the Games started clamping down heavily on amateurs, the only object a winner could receive was the laurel wreath or, later, a medal. Cups, watches, or cars were forbidden until the amateur rule was discarded in 1981.

29. Goldblatt, *The Games,* p.71.

30. Denieffe, Greg. "Athens 1896: The First Rowing Medalists?" *Hear the Boat Sing,* April 13, 2016. https://heartheboatsing.com/2016/04/13/athens-1896-the-first-olympic-rowing-medallists/. Accessed August 15, 2020.

31. *Official Olympic Report 1896*. LA84 Foundation, Digital Library Collections, 1896, p. 210. https://digital.la84.org/digital/collection/p17103coll8/id/6375/. Accessed August 20, 2020.

32. Guttmann, *The Olympics,* p. 162.

33. Lennartz, Karl. "Two Women Ran the Marathon in 1896." *Journal of Olympic History* 2, no. 1, Winter 1994.

34. The artifacts bestow special powers on the users. Of the Revithi artifact, says one character in the drama, "When held, it allows the user to accomplish astounding feats of physical and mental nature, though if not directly witnessed then no one will believe it happened." "Stamata Revithi's Document." *Warehouse 13* Artifacts Wiki. https://warehouse-13-artifact-database.fandom.com/wiki/Stamata_Revithi%27s_Document. Accessed August 15, 2020.

35. Tarasouleas, "Stamata Revithi, 'Alias Melpomeni,'" p. 54.

36. Longman, "In Footsteps…"

Chapter Two

1. As was Queen Elizabeth II.

2. For a user manual on the Polymachinon, see https://archive.org/details/gymnasticpolymac00chiorich/page/n5/mode/2up. Accessed September 4, 2020.

3. Guttmann, *The Olympics,* p. 22.

4. Goldblatt, *The Games,* p. 53.

5. Ladies' singles had been contested at Wimbledon since 1884. Men had only begun a few years earlier in 1877.

6. Tennis at the Olympics lasted until 1924 but was dropped for 60 years because of a dispute over the definition of "amateur" between the International Lawn Tennis Federation and the IOC. It returned in full when the IOC decided to drop the amateur requirement as a whole in 1988.

7. Olympic historian Professor Paula Welch tracked down the details and, ultimately, Abbott's family to give them the good news. Holmes, Tao Tao. "The First American Woman to Win an Olympic Championship Didn't Even Know It." Atlasobscura.com, August 10, 2016. https://www.

atlasobscura.com/articles/the-first-american-woman-to-win-an-olympic-championship-didnt-even-know-it. Accessed September 1, 2020.

8. Wimbledon was originally known as the All England Croquet Club, later changed to the All England Lawn Tennis and Croquet Club. Less than ten years later, croquet was dropped and only tennis remained.

9. Lucas, Charles P. *The Olympic Games, 1904*. Woodward and Tiernan, 1905, p. 15.

10. Goldblatt, *The Games*, p. 69.

11. Documenters of the time routinely identified men by first and last name, but women only as Miss or Mrs.

12. Pietri was later disqualified and American Johnny Hayes declared the winner. However, Pietri was given a special cup for his "effort." Irving Berlin memorialized his attempts in a culturally insensitive song, "Dorando, He'sa Gooda for Not."

13. There is debate about whether a woman was involved in sailing in 1900 Paris. Olympic historians ultimately identified her as an owner, so her participation was not on the boat.

14. Polley, Martin. *Sport, Gender, and Sexuality at the 1908 London Olympic Games*. Routledge Handbooks Online, March 2014. https://www.routledgehandbooks.com/doi/10.4324/9780203121375.ch3. Accessed September 1, 2020.

15. The winner in ten of the eleven years from 1901–1911 was Sweden's Ulrich Salchow, inventor of the Salchow jump, one of the key jumps in contemporary skating.

16. The ISU also expressed concerns that a judge might have to score "a girl to whom he was attached" and that "women could not be compared with men."

17. Cook, Theodore Andrea. *The Fourth Olympiad: Being the Official Report of the Olympic Games of 1908*. The British Olympic Association, May 1909, p. 336.

18. Goldblatt, *The Games*, p. 78.

19. *Daily Mirror*, July 14, 1908, p. 1. https://www.mirror.co.uk/news/gallery/classic-daily-sunday-mirror-front-10382498. Accessed September 5, 2020.

20. Polley, *Sport, Gender, and Sexuality at the 1908 London Olympic Games*, p. 9 of chapter 3. Originally from the *Daily Mirror*, July 25, 1908.

21. Figure skaters, of course, moved with speed and athleticism and were also out of breath, but with their choreography, they weren't "seen" as being athletes.

22. "Histoire de L'athetismé." Athle.fr. https://www.athle.fr/asp.net/main.html/html.aspx?htmlid=418. Accessed September 19, 2020.

23. Middleton, Lamar. "The French Renaissance in Athletics." *Outing* 44, April–September 1904, pp. 189–201.

24. Middleton, "The French Renaissance in Athletics," p. 196.

25. Barney, Elizabeth Cynthia. "The American Sportswoman." *Fortnightly Review*, no. 52, August 1894, pp. 263–267.

26. Guttmann, Allen. *Women's Sports: A History*. Columbia University Press, 1991, p. 101.

27. Bennett, Jim. "Weakness, a Crime!" www.bernarrmacfadden.com, 2013. https://www.bernarrmacfadden.com/macfadden3.html. Accessed September 21, 2020.

28. Guttmann, *Women's Sports*, p. 99.

Chapter Three

1. Guttmann, *The Olympics*, p. 46.

2. Summarized in Milliat's French Wikipedia entry as *veuve et sans enfant* (widowed and childless). "Alice Milliat," January 12, 2021. https://fr.wikipedia.org/wiki/Alice_Milliat. Accessed January 17, 2021.

3. Only one full length biography has been written. It's in French, not digitized, and out of print. Drevon, Andre. *Alice Milliat—La Pasionaria of Female Sport*. Vuibert, 2005.

4. Today, Audax refers primarily to long-distance cycling or running, with Audax long-distance rowing a thing of the past.

5. Milliat, Alice, quoted in Quintillan, Ghislaine. "Alice Milliat and the Women's Game." *Olympic Review*, no. 27, February–March 2000.

6. Goldblatt, *The Games*, p. 112.

7. One of those crazy American inventions, the "pushball," was an Indiana-Jones-boulder-sized globe that opposing groups try to push across a field. Part rugby and part tug of war, the sport never caught on, between the need for special equipment and the risk of being squashed by the ball.

8. Guttmann, *Women's Sports*, p. 167.

9. Leigh, Mary H., and Bonin, Thérèse M. "The Pioneering Role of Madame Alice Milliat and the FSFI in Establishing International Track and Field Competition for Women." *Journal of Sport History* 4, no. 1, 1977, p. 77.

10. *Ibid*.

11. Renson, Roland, and Ameye, Thomas. "Stepping out of Coubertin's Shadow: The Count and the 1932 Winter Olympics." International Society of Olympic Historians, March 2015, p. 20. http://isoh.org/wp-content/uploads/2015/03/230.pdf. Accessed September 27, 2020

12. Plenty of modern-day endurance events have proved exactly the opposite, that women's greater proportion of slow twitch muscle fibers gives them superior endurance to offset their lesser strength compared with men. Williams, Sophia. "Are Women Better Ultra-Endurance Than Men"? BBC.com, August 11, 2019. https://www.bbc.com/news/world-49284389. Accessed September 15, 2020.

13. Leigh and Bonin, "The Pioneering Role of Madame Alice Milliat and the FSFI in Establishing International Track and Field Competition for Women," p. 79.

14. Goldblatt, *The Games*, p. 114.

15. Houry, Cecile. *American Women and the Modern Summer Games: A Story of Obstacles and*

Struggles for Participation and Equality. 2011. University of Miami, Ph.D. dissertation. Olympic.org, p. 81. https://library.olympic.org/Default/doc/SYRACUSE/171142/american-women-and-the-modern-olympic-games-a-story-of-obstacles-and-struggles-for-participation-and. Accessed September 27, 2020.

16. Pruter, Robert. "Helen Filkey: How Missing the Olympics Crushed Her Dream of Track and Field Immortality: Essay by Robert Pruter." *The World of Amateur and Youth Sports in Chicago,* June 29, 2019. https://historyofsport.wordpress.com/2019/06/29/helen-filkey-how-missing-the-olympics-crushed-her-dream-of-track-and-field-immortality-essay-by-robert-pruter/. Accessed September 27, 2020.

17. Rosenfeld described it with a little more color: "we tried all over town to purchase raiment in accordance with what the best-dressed sprinter was wearing, so that we could discard our modesty-preserving pup-tent bloomers, spinnaker midi, and hip-length stockings. But ... sporting goods houses proved an absolute blank ... [our clothes] got us there, even if they didn't exemplify the ultimate in art and good taste."

Hall, M. Anne. *The Girl and the Game: A History of Women's Sport in Canada, Second Edition.* University of Toronto Press, May 2016, p. 77–79.

18. The experience of American sprinter Sha'Carri Richardson seemed eerily similar to that of Helen Filkey at the Trials for the Tokyo 2020 Olympics. Richardson was so fast in a 100 m heat that she slowed down to point at the scoreboard, which showed her 10.64 was near the second fastest time in history. But, within a few days, Richardson was booted off the U.S. team for failing a drug test and admitted to smoking marijuana after finding out a week earlier that her estranged mother had died. Richardson is young for a track star, and the marijuana ban may be overturned, but it remains to be seen whether Richardson, too, will be out of women's track history or will return for a future Games.

19. Montillo, Roseanne. *Fire on the Track: Betty Robinson and the Triumph of the Early Olympic Women.* Crown Publishing, 2017, p. 70.

20. *Ibid.*, p. 71.

21. *Ibid.*

22. The height was later remeasured and set down to 1.595 m, but it was still a gold medal. Van Rossem, G. *The Ninth Olympiad: Being the Official Report of the Olympic Games of 1928 Celebrated at Amsterdam.* J. H. Debussy Publishers, 1928, p. 476.

23. Marshall, Tabitha. "Fanny Rosenfeld." *The Canadian Encyclopedia,* June 1, 2016. https://www.thecanadianencyclopedia.ca/en/article/fanny-rosenfeld. Accessed September 27, 2020.

24. Robinson, Roger. "Eleven Wretched Women." *Runner's World,* May 14, 2012. https://www.runnersworld.com/advanced/a20802639/eleven-wretched-women/. Accessed September 27, 2020.

25. *Times* and *Tribune* both quoted in Montillo, *Fire on the Track,* p. 83.

26. Montillo, *Fire on the Track,* p. 84.

27. Goldblatt, *The Games,* p. 115.

28. Montillo, *Fire on the Track,* p. 81.

29. *Ibid.*

30. Guttmann, *Women's Sports,* p. 170.

31. Leigh and Bonin, "The Pioneering Role of Madame Alice Milliat and the FSFI in Establishing International Track and Field Competition for Women," p. 79.

32. Forster, Merna. *100 Canadian Heroines.* Dundurn Group, 2004, p. 217.

Chapter Four

1. Goldblatt, *The Games,* p. 156.

2. For example, *Boys in the Boat, Fire on the Track,* and *Olympic Pride, American Prejudice,* just to name three recent top sellers.

3. Biggs, Mary. *Women's Words: The Columbia Book of Quotations by Women.* Columbia University Press, 1996, p. 381. The original source of this most famous Didrikson quote is hard to uncover. However, there's no doubt that it has Didrikson's stamp all over it.

4. Wallace, Rich, and Wallace, Sandra Neil. *Babe Conquers the World: The Legendary Life of Babe Didrikson Zaharias.* Calkin Creeks Publishing, 2014, p. 31.

5. Cayleff, Susan E. *Babe Didrikson: The Greatest All-Sport Athlete of All Time.* Conari Press, 1995, p. 9.

6. They did exist. Lydia Reeder's book *Dust Bowl Girls: The Inspiring Story of the Team That Barnstormed Its Way to Basketball Glory,* details the plucky Cardinals of Oklahoma's Presbyterian College, which beat Employers Casualty in 1932.

7. Cayleff, *Babe Didrikson,* p. 48.

8. *Ibid.*, p. 60.

9. Soifer, Paul. "A Tale of Two Women: Babe Didrikson, Lillian Copeland, and the Women's Discus at the 1932 Olympic Games." *Southern California Quarterly* 78, no. 3, 1996, p. 248.

10. International high jump rules eventually removed the "feet-first" rule when padding was included in the pit. After that, jumpers could dive head-first, presumably in a somersault. Dick Fosbury further revolutionized the sport in the 1960s by going head-first backwards.

11. Montillo, *Fire on the Track,* p. 100.

12. Soifer, "A Tale of Two Women," p. 250.

13. Montillo, *Fire on the Track,* p. 119.

14. Wallace and Wallace, *Babe Conquers the World,* p. 121.

15. Despite Alice Milliat's negotiations with the IAAF over recognizing world records, there was still lack of standardization and consistent reporting. Today, notes about records from the 1930s vary from source to source and are sometimes contradictory. Several sources mention that Didrikson's throw was an Olympic record without pointing out that it was the *first* Olympic competition.

Wallechinsky and Loucky, whose *Book of Lists* is practically the Bible of Olympic data, call it a world record in the text but list it as an Olympic record in their tables. Two online World Progression charts note that Braumüller had thrown a longer distance weeks earlier in Berlin, which is why the Olympic record was not a world record. Perhaps Didrikson was so used to world records that she simply said it was one, and her words were repeated, like her falsified age or her ability to beat Helen Madison in the swimming pool. For the record, her Olympic javelin throw was not a world record.
16. Wallace and Wallace, *Babe Conquers the World*, p. 129.
17. *Ibid.*, p. 131.
18. Didrikson did send the bulk of her salary home to her mother and father, eventually paying off her family's mortgage and other dates. Also, a few years after marrying George Zaharias, she was supporting both of them with her golf earnings and appearances.
19. Bryan, Max. "Film Shows Complex Story of '36 Olympics." *The Sentinal Record*, October 10, 2016. https://www.hotsr.com/news/2016/oct/10/film-shows-complex-story-of-36-olympics/. Accessed October 18, 2020.
20. Cayleff, Susan. *Babe Didrikson*. Conari Press, 1995, p. 80.
21. Didrikson, Mildred. "I Blow My Own Horn." *American Magazine* 120, June 1936, p. 104.
22. Cahn, Susan K. *Coming on Strong: Gender and Sexuality in Twentieth-Century Women's Sport*. Harvard University Press, 1994, p. 216.
23. Houry, *American Women and the Modern Summer Games*, p. 89.
24. Montillo, *Fire on the Track*, p. 150.

Chapter Five

1. Including mixed gender events like sailing, the women-allowed events went from 10 in 1908 to 25 in 1936, although only a few women participated in 1908 Sailing, and none in mixed events in 1936. However, in comparison, men's events had expanded from 75 in 1908 to 129 by 1936. Men previously made up 95% of all events, but by 1936 "only" 90%.
2. Some did still argue against any participation. As late as 1953, the IOC and its president, Avery Brundage, were still seriously discussing eliminating women's events entirely. The motions were simply voted down more routinely. Houry, *American Women and the Modern Summer Games*, p. 130.
3. *Ibid.*, p. 78.
4. *Ibid.*, p. 80.
5. Montillo, *Fire on the Track*, p. 165.
6. Johnson, Jr., William O. *All That Glitters Is Not Gold: An Irreverent Look at the Olympic Games*. G. P. Putnam's Sons, 1972, p. 188.
7. Guard, Sally. "Still Very Much in the Swim." *Sports Illustrated*, June 15, 1992, p. 1. https://vault.si.com/vault/1992/06/15/still-very-much-in-the-swim-onetime-olympic-backstroke-champion-eleanor-holm-reflects-on-her-days-of-wine-and-rose. Accessed October 29, 2020.
8. Brundage was still putting a complete ban of all women's events on the Olympic organizing committee agenda all the way into the 1950s.
9. Johnson, Jr., *All That Glitters Is Not Gold*, p. 185.
10. Guard, "Still Very Much in the Swim," p. 3.
11. "Eleanor Holm." Encyclopedia.com, updated October 10, 2020. https://www.encyclopedia.com/women/encyclopedias-almanacs-transcripts-and-maps/holm-eleanor-1913. Accessed October 20, 2020.
12. Wilson, Woodrow. *A History of the American People, Volume 5*. Alfred Knopf, 1906, p. 212.
13. Anderson, Sheldon. *The Forgotten Legacy of Stella Walsh: The Greatest Female Athlete of Her Time*. Rowman & Littlefield, 2017, p. 38.
14. *Ibid.*, p. 38.
15. Tannenbaum, Rob. "The Life and Murder of Stella Walsh: Intersex Olympic Champion." www.longreads.com, August 16, 2016, pp. 5–7.
16. Tullis, Matt. "Who Was Stella Walsh? The Story of the Intersex Olympian." SBNnation.com, June 27, 2013, p. 11.
17. Anderson, *The Forgotten Legacy of Stella Walsh*: p. 41.
18. Tullis, "Who Was Stella Walsh?," p. 12.
19. *Ibid.*, p. 14.
20. See Tannenbaum, "The Life and Murder of Stella Walsh," p. 12, for the U.S. media reaction.
21. Montillo, *Fire on the Track*, p. 167.
22. *Ibid.*, p. 166.
23. Tannenbaum, "The Life and Murder of Stella Walsh," p. 16.
24. Tullis, "Who Was Stella Walsh?," p. 21.
25. *Ibid.*, p. 21.
26. *Ibid.*, p. 24.
27. Cohen, Richard. *By the Sword: A History of Gladiators, Musketeers, Samurai, Swashbucklers, and Olympic Champions*. Narrative Tension Inc., 2012, p. 354.
28. Carpenter, Les. "Nazi Germany's Jewish Champion: The Mystery of Helene Mayer Endures." *The Guardian*, July 28, 2016, p. 4.
29. Cohen, *By the Sword*, p. 348.
30. *Ibid.*, p. 353.
31. *Ibid.*, p. 357.
32. *Ibid.*, p. 354.
33. Kluge, Volker. "A 'New Woman' and Her Involuntary Myth." *International Society of Olympic Historians*, March 2015. http://isoh.org/wp-content/uploads/2015/03/214.pdf. Accessed November 2, 2020.
34. Carpenter, "Nazi Germany's Jewish Champion," p. 4.
35. Ellen Osier of Denmark, winner of the first gold medal in Women's Olympic Foil, was also Jewish.
36. Dan Coughlin of the *Cleveland Plain Dealer* tells a story that Walsh challenged him, a reporter thirty years younger, to a sprint. She gave him a 10-yard head start, and he beat her, but just barely.

She told him that was just the preliminaries and, in the "finals," they started together. She "kick[ed] cinders in my face," winning by several yards. Tullis, "Who Was Stella Walsh?," p. 30.

37. Houry, *American Women and the Modern Summer Games,* p. 89.

Chapter Six

1. Over 400 Olympic athletes died in World War II, including, for example, four members of the women's Dutch gymnastics team from 1928. Many gymnasts were Jewish; three of those Dutch gymnasts died in concentration camps with their families.

2. Chmaj, Betty E. "Some Paradox! Some Irony! Changing Images of American Woman, 1930–1974." *The Study of American Culture: Contemporary Conflicts*, edited by Luther S. Luedtke. Everett Edwards, Inc., 1977.

3. A fascinating study by Dr. Pamela Grundy details how the cultural pressure of the Feminine Mystique combined with other factors to reduce women's basketball: physical educators, who still pressed to remove competition from women's sports; the booming car industry, which allowed audiences to drive further to see entertainment; and television, which began showing men's professional sports, eliminating the need to drive entirely.

Grundy, Pamela. "From Amazons to Glamazons: The Rise and Fall of North Carolina's Women's Basketball, 1920–1960." *Journal of American History* 87, no. 1, June 2000. https://history.msu.edu/hst329/files/2015/05/Glamazons.pdf. Accessed November 11, 2020.

4. Blue, Adrienne. *Faster, Higher, Further: Women's Triumphs and Disasters at the Olympics.* Virago Press, 1988, p. 52–3.

5. Dahl, Heather. *Fearless and Fit: American Women of the Cold War.* University of New Mexico, Master's thesis, 2010 p. 15. https://www.semanticscholar.org/paper/FEARLESS-AND-FIT%3A-AMERICAN-WOMEN-OF-THE-COLD-WAR-Dahl/56d010467670c1293f2e5fa30b8e4acd78e7bff4. Accessed November 14, 2020.

6. Goldblatt, *The Games,* p. 212.

7. Ibid.

8. The AOC changed its name from American Olympic Committee to United States Olympic Committee (USOC) in 1945.

9. Johnson, Jr., *All That Glitters Is Not Gold,* p. 223. Unfortunately, while the TV spectacle was entertaining, it ended up a financial calamity. The telethon hoped to raise about $500,000 of an estimated $800,000 in funding shortfall. Pledges came in for over a million dollars, but, because the total exceeded the goal, many phoners didn't think they needed to pay their pledges. Overall, only a little over $300,000 was actually raised from the telethon, after expenses. Worst of all, since people thought so much more had been raised, they were unyielding to additional requests for money, so the USOC fell far short of its goal.

10. Ibid., p. 221.

11. Dahl, *Fearless and Fit,* p. 19.

12. Johnson, Jr., *All That Glitters Is Not Gold,* p. 224.

13. Dahl, *Fearless and Fit,* p. 6.

14. Ibid., p. 7.

15. Houry, *American Women and the Modern Summer Games,* p. 131.

16. Marriott, James. "The Strange Nationalist Origins of Modern Gymnastics." Medium.com, January 10, 2020. https://medium.com/history-of-yesterday/the-strange-nationalist-origins-of-modern-gymnastics-1a7ddb390dc9/. Accessed November 11, 2020.

17. Coubertin, Pierre de. "The Olympic Manifesto—Le Manifeste Olympique." *Civilization Magazine,* January 2008. Quoted in "Description of Item for Auction at Sothebys," Sothebys.com, 2020. https://www.sothebys.com/en/buy/auction/2019/fine-books-and-manuscripts-including-the-olympic-manifesto/coubertin-pierre-de-the-olympic-manifesto. Accessed December 12, 2020.

18. Curiously, many summaries describe the Czechs as winning easily, without mentioning that they were deadlocked at 316.7 points apiece before the last team exercise. Calculating the total team gymnastics score was complicated, involving an aggregation of the eight women's individual scores on the compulsory and free events on three separate apparatuses, with the two lowest combined scores thrown out. Using today's technology, calculating the totals and eliminating the combined low scores takes only a few minutes, but without spreadsheets and calculators, it may have been more difficult in 1948. The *New York Times* reported that at the end of the evening's competition on Saturday, the judges were unable to give the scores to the media because they were "too tired to compute the final standings." It's possible that no one—neither judges nor competitors—were aware that the teams were tied at the midpoint until after the competition was over and the Czech team had won. "Finnish Gymnasts Take Men's Title." *New York Times*, August 14, 1948, p. 8.

19. Cervin, Georgia. "Women's Artistic Gymnastics During the Cold War and Its Aftermath." *Final Report for the IOC Olympic Studies Centre,* PhD Students Research Grant Programme, December 2016, p. 7.

20. In the 21st century, North Korea also became famous for its "Mass Dances," with thousands performing exercises and dances in unison, both for audiences and for Dear Leader.

21. Guttmann, *Women's Sports,* p. 202.

22. In 1960, for comparison, the U.S. took 21 of their 71 medals in swimming and diving.

23. Cervin, "Women's Artistic Gymnastics During the Cold War and Its Aftermath." *Final* p. 12.

24. Rules were added later to prevent judges from scoring their own country's athletes. This led to vote-trading among judges from "friendly" countries and even bribery scandals. It was an

ongoing problem, but across many sports. Boxing and figure skating (most infamously) faced the same issue.

25. Reynolds, Tom. "Vera Čáslavská and the Forgotten Story of Her 1968 Olympics Protest." BBC.com, October 20, 2018. https://www.bbc.com/sport/olympics/45900544. Accessed December 8, 2020.

26. The 1968 Olympics was the site of the Black Power protests, the fists raised by sprinters Tommie Smith and John Carlos, as well as other demonstrations.

27. Dahl, *Fearless and Fit*, p. 22.

28. Those wacky Scots also threw hammers, 50-pound boulders, and tree trunks, known as cabers. They still do today in their Highland Games.

29. Guttmann, *Women's Sports*, p. 200.

30. Johnson, Jr., *All That Glitters Is Not Gold*, p. 212.

31. Dahl, *Fearless and Fit*, p. 21.

32. Schwartz, Harry. "Stalin Trains His Olympic Teams." *New York Times*, April 20, 1952, p. 58. https://timesmachine.nytimes.com/timesmachine/1952/04/20/issue.html. Accessed November 25, 2020.

33. Dahl, *Fearless and Fit*, p. 21.

34. Older sister Tamara had a rather infamous sense of humor. Ron Barak, an American gymnast at the 1964 Tokyo Games, tells a story of how his wife butted right in front of Tamara Press in the cafeteria line. According to Barak, Press picked up his "fairly tiny" wife, Barbie, and twirled her around, "holding her high like a piece of lumber," then setting her down behind them in line. A hush fell over the crowd in the restaurant. Then, Tamara gently picked Barbie up again, spun her again, and set her down in front, shaking her finger with a smile as if to say, *no cuts!* Everyone burst into relieved laughter. Barak's story is told to Tomizawa, Roy. "A Helicopter of U.S.-USSR Relations, Olympic Style." Theolympicans.co, May 22, 2015. https://theolympians.co/2015/05/22/a-helicopter-view-of-us-ussr-relations-olympic-style/. Accessed August 12, 2021.

35. Dahl, *Fearless and Fit*, p. 20.

36. Van West, Carroll. "The Tennessee State Tigerbelles: Cold Warriors of the Track." *Separate Games: African American Sport behind the Walls of Segregation*, edited by David K. Wiggins and Ryan Swanson, University of Arkansas Press, 2016, p. 63.

37. Helene Madison had done so in swimming.

38. "Brown, Earlene," Encyclopedia.com.

39. Sloper must have found it irksome, too. She placed 5th below Brown in Melbourne, 4th in Rome and 4th again in Tokyo, herself always a whisper away from a medal.

40. Aeseng, Nathan. *African-American Athletes (A to Z of African Americans)*. Facts on File Publishing, 2011.

41. This bowling alley scene of my own invention has appeared before, in ever-so-slightly different form, in another chapter, another book. Kaj, Maria. "B is for Brown." *The A to Z Olympics*, 2021, pp. 11–12.

42. Schiot, Molly. "Earlene Brown." *Game Changers: The Unsung Heroines of Sports History*. Simon & Schuster Paperbacks, 2016, p. 100.

Chapter Seven

1. Edgeworth, Ron. "The Nordic Games and the Origin of the Olympic Winter Games." *Journal of Olympic History*, International Society of Olympic Historians, Olympic Congress, Copenhagen 2009, p. 1.

2. The 1916 Summer Games had been planned for Berlin and was cancelled as WWI dragged on. Germany had also thought about holding a winter festival in tandem with their summer festival. That probably would have been the original first Winter Olympics.

3. Goldblatt, *The Games*, p. 127.

4. Adams, Mary Louise. *Artistic Impressions: Figure Skating, Masculinity, and the Limits of Sport*. University of Toronto Press, 2011, Introduction.

5. Cook, Theodore Andrea. *The Fourth Olympiad: Being the Official Report of the Olympic Games of 1908 Celebrated in London*. The British Olympic Association, 1909, p. 295.

6. "Figure Skating and Ice Hockey Make their Olympic Debut… at the Summer Games!," Olympic.org, December 20, 2017. https://www.olympic.org/news/figure-skating-and-ice-hockey-make-their-olympic-debut-at-the-summer-games. Accessed December 12, 2020.

7. Cook, *Official Report of 1908*, p. 285.

8. Gallico, Paul. "Women in Sports Should Look Beautiful." *Vogue*, June 15, 1936. Cited in Houry, *American Women and the Modern Summer Games*, p. 76.

9. Guttman, *Women's Sports*, p. 200.

10. Nordic Games were held in 1901, 1903, 1905, 1909, 1913, 1917, 1922, and 1926. In other words, quadrennially but not in Olympic years, thereby avoiding competition with the summer Games of 1920, 1924, and 1928.

11. Judging issues in skating have been especially egregious, leading to vote trading and bribes, especially in Pairs and Ice Dancing. But most Olympic events which have judges and scoring face such challenges, particularly boxing, wrestling, gymnastics, and even dressage. Curiously, there have been few judging scandals in diving.

12. The 7th first place vote in St. Moritz 1928 was the American judge voting for the American skater. Henie wasn't the only recipient of favorable judging bias.

13. Jacobs, Laura. "Sonja Henie's Ice Age." *Vanity Fair*, February 11, 2014. https://www.vanityfair.com/hollywood/2014/02/sonja-henie-ice-skating-queen. Accessed December 15, 2020.

14. Wallechinsky, David, and Jaime Loucky. *The Complete Book of the Winter Olympics: 2014 Edition*. Crossroad Press, 2014, p. 68.

15. Cook, *Official Report of 1908*, p. 295.

16. Lattimore, George M. *Official Report III Winter Games, Lake Placid 1932.* III Olympic Games Committee, 1932, p. 259.

17. Fun fact: Katharin Dewey was the daughter of the famed Melvil Dewey, who designed the library's Dewey Decimal System.

18. Rempel, Byron. "Women's Ski Jumping Takes Aim at the Winter Olympics." International Skiing History Association, 1999–2019. https://www.skiinghistory.org/history/women%E2%80%-99s-ski-jumping-takes-aim-winter-olympics. Accessed December 27, 2020.

19. Bjørnsen, Knut, and Jorsett, Per. *Skøytesportens stjerner.* J. W. Cappelens forlag, 1971, p. 183. Cited in "Speed Skating." *New World Encyclopedia,* https://www.newworldencyclopedia.org/entry/Speed_skating. Accessed December 29, 2020.

20. Until short-track speed skating debuted in 1992 and demonstrated repeatedly how all hell can break loose in a mass start.

21. Whose presidents following Victor Balck were Swedish, Dutch, British, and Swiss, not countries considered part of the Soviet bloc.

22. Franey headlined an ice revue in the Dallas Adolphus Hotel for 14 years. She also appeared endorsing Camel cigarettes in cartoon advertising nationwide, skating and smoking, as they did in the 1940s.

23. Von der Lippe, Gerd. "Primary Sources and Theoretical Analysis of Women's Sports in Norway in the 1930S: A Bastardian Exergesis or a Fruitful Point of Departure?" *The Sports Historian* 20, no. 2, November 2000, p. 80.

24. Guttmann, *Women's Sports,* p. 190.

25. Koeze, Ella. "What If Men and Women Skied Against Each Other in the Olympics?" Fivethirtyeight.com, February 14, 2018. https://fivethirtyeight.com/features/what-if-men-and-women-skied-against-each-other-in-the-olympics/. Accessed December 17, 2020.

26. Meyer, John. "Lindsey Vonn Wants to Race Against Men—But Will They Let Her?" *Denver Post,* January 14, 2017. https://www.denverpost.com/2017/01/14/lindsey-vonn-ski-race-against-men/. Accessed December 19, 2020.

Chapter Eight

1. Curiously enough, two swimming events *were* added to the Games, no doubt at Australia, the host country's, request. *Extract from the Minutes of the Conferenee* [sic] *of the Executive Board of the I.O.C. with the Delegates of the National Olympic Committees and the International Federations.* LA84 Foundation, Digital Library Collections, June 11, 1955. https://digital.la84.org/digital/collection/p17103coll1/id/26760/rec/2. Accessed December 28, 2020.

2. Xenophon also had the wrong friends and was exiled from Athens, in part, due to his friendship with Socrates.

3. Gibbon, Abby. "Xenophon, the Forefather of Dressage." *The Chronicle of the Horse,* September 29, 2011. https://www.chronofhorse.com/article/xenophon-forefather-dressage. Accessed December 19, 2020.

4. The *piaffe* is an advanced dressage move, where the horse slowly advances using an elevated trot, i.e., prancing.

5. Music was added to Olympic Dressage in 2016. While most riders choose traditional music like Tchaikovsky or Sousa, a few have used modern pieces. American rider Steffen Peters chose Vanilla Ice for his Rio 2016 performance on his way to a U.S. team bronze medal, though he later said he believed his score might have suffered slightly as a result.

6. De Haan, Donna, and Dumbell, Lucy. "Equestrian Sport at the Olympic Games from 1900–1948." *International Journal of the History of Sport* 33, nos. 6–7, May 2016, p. 18.

7. There was a dressage judging scandal in 1956. The German and Swedish dressage judges, those who had scored St. Cyr and Linselhof, ranked all their country's riders 1–2–3, irrespective of quality. It probably didn't change the outcome. But those two judges were suspended, and FEI decided after long deliberation to eliminate the team/national competition in the next Olympics and restructure the judging panel.

8. Dashper, Katharine. "'Dressage Is Full of Queens!' Masculinity, Sexuality and Equestrian Sport." *Sociology,* May 16, 2012, p. 14. http://eprints.leedsbeckett.ac.uk/id/eprint/265/1/Dressage%20is%20full%20of%20queens%20-%20final.pdf. Accessed December 22, 2020.

9. Appels, Astrid. "The New York Times Compares Dressage to 'A Poodle Scuba Diving.'" Eurodressage.com, August 23, 2016. https://www.eurodressage.com/2016/08/23/new-york-times-compares-dressage-poodle-scuba-diving. Accessed December 22, 2020.

10. "Equestrian Title to Army's Team." *New York Times,* August 14, 1948, p. 8.

11. Corbitt, Ken. "No. 5: Murdock Didn't Miss Upon Getting Her Shot." CJonline.com, August 26, 2011. https://www.cjonline.com/article/20110826/SPORTS/308269777. Accessed December 24, 2020.

12. Ibid.

13. Olympic history is full of winners pulling up the person in second due to perceived issues in the outcome. This is probably the only time the winner has been described as doing it with chivalry, the only time when a man has pulled a woman up to the top step.

14. The researchers note that claiming women have more opportunities in their own events is like suggesting baseball would have been better off for Blacks if they had stayed in the Negro Leagues rather than be subject to desegregation. Goldschmied, Nadav, and Kowalczyk, Jason. "Gender Performance in the NCAA Rifle Championships: Where Is the Gap?" *Sex Roles: A Journal of Research* 74, nos. 7–8, 2016, p. 318.

15. The top-rated shooter "of all time" according to one list is Carl Osburn, with eleven medals.

Rhode is listed as the "top female" with only three golds. Three *is* a lot less than eleven, until it's noted that medals and golds are not the same thing. Osburn has five golds to Rhode's three, which sounds less impressive; Rhode has six medals to Osburn's eleven.

16. Now that the 2032 Olympics have been provisionally awarded to Queensland, Australia, it would be possible for someone else to medal across five continents. Look for someone who started in Rio 2016, then medaled in every Olympics afterward. The list of 2016 and 2020 candidates may be long now, but who will be able to keep going through Paris, Los Angeles, and Brisbane? Keep your eye on the equestrians and the shooters.

17. "Canoe Slalom." Wikipedia.com, Updated November 27, 2020. https://en.wikipedia.org/wiki/Canoe_slalom. Accessed December 24, 2020.

18. Boulongne, "Pierre de Coubertin and Women's Sport," p. 23.

Chapter Nine

1. Boulongne, "Pierre de Coubertin and Women's Sport," p. 24.

2. *Procès Verbal de la Commission Exécutive du IOC*, Lausanne (March 1971): Annex 21, 71–72. Quoted in Houry, *American Women and the Modern Summer Games*, p. 146.

3. Guttmann, *The Olympics*, p. 112.

4. Macnaughtan, Helen. "An Interview with Kasai Masae, Captain of the Japanese Women's Volleyball Team at the 1964 Tokyo Olympics." *Japan Forum* 24, no. 4, December 2012, p. 3.

5. Metheny, Eleanor. *Connotations of Movement in Sport and Dance; A Collection of Speeches About Sport and Dance as Significant Forms of Human Behavior.* W. C. Brown & Co., 1965, p. 10.

6. "Minutes of the 53rd Session in Sofia of the International Olympic Committee." LA84 Foundation, Digital Library Collections, September 28, 1957, p. 74, https://digital.la84.org/digital/collection/p17103coll1/id/27070/rec/4. Accessed February 1, 2021.

7. Macnaughtan, "An Interview with Kasai Masae," p. 2.

8. Whitehead, Eric. "Driven Beyond Dignity." *Sports Illustrated*, March 16, 1964.

9. Tomizawa, Roy. "Japan's Team—The Oriental Witches of the 1964 Olympics Part 2: Was the Training of the Women's Volleyball Team Abuse or Tough Love?" *The Olympians: 1964 to 2020*, July 11, 2017. https://theolympians.co/2017/07/11/japans-team-the-oriental-witches-of-the-1964-olympics-part-2-was-the-training-of-the-womens-volleyball-team-abuse-or-tough-love/. Accessed January 30, 2021.

10. *Ibid.*

11. Macnaughtan, "An Interview with Kasai Masae, p. 6.

12. Tagsold, Christian. "Remember to Get Back on Your Feet Quickly: The Japanese Women's Volleyball Team at the 1964 Olympics as a 'Realm of Memory.'" *Sport in Society* 14, no. 4, 2011, pp. 444–453.

13. Macnaughtan, "An Interview with Kasai Masae," p. 3.

14. *Ibid.*, p. 7.

15. The whole women's tournament teetered briefly at the outset on the brink of cancellation, due to geopolitics. North Korea had been offered one of the six team spots, but withdrew because of disputes over a competing set of games. GANEFO (The Games of New Emerging Forces), created by Indonesia, were staged in the fall of 1963. Many countries under sanction by the IOC participated, as well as some who also went to the Olympics. Athletes were not allowed to participate in the GANEFO and the Olympics, so Japan and the USSR, for example, sent their second-tier athletes. However, North Korea opted to leave the Olympics entirely, to stick a thumb in the IOC's eye. Without North Korea, five teams were not enough to host the women's event. Japan paid South Korea a million yen to send a team, even knowing they were not of the same caliber. The South Koreans lost all fifteen of their games, which reflected a different kind of courage. Wallechinsky, p. 1166.

16. Tomizawa, "Japan's Team."

17. Daimatsu later ran for political office and wrote motivational books during his political career. He died relatively young, at age 57, of a heart attack, his body perhaps a victim of his own unrelenting requirements.

18. Von der Lippe, Gerd. "Handball, Gender and Sportification of Body-Cultures: 1900–40." *International Review for the Sociology of Sport* 29, no. 2, 1994.

19. There is a Danish Basketball League, but their encyclopedia entry says it all: "At the EuroBasket 1955 in Budapest, the national team struggled there as well as they did at the prior EuroBasket. Losing all eight of their matches in non competitive fashion, this time they finished in last place of the 18 teams at the event. After the EuroBasket 1955, the Danish national team regressed and never qualified for a major tournament again."

"Denmark's Men's National Basketball Team." Wikipedia, January 23, 2021. https://en.wikipedia.org/wiki/Denmark_men%27s_national_basketball_team. Accessed February 10, 2021.

20. Von der Lippe, "Handball, Gender and Sportification of Body-Cultures," p. 222.

21. Norway was thrilled when, at last in, Tokyo 2020, both men's and women's teams competed. Norwegian women obliterated the Swedes to take the bronze. Norwegian men finished seventh out of twelve teams.

22. Von der Lippe, "Handball, Gender and Sportification of Body-Cultures p. 222.

23. Within a few weeks, the IHF, which regulates beach handball, was already signaling a likely change in uniform standards for future games.

24. Olympic historian Wallechinsky shares a great anecdote about Lieberman playing Semjonova. Once, when Semjonova was guarding 6 ft. 8

inch Anne Donovan, Lieberman had the ball and was looking to pass. But she couldn't see her teammate: "Anne, where are you?" All she could hear was the voice, "I'm back here!" Wallechinsky, p. 445.

Chapter Ten

1. Belanger, Kelly. *Invisible Seasons: Title IX and the Fight for Equity in College Sports.* Syracuse University Press, January 2017, jacket blurb.

2. The key words in Title IX, quoted in "Introduction." *Equal Play: Title IX and Social Change,* edited by Nancy Hogshead-Maker and Andrew Zimbalist. Temple University Press, 2007, p. 1.

3. De Varona also became co-founder of the highly influential Women's Sports Foundation, making her impact on women athletes bigger and broader than just her Olympic accomplishments.

4. There are, of course, examples where clubs, leagues, and high schools together can be as powerful as colleges. A few basketball players (like LeBron James) go straight to leagues, i.e., the NBA, from high school. Soccer player Megan Rapinoe, as it happens, was a standout in high school, at a regional club, in college, and then on the Olympic team. But many strong clubs/leagues are created only after fed outstanding athletes from colleges in the first place. Regional soccer clubs for women didn't exist before women's soccer programs had been built out in college.

5. Suggs, Welch. "Heroines as Well as Heroes." *Equal Play: Title IX and Social Change,* edited by Nancy Hogshead-Maker and Andrew Zimbalist. Temple University Press, 2007, p. 17.

6. A 1973 lawsuit eventually pushed the AIAW to overturn their ban on women's athletic scholarships.

7. "Title IX and the Rise of Female Athletes in America." Women's Sports Foundation, September 2, 2016. https://www.womenssportsfoundation.org/education/title-ix-and-the-rise-of-female-athletes-in-america/. Accessed February 5, 2021.

8. According to Wikipedia, there are 800 men's soccer programs and 959 programs affiliated with NCAA. Including junior colleges and others schools raises the totals to 1,500 for women and 1,400 for men. For Division I only, the elite athletics programs, there are 300 for women and 200 for men. All numbers from 2019/2020.

9. Chuck, Elizabeth. "A Level Playing Field: Why the USA Is So Strong in Women's Soccer." *NBC News,* July 5, 2015. https://www.nbcnews.com/storyline/world-cup/level-playing-field-why-usa-so-strong-womens-soccer-n385346. Accessed February 12, 2021.

10. *Title IX at Forty: Working to Ensure Gender Equity in Education.* The National Coalition for Women and Girls in Education, 2012, p. 8. https://www.ncwge.org/TitleIX40/TitleIX-print.pdf. Accessed February 10, 2021.

11. Wrestling had been vocal about cuts but is recovering, according to NCAA statistics: 9,000 men wrestled at 400 schools in the early 1970s, which had dropped to 6,300 at 257 schools by the 1990s. However, by 2020, the number of schools had increased again to 419, while 11,366 men were in programs—along with 1,070 women. 260,000 boys wrestled in high schools—along with 22,236 women. "Odds of a High School Wrestler Making a College Varsity Roster 2020." Scholarshipstats.com, February 2021. https://scholarshipstats.com/wrestling. Accessed February 12, 2021.

12. Acosta, Vivian, and Carpenter, Linda Jen. "Women in Intercollegiate Sport: A Longitudinal, National Study, Twenty-Nine Year Update, 1977–2006." *Equal Play: Title IX and Social Change,* edited by Nancy Hogshead-Maker and Andrew Zimbalist. Temple University Press, 2007, p. 169.

13. Bevan, William. "Pulling Together." *Cambridge Alumni Magazine,* no. 75, May 1, 2015, p. 34.

14. Schweinbenz, Amanda Nicole, and Cronk, Alexandra. "Femininity Control at the Olympic Games." *Thirdspace: A Journal of Feminist Theory and Culture* 9, no. 2, 2010. https://journals.sfu.ca/thirdspace/index.php/journal/article/view/schweinbenzcronk/0. Accessed February 10, 2021.

15. State-sponsored drug distribution for sport had begun in the 1950s before testing had been established. Not until the 1970s would athletes "fail" tests, after which the focus was on making the drugs less detectable. In the 1990s, after the fall of the Berlin Wall, Stasi records documented large-scale, centralized drug experimentation and distribution, which would lead to medical problems for many athletes for the rest of their lives.

16. Individual Romanians have had issues with failed drug tests, but not in rowing and not to the state-sanctioned level as in East Germany (or, more recently, Russia).

17. Ergo, "Oarsome Foursome v Romanian Women's 8—A Technique Lesson." *Erg Rowing,* April 12, 2011. https://ergrowing.com/rowing-technique-lesson/. Accessed February 5, 2021.

18. Brewer, Jerry. "The Best Team in Rio? The U.S. Women's Eight: They're Rowers, and They're Awesome." *Washington Post,* August 13, 2016. https://www.washingtonpost.com/sports/olympics/the-best-team-in-rio-the-us-womens-eight-theyre-rowers-and-theyre-awesome/2016/08/13/426845c6-6155-11e6-9d2f-b1a3564181a1_story.html?utm_term=.c4bd9ffe9cd2. Accessed September 12, 2017.

19. Sides, Annabel Jane. "Making a Splash in 2000: A Historical Case Study of Women's Water Polo at the Olympic Games." *Fifth International Symposium for Olympics Research,* LA84 Foundation, Digital Library Collections, September 2000. https://digital.la84.org/digital/collection/p17103coll10/id/13463/rec/2. Accessed February 12, 2021.

20. *Ibid.,* p. 4.

21. *Ibid.,* p. 5.

22. FINA allowed every country to send two swimmers, even if they couldn't qualify. The most infamous of these was Eric Moussambani from Equatorial Guinea. He had only recently learned to

swim, and his coach changed his race from the 50 to 100 m on race day. He expended all his energy on the first half, then barely made it to the end. The TV announcers repeated his story of brave struggle multiple times, without mentioning that such swimmers were taking spots that might have gone to women's water polo.

The argument against women competing has often been (and still is) that their lesser athleticism makes them less interesting to watch. In this case, though, FINA was arguing that significantly inferior "athletes" were more interesting to watch than skilled women.

23. Suggs, Welch. *A Place on the Team: The Triumph and Tragedy of Title IX.* Princeton University Press, 2006, p. 2.

24. Schaaf, Phil. *Sports, Inc.: 100 Years of Sports Business.* Prometheus, 2003, p. 106. Accessed via Google books, January 6, 2018.

Chapter Eleven

1. Suggs, *A Place on the Team*, p. 138–9.
2. Verbrugge, Martha H. "Gender, Science & Fitness: Perspectives on Women's Exercise in the United States in the 20th Century." *Health and History* 4, no. 1, 2002, p. 61.
3. Wolven, E. L. "College Sports and Motherhood." *New York Times,* July 3, 1921, p. 42. Also cited in Houry, *American Women and the Modern Summer Games,* p. 31.
4. Dr. M. A. Ribble cited in Houry, *American Women and the Modern Summer Games,* p. 82.
5. Verbrugge, "Gender, Science & Fitness," p. 52.
6. Hutchinson, Andrew Boyd. "Separate but Unequal: Cross-Country's Great Distance Debate." Medium.com, February 2, 2016. https://medium.com/@Real_XC/separate-but-unequal-cross-country-s-great-distance-debate-dbd395c2767. Accessed February 24, 2021.
7. Beresini, Erin. "The Myth of the Falling Uterus." Outsideonline.com, March 25, 2013. https://www.outsideonline.com/1783996/myth-falling-uterus. Accessed November 10, 2020.
8. Schultz, Jaime. "Breaking into the Marathon: Women's Distance Running as Political Activism." *Frontiers: A Journal of Women's Studies* 40, no. 2, 2019, p. 6.
9. Berkowitz, Ira. "Players: Olympian Ahead of Her Time." *New York Times*, October 2, 1982. https://www.nytimes.com/1982/10/02/sports/players-olympian-ahead-of-her-time.html. Accessed November 14, 2020.
10. Longman, Jeré. "At the Olympics in Bombed-Out London, She Forever Changed Women's Sports." *New York Times Magazine,* July 24, 2020. https://www.nytimes.com/2020/07/24/magazine/1948-olympics-fanny-blankers-koen.html. Accessed February 25, 2021.
11. Marion Jones attempted to repeat Jesse Owens's and Carl Lewis's feat of four golds. Jones won three golds and two bronze medals (long jump, 4 × 100 relay) in Sydney 2000, but all her medals were stripped when she later admitted to steroid use.
12. Ironically, Blankers-Koen was so bent on proving her critics wrong that—according to a tell-all biography by Kees Kooman—she may have neglected her family in favor of international competition. Her daughter Fanneke, in a bit of a *Mommie Dearest* play, claims in the book that her mother didn't show affection and was more focused on winning competitions than on her children. Her son, Jan, countered some of the claims by fondly describing their mother as simply determined and displaying affection in the stoic manner of the Dutch.
13. Schultz, "Breaking into the Marathon," p. 17.
14. Over time, the ACSM would address a different problem, which they labeled the Female Triad. Women athletes who over-exercised without adequate nutrition—whether runners, gymnasts, or any other type of athlete—could develop health problems, ranging from eating disorders to gynecological disruptions. There was no harm in exercise *per se*, but there were unique medical needs for women athletes if they overtrained without enough calories.
15. In her first Boston run, in 1979, Benoit took eight minutes off the previous women's record. Late in the run, she had leaned toward one of the men nearby to ask, "Where are the famed heartbreak hills?" He had growled, "You already passed them" In 1983, she completed the Boston run in 2:22, two minutes faster than Waitz's time. That record stood for eleven more years. *1984 Los Angeles Olympics: Bud Greenspan Remembers*. Dir. Bud Greenspan. Showtime, July 19, 2004.
16. Even a book published in 2020 for the Tokyo Games still got it wrong: "the collapse of several of the women following the completion of the event led to its elimination." This, despite evidence to the contrary being one YouTube click away. The Olympic Foundation for Culture & Heritage. *The History of the Olympic Games*. Welbeck, 2020, p. 49.
17. Hutchinson, "Separate but Unequal."
18. Schultz, "Breaking into the Marathon," p. 7.
19. *Ibid.,* p. 1.
20. Blue, Adrienne. *Faster, Higher, Further: Women's Triumphs and Disasters at the Olympics.* Virago Press, 1988, p. 149.
21. *1984 Los Angeles Olympics: Bud Greenspan Remembers.*
22. *Ibid.*
23. Schultz, "Breaking into the Marathon," p. 10.
24. *Ibid.,* p. 11.
25. *Ibid.,* p. 14.
26. *Ibid.,* p. 10.
27. Eskenazi, Gerald. "2 Women Marathoners Abandon Marital Route." *The New York Times,* March 19, 1973, p.52.
28. *1984 Los Angeles Olympics: Bud Greenspan Remembers.*
29. Lovett, Charlie. "The Fight to Establish the Women's Race." Excerpt from *Olympic Marathon:*

A Centennial History of the Games' Most Storied Race, 1997. http://www.marathonguide.com/history/olympicmarathons/chapter25.cfm. Accessed February 25, 2021.

30. *1984 Los Angeles Olympics: Bud Greenspan Remembers*.

31. Blue, *Faster, Higher, Further*, p. 149.

32. *Ibid.*, p. 144.

33. Leder, Jane Mersky. *Grace & Glory: A Century of Women in the Olympics*. Triumph Books, 1996, p. 72.

34. *1984 Los Angeles Olympics: Bud Greenspan Remembers*.

35. Hutchinson, "Separate but Unequal."

36. Berkow, Ira. "TV Sports: Sensitive and Acute Coverage of Marathon Finish." *New York Times*, August 7, 1984, p. A18.

37. Vecsey, George. "Sports of the Times: 'I Was Hurting.'" *New York Times*, August 7, 1984, p. A17.

38. Decker even planned for two medals, as she had recent records in the 1500 and 3000, but decided to pull out of the 1500 because there would be too many heats and races. "I'd rather have one gold than two silvers." "Sports People; Mary Decker's Decision." *New York Times*, July 13, 1984, p. A18.

39. Parker-Pope, Tara. "An Olympic Blast from the Past." *New York Times*, August 1, 2008. https://well.blogs.nytimes.com/2008/08/01/an-olympic-blast-from-the-past. Accessed February 25, 2021.

40. Dawson, Louise. "How the Bicycle Became a Symbol of Women's Emancipation." *The Guardian*, November 4, 2011. https://www.theguardian.com/environment/bike-blog/2011/nov/04/bicycle-symbol-womens-emancipation. Accessed February 22, 2021.

41. De Visé, Daniel. "The Outer Line: The All-time Greatest Female Cyclists." Velonews.com, March 13, 2019. https://www.velonews.com/events/the-outer-line-the-all-time-greatest-female-cyclists/. Accessed February 22, 2021.

42. It was hard work especially when the British delegation, the National Cyclists' Union (NCU), "forgot" to put forward the motion for records to be recognized, after agreeing with Gray and women to do so.
Fotheringham, William. "Eileen Gray Obituary." *The Guardian*, June 2, 2015. https://www.theguardian.com/sport/2015/jun/02/eileen-gray. Accessed February 25, 2021.

43. Sinclair, Belinda. "Interview: Eileen Gray, CBE." *British Cycling*, June 2, 2010. https://www.britishcycling.org.uk/road/article/spor20100602-Interview--Eileen-Gray-CBE-0. Accessed March 11, 2021.

44. "Connie Carpenter-Phinney Inducted into Hall of Fame." *U.S. Biking Hall of Fame*. https://usbhof.org/inductee/connie-carpenter-phinney-2/. Accessed February 25, 2021.

45. Lucas, Shelley. "Women's Cycle Racing: Enduring Meanings." *Journal of Sport History*, Summer 2012, p. 230.

46. *Ibid.*, p. 231.

47. Star power probably helped. U.S. distance freestyle swimmer Katie Ledecky was a marquee athlete in America, which may have put the event more "in demand," at least for audiences. Ledecky had been setting records in the event outside the Games since she was 16.

48. Moran, Malcolm. "Benoit Gears Down to Life's Other Joys." *New York Times*, August 7, 1984, p. A19.

49. "Tirunesh Dibaba." Wikipedia, January 25, 2021. https://en.wikipedia.org/wiki/Tirunesh_Dibaba.
Accessed February 25, 2021.

50. Brown, Meghan. "The Longer the Race, the Stronger We Get." *Outside*, April 11, 2017.
https://www.outsideonline.com/2169856/longer-race-stronger-we-get. Accessed February 25, 2021.

51. Carter, Kate. "'Women Have Less Ego. Men Think: How Hard Can This Be?': The Female Ultra-Athletes Leading the Field." *The Guardian*, January 3, 2020. https://www.theguardian.com/lifeandstyle/2020/jan/03/female-ultra-athletes-leading-field-women-less-ego. Accessed February 25, 2021.

52. Goldblatt, *The Games*, p. 318.

Chapter Twelve

1. Guttmann, *Women's Sports*, p. 74.

2. Ruz, Camila, and Parkinson, Justin. "'Suffrajitsu': How the Suffragettes Fought Back Using Martial Arts." *BBC News*, October 5, 2015. https://www.bbc.com/news/magazine-34425615. Accessed July 10, 2021.
Antonia Raeburn also tells of a group of British suffragettes who retreated from an afternoon of stone throwing at the cops to their hideaway, Mrs. Garrud's jiu-jitsu gymnasium. Quickly hiding their remaining rocks under floorboards covered by tatami mats, the women began practicing throws as the bobbies banged on the door. The matron allowed only one quick and unsuccessful look. Raeburn, Antonia. *Militant Suffragettes*. NEI, 1974.

3. Jennings, L. A. "She's a Knockout!: A History of Women in Fighting Sports." Rowman & Littlefield, ePub edition, 2015, Preface.

4. Project Rusty, LLC, Rustykanokogi.com, 2020. https://www.rustykanokogi.com/. Accessed March 8, 2021.

5. Van der Veere, Anoma P. "Wrestling with Gender: Coverage of the Olympic Games in Japanese Media." *Yearbook of Women's History: 38*, January 2019, p. 59.

6. Miarka, Bianca, Marques, Juliana Bastos, and Franchini, Emerson. "Reinterpreting the History of Women's Judo in Japan." *The International Journal of the History of Sport* 28, no. 7, May 2011, p. 1024.

7. *Ibid.*, p. 1024.

8. Late in life, Fukuda taught judo to Dr. Shelley Fernandez, Northern California president of the National Organization of Women. Fernandez

petitioned the Kodokan to raise Fukuda's rank, and they finally did, in 1972, to 9th rank. Fukuda also earned Japan's Order of the Sacred Treasure in 1990.

9. "Rumbling with Rusty: She Started Life as Rena Glickman, and Today Brooklyn's Rusty Kanokogi Is the Queen of Judo." *Sports Illustrated*, March 24, 1986, p. 6. https://vault.si.com/vault/1986/03/24/rumbling-rusty. Accessed August 15, 2021.

10. Lewellen, Wendy. "Rena Kanokogi, Mother of Women's Judo." *Women's Sports Foundation*, 2008. https://web.archive.org/web/20101222203350/http://www.womenssportsfoundation.org:80/Content/Articles/Athletes/About-Athletes/R/Rena-Kanokogi-Mother-of-Womens-Judo.aspx. Accessed March 13, 2021.

11. Rusty knew Ryohei was the one for her. After she broke her hand in a bar fight with a woman who had insulted the Japanese, rather than admonishing her Ryohei said, "When you punch head, always wrap handkerchief around hand." "Rumbling with Rusty," p. 7.

12. West, Karen. "Judo Group Charges IOC with Discrimination Against Women's Judo." UPI, August 8, 1984.

13. "Rumbling with Rusty," p. 2, 9.

14. Moshe Feldenkrais was a Ukrainian-Israeli engineer interested in body mechanics. Feldenkrais became so passionate about judo that he founded a club which is one of the oldest still existing in France. He later developed his ideas about posture and physical therapy into the Feldenkrais method. Meanwhile, the seed he planted in France blossomed, and in 2016 the country had over 200,000 registered judokas.

15. Bouteiller, Florent. "Audrey Tcheuméo, le Tank du Judo Français." LeMonde.fr., August 11, 2016. http://combat.blog.lemonde.fr/2016/08/11/audrey-tcheumeo-le-tank-du-judo-francais/. Accessed September 25, 2016. Translated from the French by Nancy Castille.

16. Krieger, Daniel. "Japanese Women Kick and Punch Out a Space for Themselves in Sports." *New York Times*, nytimes.com, -for-themselves-in-sports.html. Accessed March 11, 2021.

17. Curby, David G., and Jomand, Guillaume. "The Evolution of Women's Wrestling: History, Issues and Future." *International Journal of Wrestling Science* 5, May 28, 2015, p. 3.

18. Fields, Sarah K. *Female Gladiators: Gender, Law, and Contact Sport in America*. University of Illinois Press, 2005, p. 104.

19. *Ibid.*, p. 104.

20. Fields, *Female Gladiators*, p. ix.

21. Brake, Deborah L. "Wrestling with Gender: Constructing Masculinity by Refusing to Wrestle Women." *Nevada Law Journal* 13, Winter 2013, pp. 101–150.

22. The *Foxcatcher* scandal brought the wrong kind of notoriety to wrestling. Because of the scarcity of funding, some former Olympians began working with millionaire John DuPont, who built them a state-of-the-art training facility at his estate in Pennsylvania. However, the eccentric and psychologically disturbed recluse DuPont ended up murdering wrestler Dave Schultz. Schultz's brother wrote a book, and the 2012 movie based on the story was released just when Olympic wrestling faced its worst crisis.

23. Curby and Jomand, "The Evolution of Women's Wrestling," p. 9.

24. The other two women torch carriers were paralympian Tsuchida Wakako and tennis player Osaka Naomi, who lit the cauldron. Male judoka Nomura Tadahiro and baseball players Oh Sadaharu, Matsui Hideki, and Nagashima Shigeo also carried the torch.

25. Risako had dropped weight to allow her sister, Yukako, to wrestle without being in the same category. Both sisters won gold.

26. In the Bollywood movie, the girls sing, "You ask delicate dolls to toughen up," but coach/father Phogat responds with the quintessential father's argument: "I am going to make my girls so capable that they can choose boys." *Dangal*. Dir. Tiwari, Nitesh. Aamir Khan Productions, 2016.

27. *Ibid.*

28. Walton, Theresa A. "Title IX: Forced to Wrestle Up the Backside." *Women in Sport and Physical Activity Journal* 12, no. 2, Fall 2003, p. 20.

29. Data from the National Federation of State High School Associations.

30. Thompson, Bill. "Am I the Only One or Was It Weird Watching Two Girls in a Boxing Ring?" *Fort Worth Star-Telegram*, February 23, 1997, p. 4.

31. Guttmann, *Women's Sports*, p. 75.

32. Thrasher, Christopher. "Disappearance: How Shifting Gendered Boundaries Motivated the Removal of 18th Century Boxing Champion Elizabeth Wilkinson from Historical Memory." *Past Imperfect* 18, 2012, p. 53.

33. *Ibid.*

34. Boulongne, "Pierre de Coubertin and Women's Sport," p. 25.

35. Shields, p. 124.

36. "Lisa Warren: Junior Missy Gloves." Women's Boxing Archive Network, 1979. https://www.womenboxing.com/fight1979juniormissygloveslisawarren.htm. Accessed August 15, 2021.

37. Jennings, "She's a Knockout!," p. 130.

38. Schweinbenz, Amanda. "'Float Like a Butterfly, Sting Like a Bee'—But Only If You Dress Like a Girl: An Analysis of the Feminization of Female Olympic Athletes through Athletic Attire." *Eleventh International Symposium for Olympic Research, Olympic World Library*, 2012, p. 94.

39. Weaving, Charlene. "'Babes Boxing in Skirts': A Critique of the Proposed AIBA Uniform Rule." *Eleventh International Symposium for Olympic Research, Olympic World Library*, 2012, p. 90.

40. *Ibid.*

41. *Ibid.*

42. One fighter staged a "ringside protest" for an hour after he was disqualified for head-butting his opponent, while another refused to wear his silver medal during the podium ceremony.

43. Macur, Juliet. "Samaranch Pushed for Inclusion of Women." *New York Times*, April 21, 2010. https://www.nytimes.com/2010/04/22/sports/olympics/22olympics.html. Accessed May 14, 2021.

44. Goldblatt, *The Games*, p. 422.

Chapter Thirteen

1. Myers, Dvora. *The End of the Perfect Ten: The Making and Breaking of Gymnastics' Top Score—From Nadia to Now*. Touchstone Press, 2017, p. 12.

2. Brown, Les. "Olympic Games Average 35% of the TV Audience." *New York Times*, p. 91, February 11, 1976. https://www.nytimes.com/1976/02/11/archives/olympic-games-average-35-of-the-tv-audience-growing-interest-seen.html. Accessed Mary 12, 2021.

3. A time delay for American television, which was often the feed used elsewhere, applied to most Games. Only Olympics contested in the North American time zones would have any live segments, and those were often carefully curated. The networks would even try to persuade the Olympic organizing committees to schedule American-preferred competitions at odd times—8 am for example—so that they could be shown live in Eastern Daylight Time. But even those would have a director choosing which camera, which event, and which person to highlight.

4. Enberg, Dick. "1988 Olympics Women's Gymnastics—All Around Final—complete." NBC TV, uploaded to YouTube by kentiemac gymnastics, July 16, 2020, https://www.youtube.com/watch?v=zE_0CcHdd2k. Accessed August 15, 2021.

5. Guttmann, *Women's Sports*, p. 205.

6. Beechum, Justin. *Olga*. Paddington Press, 1975, p. 7.

7. To take on the Soviet teams, with their world-class coaches and state-sponsored funding, was no easy task. Even without any medals, Rigby received commercial endorsements plus an offer for a Broadway musical. It turned out she could sing and act, and she was able to play Peter Pan on and off Broadway for more than thirty years. Having Rigby play an ageless boy for three decades seems particularly ironic.

8. Fourth behind the USSR, East Germany, and Czechoslovakia.

9. Moore's floor exercise routine placed a highly respectable 11th place in Munich. Maddux, Gordon with McKay, Jim. "Joan Moore 1972 Olympics Team Optionals FX." ABC, August 27, 1972, uploaded to YouTube August 20, 2012. https://www.youtube.com/watch?v=-x3alQf96gI. Accessed May 12, 2021.

10. Myers, *The End of the Perfect Ten*, p. 45.

11. The first ten awarded in competition had actually been awarded to Vera Čáslavská back at the 1967 European Championships, but Olympic judges were not supposed to go above 9.95.

12. Guttmann, *The Olympics*, p. 137.

13. Goldblatt, *The Games*, p. 281.

14. Myers, *The End of the Perfect Ten*, p. 39.

15. According to Comaneci, the Karolyis asked if she wanted to defect with them, and she declined. When she didn't leave, Romania retaliated against her coach's defection with harsh measures. She no longer competed, which left her with far less money, and she couldn't travel, so she ended up with far fewer freedoms than even the average Romanian. She finally defected in 1989, shortly before the fall of the government.

16. Myers, *The End of the Perfect Ten*, p. 39.

17. Comaneci was 5'4" and Latynina 5'3", while Simone Biles is 4'8" like Retton.

18. Whiteside, Kelly. "Looking Back at 'the Most Beautiful Face of Socialism.'" *USA Today*, August 6, 2013. https://www.usatoday.com/story/sports/olympics/2013/08/06/katarina-witt-figure-skating-yuna-kim-cold-war/2623483/. Accessed June 2, 2021.

19. Guttmann, *The Olympics*, p. 168.

20. Guttmann, *Women's Sports*, p. 262.

21. *Ibid*.

22. Witt's American counterparts struggled with threading the needle of sex appeal. U.S. audiences could be alternately lascivious and prudish. They wanted their female athletes pretty, not nude. Thomas tried a compromise by wearing a unitard, but that was also somehow too daring. The IOC augmented the costume regulations with a "Thomas rule." Skirts would also be required—until 2003—when women's unitards gained approval.

23. Hiller, Stephanie A. "Katarina Witt, Socialism's Most Beautiful Face." DW.com, July 1, 2009. https://www.dw.com/en/katarina-witt-socialisms-most-beautiful-face/a-3817281. Accessed May 9, 2021.

24. Gallico, Paul. "Women in Sports Should Look Beautiful." *Vogue*, June 15, 1936. Cited in Houry, *American Women and the Modern Summer Games*, p. 76.

25. Hamilton, Scott. "Midori Ito (JPN)—1992 Albertville, Ladies' Free Skate." YouTube, uploaded by 3Axel 1996, November 29, 2009.

26. Adam Rippon and Brian Boitano both described how judges' body-shaming remarks also extended to male skaters, who would eat only a few slices of bread per day in order to look "like matchsticks." "If judges tell you to lose weight," said Boitano, "you don't have time to figure out how to do it healthily." Rippon developed an eating disorder.

Crouse, Karen. "Adam Rippon on Quiet Starvation in Men's Skating." *New York Times*, February 13, 2018. https://www.nytimes.com/2018/02/13/sports/olympics/figure-skating-adam-rippon.html. Accessed May 15, 2021.

27. Schwiegershausen, Erica. "Was Tonya Harding a Victim, Too? A New Essay Investigates." *New York Magazine*, January 8, 2014. https://www.thecut.com/2014/01/new-essay-was-tonya-harding-a-victim-too.html. Accessed May 17, 2021.

28. Baum, Greg. "Australia Ganged Up on Perec: She Deserves an Apology." *Sydney Morning*

Herald, September 22, 2020. https://www.smh.com.au/sport/athletics/australia-ganged-up-on-perec-she-deserves-an-apology-20200917-p55wq6.html. Accessed August 15, 2021.

29. Murray, Oliver. "Horrible Racism Behind Cathy Freeman's Famous Moment." *Daily Mercury,* September 18, 2020. https://www.dailymercury.com.au/news/horrible-racism-behind-famous-moment/4101975/. Accessed May 30, 2021.

30. "Perec Said Harassment Made Her Leave." ESPN.com, September 28, 2000. https://www.espn.com/oly/summer00/news/2000/0928/785656.html. Accessed June 4, 2021.

31. Berlin, Peter. "Why Did French Runner Run Away?" *New York Times,* September 22, 2000. https://www.nytimes.com/2000/09/22/news/why-did-french-runner-run-away.html. Accessed June 3, 2021.

32. *Ibid.*

33. Baum, "Australia Ganged Up on Perec."

34. "Marie-Jose Perec on Track." *Sydney Morning Herald,* December 6, 2002. https://www.smh.com.au/sport/marie-jose-perec-on-track-20021206-gdfx9o.html. Accessed June 2, 2021.

35. Baum, "Australia Ganged Up on Perec."

Chapter Fourteen

1. For the record, had Galieva scored a 10, Strug's second vault *would* have been needed. It was unlikely Galieva would have earned such a score, given her history, but it was theoretically possible.

2. Leavy, Jane. "A Year After Her Olympic Vault to Fame, Kerry Strug Is in College, Learning to Live Like an Ordinary Kid." *Sports Illustrated,* August 11, 1997, p. 3.

3. Ryan, Joan. *Little Girls in Pretty Boxes.* Doubleday Books, 1995.

4. Leavy, "A Year After her Olympic Vault to Fame, Kerry Strug Is in College."

5. The Female Triad is not limited to gymnasts. Runners, soccer players, and other athletes could develop the condition. But it was especially prevalent where coaches knew judging bias extended to overall appearance.

6. Dantzscher, Jamie. "Book Excerpt: 'Little Girls in Pretty Boxes' With New Forward by Olympic Gymnast Jamie Dantzscher." Espn.com, August 6, 2018. https://www.espn.com/espnw/culture/story/_/id/24300690/little-girls-pretty-boxes-new-forward-olympic-gymnast-jamie-dantzscher. Accessed May 27, 2021.

7. Myers, *The End of the Perfect Ten,* p. 44.

8. Leavy, p. 4.

9. *Ibid.*, p.4.

10. Kerri Strug responded to Q&A on the website https://www.kerristrug.info/faq/. Accessed May 18, 2021.

11. Pieper, Lindsay. "Star-Spangled Fingernails: Florence Griffith-Joyner and the Mediation of Black Femininity." USSportshistory.com, April 20, 2015. https://ussporthistory.com/2015/04/20/star-spangled-fingernails-florence-griffith-joyner-and-the-mediation-of-black-femininity/. Accessed August 15, 2021.

12. Cahn, *Coming on Strong,* p. 216.

13. *Ibid.*

14. In many polls, Babe Didrikson and Jackie Joyner-Kersee ranked #1 and #2 (or #2 and #1) as World's Greatest Female Athletes, either of the 20th century or of all time. *Sports Illustrated,* for example: https://www.topendsports.com/world/lists/greatest-all-time/women-si100.htm. Accessed June 10, 2021.

15. Moore, Kenny. "Our Woman in Moscow Jackie Joyner Was Queen of the Goodwill Games with a Stunning World Record in the Heptathlon." *Sports Illustrated,* 21, 1986. https://vault.si.com/vault/1986/07/21/our-woman-in-moscow-jackie-joyner-was-queen-of-the-goodwill-games-with-a-stunning-world-record-in-the-heptathlon. Accessed June 6, 2021.

16. Cahn, *Coming on Strong,* p. 271.

17. Moore, "Our Woman."

18. Eaton's coach was Harry Marra and Thompson's coach was Frank Dick.

19. Brennan, Kristine. "There Are Sprinters, Then There's Griffith-Joyner." *Washington Post,* September 30, 1988. https://www.washingtonpost.com/archive/sports/1988/09/30/there-are-sprinters-then-theres-griffith-joyner/df3dd044-9be9-4fab-a903-57d3d8c0ac3f/. Accessed June 8, 2021.

20. The winner was Silke Gladisch Möller, whose East German doping records later revealed she had been systematically and periodically taking steroids for years.

21. Pieper, "Star-Spangled Fingernails," p. 8.

22. Cahn, *Coming on Strong,* p. 270.

23. Guttmann, *Women's Sports,* pp. 249 and 260.

24. *Ibid.*

25. Cahn, *Coming on Strong,* p. 270.

26. "Florence Griffith-Joyner—Women's 100m (WR)—1988 U.S. Olympic Trials." NBCSports, YouTube, uploaded by Jim Muchmore, August 19, 2018. https://www.youtube.com/watch?v=9CMM2lQDMDI. Accessed June 12, 2021.

27. Montague, James. "Savings Flo Jo: Taking Back a Legacy." CNN, August 10, 2012. https://edition.cnn.com/2012/08/10/sport/olympics-flo-jo-seoul/index.html. Accessed June 10, 2021.

28. Manko, Katina. *Ding Dong! Avon Calling!: The Women and Men of Avon Products, Incorporated.* Oxford University Press, 2021, p. 234. Some writers take a curious approach when using the ad to extol Joyner-Kersee's accomplishments. Manko references the actual ad copy, whereas others seem to be inventing numbers as they might for a comic book hero. One writer quotes, "I can throw a shot putt [sic] 29 feet and run 100 m in under 11 seconds," which would have been close to sister-in-law Flo-Jo's time but only half JJK's typical shot put distance (https://www.irishtimes.com/sport/worlds-best-give-comfort-and-joy-1.74035). Another

claims the ad says, "I can throw a shot put 100 yards and I can run faster than all but 128 men in the world," which would make JJK into a demi-god rather than just the world's greatest female athlete. On the other hand, watching Jackie Joyner-Kersee would make any viewer believe she could do anything. https://books.google.com/books?id=sqhoAgAAQBAJ&pg=PA192&lpg=PA192&dq=jackie+joyner+kersee+and+red+toenail&source=bl&ots=9g7gCInC0W&sig=ACfU3U3PtJLWP-tE-pJNXHS8CoShEXJzRQ&hl=en&sa=X&ved=2ahUKEwi5vuD4spLxAhWI_p4KHdBEAYIQ6AEwHHoECCYQAw#v=onepage&q=jackie%20joyner%20kersee%20and%20red%20toenail&f=false.

29. Desmond-Harris, Jenee. "Serena Williams Is Constantly the Target of Disgusting Racist and Sexist Attacks." Vox, September 7, 2016. https://www.vox.com/2015/3/11/8189679/serena-williams-indian-wells-racism. Accessed June 10, 2021.

30. Carter, Michelle. "Michelle Carter Is the Body Positive Champion We Can't Wait to See in Rio." *Redbook,*, July 28, 2016. http://www.redbookmag.com/body/mental-health/a45271/michelle-carter-body-olympics/. Accessed January 24, 2017.

31. Houry, *American Women and the Modern Summer Games,* p. 146.

32. Pilon, Mary. "You Throw, Girl: An Olympic Shot Putter's Feminist Mission." *The New Yorker,* August 11, 2016. http://www.newyorker.com/news/sporting-scene/you-throw-girl-an-olympic-shot-putters-feminist-mission. Accessed January 24, 2017.

33. Rosen, Karen. "Michelle Carter Plans to Win in Rio, Following Footsteps of Olympian and Super Bowl Winning Dad." *TeamUSA Sports News,* July 7, 2017. http://www.teamusa.org/News/2016/July/07/U.S.-Olympic-Team-Trials-For-Track-And-Field. Accessed January 23, 2017.

34. Indeed, for Paris 2024, the teams will return to five members rather than four.

35. As far as medals go, Karolyi was right, given that Kocian earned a silver on the uneven bars.

36. Meyers, *The End of the Perfect Ten,* pp.189–190

37. Biles, Simone [@Simone_Biles]. "Can't tell you how hard…" Twitter, November 22, 2019. https://t.co/UrDXIrTng9. Accessed June 19, 2021.

38. Bengel, Chris. "Simones Biles Tells '60 Minutes' 2020 Summer Olympics Postponement Gave her Doubts about Competing Again." CBS, February 14, 2021. https://www.cbssports.com/olympics/news/brisbane-australia-set-to-be-named-2032-summer-olympics-host-city-as-only-candidate/. Accessed June 19, 2021.

Chapter Fifteen

1. Cahn, *Coming on Strong,* p. 168.
2. *Ibid.*
3. *Ibid.,* p. 166.
4. *Ibid.,* p. 170.
5. Gallico, Paul. "Muscle Molls—You Can Have Them." *Vanity Fair,* May 1931. https://archive.vanityfair.com/article/1931/5/muscle-molls-you-can-have-them. Accessed June 14, 2021.
6. Cahn, *Coming on Strong,* p. 115.
7. McKenna, Dave. "Remembering Paul Gallico, The Sportswriter Who Hated Women but Was Okay with Nazis." *Deadspin,* December 29, 2015. https://deadspin.com/remembering-paul-gallico-the-sportswriter-who-hated-wo-1749309043. Accessed June 14, 2021.
8. Houry, *American Women and the Modern Summer Games,* p. 90.
9. Beschloss, Michael. "A Maverick Golfer's Struggles in a More Conformist Time." *New York Times,* August 8, 2014. https://www.nytimes.com/2014/08/09/upshot/a-maverick-golfers-struggles-in-a-more-conformist-time.html. Accessed June 24, 2021.
10. Cahn, *Coming on Strong,* p. 185.
11. Zipter, Yvonne. *Diamonds Are a Dyke's Best Friend.* Firebrand Books, 1988, p. 48.
12. Suggs, *A Place on the Team,* p. 121.
13. *Ibid.*
14. Tinsley, Justin. "Twenty-five Years Ago Today, Magic Johnson Announced He Had HIV." *The Undefeated,* November 7, 2016. https://theundefeated.com/features/twenty-five-years-ago-today-magic-johnson-announced-he-had-hiv-los-angeles-lakers/. Accessed July 21, 2021.
15. "Martina Navratilova." Wikipedia, updated July 21, 2021. https://en.wikipedia.org/wiki/Martina_Navratilova. Accessed July 21, 2021.
16. Cahn, *Coming on Strong,* pp. 1–2.
17. Penn State, which was harboring notorious pedophile Jerry Sandusky, for the same 30-year time period.
18. Figel, Bill. "Lesbians in World of Athletics". *Chicago Sun-Times,* June 16, 1986.
19. Gleeson, Scott, and Brady, Erik. "Why Haven't More…" *USA Today,* October 8, 2015. https://www.usatoday.com/story/sports/ncaab/2015/10/08/coaches-gay-sports-homophobia-closet-chris-burns-sherri-murrell/73409216/. Accessed June 20, 2021.
20. Bledsoe, Lucy Jane. "No Victims, No Fear: Reflecting on Title IX Lesbians." *Aethlon* 15, no. 1, Fall 1997, p. 106.
21. Roger Ebert gave the movie 4 stars, praising its "honesty." It was groundbreaking in showing two young women falling for each other, but it was not groundbreaking in resolving the relationship problems by having one of them end up with a man.
22. *Personal Best,* Warner Brothers, 1982.
23. Visibility is a function of the press, and reviewing past press is a little like looking at the fossil record. Athletes might have told the press that they were LGBTQ but been ignored. Reports which mentioned it in tiny print might not be in the public domain now. Thus, it's hard to gauge exactly who came out when, unless the athlete called a press conference or did a special interview to make the announcement. But it was less than a dozen, and at best only a few.

24. Zeigler, Cyd. "Robert Dover Was the First Out Gay Olympic Athlete, in 1988. SBNation, February 19, 2020. https://www.outsports.com/platform/amp/2020/2/19/21138643/gay-olympic-robert-dover-equestrian-horse-riding-five-rings-athlete. Accessed June 22, 2021.

25. France, Louise. " Without Prejudice." *The Observer: Tennis*, November 26, 2006. https://www.theguardian.com/sport/2006/nov/26/tennis.features1. Accessed June 22, 2021.

26. Billie Jean King was a little too old to compete when tennis was re-admitted in 1988, although she did coach two U.S. teams to a handful of medals.

27. Smith, Gary. "In Love and War." *Sports Illustrated*, October 2, 2000. https://vault.si.com/vault/2000/10/02/in-love-and-war-team-handball-stars-camilla-andersen-and-mia-hundvin-are-the-first-spouses-ever-to-oppose-each-other-in-the-games. Accessed August 16, 2021.

28. Bledsoe, "No Victims, No Fear," p. 106.

29. Hauser, Melanie. "Life after Golf Has Been All about Family for Patty Sheehan." ESPN, July 28, 2015. https://www.espn.com/espnw/news-commentary/story/_/id/13333239/life-golf-all-family-patty-sheehan. Accessed June 20, 2021.

30. Swopes has since separated and married a longtime male friend, which prompted some to label her NGAA (Not Gay After All) rather than bisexual.

31. Thomas, June. "Gold-Medal-Winning Dutch Speedskater Ireen Wüst Doesn't Want to Be a Model Queer." Slate.com, February 9, 2014. https://slate.com/human-interest/2014/02/gold-medal-winning-dutch-speedskater-ireen-wust-doesnt-want-to-be-a-model-queer.html. Accessed March 25, 2021.

32. "Gro Hammerseng & Katja Nyberg." YouTube, uploaded by grokatjahandball, November 11, 2007. https://www.youtube.com/watch?v=3MBN7i8xNX4. Accessed July 21, 2021.

Chapter Sixteen

1. "Sex" and "gender"—these words have been used interchangeably throughout this book, until now. In prior chapters, the terms were treated as equal synonyms for variety.

In this specific chapter, words will be used more precisely. *Sex* will refer to the body parts. A person may have the sexual parts of a male or a female or some of both. A person can also exchange the body parts of one sex for another through medical intervention.

Gender refers to the conceptual image. A person can perceive themself as belonging to either a male or female gender, or possibly neither, although "non-binary" was not a well-known concept prior to the 21st century, even though it did exist in several cultures. When a person's gender perception doesn't match their body parts, they may experience gender dysphoria.

However, there is the additional cultural concept of *gender*. Social ideas of masculine and feminine have historically treated them as neat little boxes. When people don't match the cultural image—when a person's sex doesn't entirely match the image of their gender—those with influence have criticized or tried to apply regulations. Thus, women with large muscles have been called "unnatural beings." Hence, the IOC's experiments with sex verification has been to enforce gender verification. Hence, nearly a century of mess.

2. Erikainen, Sonja. "Policing the Sex Binary: Gender Verification and the Boundaries of Female Embodiment in Elite Sport." Report for the IOC Olympic Studies Centre, University of Leeds School of Sociology and Social Policy, December 31, 2016.

3. Houry, *American Women and the Modern Summer Games*, p. 126.

4. Guttmann, *Women's Sports*, p. 96.

5. Tannenbaum, "Stella Walsh," p. 29.

6. Houry, *American Women and the Modern Summer Games*, p. 127.

7. Heggie, Vanessa. "Testing Sex and Gender in Sports; Reinventing, Reimagining and Reconstructing Histories." *Endeavor* 34, no. 4, December 2010, pp. 159–160.

8. "Medicine: Change of Sex." *Time*, August 24, 1936. http://content.time.com/time/subscriber/printout/0,8816,756527,00.html#. Accessed June 25, 2021.

9. Houry, *American Women and the Modern Summer Games*, p. 126. The (?) notations are from Brundage.

10. Andrew (one-name only), "The Opposite of Fair Play: Part I," The Victory Press blog, October 18, 2017. https://victorypress.org/2017/10/18/the-opposite-of-fair-play-part-i/. Accessed July 3, 2021.

11. Walsh still made news, and in December 1935 told a newspaper upon returning from an international meet that she saw Germans discriminating against Jewish athletes. Her comments lent support to those who wanted to boycott the Berlin Games. Brundage and others were against the boycott and chose the example of Helene Mayer, the Jewish fencer accepted by Germany, as their rationale to move forward. If Brundage really held a grudge because of Walsh's "interference," he could have recommended examining everybody.

"Battle Lines Sharply Drawn as Fight Continues..." *Detroit Jewish Chronicle*, November 1, 1935, p. 3.

12. Dohle, Max. *Ze zeggen dat ik geen meid ben: De schorsing van Foekje Dillema* ('They say I'm Not a Girl': The Suspension of Foekje Dillema). Max Dohle, June 2011, p. 17. https://web.archive.org/web/20160422082250/http://www.foekjedillema.nl/. Accessed June 28, 2021. Translation by Google Translate.

13. Turnbull, Simon. "Blankers Jnr: 'My Mother Only Enjoyed Herself When She Was Being Worshipped.'" *The Independent*, October 23, 2011. https://www.independent.co.uk/sport/olympics/blankers-jnr-my-mother-only-enjoyed-herself-

when-she-was-being-worshipped-2319488.html. Accessed June 29, 2021.
  14. *Ibid.*
  15. Ballantyne, Kaye N., Kayser, Manfred, and Grootegoed, J. Anton. "Sex and Gender Issues in Competitive Sports: Investigation of a Historical Case Leads to a New Viewpoint." *British Journal of Sports Medicine* 46, no. 8, 2012, 614–617.
  16. Dohle, *Ze zeggen dat ik geesn meid ben,* p. 17.
  17. Erikainen, "Policing the Sex Binary," p. 16.
  18. Schweinbenz and Cronk, "Femininity Control at the Olympic Games," p. 4.
  19. Erikainen, "Policing the Sex Binary," p. 15.
  20. "Track & Field: Preserving la Différence." *Time,* September 16, 1966. http://content.time.com/time/subscriber/article/0,33009,836386,00.html. Accessed August 15, 2021.
  21. *Ibid.*
  22. Larned, D. "The Femininity Test: A Woman's First Olympic Hurdle." *Womensports* 3, 1976, p. 8.
  23. Heffie, p. 158.
  24. UPI, "Tamara Press Retires as Track Competitor." *New York Times,* December 5, 1967, p. 63.
  25. Schweinbenz and Cronk, "Femininity Control at the Olympic Games," p. 8.
  26. Henne, p. 798.
  27. *Ibid.*
  28. Pieper, Lindsay Parks. *Policing Womanhood: The International Olympic Committee, Sex Testing and the Maintenance of Hetero-Femininity in Sport.* 2013. Ohio State University, Ph.D. dissertation, p. 13. https://etd.ohiolink.edu/apexprod/rws_olink/r/1501/10?clear=10&p10_accession_num=osu1366280376. Accessed August 15, 2021.
  29. Schweinbenz and Cronk, "Femininity Control at the Olympic Games," p. 7.
  30. "Question of Gender: The Sex Testing of Female Athletes." Rear Vision Podcast, ABC Radio National, August 14, 2016.
  31. Erikainen, "Policing the Sex Binary," p. 19.
  32. Dr. Lothar Kipke, who oversaw the East German swim program, was convicted in 2000 of causing harm to 58 swimmers. Maimon, Alan. "Doping's Sad Toll: One Athlete's Tale from East Germany." *New York Times*, February 6, 2000. https://www.nytimes.com/2000/02/06/sports/dopings-sad-toll-one-athletes-tale-from-east-germany.html. Accessed July 8, 2021.
  33. Schweinbenz and Cronk, "Femininity Control at the Olympic Games," p. 11.
  34. Elsas, Louis J., Linqvist, Arne, and Ferguson-Smith, Malcolm. "Gender Verification of Female Athletes." *Genetics in Medicine*, July/August 2000, p. 251.
  35. Semenya took silver in her first Olympics in London, but the winner of the 800 m was later excluded due to a failed drug test.
  36. Shapiro, Samantha. "Caught in the Middle." ESPN, July 23, 2012. https://www.espn.com/olympics/story/_/id/8192977/failed-gender-test-forces-olympian-redefine-athletic-career-espn-magazine. Accessed July 4, 2021.
  37. Ferguson-Smith, M. A., and Ferris, E. A. "Gender Verification in Sport: The Need for Change?" *British Journal of Sports Medicine* 25, no. 1, March 1991, pp. 17–20.
  38. Fordyce, Tom. "Semenya Left Stranded by Storm." BBC, August 19, 2009. https://www.bbc.co.uk/blogs/tomfordyce/2009/08/semenya_left_stranded_by_storm.html. Accessed July 4, 2021.
  39. Padawer, Ruth. "The Humiliating Practice of Sex Testing Athletes." *New York Times,* June 28, 2016. https://www.nytimes.com/2016/07/03/magazine/the-humiliating-practice-of-sex-testing-female-athletes.html. Accessed July 4, 2021.
  40. Critchley, Mark. "Rio 2016: Fifth-Placed Joanna Jozwik 'Feels Like Silver Medalist' after 800m Defeat to Caster Semenya." *The Independent*, August 22, 2016. https://www.independent.co.uk/sport/olympics/rio-2016-joanna-jozwik-caster-semenya-800m-hyperandrogenism-a7203731.html. Accessed July 10, 2021.
  41. Coleman, Doriane Lambelet. "Sex, Sport, and Why Track and Field's New Rules on Intersex Athletes Are Essential." *New York Times,* April 30, 2018.
  42. Pielke, R., Tucker, R. & Boye, E. "Scientific Integrity and the IAAF Testosterone Regulations." *Int Sports Law*, no. 19, 2019. https://doi.org/10.1007/s40318-019-00143-w. Accessed August 15, 2021.
  43. Sudai M. "The Testosterone Rule-Constructing Fairness in Professional Sport." *Journal of Law and Bioscience* 4, no. 1, 2017. doi:10.1093/jlb/lsx004. Accessed August 15, 2021.
  44. Coubertin, Pierre. *The Women at the Olympic Games.* 1912. Quoted in Muller, M., editor, *Pierre de Coubertin: 1863–1937—Olympism: Selected Writings.* International Olympic Committee, pp. 711–713.
  45. Guttmann, *Women's Sports*, p. 254.
  46. While, 30 years later no women are yet playing in the NFL, there are successful kickers on college teams as well as a rising number of assistant coaches, referees, and announcers. Also, while no woman weightlifter has yet done a clean and jerk of Guttmann's "improbable" ceiling of 250 kg, women's records are up to 193 kg, after only two decades of competition.
  47. Boulongne, "Pierre de Coubertin and Women's Sport," p. 24.

Afterthoughts

  1. Bane, Colin. "Huston Sorry for Comments about Female Skaters." *ESPN,* June 4, 2013. http://www.xgames.com/skateboarding/article/9342843/nyjah-huston-apologizes-comments-female-skateboarders. Accessed July 13, 2021.
  2. Houston, who was heavily favored and had won so many street events before that he had attained legendary status, did not medal and finished 7th out of 8 in the finals.

Bibliography

Primary Sources

Extensive resources about the Olympics have been collected and curated by the LA 84 Digital Foundation Library (https://digital.la84.org/digital). The following were used as primary reference materials:

Official Olympic Reports. Produced by the host city, these provide an overview not only of the schedule at the Games, but also detail the banquets, meetings, VIP attendees, ticket sales, construction schedule, and budget. They also are the formal and complete list of event rules, results, and statistics. As the Games have expanded, these have grown from 241 pages in 1896 Athens and 141 pages in 1908 St. Louis to 1525 pages, spread across three books, for Montreal 1976. By Rio 2016, these took the form of 30 separate PDF files, each between 50 to 100 pages, with statistics covering every event and sport.

Extract from Meeting Minutes from the Executive Board Meetings, speeches from the General Assembly Sessions, and programs for meetings hosted by the International Olympic Committee (IOC).

Oral Histories: Evelyn Hall Adams, Monique Berliox, Anita L. DeFrantz, Bob Mathias, Jean Shiley Newhouse, Simone Schaller Kirin, and Anne Vrana O'Brien.

Key periodicals sourced for historical articles reporting from each Olympic Games at the time:
Harper's
The New York Times
Sports Illustrated
TIME Magazine

Secondary Sources

Baker, Keith. *The 1908 Olympics.* SportsBooks, 2008.

Blue, Adrienne. *Faster, Higher, Further: Women's Triumphs and Disasters at the Olympics.* Virago Press, 1988.

Boulongne, Yves-Pierre. "Pierre de Coubertin and Women's Sport." *Olympic Review,* No XXVI-31, February-March 2000. LA84 Foundation, Digital Library Collections, *Digital.la84.org,* https://digital.la84.org/digital/collection/p17103coll1/id/36808/.

Cahn, Susan K. *Coming on Strong: Gender and Sexuality in Twentieth-Century Women's Sport.* Harvard University Press, 1994.

Cohen, Richard. *By the Sword.* Narrative Tension, 2002.

Dahl, Heather. *Fearless and Fit: American Women of the Cold War.* 2010. University of New Mexico, Masters dissertation. *SemanticScholar.org,* May 2010. https://www.semanticscholar.org/paper/FEARLESS-AND-FIT%3A-AMERICAN-WOMEN-OF-THE-COLD-WAR-Dahl/56d010467670c1293f2e5fa30b8e4acd78e7bff4.

Draper, Deborah Riley, and Thrasher, Travis. *Olympic Pride, American Prejudice: The Untold Story of 18 African Americans who Defied Jim Crow and Adolf Hitler to Compete in the 1936 Berlin Olympics.* Simon & Schuster, 2020.

Fields, Sarah K. *Female Gladiators: Gender, Law, and Contact Sport in America.* University of Illinois Press, 2005.

Goldblatt, David. *The Games: A Global History of the Olympics.* W.W. Norton, 2016.

Goldblatt, David, and Acton, Johnny. *How to Watch the Olympics: An Instant Initiation into Every Olympic Sport at Rio 2016.* Profile Books, 2016.

Guttmann, Allen. *The Olympics: A History of the Modern Games, Second Edition.* University of Illinois Press, 2002.

———. *Women's Sports: A History.* Columbia University, 1991.

Hogshead-Makar, Nancy, and Zimbalist, Andrew. *Equal Play: Title IX and Social Change.* Temple University Press, 2007.

Houry, Cecile. *American Women and the Modern Summer Games: A Story of Obstacles and Struggles for Participation and Equality.* 2011. University of Miami, Ph.D. dissertation. *Olympic.org.* https://library.olympic.org/Default/doc/SYRACUSE/171142/american-women-and-the-modern-olympic-games-a-story-of-obstacles-and-struggles-for-participation-and.

Johnson, William O., Jr. *All that Glitters Is Not Gold: An Irreverent Look at the Olympic Games.* G. P. Putnam's Sons, 1972.

Leder, Jane Mersky. *Grace & Glory: A Century of Women in the Olympics.* Triumph Books, 1996.

Macy, Sue. *Swifter, Higher, Stronger: A Photographic History of the Summer Olympics.* National Geographic Publishing, 2004.

Montillo, Roseanne. *Fire on the Track: Betty Robinson and the Triumph of the Early Olympic Women.* Crown, 2017.

Myers, Dvora. *The End of the Perfect Ten: The Making and Breaking of Gymnastics' Top Score—From Nadia to Now.* Touchstone Press, 2017.

Schiot, Molly. *Game Changers: The Unsung Heroines of Sport History.* Simon & Schuster Paperbacks, 2016.

Suggs, Welch. *A Place on the Team: The Triumph and Tragedy of Title IX.* Princeton University Press, 2006.

Tarasouleas, Athanasios. "Stamata Revithi, 'Alias Melpomeni.'" *Olympic Review* 26, no. 17, October–November 1997.

Wallace, Rich, and Neil Wallace, Sandra. *Babe Conquers the World: The Legendary Life of Babe Didrikson Zaharias.* Calkin Creeks Publishing, 2014.

Wallechinsky, David, and Loucky, Jaime. *The Book of Olympic Lists.* Aurum Press, 2012

_____. *The Complete Book of the Olympics: 2012 Edition.* Aurum Sport, 2012.

_____. *The Complete Book of the Winter Olympics: 2014 Edition.* Crossroad Press, 2014.

Young, David C. *A Brief History of the Olympic Games.* Blackwell Publishing, 2004.

Index

Numbers in **_bold italics_** indicate pages with illustrations

Abbott, Margaret 29, 270*n*7
Academia 40
ACLU 176, 178–9, 182
Adams, Nicola **_188_**
aesthetics in sport 17, 33–34, 93, 110, 112–114, 181, 202, 240
AIDS, impact on women's sports 231–232
Albertville Winter Olympics (1992) 202–203
Albright, Tenley 113
Ali, Laila 187
Amateur Athletic Union (AAU) 15, 31, 46–48, 61, 70, 79–80, 102, 157, 178, 217, 228; restrictions on women's sports 35–38, 55, 64–65, 160, 162–165, 171
amateurism 14–16, 17, 80, 111–113; end of 190; "gentleman athlete" 14–16, 19; violations of 70, 72, 111, 113
American Olympic Committee (AOC) *see* United States Olympic Committee
American Physical Education Association (APEA) 37
Amsterdam 160
Amsterdam Summer Olympics (1928) 1, 45, 49–54, 62–63, 74–5, 83, 158, 162, 274*n*1
Andersen, Camella 236–237
Andersen-Schiess, Gabriela 167–168
Andreeva, Anna 98
Andrianov, Konstantin 91, 135, 140
androgen insensitivity syndrome (AIS) 250
Anker-Doedens, Alida Geertruida van der 131
Anne, Princess Royal 125
Anthropology Days 31–32
anti-Polish sentiment 77
Antwerp Summer Olympics (1920) 35–36, 38–39, 41–42, 110, 127
appearance in sport, feminine 33, 54, 73, 95, 162–163, 196, 202, 204, 214, 229–230; *see also* aesthetics
aquatics *see* diving; swimming; water polo
archery 27, 31–33, 36, 83, 239
Arledge, Roone 194–195
art competitions at Olympics 33–34
Association for Intercollegiate Athletics for Women (AIAW) 146–149, 155–156, 162, 278*n*6
Astakhova, Polina 7, **_95_**
Asty (Greek newspaper) 11, 269*ch*1*n*2
Atalanta 26, 180
Athens, non-Olympic meets 105, 161
Athens Summer Olympics (1896) 10–25, **_24_**, 108
Athens Summer Olympics (2004) 181, 223, 227, 235
athletics *see* track and field
Atlanta Summer Olympics (1996) 129, 152, 180, 207–208, 211–212, 218, 222–223
Australia 92, 96, 142–143, 153–155, **_154_**, 206–209, 219, 235–236; *see also* basketball; water polo
Australian Open Tennis 220

Babilonia, Tai 206
Bach, Thomas 2, 191
badminton 136
Baillet-Latour, Henri de 43, 90
Baiul, Oksana 205
Balck, Victor 108–111, 115
Barak, Ron 275*n*34
Barcelona Summer Olympics (1992) 125, 179
Barnes, Leanne 153
Barnett, Courtney 182

Barr body 249
baseball 134–5, 230
basketball 121, 134–6, 141–144, 143, 231, 274*n*3; lesbians on team 230, 233, 236–238; special rules for 159; Title IX intersection 146, 148, 182; *see also* netball
Bassham, Lenny 127–**_129_**
Battle of Marathon 20
"Battle of the Carmens" 201–202
Beaumont, Texas 59–62
Beijing Summer Olympics (2008) 152, 154, 180, 187, 219, 223, 237
Bell, Terrell 231
Belokas, Spiridon 21
Benoit-Samuelson, Joan 161–**_167_**, 172–173
Berlin 36 242
Berlin Summer Olympics (1936) 23, 56, 58, 71, 73–75, 82–88, 93, 130, 241–244, **_243_**, 285*n*11
Berlioux, Monique 150, 246
Biles, Simone 6, 223–**_225_**, 257
Bird, Sue 238
Blake, Arthur 23–24
Blanc, Camille 42
Blankers-Koen, Fanny 90, 159–161, **_160_**, 244–**_245_**, 279*n*12
Blazejowski, Carol 157
bobsled/bobsleigh 108, 114–115
Boitano, Brian 201, 204, 282*n*26
Bonaly, Surya 203
Boston Marathon 161–165, **_164_**, 173, 279*n*15
Bowers v. Hardwicke 231
Bowlarama 6, 105–106
Bowman, Norris 113
boxing 33, 110, 175–176, 181–182, 185–189, 188; and masculinity 175, 185–186; in skirts 187–188
boycotts *see* Moscow Summer Olympics 1980
Braumüller, Ellen 67

Bréal, Michel 15, 22
British Figure Skating Union 33
British Journal of Medicine study 255
Brookes, Dr. William Penny 13
Brown, Earlene 103–107, 221, 247
Brown, Rita Mae 233
Brown, Sky 260
Brundage, Avery 64, 75–76, 84–85, 91, 96, 285n11; amateurism, attitude toward 70, 113; gender testing 240–242, 248; women, opposition to 55, 97, 121, 220, 273n2
Budd, Zola 169–170
Bull Montana 78
Burger, Fritzi 111
Burghley, Lord 50, 270n22
Burton, Beryl 170
Bush, (George W.) administration 148
Button, Dick 113

Calgary Winter Olympics (1988) 201–204, *203*
Canada 52, 149, 188, 257
Canadian Female Athlete of Half Century 56
Canadian Olympic Trials 49
canoe 130–132, 150, 170
Carman, Lyn 163
Carpenter-Phinney, Connie 171–172
Carroll, Helen 234
Carter, Michelle 220–*221*
Cartwright, Elta 49–50
Caslavska, Vera 96–97, 195–197, 282n11
Casper, Gian Franco 190
Catherwood, Ethel 49, 52
Chaffee, Suzy 231
Chamonix Winter Olympics (1924) 108–110
Chand, Dutee *253*–255
Chariots of Fire 19
Chase-Brand, Julia 162
Chastain, Brandi 149
Cheeseborough, Chandra 102
cheveaux de selle 28
Chicago 28, 30, 46–48, 64
Chiosso, James 27
cholitas 180
Chukarin, Victor 94
Chung-Kuo Wu 187
Clement, Kerron 125
Cleveland Junior Olympics 78
Clinton administration 148
Cold War (of Sport) 89–107, 201–202; basketball 142–144; Feminine Mystique 90, 92; figure skating 201–202; good will tours 105–107;

gymnastics 93–97; impact on fitness programs 92; propaganda 91–92; shot put 97–106; telethon 91, 274n9
Coleman, Georgia 67
Colledge, Cecilia 86, 111–112
Comaneci, Nadia 197–202, *198*, 282n15
Commission on Intercollegiate Athletics for Women 146; *see also* AIAW
Commonwealth Games 184, 207, 247, 250
Compton, California 104, 106
contact sports 175–190, 230
Cook, Myrtle 49–52
Cooper, Charlotte 28
Copeland, Lillian 52, 63–64, 66–68, 98
Cortina d'Ampezzo Winter Olympics (1956) 113
costumes and women's sports 34, 110–111, 201–204; *see also* fashion
Coubertin, Baron Pierre Fredy de 12–19, *18*, 22, 28, 43, 108, 110, 126, 176, 185, 240, 261, 270n24; amateurism, attitude toward 17; arts competition 33; early life 13–14; women, opposition to 15–18, 34, 41–42, 131, 134
Courmayeur-Champex-Chamonix race 173
Court of Arbitration for Sport (CAS) 251
Cousins, Robin 201
COVID impact 220, 259–260
Cranz, Christl 117
croquet 26–31, 110
Crosby, Bing 91
Curry, John 201
Cuthbert, Betty 103, 207
cycling 170–172
Czechoslovakia 91, 93, 195, 212, 274n18

Daimatsu Hirobumi 135–140, 277ch9n17
Daley, Arthur 63, 72, 91, 247
"Danish Dianas" 34
d'Aubigny, Julie 83
Davenport, Lindsay 235
Davis, Cat 186
Decker, Mary *see* Slaney, Mary Decker
Defoe, Frances 113
DeFrantz, Anita 150, 189–190
Denmark 141, 149, 155, 236, 277n19
Després, Andre & Mme 30
De Varona, Donna 145–146, 231, 278n3
Dewey, John 176

Dewey, Katharin 114
Diaz de Cano, Leda 167
Dibaba family of runners 173
Didrikson, Babe 58–72, 88, *62*, *69*, 99, 128, 142, 217–8, 273n15, 273n18, 283n14; basketball 60–61; competing at Olympics 66–70; early life 59–61; golf 71–72, 88; later years 88, 229; lesbian 229; one-woman team 63–66; racism 67
Dieterle, Ingrid 150
Dillema, Foejke 244–*245*
disabled Olympic athletes 56, 103, 123–126
discus *see* track and field, discus
diving 33–36, 43, 65, 92, 131, 159, 214, 267, 274n22, 275n11
Dodd, Betty 229
Doherty, Laurie 28
Doherty, Reggie 28–29
Dohle, Max 244
Donnelly, Patrice 234
doping 150, 246, 250, 278n15, 283n14, 286n32
Douglas, Gabby 221–223, *225*
Dover, Robert 125–126, 235
drug testing 216–218, 246, 250, 252
drug use *see* doping
DSD (disorder of sex development) *see* mosaicism
Durack, Fanny 35
Durham, Dianne 199

East Germany 150–151, 201–202, 246, 250, 286n32
eating disorders 206, 279n14
Eaton, Ashton 215
Eckhardt, Shawn 204
Ederly, Gertrude 59, 228
800m *see* track and field, 800m
Eisenhower, Dwight 92
Elizabeth I, Queen 27
Employers Casualty 61, 63–64, 66, 80; Golden Cyclones basketball team 61–62; *see also* Didrikson, Babe
equestrian 121–126; dressage 122, 124, 276n7; eventing 123, 125; jumping 123, 125
Estia (Greek newspaper) 11
Edström, Sigfrid 41, 43–44, 91
Evert, Chris 232–233
exceptionalism 71–72
expansion of events 34, 36, 38, 45, 92–93, 95, 120–130

"face of the Olympics" 224
fairness in sport 75, 131, 169, 204, 239

Index

fashion, sports 219–220; *see also* costumes
FBI, Indiana Field Office 224
Fédération des Sociétés Féminines Sportives de France (FSFSF) 41
Fédération Équestre Internationale (FEI) 121–126
Fédération Internationale de Football Association (FIFA) 148–149
Fédération Internationale de Natation Amateur (FINA) 153–154, 278n22
Fédération Internationale de Volleyball (FIVB) 136
Fédération Internationale des Sociétés d'Aviron (FISA) 238
Federation Sportive Feminine Internationale (FSFI) 43
Feldenkrais, Moshe 179, 281n14
Felix, Allyson 174, 257
Female Triad 213, 279n14, 283n5
Femina Sport 40–41
Feminine Mystique 89–90, 102
femininity control *see* gender verification
femininity standards 33, 73, 87, 94, 114, 181
fencing **29**, 83–88, **86**
Ferguson-Smith, Malcolm 250
1500m *see* track and field, 1500m
Figg, Jim 185
figure skating *see* skating, figure
Filkey, Helen 46
"Final Five" 224–**225**
Finland 32, 189
first, women's 28–29, 112, 124, 129, 143, 150, 170, 186, 199, 201, 203, 235–236
Fischer, Birget 7
Flack, Edwin 21–22
Fleischer, Tilly 67
Fleming, Peggy 113, 231
"Flying Housewife" 159
football *see* soccer
Forsberg, Emelie 173
46,XX/46,YY *see* mosaicism
Foss, Marit 181
400m *see* track and field, 400m
Foxcatcher 281n22
fragility, women in sport 98, 100, 117, 158, 212–214
França (Maestrini), Larissa 237
France 30, 36, 43, 83, 92, 144, 179; *see also* Coubertin, Baron Pierre Fredy de; judo; Milliat, Alice; wrestling
Franey, Dot 114
Fraser, Dawn 75, 207

Fraser, Gretchen 118
Freeman, Cathy 206–**210**
Friedan, Betty 90, 231
Fukuda Keiko 177, 280n8

Galieva, Rosa 212, 283n1
Galindo, Vicky 237
Gallico, Paul 71, 110, 202, 218, 229
Gambon-de-Vos, Nelly 150
Games of Hera 37
GANEFO 277ch9n15
Garmisch-Partenkirchen Winter Olympics (1936) 111–112, 114–117
"La Gazella Nera"/"La Perle Noire" 103, 208
Geddert, John 223
gender dysphoria *see* gender verification
gender parity 5, 115, 175, 190–191, 257, 265–266
gender reassignment 241
gender verification/gender testing 239–248, 285n1
Gentzel, Inga 52–**53**
Germany 41, 52, 73–74, 83, 87, 91, 94, 117, 125, 130, 140–141, 151
Gibb, Roberta 163–164
gigantism 36, 120–132; *see also* expansion of events
Gilooly, Jeff 204
Gioga, Nicolae 151–152
Gira Rosa race 172
Gogarty, Deirdre 186
Gold, Gracie 206
Golden Gloves 186
golf 27–29, 31, 71–72, 88, 90, 229, 236
Göring, Hermann 75
Gorokhovskaya, Maria 94
Graf, Steffi 232
Gray, Eileen 170–171
Great Britain 36, 41–42, 49, 92, 151–152
greatest *see* world's greatest woman athlete
Greece 10–27; *see also* Olympic Games, ancient Greeks
Green, Edith 146
Grenoble Winter Olympics (1968) 249
Grier, Barbara 230
Griffith-Joyner, Florence 216–218, **217**, 233
Grosse, Rosa 47
Grove City College v. Terrell H. Bell 148
Grunsven, Anky van 124
Guerra, Elvira 28
Gundersen, Ove 181
gym teachers *see* APEA; P.E. teachers

gymnastics 19, 92–97, 194–201, 198, 221–226, 225, 274n18; balance beam **97**, 225; disproving female fragility 213–214; floor exercise 95–96, 199–**200**; injuries in 212–214; men's vs. women's events 93–94; origin of 92–93; parallel bars **95**; rhythmic 174; uneven bars 95, 194, **198**; vault 196, 200, 211–214; *see also* Nassar, Larry; Perfect Ten;

Haëntjens, Marcel 29
Häggman, Pirjo 189
Hall, Evelyn 63, 68–69, 128
Hamill, Dorothy 113, 200–1
Hammerseng, Gro 237
handball 117, 134–135, 140–142, 236–237; beach 142; origin of, by gender 141
Haney, Maggie 224
Harding, Tonya 203–204
Harrison, Kayla 179
Hartel, Lis 123–**125**
Haß, Hedwig 86
Hayes, Quanera 257
Heines, Jackson 109
Helsinki Summer Olympics (1952) 91, 94, 99, 102, 123, **124**, 130
Hemingway, Mariel 234
Henie, Sonja 86, 110–**113**, 203, 275n12
Henrietta's Beauty College 105
heptathlon 46, 29, 215
Hernandez, Laurie 224–**225**
Higgins, Yvette 154
high jump *see* track and field, high jump
Hingis, Martina 235
Hiraki Kokona 260
Hitomi Kinue 52–**53**
hockey: field 33, 41, 66, 135; ice 47, 120, 141, 182
Hoff, Karen 131
Holm, Eleanor 72, 74–**76**, 88
Hope, Bob 91
horse ballet *see* dressage
Houston, Nyjah 260, 286n2
Howell, Matilda Scott 32
Hubbard, Laurel 256
huka huka 180
Hundvin, Mia 236–237
Hungary 27, 83, 96, 154, 212, 274n18
Hunter, Jerry 181
hurdles *see* track and field, hurdles
hyperandrogenism 245, 249, 253

"Ice Queen of Norway" *see* Henie, Sonja

Index

Icho Kaori 183
Illinois Women's Athletic Club (IWAC) 46–48, 63
India 135, 252–253; *see also* Chand, Dutee; wrestling
International Amateur Athletic Federation (IAAF) 36, 41, 43–44, 55, 162; involvement in gender testing 101, 246–253
International Boxing Association (AIBA) 187
International Canoeing Federation (ICF) 130–131
International Equestrian Federation *see* FEI
International Federation of Association Football *see* FIFA
International Gymnastics Federation (FIG) 93–94, 197
International Handball Federation (IHF) 136
International Judo Federation (IJF) 1795
International Olympic Committee (IOC) 16, 84, 251
International Shooting Sport Federation (ISSF) 127
International Skating Union (ISU) 33, 109–110
International Volleyball Federation *see* FIVB
Isava-Fonseca, Flor 189

Jahn, Friedrich Ludwig 93
Japan 87, 116, 277*n*15; *see also* judo; Tokyo; volleyball; wrestling
javelin *see* track and field, javelin
Jews on the 1936 German team 82–85
jiu-jitsu 175–176
Joao Havelange Stadium 221
Johnson, Ben 217
Jones, Marion 279*n*11
Jones, Rosie 237
Jowzik, Joanna 254, **255**
Joyner, Al 216
Joyner-Kersee, Jackie 142, 215, 218, 283*n*14, 283*ch*14*n*28
judges, impact on competition 111, 116, 127, 196–197, 202, 204–205, 212–213, 239
judo 175–180; *kata* 177–178

Kahn, Elfriede 242
kaiten reeshibu *see* rotate and receive
Kanō Jigorō 176–177
Kanō Noriko 177
Kanokogi, Rusty 176–**179**, 281*n*11

Karolyi, Bela 197–198, 222–223, 282*n*15
Karolyi, Marta 197–198, 222–223, 282*n*15
Kasai Masae 135–**140**
Katarina Witt rule 202–**203**; *see also* "Thomas rule"
Kawai Risako 184
Keller, Thomas 150
Kellner, Gyula 21–22
Kennedy, John 92
Kerrigan, Nancy 203–206
Kersee, Bob 215
Killanin, Lord 170
Kim, Nellie 197
King, Billie Jean 146, 231–**232**, 285*n*26
Kipke, Dr. Lothar 286*n*32
Kirby, Gustavus 55
Kirkorian, Adam 155
Klobukowska, Eva 249
Knox, Walter 47
Kocian, Madison **225**, 284*n*35
Konopacka, Halina 52
Kooman, Kees 244
Korbut, Olga 94, 194–199, 224
Koubek, Zdenek (Zdenka) 241
Krajewski, Julia 125
Kristiansen, Ingrid 161–166, 173
Kucsik, Nina 165
Kurrell, Pamela 99
Kuznetsva, Yevgeniya 106

Lake Placid Winter Olympics (1932) 111, 114, 116
Lake Placid Winter Olympics (1980) 201
Lamberg, Paula 260
Lapin, Lauren 237
Latynina, Larisa 89–97, **95**, 194, 196–197
lavender menace 231
law and sport 148–149, 154, 157, 182, 186, 251, 253, 278*n*6; *see also* Title IX
Lawrence, Andrea Mead 118
Leal, Rayssa 260
Ledecky, Katie 146, 280*n*47
Lenglen, Suzanne 59, 228
Lepper, Merry 163
Lermusiaux, Albin 21–22
lesbianism 71, 227–238, 259
Libaud, Paul 136
Lieberman, Nancy 143–144, 231, 233, 277*n*24
Lillehammer Winter Olympics (1994) 204–206
Lines, Mary 42–44
Linselhoff, Liselott 124
Lipă, Elisabeta 151
Liquori, Marty 168
"Little Miss Moneybags" *see* Henie, Sonja
London Summer Olympics (1908) 20, 32–34, 11, 114, 273*n*1
London Summer Olympics (1948) 87, 90, 93, 98, 102, 122, 125, 130–131, 158–160, 244
London Summer Olympics (2012) 152, 155, 187–188, 219, 223, 237, 253
long jump *see* track and field, long jump
Longman, Jere 25
Longo, Jeannie 171–172
Los Angeles Summer Olympics (1932) 55–56, 58, 67–70, **69**, 74, 80–82, 84
Los Angeles Summer Olympics (1984) 151, 157, 162–172, **167**, 174, 176, **200**, 207, 216; Los Angeles Olympic Organizers (LAOOC) 165
Louganis, Greg 214
Louis, Spyridon 19–20
Lysenko, Lyudmila 162

Macarthur, General Douglas 49, 74
Maccabiah Games 178
Macfadden, Bernard 38
"Mademoiselle la Chicken!" 209
Madison, Helene 58, 67
Maestrini, Liliane 237
"Magnificent Seven" 214
Makray, Katalin **95**
Malloy, "Bruising Peg" **185**
S.S. *Manhattan* 74
"mannish" as descriptor 216, 228–229, 236
marathon *see* track and field, marathon
Marathon, source of race 1–3, 270*n*26
Maroulis, Helen 182–183
martial arts *see* judo; taekwondo
Martin, Christy 186
Martinez-Patino, Maria 250–251
Mary, Queen 27
"Match of the Century" 59
"Matchless Six" 45, 56
Mathias, Bob 91
Mauresmo, Amelie 235–236
Mayer, Helene 82–88, **86**, 285*n*11
Mayer, Sarah 177
McCombs, Colonel Melvin 61–71, 215
McCormick, Pat 159
McGee, William J. 31–32
McNamara, Mike 170
media/press impact on: Babe Didrikson 61, 63; the 800m 53–54; gymnastics 194–195,

200–201, 221–226; Harding/
  Kerrigan 204–206; lesbian
  athletes 232–237; Marie-Jose
  Péréc 208–209; Stella Walsh
  78–82
medical objections to women in
  sport 158–160, 228; *see also*
  800m; Female Triad
Meese, Ed 231
Melbourne Summer Olympics
  (1956) 87, 94–95, 100, 102–
  104, 120, 159, 207, 276n7
Melpomene *see* Revithi,
  Stamata
men in disguise 99, 229; *see
  also* gender verification
Mexico Summer Olympics
  (1968) 96–**97**, 248–250
Meyer, Ann 143–144, 231
Michaels, Al 168
Midori Ito 203
Milliat, Alice 39–55, **40**
Millrose Games 78
"Min Bebe" 59
Mink, Patsy 146
Miss Stadium beauty contest
  80
Missy Junior Gloves Program
  186
mixed gender competitions
  30, 110, 114, 118–119, 124, 130,
  218–219, 256–258, 273n1
Moceanu, Dominic 212
Möller, Silke Gladisch 283n20
Monte Carlo 42
Montreal Summer Olympics
  (1976) 125, 127–**129**, **143**–144,
  149–150, 168, 195, 197–**198**
Moody, Helen Wills 59
Moore, Joan 196
Moran, Gertrude "Gussie" 90
mosaicism 245, 255; *see also*
  hyperandrogenism
Moscow Summer Olympics
  (1980) 143, 150, 157, 168, 178,
  199–200, 207
Mota, Rosa 161–164
Mother of Women's Judo *see*
  Kanokogi, Rusty
motherhood, impact from sport
  67, 90, 158; *see also* Feminine
  Mystique
movies, Olympic-themed 105,
  112, 234, 242
Much Wenlock Olympian
  Games 13, **14**, 269n5
multi-sport women athletes 46,
  49, 59, 62, 66, 100, 116, 171,
Munich Summer Olympics
  (1972) 124, 131, 146, 162,
  194–196
murderous exercise 137
Murdock, Margaret 127–**129**
muscle moll 71, 228–229, 240

muscular feminity 98, 200, 203,
  216–221, **219**

Nakanishi Michi **69**
Nassar, Larry 223
National Collegiate Athletic
  Association (NCAA) 147,
  149, 162, 278n8
National Cycling Union
  (Britain) (NCU) 280n42
National Organization of
  Women (NOW) 230–231
National Wrestling Coaches vs.
  Dept. of Education 148
nationalism 134–144 *see also*
  Cold War
Navratilova, Martina 232–233
Nazis 82–88, 242–243
Nelson, Judy 233
Nemov, Alexei 214
netball 142–143
New Jersey 48
New South Wales Ladies
  Amateur Swimming
  Association 35
New York Bombers 106
New York Central Railroad
  79–80
New York City Marathon 165
New York, ruling on female
  boxers 186
Nichibo Corporation 137–139
Nichols, Maggie 223
Nilsen, Laila Schou 116–**117**,
  141
Nippon Budokan 176
Nordic Games 108–109
North Korea 277ch9n15
Norway 109, 116, 140–142, 155,
  181, 236, 251
Novotna, Jana 235
Nurmi, Paavo 17, 111
Nyberg, Katja 237

"Ode to Sport" 270n24
Office of Civil Rights (OCR)
  148
Okamoto, Misugu 260
Okino, Betty 213
Olympia 258
Olympic Games: alternatives
  108 (*see also* Spartakiads;
  Women's World Games);
  ancient Greek Games 27,
  269n2; origin of 108–109 (*see
  also* Nordic Games)
Olympic Games (1900) *see*
  Paris
Olympic Games (1904) *see* St.
  Louis
Olympic Games (1908) *see*
  London
Olympic Games (1912) *see*
  Stockholm

Olympic Games (1920) *see*
  Antwerp
Olympic Games (1924) *see*
  Paris
Olympic Games (1928) *see*
  Amsterdam
Olympic Games (1932) *see* Los
  Angeles
Olympic Games (1936)
  see Berlin; Garmisch-
  Partenkirchen
Olympic Games (1948) *see*
  London; St. Moritz
Olympic Games (1952) *see*
  Helsinki; Oslo
Olympic Games (1956) *see*
  Melbourne / Stockholm;
  Cortina d'Ampezzo
Olympic Games (1960) *see*
  Rome
Olympic Games (1964) *see*
  Tokyo
Olympic Games (1968) *see*
  Mexico City
Olympic Games (1972) *see*
  Munich; Sapporo
Olympic Games (1976) *see*
  Montreal
Olympic Games (1980) *see*
  Moscow; Lake Placid
Olympic Games (1984) *see* Los
  Angeles; Sarajevo
Olympic Games (1988) *see*
  Seoul; Calgary
Olympic Games (1992) *see*
  Barcelona; Albertville
Olympic Games (1994) *see*
  Lillehammer
Olympic Games (1996) *see*
  Atlanta
Olympic Games (2000) *see*
  Sydney
Olympic Games (2002) *see* Salt
  Lake City
Olympic Games (2004) *see*
  Athens
Olympic Games (2008) *see*
  Beijing
Olympic Games (2012) *see*
  London
Olympic Games (2014) *see*
  Sochi
Olympic Games (2016) *see* Rio
  de Janeiro
Olympic Games (2018) *see*
  Pyeongchang
Olympic Games (2020) *see*
  Tokyo
Olympic Trials *see* Canadian
  Olympic Trials; United States
  Olympics Trials
"Olympics of Spectacle" 58
100m *see* track and field, 100m
Oregon Supreme Court 181

Oriental Witches *see* volleyball
Oslo Winter Olympics (1952) 118
Ostermeyer, Micheline 98–99
Owens, Jesse 71, 102, 159

Panathenaic Stadium 21–22
Papadiamantopoulos, Major 21–22
Paris, Jasmin 173
Paris Summer Olympics (1900) 28–30, **29**, 36
Paris Summer Olympics (1924) 42–43
patriotism and sport 73, 80, 82–93
Paulsen, Axel 109
Payseé, Pierre 40
P.E. teachers 230, 238, 274*n*3 *see also* APEA
pedestriennes 26
Peleus 180
Penn State 233, 284*n*17
Penny, Steve 223
pentathlon: modern 34, 126; women's 100, 234
Péréc, Marie-José 207–210, 215
Perfect Ten 197, 282*n*11
Pershing Stadium, Paris 43
Personal Best 234, 284*n*21
Persson, Gehnäll 122–123
Peter the Great 94
Peters, Don 200, 223
Petrik, Larisa 96
Phinney, Davis 171
Phogat, Geeta **184**
Phogat, Mahavit 184, 281*n*26
Physical Culture magazine 38
piaffe 276*n*4
Pickett, Tidye 67, 102, 215
Pikhala, Laurie 44
play days 37, 228
"Play It, Don't Say It" 229
Poage, George 102
Poland 52, 77, 79–80, 248–249
policing the binary 240
polio 93, 103, 113, 123–124
Polymachinon 27
Ponmareva, Nina 99
"poodle scuba diving" 125–126
Portland, Rene 233
Preece, Helen 126
Preis, Ellen 83–86
Presidential Council of Physical Fitness 92, 218
presidents, U.S. impact on sport 92, 148
Press, Irina 100–**101**, 105–106, 247–248, 275*n*34
Press, Tamara 100–**101**, 105–106, 247–248, 275*n*34
Price, Coach Charles 45–46

Protopopovs 113
Puica, Marcica 169–170
pushball 271*n*7
Pyeongchang Winter Olympics (2018) 237

"Queen of the Waves" 59
Queensland, Australia 277*ch*8*n*16
Quinn 257

race, role in sport 31–32, 67, 71, 102, 203, 206–207, 215–216, 254–255, 276*n*14
Radke, Lina 52–**53**
Raisman, Aly 223, **225**
Rapinoe, Megan 146, 237–238, 278*n*4
Ratjen, Heinrich (Dora) 242–**243**
reproduction and sports *see* medical objections
Retton, Mary Lou 199–**200**
reverse discrimination arguments 148, 182; *see also* Title IX
Revithi, Stamata 10–25, **24**
Rhode, Kim 129–130
Rice, Grantland 71–72
Richardson, Sha'Carri 272*n*18
Rigby, Cathy 196, 282*n*7
Rio de Janeiro Summer Olympics (2016) 130–131, 152, 172, 173, 179, 183, 188, 219–220, **225**
Rippon, Adam 206, 282*n*26
Road Runners Club of America 163
Robinson, Betty 45–56, 128
Rodnina/Zaitsev 201
Rogge, Jacques 191
Roller Derby Hall of Fame 106
Romania **151**, 198–200, 278*n*16, 282*n*15; *see also* rowing
romantic primitivism 31–32
Rome Summer Olympics (1960) 95, 100, 103–106, 113, 116, 125, 131, 162
S.S. *Roosevelt* 49
Rose, Billy 88
Rosenfeld, Fanny (Bobbie) 45–56, 128, 229, 272*n*17
rotate and receive 137–138; *see also* Daimatsu Hirobumi
rowing 28, 40, 150–152, **151**; pairs sculling 22–23; women's eight 151–152; *see also* Yale rowing team
Rudolph, Wilma 103–104
rugby 41, 131, 182
running **24**, 45–55, 157–174, **164**; distance limitations for women 54–55, 160, 163–165; history of women participating 26, 36–38; superiority to men over distances 173; *see also* track and field (events)
Russia 90, 94, 101, 143, 205, 224; *see also* Soviet Union
Ryan, Joan 212

sailing 32, 271*n*13, 273*n*1
St. Cyr, Henri 123–124
St. Louis Summer Olympics (1904) 30–32
St. Moritz Winter Olympics (1928) 111–112, 275*n*11
St. Moritz Winter Olympics (1948) 118
St. Petersburg 143
Sakae Kazuhito 183
Salchow, Ulrich 109
Salt Lake City Winter Olympics (2002) 114–115, 117
Samaranch, Juan Antonio 190
Sandler, Bernice 146
Santa Monica 161
Sapporo Winter Olympics (1972) 171
Sarajevo Winter Olympics (1984) 201, 203
"Saskatoon Lily" 52
satsujin taiso see murderous exercise
Saunders, Raven "Hulk" 227, 238
Schacherer-Elek, Ilona 85–86
Schaller, Simone **69**
Schartau, Professor Gustav 13
Schelenz, Karl 141
Schinegger, Erik (Erica) 249–250
Schwingl, Fritzi 131
"scissors-kick" high jump style 65, 69–70
Scott, Barbara Ann 112–113
Scurlock, "Tiny" 61
Seidler, Maren 247
Semenya, Caster 251–256, **255**, 286*n*35
Semjonova, Uljana **143**, 277–278*n*24
Semple, Jock **164**
Seoul Summer Olympics (1988) 144, 217–218
Sharp, Lynsey 254–**255**
Sheehan, Patty 236–237
Shields, Claressa 188–189
Shiley, Jean 63, 65–66, 69–70
shooting 126–130, **129**
Shot Diva 220
shot put *see* track and field, shot put
Simon, Lou Anna 224
Simon Fraser University 183
Sin Kim Dan 246
skateboarding 260–261, 286*n*2

skating, figure 32–33, 109–114, *113*, 201–206, ***203***
skating, speed 115–116
ski jumping 108, 260; rationale for barring women 3, 114–116, 159, 190–191
skiing: alpine 108, 115–118, ***117***, 131, 260; cross-country 108, 114–115
Slaney, Mary Decker 168–170, 280n38
Sloper, Valerie 105
Sly, Wendy 169
Smith, Ethel 49
Smith, Joyce 166–167
Smith, Leni 50–51
Smith, Stephen A. boxing attitude 189
soccer 7, 27, 41, 90, 145–146, 148–149, 237–238, 257, 278n8
Sochi Winter Olympics (2014) 237
softball 230, 237
sokol 78, 94; *see also* gymnastics
Soundarajan, Santhi 252
South Korea 137, 231, 277n15
Soutsos, Panagiotis 13
Soviet Union 89, 91–92, 94, 96–97, 99, 116, 135, 201, 207; *see also* basketball; gymnastics; track and field; volleyball
Spartakiads 91, 94, 108
Sports Illustrated 87, 92, 137, 186, 199, 215
Stalin 90, 94
Steers, Fred 63
Steinberg, Erna 50
"Stella the Fella" *see* Walsh, Stella
Stephens, Helen 81–82, 229, 241–2
Stewart, Breanna 146
Stockholm Summer Olympics (1912) 32, 34–35, 41, 110, 270n24
Stokes, Elizabeth Wilkinson 185
Stokes, Louise 67, 215
Strickland, Shirley 103, ***160***, 207
Strug, Kerri 211–214, 283n1
suffragettes 39, 43–44, 175, 185, 280n2
Sullivan, James E. 31–32, 35–36, 41
Sumners, Rosalyn 201
Swahn, Oscar 126
Sweden 13, 32–34, 42–43, 108–109, 122–123
Swedish Olympic Union 13
swimming 34–***35***, 92, 95, 110, 146, 220, 228–229, 239; artistic (synchronized) 153–154, 174
Switzer, Kathrine ***164***
Swopes, Sheryl 237, 285n30
Sydney Summer Olympics (2000) 130, 153–155, 206–***210***, 219, 236, 279n11; Sydney Organizing Committee (SOCOG) 153
Syers, Madge 102–106
synchronized swimming *see* swimming, artistic
Szabo, Ecaterina 200

taekwondo 175, 180, 189–190
Takács, Károly 126
Talbot, Monsignor Ethelbert 16
Tani Ryoko 180
Taylor, John 102
Taylor, Katie 187–188
Taylor, Megan 111
Tcheuméo, Audrey 179
team sports 134–147
Team USA *see* United States
telethon, USOC 91
television, impact from 194–195, 206–208, 282n3
Temple, Ed 102–105, 215
10 nannomoles/liter 253
tennis 14, 19, 26–29, 31–32, 59, 90, 218–***219***, 230, 232–235
Terhaar, Tom 151–152
testosterone 245, 252–256
Tewksbury, Mark 125
"Texas Tornado" 59
Thomas, Debi 201–203
"Thomas rule" 282n22
Thompson, Daley 215
Thompson, Jenny 7
Thorntown Township High School 45
Thorpe, Jim 17, 72
Thunberg, Clas 116
Tigerbelles 102–106
TIME magazine 241, 247
Title IX 145–156, 182, 230–231, 233–234; court decisions 148; women's improved participation from 149, 267; *see also* Yale rowing team
Todd, Nellie 48
toe jiu-jitsu hold 152
Tokyo Summer Olympics (1964) **95**, 96, ***100–101***, 105, 135–***140***
Tokyo Summer Olympics (2020) 2, 125, 131, 152, 172, 189, 191, 224, 254
Tonawanda, Jackie 186
torch relay 207, 258, 281n24
Torres, Dara 146
Tour de France/Tour de France Feminina 170
Tourischeva, Ludmilla 195–196
track and field: discus 28, 34, 45, 49, 52, 62, 65–66, 68, 79, 97–105, ***101***; 800m 52–56, ***53***, 158, 160, 162, 212, ***255***, 279n16; 1500m 168–170; 400m 206–210; high jump 42, 62, 65–66, 70, 241–***243***; hurdles 66, 68, **69**, *160*; javelin 67–68; long jump 42, 48–49, 62, 100, 215; marathon 10–12, 15, 18–22, 24–25, 157–158, 161–168, ***164***, *167*, 173; 100m 45–52, 216–218; pole vault 260; relay ***253***; shot put 97–107, ***100***, 220–***221***, 283n28; 200m 12, 79, 104
transgender athletes 241–242, 256–257
Trimiar, Marion "Tyger" 186
tug of war 32
Tulu, Derartu *see* Dibaba family
Tunis, John R. 1, 53, 120
Twigg, Rebecca 171–172
200m *see* track and field, 200m
Tyrš, Miroslav 93
Tyskevich, Tamara 103
Tyus, Wyomia 102. 249

Ueberroth, Peter 165
Underwood, Queen 187
Union Cycliste Internationale (UCI) 170–172; *see also* cycling
Union des Societies Francaises de Sports Athletiques (USFSA) 15
unitards *see* "Thomas rule"
United States 91–92, 218; Team USA 27, 69, 128–129, 151–152, 157, 182–183, 186, 200, 212, 217, 220, 222–224; United States Olympic Committee (USOC) 75, 84, 91, 145, 157, 274n8; United States Olympic Trials 48–49, 63, 74, 78, 173, 217, 222, 257; United World Wrestling Federation (FILA) 181–182
USSR *see* Soviet Union
uterine prolapse 158–160

Vaillancourt, Sarah 237
Victoria, Queen 27, 228
Vikelas, Dimitrios 16
Villa, Brenda 154
visibility 194–195, 211, 215–217, 219–221, 226–229, 238, 259, 284n23
vital force *see* medical objections
VO2 max 173
volleyball 135–***140***
volleyball, beach 142, 235, 237
Von der Lippe, Gerd 140–141
Vonn, Lindsey 118–119
Vrana, Anne 49–50

Waitz, Greta 161–166
Wakefield, Kelsey *154*
Walasiewicz, Stanislawa *see* Walsh, Stella
Walsh, Stella 49, *62*, 67, 76–82, *81*, 87–88, 242–243, 260, 273*n*36, 285*n*11
Warehouse 13 23, 270n34
water polo 152–155, *154*
"water rugby" *see* water polo
Weaver, Doyle 186
weightlifting 286n46
Weissmuller, Johnny 50, 58, 88
Welsh, Priscilla 166
Werth, Isabell 124
"Western roll" high jump style 65, 69–70
Weston, Mark (Mary) 241
Whalen, Eleanor Holm Jarrett *see* Holm, Eleanor
Whipple, Mary 152
Williams, Serena 218–220, *219*
Williams, Venus 218–219
Witt, Katarina 201–*203*; *see also* "Thomas rule"

Women's Basketball League 231
Women's Challenge Race, Spokane 172
Women's Cycle Racing Association 170
Women's Olympics *see* Women's World Games
Women's Sports Foundation (WSF) 190, 231
Women's Tennis Association (WTA) 231
Women's World Cup (FIFA) 149
Women's World Games 42–45, 44, 55; *see also* Milliat, Alice
workers' sport movements *see* Spartakiads
World Rowing Federation *see* FISA
World's Fair 22, 28–30
World's Greatest Woman Athlete 46, 58, 79, 160, 215, 283*n*14
wrestling 180–185, *184*, 278n11, 278n26; freestyle 175, 180–185; Greco-Roman 181; *see also Foxcatcher*
Wüst, Ireen 237
Wylie, Mina 35

Xenophon 122

Yale rowing team 147–148, 153
Yamaguchhi, Kristy 202
Yoshida Eikatsu 183
Yoshida Saori 183–184
Youth Olympics (2020) 142
Yugoslavia 135

Zaharias, Babe *see* Didrikson, Babe
Zaharias, George 72, 229
Zappas Olympic Games, Zappas Evangelis 13
zero sum game 130–132, 148–149, 189
Zhang Shan 129
Zybina, Galina 99, *100*, 105

www.ingramcontent.com/pod-product-compliance
Lightning Source LLC
Chambersburg PA
CBHW060336010526
44117CB00017B/2851